NATIONAL CLIMATE (

This groundbreaking book collects contributions from many of the world's leading climate and energy law scholars and provides the first major study of national Climate Change Acts. This cutting-edge type of legislation originated with the first Climate Change Act framework which was passed in the United Kingdom in 2008, and is intended to enable the law to grapple effectively with one of the great problems of our times – anthropogenic climate change.

Since 2008, national framework climate legislation has been slowly but steadily emerging in countries across the world. This trailblazing collection employs a comparative analytical legal methodology and offers the first comprehensive study of this new, innovative form of legislative regime.

In addition to containing broad internationalist chapters, deep-dive national case study chapters are included that focus on individual countries and provide analytical depth. A final chapter draws together the threads of the book's foregoing contributions to deduce generalisable conceptual insights based on current knowledge and experience. Uniquely, the book provides a conceptual model for Climate Change Acts that can usefully inform the development of national framework climate legislation in all countries.

Global Energy Law and Policy: Volume 4

Global Energy Law and Policy

Series Editors

Peter D Cameron

Pieter Bekker

Volker Roeben

Energy policy and energy law are undergoing rapid global transformation, characterised by the push in favour of decarbonisation. The 2015 Sustainable Development Goals and the 2015 Paris Agreement on international climate action have forged a consensus for a pathway to a universal just transition towards a low-carbon economy for all states and all societies.

This series publishes conceptual works that help academics, legal practitioners and decision-makers to make sense of these transformational changes. The perspective of the series is global. It welcomes contributions on international law, regional law (for example, from the EU, US and ASEAN regions), and the domestic law of all states with emphasis on comparative works that identify horizontal trends, and including transnational law. The series' scope is comprehensive, embracing both public and commercial law on energy in all forms and sources and throughout the energy life-cycle from extraction, production, operation, consumption and waste management/decommissioning. The series is a forum for innovative interdisciplinary work that uses the insights of cognate disciplines to achieve a better understanding of energy law and policy in the 21st century.

Recent titles in this series:

Decarbonisation and the Energy Industry
edited by Tade Oyewumni, Penelope Crossley, Frédéric Gilles Sourgens
and Kim Talus

*The Global Energy Transition: Law, Policy and Economics
for Energy in the 21st Century*
edited by Peter Cameron, Xiaoyi Mu and Volker Roeben

The Law and Governance of Mining and Minerals: A Global Perspective
by Ana Elizabeth Bastida

National Climate Change Acts

The Emergence, Form and Nature of National Framework Climate Legislation

Edited by
Thomas L Muinzer

•HART•

OXFORD • LONDON • NEW YORK • NEW DELHI • SYDNEY

HART PUBLISHING

Bloomsbury Publishing Plc

Kemp House, Chawley Park, Cumnor Hill, Oxford, OX2 9PH, UK

1385 Broadway, New York, NY 10018, USA

29 Earlsfort Terrace, Dublin 2, Ireland

HART PUBLISHING, the Hart/Stag logo, BLOOMSBURY and the Diana logo are
trademarks of Bloomsbury Publishing Plc

First published in Great Britain 2020

First published in hardback, 2020
Paperback edition, 2022

A catalogue record for this book is available from the British Library.

Library of Congress Cataloging-in-Publication Data

Names: Muinzer, Thomas L, editor.

Title: National climate change acts: the emergence, form and nature of national framework climate
legislation / edited by Thomas L Muinzer.

Description: Oxford, UK ; New York, NY: Hart Publishing, an imprint of Bloomsbury Publishing,
2020. | Series: Global energy law and policy; volume 4 | Includes bibliographical references and index.

Identifiers: LCCN 2020040406 (print) | LCCN 2020040407 (ebook) |
ISBN 9781509941711 (hardback) | ISBN 9781509943098 (paperback) |
ISBN 9781509941728 (epdf) | ISBN 9781509941735 (Epub)

Subjects: LCSH: Climatic changes—Law and legislation. | Environmental law, International.

Classification: LCC K3585.5 .N38 2020 (print) | LCC K3585.5 (ebook) | DDC 344.04/6342—dc23

LC record available at https://lccn.loc.gov/2020040406

LC ebook record available at https://lccn.loc.gov/2020040407

ISBN: HB: 978-1-50994-171-1
PB: 978-1-50994-309-8
ePDF: 978-1-50994-172-8
ePub: 978-1-50994-173-5

Typeset by Compuscript Ltd, Shannon

To find out more about our authors and books visit www.hartpublishing.co.uk. Here you will find
extracts, author information, details of forthcoming events and the option to sign up for our newsletters.

FOREWORD

Lord Carnwath

I am delighted to welcome this new and timely study of framework climate change legislation. I recall that the 2015 Paris Agreement under the United Nations (UN) Framework Convention on Climate Change required states parties not only to prepare and maintain successive 'nationally determined contributions', but also to 'pursue domestic mitigation measures with the aim of achieving the objectives of such contributions' (Article 4(2)). There seems to have been little discussion of what is required for effective 'domestic ... measures' under this article. To my mind, this must involve an effective overall legislative framework, supplemented by detailed laws across the different sectors and effective means of judicial enforcement.

As is explained in the chapter by Professor Macrory and Dr Muinzer, the UK led the way with the Climate Change Act 2008. This Act continues to command all-party support. It was recently amended by statutory order to incorporate a mandatory target of net-zero emissions by 2050. Central to the statutory scheme is the expert advice of the independent Climate Change Committee, which reports to Parliament on the success or otherwise of the government's proposals.

In November 2021, this country will be hosting in Glasgow the postponed COP26 conference under the UN Framework Convention on Climate Change. As the Climate Change Committee said in its latest report:

> Strong domestic action will provide the basis for the UK Government's vital international leadership in the coming year as it takes on the presidency of the COP26 climate summit in 2021. The UK's international credibility is on the line.

I believe this applies as much to the law as it does to other areas of public life. It is time for us, as members of the legal community – whether as judges, practitioners or academics – to be thinking what we can do to assist the development and improvement of effective laws and legal institutions here and elsewhere, and how we can feed that thinking into the COP26 process.

This valuable collection contains substantial contributions from a range of leading-edge experts in climate law and policy from around the world. Two broad conceptual and internationalist chapters begin by helping to set an overall framework for discussion, and these are followed by national case study chapters that focus individually on the small number of states that have set major versions of these regimes in place to date. A concluding chapter by the editor then reflects back on the collection as a whole and draws evaluative and analytical lessons in order to provide new insights into what are in essence novel legal regimes crafted to engage with a similarly novel problem (climate change).

More generally, I welcome this comparative study as another step in the journey to achieving effective and coordinated legal protection for the environment and environmental rights at the national and international levels. Climate change is perhaps the greatest challenge to our environment facing present and future generations, but it is one of many. The Global Pact for the Environment, launched by President Emmanuel Macron in 2017 and later presented to the UN is an important attempt to encapsulate our shared rights and responsibilities in concise and compelling form.

The underlying principles are simply expressed in the first two articles:

Article 1

Right to an ecologically sound environment

Every person has the right to live in an ecologically sound environment adequate for their health, well-being, dignity, culture and fulfilment.

Article 2

Duty to take care of the environment

Every State or international institution, every person, natural or legal, public or private, has the duty to take care of the environment. To this end, everyone contributes at their own levels to the conservation, protection and restoration of the integrity of the Earth's ecosystem.

Effective climate change legislation is one indispensable means by which nation-states can honour these commitments. This pioneering study of emerging legislative schemes provides valuable guidance for lawyers and policy-makers grappling with these difficult issues.

ACKNOWLEDGEMENTS

The editor extends special thanks to Anna-Marie McAlinden (Director, Mills Selig solicitors). Particular thanks are also extended to Professor Sharon Turner (European Climate Foundation) and Professor Gavin Little (University of Stirling).

Thanks also to Professor Volker Roeben (University of Dundee) and the team involved with this book at Hart Publishing, especially Roberta Bassi. And special thanks to Lord Carnwath for kindly providing a Foreword to the collection.

CONTENTS

Foreword..v
Acknowledgements... vii
Contributors xi

Introduction 1
Thomas L Muinzer

1. What Do We Mean When We Talk about National
   'Climate Change Acts' and How Important are They
   in the Context of International Climate Law?....................................11
   Thomas L Muinzer

2. 'Paris Compatible' Climate Change Acts? National Framework
   Legislation in an International World..43
   Matthias Duwe and Ralph Bodle

3. The UK's Climate Change Act 69
   Richard Macrory and Thomas L Muinzer

4. Mexico's Framework Legislation on Climate Change: Key Features,
   Achievements and Challenges Ahead...93
   Alina Averchenkova

5. Denmark's Climate Change Act(s) 111
   Sarah Louise Nash

6. Ireland's Climate Action and Low Carbon
   Development Act 2015: Symbolic Legislation,
   Trojan Horse, Stepping Stone?..129
   Andrew Jackson

7. The Swedish Climate Policy Framework Including
   the Climate Act..153
   Åsa Romson and Kristina Forsbacka

8. The Dutch Response to Climate Change: Evaluating
   the Netherlands' Climate Act and Associated
   Issues of Importance..175
   Otto Spijkers and Sofie Oosterhuis

9. *The New Zealand Legislation: Pursuing the 1.5°C Target
    Using a Net Zero Approach* *199*
    Prue Taylor

10. *Conceptualising and Formulating
    National Climate Change Acts* *227*
    Thomas L Muinzer

Index *259*

CONTRIBUTORS

Alina Averchenkova is a Distinguished Policy Fellow at the Grantham Research Institute on Climate Change and the Environment, London School of Economics. She leads the Governance and Legislation research theme at the institute and focuses on the analysis of the implementation of the Paris Agreement, national climate governance and climate legislation. She has over 18 years of experience in this area, having worked previously for the international consultancy KPMG and the United Nations Framework Convention on Climate Change, and as a carbon asset manager with First Climate and the Environmental Defence Fund. She holds a BSc in Geography from Moscow State University, and an MSc and a PhD in Economics and International Development from the University of Bath.

Ralph Bodle has been a Senior Fellow at the Ecologic Institute, Berlin since 2007. He specialises in international and European environmental law and policy. He has supported the German delegation at the UN climate negotiations since 2008 and been a member of the EU negotiating team on legal aspects of climate finance and the Paris Agreement. He has also been involved in other international environmental treaty negotiations. He was a researcher and lecturer in public and international law at Humboldt University, Berlin, taught administrative law at the Berlin Academy for Administration, and was a practising lawyer at law firms advising and representing the public sector on environmental and public law.

Matthias Duwe is Head of Climate at the Ecologic Institute, Berlin. His main role involves the coordination of the institute's climate change-related work strands. His work focuses primarily on the EU's energy and climate policies, including their connections to national policy and the international regime. At Ecologic Institute, he also serves as senior project leader and expert contributor to a variety of projects looking at EU climate policy. He also acts as co-moderator for the European ETS Summer School courses and frequently acts as an expert speaker and host moderator for the Institute's Public Diplomacy Programme.

Kristina Forsbacka is a Swedish lawyer specialising in renewable energy and climate law. She currently conducts a research project on climate finance in collaboration with the Stockholm Sustainable Finance Centre, holding a position as a PhD student at Luleå University of Technology. She is also Expert in the Government Committee investigating Climate Law and Secretary of the Government Committee investigating stricter regulation for when extraction of metals and minerals from alum slate can take place.

Andrew Jackson is Assistant Professor of Environmental Law at University College Dublin. He previously worked for the international law firm Slaughter and May, the UK government's legal service at the Department for Environment, Food and Rural Affairs (DEFRA) and with the non-governmental organisations Friends of the Irish Environment and An Taisce, the National Trust for Ireland, where he was Natural Environment Officer and In-house Solicitor. He has been involved in public interest environmental and planning litigation for many years, including before the Irish, English and EU courts. He is a graduate of Oxford University (BA, Law) and Cambridge University (LLM). He also holds an MSc in Biodiversity and Conservation as well as a PhD from Trinity College Dublin (TCD).

Richard Macrory is a barrister and a member of Brick Court Chambers, London. In 2000 he was awarded a CBE for his services to the environment and law, and in March 2008 he was made honorary Queen's Counsel. In 2010 he was elected a Bencher of Gray's Inn. He joined the Faculty of University College London in 1999, having previously taught at Imperial College London, and was Director of the Environmental Change Institute at Oxford University. He was a Member of the Royal Commission on Environmental Pollution between 1992 and 2003, and was a Board Member of the Environment Agency in England and Wales between 1999 and 2004. He was also the founding editor-in-chief of the *Journal of Environmental Law* and is currently legal correspondent to the *ENDS Report*.

Thomas L Muinzer BA, Dip Eng, MA, Mlegsci, LLM, PhD, FRSA is Senior Lecturer in Energy Transition Law at the Aberdeen University Centre for Energy Law, University of Aberdeen. He undertook his qualifying law degree and other legal qualifications in Northern Ireland at Queen's University Belfast. Prior to commencing his post at Aberdeen, he was Lecturer in Energy Law at the University of Dundee's Centre for Energy, Petroleum and Mineral Law and Policy (2018–20). Previously, he was Lecturer in Law at Stirling University, where he was Co-director of the Law School's major dual-stream LLM/MSc Master's programme (2016–18). He is the author of two books, co-editor of a leading Irish sustainability magazine and sits on two of the Committees of the Law Society of Scotland that regulate aspects of solicitors' training in Scotland.

Sarah Louise Nash is a postdoctoral researcher in the Institute of Forest, Environmental and Natural Resources Policy at the University of Natural Resources and Life Sciences in Vienna, where she holds a Marie Skłodowska-Curie Individual Fellowship for the CLIMACY project (Climate Diplomacy and Uneven Policy Responses on Climate Change on Human Mobility). She previously worked on the 'Climate Change Acts: Comparing Diffusion, Governance and Policy Relevance' project and has conducted case studies of the Austrian, Danish, Scottish and Swedish Climate Change Acts. She holds a PhD in political science from the University of Hamburg. Her first book, *Negotiating Migration in the Context of Climate Change: International Policy and Discourse*, was published in 2019 by Bristol University Press.

Sofie Oosterhuis is currently conducting research at Utrecht University. She has a strong interest in European administrative law and climate change law. She holds an LLB from Utrecht University and a BA from University College Roosevelt, Middelburg, where she majored in political science, legal studies and anthropology.

Åsa Romson is Senior Researcher in Environmental Law and Policy at the IVL Swedish Environmental Research Institute. She holds a LLD (*juris doctor*) in Environmental Law from Stockholm University, where she is board member of the Centre for Environmental Law and Policy. She has been an acting politician and was Sweden's Minister of Climate and the Environment (2014–16) at the time of the Paris Agreement and the formation of the new Swedish Climate Policy Framework.

Otto Spijkers is Professor of Public International Law at the China Institute of Boundary and Ocean Studies (CIBOS), Wuhan University. He is a member of the Committee on the Role of International Law in Sustainable Natural Resource Management for Development of the International Law Association. He was a visiting lecturer at the University of Malta, Xiamen University's China International Water Law Programme (China), the Università degli Studi di Salerno (Italy) and the Association pour la promotion des droits de l'homme en Afrique centrale (APDHAC) of the Université Catholique d'Afrique Centrale (Yaoundé, Cameroon). Previously, he was a lecturer at the Grotius Centre for International Legal Studies at the University of Leiden.

Prue Taylor received her legal qualifications from Victoria University, New Zealand and Tulane University, the US. She currently teaches environmental and planning law at the School of Architecture and Planning. She is the Deputy Director of the New Zealand Centre for Environmental Law and is an elected member of the International Union for Conservation of Nature (IUCN) Commission of Environmental Law and its Ethics Specialist Group. She has authored numerous books and articles. Her book *An Ecological Approach to International Law: Responding to the Challenges of Climate Change* (Routledge, 1998) won a New Zealand Legal Research Foundation Prize. In 2007 she received an outstanding achievement award from the IUCN in recognition of her contribution to law, ethics and climate change.

Introduction

THOMAS L MUINZER

Since the creation of the world's first national framework Climate Change Act in the UK in 2008, major national Climate Change Acts have been starting to emerge in countries across the world. This collection, written by leading scholars and thinkers working in the area of climate law and governance, provides the first comprehensive book-length study of these novel emerging regimes.

The collection offers deep-dive case study chapters that explore specific major national regimes in depth: the UK, Mexico, Denmark, Ireland, Sweden, the Netherlands and New Zealand. In addition to providing useful outlines and analytical evaluations of important Climate Change Acts specific to particular national settings, which have scholarly value in their own right, these chapters also speak in concert with each other. In particular, they actualise the broader definitional, conceptual and internationalist studies of Climate Change Acts set down in Chapters 1 and 2 by rooting those chapters in concrete national experiences.

Further, the evaluative analyses set out in those chapters also feed empirical data into the broader book as a whole, most notably in the case of Chapter 10, 'Conceptualising and Formulating National Climate Change Acts'. This chapter offers the first detailed consideration of how one might usefully conceptualise an optimum Climate Change Act and investigates the sorts of components one might expect to find there and on what basis. In doing so, it is heavily informed by the data and findings embodied by the deep-dive national studies.

Arrangement and Content of the Chapters

Chapters 1 and 2: National Climate Change Acts and the International Sphere

The book's investigations begin with Chapter 1 by Thomas L Muinzer, 'What Do We Mean When We Talk about National "Climate Change Acts" and How Important are They in the Context of International Climate Law?' Following the logical thread inferred by its title, the chapter begins by defining 'Climate Change Acts' ('national framework climate legislation'), after having pointed out and elaborated on definitional and linguistic problems that persist in relation to the term. The relationship of 'Climate Change Acts' to 'climate law' more broadly is also discussed, and a specific 'ICL Regime' concept – standing for 'International Climate Law Regime' – is formulated and fleshed out. This latter device permits the study to situate national framework climate legislation in the context of a complex, emerging international legal tradition in a manner that helps certain evaluative insights to be drawn out pertaining to Climate Change Acts and their relationship to broader international developments.

Chapter 1 can be read fruitfully with Chapter 2, provided by leading climate law and policy authorities Matthias Duwe and Ralph Bodle, entitled '"Paris Compatible" Climate Change Acts? National Framework Legislation in an International World'. Their contribution, read in concert with Chapter 1, provides the first substantial analysis available in the literature on the theme of national framework climate legislation in the context of broader international-level climate developments. Duwe and Bodle enhance the condition of knowledge concerning the complex relationship between national framework climate legislation and the international sphere of law and governance by probing the role and influence of the Paris Agreement, and they also afford special consideration in the latter part of their study to complexities arising for national Climate Change Acts in the European Union (EU) setting. Here, the EU's dense supranational governance tradition can be seen to pose both problems and opportunities as national climate law continues to emerge and evolve. For a range of reasons set out in their chapter, the authors 'conclude that there is a clear connection between the Paris Agreement and the establishment of national climate legislation'.

Duwe and Bodle also find that there has been a significant 'Paris momentum' behind the spread of these national climate laws that is arguably detectible. This serves to emphasise to analysts and researchers that it can be over-simplistic to approach a particular state's 'national' framework climate law in insular terms specific to the internal workings of that state, when in fact significant international regime drivers also exist and, by logical implication, need to be accounted for if the analysis is to be comprehensive. Duwe and Bodle also highlight that although the Paris Agreement employs the device of Nationally Determined Contributions (NDCs) to drive internal state responses to climate change, the NDCs themselves are subject to a degree of short-termism, insofar as they are arranged around timeframes of 5 or 10 years. Depending on one's perspective, 5 and 10-year time blocks may appear to be substantial timescales; however, relative to the Paris Agreement, they are narrow, given that this agreement is concerned with working towards 'net zero' carbon emissions for the second half of this century. Thus, set in this broader time register, the NDCs are short-term in design. One useful means of bridging an arguably problematic gap between short-term NDC framing and necessary long-term objective framing is to employ state-level framework climate legislation. The UK's Climate Change Act 2008 provides a working example of this type of approach, where it incorporates a legally binding milestone emissions reduction date of 2050 (satisfying the longer-term perspective to some extent) and NDC-style 'carbon budgets' that are strung across five-year time blocks, occurring one after another up to 2050 and beyond (satisfying the shorter-term element).

The authors also make a convincing case for the utility of Climate Change Acts in providing a means of usefully absorbing and locking in additional imperatives that filter down from the international level to the national level under the terms of the Paris Agreement. These could include directly required forms of imperatives, such as the implementation of progress reporting measures, to more indirectly useful forms of imperatives, such as opportunities to broaden and formalise the inclusion of public participation. Furthermore, and amongst a range of other insights offered across the analysis as a whole, Duwe and Bodle also find that Climate Change Acts can contribute to achieving the goals of the Paris Agreement, due, in effect, to their capacity to build usefully and in an improving manner on the legal dimensions of the Paris Agreement itself within states. A similar conclusion is reached by Muinzer towards the end of Chapter 1, who engages with the Paris Agreement as one component of the ICL Regime and who points to national framework climate legislation as a means of shoring up significant weaknesses that underpin the Paris arrangements.

Chapters 1 and 2 provide a framing background that enables the deep-dive national case study chapters that follow them to enrich the unfolding elucidation of national Climate Change Acts with reference to concrete national facts, settings and legislation.

Chapters 3–9: National Case Studies

In Chapter 3, 'The UK's Climate Change Act', Richard Macrory and Thomas L Muinzer provide a deep-dive summary and analysis of the world's first example of *national framework climate legislation*, the UK's Climate Change Act 2008. They do so with reference to a basic conceptual scheme posited as a means of outlining and examining the framework, which relates matters to: *mitigation* and *adaptation* characteristics; *substantive* duties and *procedural* duties; and (in looking to the future), *strengthening* and *deepening* opportunities and effects. After addressing the background to the Act, they outline that the framework is designed to drive an economy-wide UK decarbonisation transition, where a pinpointed basket of 'targeted greenhouse gases' is required to be driven down over time. The burden to secure the reductions falls to the Secretary of State, that is, a senior minister in the UK government.

The UK framework is broad, and the legislation is detailed and far-reaching. Drawing on previous discussion of the regime, the authors suggest that the Climate Change Act amounts to something resembling a 'skeleton' framework and that 'flesh' is put on the bones through a variety of secondary legislation and policy practices that are enabled or stimulated by that skeleton regime:

> [The Climate Change Act's] 'blanket-style approach can be construed as a "skeleton" framework that facilitates a potentially broad range of targeted and/or pragmatic political-legal action'; thus, through 'realising and employing' the 'capacities for innovative action' actively enabled by the CCA 2008, which must be realised 'within the framework's permitted parameters' – parameters that both enable action and simultaneously impose constraints upon it – such 'action serves to put flesh on the bones of the skeleton framework and contributes towards the achievement of practical outcomes'. Much of the form and nature of the 'flesh' that is added to the bones arises through capacities for secondary legislation, policy innovation and so on, created by and operating within the acceptable parameters of the skeleton framework.

Extending the skeleton-flesh metaphor, it can be said that the spine or backbone of the legislation is embodied by milestone emissions reduction targets imposed by the Act for 2020 and 2050, and by an associated carbon budgeting scheme created in order to drive down emissions with reference to those targets, strung out in successive five-year carbon accounting blocks. The authors outline that the 2020 target requires a 34 per cent reduction in greenhouse gas emissions based on 1990 levels, and the 2050 target requires a 100 per cent (ie, net zero) reduction. The legislation also creates a Committee on Climate Change, opens up special capacities to implement trading schemes, engages with climate adaptation in a number of ways, and includes various other measures and features.

Mexico's pioneering Climate Change Act is considered in Chapter 4, 'Mexico's Framework Legislation on Climate Change: Key Features, Achievements and Challenges Ahead'. Written by Alina Averchenkova, a leading international expert on the Mexican climate regime, the study provides a detailed analysis of Mexico's General Law on Climate Change 2012 (in Spanish, Ley General de Cambio Climático or LGCC).

It is clear that Mexico's energy circumstances are complex: the country is a substantial oil producer and the tenth largest producer of fossil fuel emissions in the world, yet it is also a climate law pioneer and has a natural environment that is very favourable to a range of renewable energy sources, including solar and wind energy. In passing its Climate Change Act, Mexico's Parliament played a very important role in the development and evolution of national framework climate legislation, as its creation rendered Mexico not only one of the first states to pass such legislation in the world, but also the first nation in the *developing* world to do so. Averchenkova also points out that the Mexican Act has been 'an important achievement for Mexico politically' that has helped the decarbonisation movement face down 'strong opposition from fossil fuel-intensive industry', which exerts a substantial influence on Mexican governance. The framework has 'set the direction of travel for domestic climate policy in the country and laid the foundation for a subsequent ratcheting of ambition'.

The chapter offers an outline of the main features of the Act, which provides for 'long-term objectives for emission reduction, clean energy targets and set[s] up the institutional infrastructure required to deal with climate change'. The framework has been bolstered by an Energy Transition Law, set in place in 2015 and extending to energy production and consumption. Mexico's Climate Change Act itself was also amended in 2018 in order to help it align more effectively with the Paris Agreement. Over the course of her inquiry, Averchenkova emphasises Simone Pulver's thoughtful work on Mexican climate policy and politics, which stresses the important influence of international-level developments over time in stimulating progressive action and responsiveness within Mexico.[1]

For all its strengths, Mexico's Climate Change Act eschews the incorporation of legally binding reduction targets for greenhouse gas emissions. This is an absence that stands out in particular where one compares the final outcome legislation with the account of the UK's equivalent Act, which helped to inspire the Mexican framework, provided in Chapter 3. Nevertheless, it is noteworthy that the Mexican framework does include 10 'transitory articles', which do make reference to specific targets. Transitory articles are a nuanced device employed at times in Mexican law. Averchenkova explains that, in Mexican law, transitory articles:

> [H]ave a temporary validity and are viewed as secondary or auxiliary to the main articles ... Transitory articles are viewed as complementary legislation to existing legislation and they cannot stand on their own ... When it comes to the enactment of a new law, articles of a permanent nature and transitory articles are separated.

Here, then, one finds that reduction targets for greenhouse gas emissions are included in the Mexican Climate Change Act, but they feature in such a way that their legal weighting is in effect voided and they are not legally enforceable.

In Chapter 5, entitled 'Denmark's Climate Change Act(s)', Sarah Louise Nash examines the Danish Climate Change Act and its associated governance context. She emphasises that Denmark is both an early adopter of a Climate Change Act and a state that is a frontrunner in relation to renewable energy. Her treatment of the Danish experience, which, unlike many other countries covered in this volume, has a pronounced tradition of coalition governments, conveys an acute sense of the extent to which the shifting sands of changing governments and coalition alliances can impact climate planning in this sort of environment.

The Danish framework displays a particular sensitivity to transparency and openness, and lays a stress on reporting processes. It also establishes an important independent advisory expert body, the Climate Council. Nash also outlines the role and relevance of a subsidiary document, which she describes as the 'Comments on the Bill', and highlights and discusses the relationship between the Danish Climate Change Act and aspects of national policy. She also discusses a 'Citizens' Initiative' that is likely to result in the creation of a new Danish Climate Change Act.

---

[1] Simone Pulver, 'Climate Change Politics in Mexico' in Henrik Selin and Stacy van Deveer (eds), *Changing Climates in North American Politics* (Cambridge, MA, MIT Press, 2009) 25–46; and Simone Pulver, 'A Climate Leader? The Politics and Practice of Climate Governance in Mexico' in David Held, Charles Roger and Eva-Maria Nag (eds), *Climate Governance in the Developing World* (Cambridge, Polity Press, 2013) 174–95.

Nash's exposition of the Danish experience in Chapter 5 is followed by Andrew Jackson's contribution in Chapter 6, entitled 'Ireland's Climate Action and Low Carbon Development Act 2015: Symbolic Legislation, Trojan Horse, Stepping Stone?' Here, Jackson sketches out the background and content of Ireland's Climate Action and Low Carbon Development Act 2015, interrogating the form and impact of the regime from a range of perspectives. Ireland's recent economic evolution in the context of its EU membership is particularly notable, insofar as Jackson points out that 'Ireland went abruptly from being permitted to grow its emissions to being required to rapidly reduce them, based on its transition during the Celtic Tiger years from a relatively poor to a relatively wealthy country in EU terms'. As a consequence of these developments, Ireland had been subject to a 1993 climate strategy that permitted a greenhouse gas emissions *increase* up to 20 per cent between 1990 and 2000, followed by a permitted 13 per cent emissions increase over the period 2008–12. Next, the state found itself suddenly in the contrary position of 'having one of the highest reduction targets in the EU under the Effort Sharing Decision of 2009, based on its relatively high per capita GDP at that time'. Thus, Ireland's recent economic boom shifted the state's position relatively rapidly from that of an EU Member State that was permitted to increase emissions to one that was expected to decrease them significantly. As the chapter outlines, Ireland has failed to satisfy reductions requirements over the course of this change of direction.

Jackson sketches out what amounts in the context of the developed West to a fairly fiery tradition of cumulative resistance to climate legislation amongst certain sections of Irish society (eg, elements of the Irish Farmers' Association), the government apparatus (including elements of the civil service) and others. These circumstances have emerged from within a socio-political environment where influential narratives misinterpreting climate change as a net benefit have gained some significant degree of traction in elite spheres of governance downwards across the Irish social setting:

> [F]rom the early days of Ireland's response to climate change, an official narrative developed, from State level down, that climate change would be *beneficial* for Irish agriculture. This perspective informed Ireland's first national climate strategy in 1993, which listed as the first bullet point under the implications of climate change for Ireland: 'broadly beneficial effects for the agriculture sector'. This view influenced and arguably continues to influence the views of prominent figures in Irish agriculture.

As to the substance of Ireland's Climate Change Act itself, the chapter captures much that is positive and significant in its development. However, in addition, Jackson is explicit in identifying and highlighting key weaknesses that he detects in the legislation, which serve to foreshadow discussion and analysis in this book's final chapter, where the substantive features of Climate Change Acts are explored from a conceptual and evaluative perspective. In order to inform his broader analytical and evaluative thinking, Jackson draws usefully on the work of Jens Newig. Newig distinguishes four prototypes of legislation, with one of the four varieties being classified as 'symbolic legislation'. This form of legislation 'encompasses those pieces of legislation which are not intended and expected to be legally and substantively effective but which are enacted with certain political-strategic intentions'. Jackson draws on this concept in order to elucidate aspects of the Irish Climate Change Act. He notes that 'symbolic legislation' exists in Newig's thinking on a sliding scale, such that some legislation can be more symbolic than other legislation. He finds that Ireland's Climate Act seems 'to be at the "very symbolic" end of the ["symbolic legislation"] spectrum'.

The examination of Ireland is followed by Chapter 7, 'The Swedish Climate Policy Framework, Including the Climate Act' by Åsa Romson and Kristina Forsbacka, which examines the workings of Sweden's Climate Change Act, which has been in force since January 2018. Romson in particular is especially well placed to open up the mechanics of the Swedish Climate Change Act and highlight key issues arising from its governance setting and schematic design due to her substantial political experience in the country. This culminated (so far as climate matters are concerned) with her appointment as Minister of Climate and the Environment from 2014 to 2016. This tenure covered a period where the foundations of Sweden's Climate Change Act were laid down, and also paralleled a crucial period of international development as the Paris Agreement was finalised and set in place (it was agreed in 2015).

The development of Sweden's Climate Change Act is not as isolated a Bill-to-Act process as one might expect, insofar as the authors clarify that the legislation is to be understood as being nested within the country's Climate Policy Framework, which was decided in 2017 by the Swedish Parliament and placed particular progressive climate obligations on the government. The authors outline that this overall regime divides into three parts: 'The [Climate Policy Framework] adopted consists of three parts: (i) a Climate Act; (ii) new ambitious interim and long-term climate targets; and (iii) a Climate Policy Council.'

Thus, the Climate Policy Framework includes climate mitigation targets *and* a Climate Change Act, with those headline targets being external to the Act itself. The major target goal is to achieve net zero emissions by 2045. The Climate Policy Framework also applies a number of interim milestone targets.

The Act is short, running only to five sections. It places an obligation on the Swedish government to pursue climate policies that will ensure that climate targets adopted by the Swedish Parliament are secured. It also requires the government to present a climate report every year in the Budget Bill and produce a new action plan every four years setting out the ways that national climate objectives will be achieved. The budget and climate policy strands are to be carried out in an integrated, harmonious way, with section 3 of the Climate Act asserting that climate and budgetary targets can interact strategically. The authors summarise that: 'This framework is the most comprehensive climate reform ever approved in Sweden, and it includes one of the world's most ambitious climate targets, as well as a Climate Act.'

In Chapter 8, 'The Dutch Response to Climate Change: Evaluating the Netherlands' Climate Act and Associated Issues of Importance', Otto Spijkers and Sofie Oosterhuis engage with the Dutch Climate Change Act, which entered into force on 1 September 2019. This makes it the second most recently created Climate Change Act treated in an in-depth chapter in this volume – or, indeed, the most recent depending on one's perspective, given that the more recent New Zealand Climate Change Act has taken the form of amendments to pre-existing legislation (see below). Spijkers and Oosterhuis provide an outline of the Netherlands' Climate Act ('klimaatwet') and also, by necessity of the subject matter, the inter-related Netherlands Climate Agreement ('klimaatakkoord'). The Climate Act includes a 95 per cent greenhouse gas reduction target for 2050 based on 1990 emissions levels, which, amongst other things, is bolstered by a parallel requirement for the Netherlands to achieve complete CO_2-neutral electricity production by 2050. The Netherlands is also subject to an intermediate goal of reaching a 49 per cent emissions reduction target on 1990 levels for 2030.

The Climate Agreement is designed to both secure the achievement of the Climate Act's objectives and to implement the Paris Agreement, with its substance having been negotiated by both private and public Dutch parties. It is notable that an Agreement is different in terms of robustness to a Climate Change Act; in particular, the Dutch Climate Act is a law that is binding on the government and thus, in terms of general principle, it is legally enforceable in the courts, whereas the Agreement is not. The authors also devote marked attention to the important *Urgenda* decision in the Dutch courts, which has exerted a ripple effect not just across climate governance in the Netherlands, but also around the world.

Chapter 9, 'The New Zealand Legislation: Pursuing the 1.5 Target Using a Net Zero Approach' by Prue Taylor, provides the last of the deep-dive case study analyses. Here, Taylor opens up the creation and workings of New Zealand's Climate Change Act. It was initially thought that this Act would be stand-alone legislation, but it was ultimately introduced as an amendment to New Zealand's Climate Change Response Act 2002, which had set out the country's emissions trading scheme. The amending legislation that is treated as embodying the New Zealand Climate Change Act was entitled the Climate Change Response (Zero Carbon) Amendment Bill. The amendments were granted assent over the time of this book's preparation, on 13 November 2019, such that the amendments have been passed and received into the Climate Change Response Act 2002. Taylor states that: 'According to the Minister for Climate Change … it will be the first legislation in the world to create a legally binding commitment to "living within 1.5 degrees Celsius of global warming".' This commitment is derived from the Paris Agreement's requirement to 'pursue efforts' to hold global warming to 1.5°C on pre-industrial levels.

Chapter 10

The final chapter concludes the collection by tying together the insights in the preceding chapters, and drawing key lessons and conclusions from the experiences and understandings of national framework climate legislation. It addresses the conceptualisation of Climate Change Acts and their associated design in a general, abstracted way, raising the question of what sort of features might usefully underpin optimal national framework climate legislation. The investigation is informed by the deep-dive case studies in Chapters 3–9, which have elucidated a variety of major national Climate Change Acts in states that have pioneered the form to date. This assists in permitting an overall conceptual outline of an approximately optimum form of Climate Change Act to be speculated upon meaningfully. Based on current knowledge, this theorised general type of framework, which endeavours to highlight, foreground and preserve the paramount and most effective elements of this new form of governance regime, provides a conceptual model that can usefully inform the development of national framework climate legislation in countries that are seeking to adopt a Climate Change Act. It can also make a useful contribution where countries that already employ a Climate Change Act are seeking to review that existing regime with a view to enhancing it.

1

What Do We Mean When We Talk about National 'Climate Change Acts' and How Important are They in the Context of International Climate Law?

THOMAS L MUINZER

I. Introduction

This book is concerned with Climate Change Acts. This chapter, however, begins by pointing out the definitional and linguistic problems that persist when one seeks to apply the term 'Climate Change Act' in a meaningful way in the context of (climate) law. It therefore addresses how one might reduce or avoid such problems in the future. In the course of doing so, it provides a definition of this emerging, innovative form of legislation in careful and exacting terms, equating its intended meaning with *national framework climate legislation*. The discussion then addresses 'climate law' and its general importance, and proceeds to establish and trace a specific 'ICL Regime' ('International Climate Law Regime') that makes it possible to say both meaningful things about climate law in general and to locate national framework climate legislation within that emerging legal tradition in order to interpret its role and significance in the context of a complicated world.

II. What are Climate Change Acts?

The subject of this chapter, in keeping with this book as a whole, is Climate Change Acts.[1] The nature of semantics and linguistic fluidity is such that this compound

---

[1] 'Climate Change Acts' are a particular form of climate legislation (see further the discussion below). Climate legislation has arisen as an increasingly targeted object of research inquiry over the last decade. See, eg, Alina Averchenkova, Sam Fankhauser and Michal Nachmany, *Trends in Climate Change Legislation* (Cheltenham, Edward Elgar, 2017); Rachel Brewster, 'Stepping Stone or Stumbling

term – 'Climate Change Act' – might, in principle, be used as an expression by a range of people who are in fact endeavouring to convey significantly different meanings. While the term clearly indicates that the person employing it is proffering a form of legal designation (ie, it pertains to a legislative 'Act'), the overall linguistic construction does not place much overt qualification on the nature of the Act itself. This is in part due to the fact that although the root issue engaged by the legislation is clearly stated ('Climate Change'), this issue itself, articulated in this general way, is unusually broad and somewhat nebulous. This condition arises chiefly as a consequence of the 'climate' itself being (globally) pervasive[2] and is added to by climate change amounting to a problem that is shared by humanity in general.[3] It is further contributed to by the fact that climate change law and policy, taken broadly, tends to involve economy-wide decarbonisation transitions that are to some extent socio-economically pervasive.[4] Contrast a 'Climate Change Act', for example, with the 'Wild Animals in Circuses Act 2019' passed in England during the course of this book's development:[5] the title of the 2019 Act clearly indicates that it is an Act of Parliament narrowly concerned with some particular creatures (wild animals) in some particular way (their use in circuses). Such narrow clarity is absent from the designation 'Climate Change Act'.

Block: Incrementalism and National Climate Change Legislation' (2009) 28 *Yale Law and Policy Review* 245; Richard Cowart, 'Carbon Caps and Efficiency Resources: How Climate Legislation Can Mobilize Efficiency and Lower the Cost of Greenhouse Gas Emission Reduction' (2008) 33 *Vermont Law Review* 201; Sam Fankhauser, Caterina Gennaioli and Murray Collins, 'Do International Factors Influence the Passage of Climate Change Legislation?' (2016) 16(3) *Climate Policy* 318; Sam Fankhauser, Caterina Gennaioli and Murray Collins, 'Domestic Dynamics and International Influence: What Explains the Passage of Climate Change Legislation?' (2014) Centre for Climate Change Economics and Policy Working Paper 156; Sam Fankhauser, Caterina Gennaioli and Murray Collins, 'The Political Economy of Passing Climate Change Legislation: Evidence from a Survey' (2015) 35 *Global Environmental Change* 52; David Feldman, 'Legislation Which Bears No Law' (2016) 37(3) *Statute Law Review* 212; Steen Gade, *Clever Climate Legislation: A Hands-on Guide for Parliamentarians to Achieve the Paris-Agreement* (Copenhagen, Nordic Council, Denmark, 2017); Janelle Knox-Hayes, 'Negotiating Climate Legislation: Policy Path Dependence and Coalition Stabilization' (2012) 6(4) *Regulation & Governance* 545; Michal Nachmany et al, *The 2015 Global Climate Legislation Study: A Review of Climate Change Legislation in 99 Countries, Summary for Policy-Makers* (Grantham Research Institute, GLOBE, IPU, 2015); Michal Nachmany, Sam Fankhauser and Joana Setzer, 'Global Trends in Climate Change Legislation and Litigation' (Grantham Research Institute on Climate Change and the Environment, May 2017); Navroz Dubash et al, 'Developments in National Climate Change Mitigation Legislation and Strategy' (2013) 13(6) *Climate Policy* 649; Marjan Peeters, Mark Stallworthy and Javier de Cendra de Larragán (eds), *Climate Law in EU Member States: Towards National Legislation for Climate Protection* (Cheltenham, Edward Elgar, 2012); Jim Rossi, 'The Political Economy of Energy and its Implications for Climate Change Legislation' (2009) 84 *Tulane Law Review* 379; Terry Townshend and Adam Matthews, 'National Climate Change Legislation: The Key to More Ambitious International Agreements', CDKN/Globe International (2013); Terry Townshend, Sam Fankhauser, Rafael Aybar, Murray Collins, Tucker Landesman, Michal Nachmany and Carolina Pavese, 'How National Legislation Can Help to Solve Climate Change' (2013) 3(5) *Nature Climate Change* 430.

[2] Roger Barry and Eileen Hall-McKim. *Essentials of the Earth's Climate System* (Cambridge, Cambridge University Press, 2014).

[3] Wolfgang Behringer, 'Global Warming: The Modern Warm Period' in *A Cultural History of Climate* (Cambridge, Polity, 2010).

[4] Sam Fankhauser, 'A Practitioner's Guide to a Low-Carbon Economy: Lessons from the UK' (2013) 13(3) *Climate Policy* 345.

[5] Wild Animals in Circuses Act 2019, c 24.

A common presumption has arisen that typically assumes that a 'Climate Change Act' refers to an item of broadly construed general legislation that has been purpose-built in order to tackle the problem of anthropogenic climate change in some sort of overarching way. The origins of this assumption can be traced to the world's first major Climate Change Act, the UK's Climate Change Act 2008, which has exerted a profound influence.[6] Here, under the terms of the world's first legislative framework climate regime, the UK Parliament became the first national parliament to set long-term legally binding carbon budgets and targets in legislation. Clare et al, drawing on the work of Townshend and others,[7] highlight that 'framework legislation' involves 'wide-ranging laws that define a strategic approach to climate policy'[8] and note that this type of climate legislation is sometimes construed or described as 'flagship' legislation:

> These so-called flagship laws are, by definition, fairly comprehensive pieces of legislation, but they do not offer a complete treatment of all issues … Instead, framework laws often establish institutional structures that facilitate and guide future policy making.[9]

The broader international influence of the UK's pioneer framework, described by Fankhauser, Averchenkova and Finnegan as a 'progressive, world-leading piece of environmental legislation',[10] has been addressed elsewhere by the present writer,[11] is raised at many points across this book[12] and is discussed in depth in the concluding chapter.[13]

As noted above, a form of commonly presumed meaning has emerged from this background, namely, that a 'Climate Change Act' refers to an item of broadly construed framework legislation that has been set in place to deal with anthropogenic climate change in a strategic way. While this sort of presumed meaning seems reasonable given the contextual factors that have just been noted, it is also possessed of a degree of logical force, insofar as the descriptor 'Climate Change Act' is characterised by a degree of linguistic generality (as noted above) that is useful in its own right in signifying the sort of generality indicative of a broadly designed framework Act.[14] Thus, this variety of commonly presumed meaning

---

[6] Climate Change Act 2008, c 27 (UK).

[7] Townshend, Fankhauser et al (n 1); Terry Townshend, Sam Fankhauser, Adam Matthews, Clément Feger, Jin Liu and Thais Narciso. 'Legislating Climate Change on a National Level' (2015) 53(5) *Environment: Science and Policy for Sustainable Development* 5.

[8] Abbie Clare, Sam Fankhauser and Caterina Gennaioli, 'The National and International Drivers of Climate Change Legislation' in Alina Averchenkova, Sam Fankhauser and Michal Nachmany (eds), *Trends in Climate Change Legislation* (Cheltenham, Edward Elgar, 2017) 23.

[9] ibid.

[10] Sam Fankhauser, Alina Averchenkova and Jared Finnegan, '10 Years of the UK Climate Change Act', Grantham Research Institute on Climate Change and the Environment, 19.

[11] Thomas L Muinzer, *Climate and Energy Governance for the UK Low Carbon Transition: The Climate Change Act 2008* (Dordrecht, Springer, 2018) 96–99.

[12] The Act itself is also examined in detail by Richard Macrory and Thomas L Muinzer in ch 3 of this volume.

[13] See Thomas L Muinzer, ch 10 in this volume, section III.A.

[14] For more on these dimensions of the UK Act, see ch 3 in this volume, where it is described by Macrory and Muinzer in this volume as a 'skeleton' regime.

is useful both in terms of emergent shared presumptions within the discipline of climate law and in relation to the manner in which the descriptor term points to a sense of the legislative content. However, one consequence of the sort of descriptive ambiguity that has been flagged up above as being inherent in the term 'Climate Change Act' is that the term might also be employed to describe something that in actuality departs quite considerably from the commonly presumed type of meaning that has just been noted. Indeed, this occurs in practice, with the result that an underlying degree of discursive confusion can arise in relation to this particular type of law. Taking Australia, for example, the 'Climate Change Authority Act 2011' tends through the construction of its title to create a semantic impression that Australia has a 'Climate Change Act' in place, but it does not; this Act is actually narrow in scope and concerns a climate change research and review body.[15]

Uncertainty arising from this type of practice is not limited to the matter of the title of legislation. In other words, it is not merely limited to cases where the legislation in question is actually entitled 'Climate Change Act' or similar; far more commonly, it arises through the function of formal or informal *descriptions* being attached to Acts that may be possessed of clearer or otherwise differing official titles. In other words, the extent to which a particular Act is formally or informally *described* as a 'Climate Change Act' or similar also contributes to the degree of descriptive ambiguity underlying the term's usage.[16] For example, a very narrow legal measure enacted by a parliament that, say, applies a tax on a heavy greenhouse gas-emitting diesel transport fuel in order to incentivise the public to reduce diesel usage and/or move towards less pollutant transport fuel sources might credibly be described as a 'Climate Change Act'.[17] Yet such usage of the term 'Climate Change Act' to describe or refer to this legislation might conceivably mislead a person who first hears 'Climate Change Act' as a description of this fuel tax

---

[15] Climate Change Authority Act 2011 (Australia).

[16] This is illustrated, for example, where a Friends of the Earth publication notes that: 'In addition to the UK [Climate Change Act 2008] there are Climate Change Acts in Wales and Scotland, since action is needed at the devolved level as well' ('What Has the UK Climate Law Achieved and Where Next?', Friends of the Earth briefing paper, 8 July 2018). It is the case that a sub-state Climate Change (Scotland) Act 2009 operates in Scotland at the devolved level within the context of the UK's national Climate Change Act and that it bears all the major hallmarks of framework climate legislation, but an equivalent sub-state Act does not operate in Wales. Instead, certain Wales-specific climate provisions are laid down within the Environment (Wales) Act 2016 and certain other items of legislation. Thus, titular usage of the term (Climate Change Act 2008), quasi-titular quasi-descriptive usage (the Climate Change (Scotland) Act) and quasi-analogous usage (the Environment (Wales) Act 2016) tend to contribute to ambiguity here.

[17] The main text here takes a hypothetical fuel tax Act by way of example; however, numerous real-life examples also exist. For instance, Germany's Offshore Wind Energy Act 2017 (WindSeeG 2017) endeavours to expand offshore wind energy in Germany, in part due to climate change concerns, and might credibly be described as a Climate Change Act. Similarly, Armenia's Law on Energy Efficiency and Renewable Energy 2004 seeks to augment Armenia's energy efficiency and renewable energy levels in order to strengthen the national economy, improve the power system and energy independence, and lower greenhouse gas emissions, and might credibly be described as a Climate Change Act.

legislation without having prior knowledge of the content of the legislation. He or she may assume in the first instance that the term is intended to connote the kind of broadly construed general legislation designed to tackle anthropogenic climate change, commonly known as a 'Climate Change Act', which has been noted above. Nevertheless, the fuel measure, set out in the form of an Act, might still attract the formal or informal description of 'Climate Change Act' (or indeed be officially titled as such).

These circumstances are somewhat unhelpful and reduce clarity, both through departing from headline definitional assumptions persisting in the field and insofar as the broad designation 'Climate Change Act', which is suitable by virtue of this degree of breadth and generality to indicating a broadly designed framework Act, is being applied in the type of scenario just outlined to a narrow Act that does not conform to this sense of meaning. Indeed, according to this line of thinking, numerous countries could be said to have numerous Climate Change Acts in place and even within one country, there might be many 'Climate Change Acts' on the statute books when one tots up the primary legislation designed to deal expressly with climate-related issues or that deals with them indirectly but significantly.[18] An example of this latter form of Act – one that deals *indirectly* but significantly with climate change – will arise where any Act of a national parliament (or of an equivalent national assembly) set in place for non-climate related primary reasons also serves to impact usefully on governance in the sphere of climate change to a greater than negligible extent.[19] Thus, for example, it could just as well be the case that the hypothetical fuel tax Act just mentioned above, which is designed to increase the cost of a heavy greenhouse gas-emitting transport fuel in order to change consumer behaviour, has been enacted for the primary purpose of steering drivers away from particular fuel imports for macro-economic reasons pertinent to the country's economy rather than for climate-related reasons. It might also be the case that the legislation has been officially titled the Diesel Levy Act, as opposed to anything directly climate-related, including 'Climate Change Act'. Yet the net result in climate terms is just the same: if its intended outcomes are realised, the Act will serve to steer consumers away from a fuel source that is higher in fossil fuel emissions, thus contributing to climate change mitigation and falling just as before into the category of an Act that has significance in the sphere of climate law and governance.

Referring to an officially titled 'Diesel Levy Act' as a 'Climate Change Act' for rhetorical convenience does no particular harm per se if the intention and

---

[18] In the UK, for example, such 'Climate Change' Acts would include the Energy Act 2016, the Finance Act 2011 and the Climate Change and Sustainable Energy Act 2006.

[19] In the UK, for example, the Climate Change Levy – a carbon tax levied on the energy bills of non-domestic energy consumers in the UK that forms an important part of the government's climate change strategy – first came into force on April 1 2001 and was introduced under the Finance Act 2000. The Finance Act was set in place for non-climate-related primary reasons, but has also served to impact substantially on governance in the sphere of climate change in the UK via this Climate Change Levy.

implications behind the reference are made clear. However, the consequences become much more problematic where the term 'Climate Change Act' is integrated in a casual rhetorical manner into areas of the technical vocabulary of climate law and governance discourse, or indeed into the official title of an Act where it does not appear to belong.[20] The casual integration of this level of linguistic elasticity into the technical discourse is undesirable and problematic for two main reasons. First, it undermines the general implication that a 'Climate Change Act' pertains to what has been loosely described above as an item of broadly construed general legislation that has been purpose-built in order to tackle the problem of anthropogenic climate change in some sort of overarching way. Second, and quite apart from this first point, it creates confusion by integrating multiple meanings into the discourse under the guise of one compound term, such that it can become very difficult to say things about 'Climate Change Acts' in clear terms as a result.

Indeed, the sorts of confusions and uncertainties pointed to here as arising from the imprecise and inconsistent use of the term 'Climate Change Act' are but the tip of an iceberg, because the problems noted so far operate under the assumption that the interpretive implications pertaining to Climate Change Acts constrict the meaning to Acts of Parliament (Climate Change *Acts*). Yet this is not always the case.[21] Further confusion arises in the technical discourse where it is taken for granted that the term 'climate legislation' – thus including Climate Change Acts – can be used relatively freely to indicate not only executive orders but also other diverse forms of policy-oriented action, with the result that a concrete technical term is used to describe something that it technically is not;[22] in other words, a legislative term (an Act) is employed to indicate something that it is not (a non-Act). Such instances contribute further to an unhelpful degree of applied

---

[20] eg, in the case of the example just discussed, 'Diesel Levy Act' is to be preferred as an official title over 'Climate Change Act': it more suitably indicates the Act's legislative content and it avoids going against the grain of the prevalent understanding of what a Climate Change Act is most commonly understood to connote, namely legislation of a broader, framework-style character.

[21] For example, *Trends in Climate Change Legislation* draws on the cutting-edge Climate Change Laws of the World database in order to generate important research insights. In the introduction to the book, it is noted that: 'There are today *over 1,300 national climate laws* worldwide, broadly defined as laws that address issues of climate change mitigation and adaptation' (Averchenkova, Fankhauser and Nachmany (n 1) 1 (emphasis added)). This is an interesting and helpful statistic, but presently it is stated that: 'As of October 2017 … over *1,300 laws and policies* that directly address climate change mitigation or adaptation' have been detected (ibid 2 (emphasis added)). The uncertainty introduced as to whether national climate laws *or* national climate laws plus policies are part of the stated 1,300 figure renders the meaning and legal (and indeed policy) import of the statement elusive. Presently the text goes on to discuss 'the passing of over *1,300 legislative acts*', such that the meaning of the 1,300 figure is by now unclear (ibid 14 (emphasis added)).

[22] This arises, for example, in the case of the (otherwise excellent) study by Isabella Neuweg and Alina Averchenkova, 'Climate Change Legislation and Policy in China, the European Union and the United States' in Averchenkova, Fankhauser and Nachmany (n 1). The study raises confusion at the outset by asserting that '[t]he focus of the chapter *lies on climate policy, conceptualized as legislation*, objectives and instruments targeted to reduce carbon emissions' (ibid 37 (emphasis added)). Thus, a problematic disjunction arises from the title presenting 'legislation' and 'policy' as two distinct matters on the one hand and, on the other hand, the conceptual treatment rolling legislation *into* the concept of policy in the manner just quoted.

rhetorical elasticity that renders the meaning of the term 'Climate Change Act' uncertain in any generalisable sense. If clarity and lucidity are to be improved in the field of climate law, this tendency must be reduced in the immediate term and avoided wherever possible over the longer term going forward. If a crucial technical term like 'Climate Change Act' can be used in a more sharply defined and consistent way, research, literature, commentary and law itself can proceed more rapidly to a place where it is possible to say considerably more useful and precise things. Given that the discipline of climate law is inherently challenging in its own right,[23] it is in the field's best interests to guard against the layering in of additional further challenges via the integration of imprecise and hazy meanings into the technical discourse.

A great deal more could be said about the semantic and definitional dimensions of the term 'Climate Change Act', but the chief point for the present purposes in the express context of this chapter and the book of which it is a part is to flag up the nature of the definitional uncertainty that presently muddies the waters of law where one seeks to say something of importance about 'Climate Change Acts' in any general way. It has been emphasised that it is difficult at the present time to speak as lawyers or others in an adequately precise manner on the subject of 'Climate Change Acts', or on subjects to which such legislation relates, due to the 'antics of semantics' and the definitional and linguistic imprecision that presently has some tendency to characterise the usage of the term. Thus, if one wishes to say something serious and meaningful in the immediate term – as in the case of this book – one is required to find a way around this problem. The primary means of getting around the problem is to define in precise terms from the outset of any serious study on the subject what it is that one means by 'Climate Change Act' where one seeks to employ the term in any technical sense.[24]

In doing so here for the purposes of this chapter and book, the definitional outline is influenced by the points raised over the course of the discussion above, where it has been noted favourably that the term 'Climate Change Act' is commonly assumed to refer to some variety of broadly construed general legislation that has been designed and set in place by a national parliament (or equivalent national assembly) in order to tackle the problem of anthropogenic climate change in an overarching or otherwise broadly strategic way. As noted above, Townshend and

---

[23] See, eg, Peel's treatment of certain cross-cutting complexities common to climate change litigation, which, she notes, 'are a reflection of the complexities of the problem of climate change itself' and of 'the challenges it poses for conventional legal forms'. Jacqueline Peel, 'Issues in Climate Change Litigation' (2011) 5(1) *Carbon & Climate Law Review* 15, 15.

[24] An alternative way around the problem that is suitable to narrower critiques focused on particular items of legislation is to state at the outset in clear terms the particular legislation that one intends to refer to as a 'Climate Change Act' and then provide a sense of that legislation for the reader. Reid adopts this approach, addressing in detail both the UK Climate Change Act 2008 and the sub-state Climate Change (Scotland) Act 2009 passed by the UK and Scottish Parliaments, respectively. He opens with the words 'The Climate Change Acts ... [etc]' and adds a footnote to indicate that this expression refers specifically across his study to the 2008 and 2009 Acts: Colin T Reid, 'Climate Law in the United Kingdom', in Erkki Hollo, Kati Kulovesi and Michael Mehling (eds), *Climate Change and the Law* (Dordrecht, Springer, 2013), 537.

others have helpfully characterised this sort of regime as both a 'framework' and a 'flagship' law:

> In most countries there is … what Townshend et al. (2013) call a 'flagship' law[25] – a wide-ranging piece of legislation that fundamentally defines a country's approach to climate change, often setting emissions targets or unifying earlier policies under one umbrella. Good examples are Mexico's General Law on Climate Change, passed in 2012, and the French Grenelle laws of 2009 and 2010.[26]

Interestingly, Fankhauser, Gennaioli and Collins have hypothesised and confirmed through data analysis that this sort of strategic framework 'flagship' climate law exhibits a tendency to drive an increase in the quantity of existing climate laws over time in the country in question.[27] On the one hand, this is unsurprising, given that these sorts of laws tend to be designed by their very nature to stimulate action, which presupposes in turn the likely creation of further substantial laws. On the other hand, the finding is also interesting in the broader context of 'law' in general insofar as one may more naturally intuitively expect the creation of an expansive law in a given area of governance to *minimise* the creation of further law (ie, by plugging legal gaps in its own right or by otherwise attending to some legal issue in need of repair or development). The fact that the situation in this area of climate law appears to be the opposite of what might be conventional normative legal expectations arguably stands as further testament to certain novel aspects underpinning climate law itself.

As to the definition set out below for the purposes of this chapter and book, which other commentators may see cause or opportunity to either accept or develop/advance in useful directions going forward, it is notable that the overall approach advocated here has pertinence for 'climate law' as a general field and should not be narrowly confined to discussion of 'Climate Change Acts' within that discipline. The overall methodological point is clear: any loaded technical term that is both employed within the emerging field of climate law and is subject to some notable degree of semantic ambiguity should be carefully and clearly defined from the outset of any major study that endeavours to say something serious with reference to that term.

A. Definition of 'Climate Change Act' for the Purposes of This Book

It is by now clear that this book seeks to provide a first extensive inquiry into a fledgling legislative innovation that has emerged within the sphere of climate law.

---

[25] Townshend, Fankhauser et al (n 1).

[26] Fankhauser, Gennaioli and Collins, 'Do International Factors Influence the Passage of Climate Change Legislation?' (n 1) 322.

[27] Fankhauser, Gennaioli and Collins, 'The Political Economy of Passing Climate Change Legislation' (n 1).

This legislative form tends to be known as a 'Climate Change Act', but it has been clarified above that this term is problematic in nature due to its linguistic elasticity, the imprecise or conflicting way in which it is sometimes employed and the pervasiveness of its primary referent (ie, climate change). Thus, it is helpful to anchor the term and rein in its breadth in order to distinguish the intended narrower object of analysis: here, the intended meaning of the term 'Climate Change Act' should be interpreted as being synonymous with the term 'national framework climate legislation'. National framework climate legislation should be interpreted as follows:

> Reduced to its minimum logical foundations, this form of legislation should be taken to indicate a broad national legislative framework that has been set in place by a state legislature as an Act of Parliament (or equivalent) for the purpose of redressing specific problems posed by climate change in an overarching or otherwise broadly strategic manner within that particular country.[28]

On the concluding point raised in this definition – 'within that particular country' – this feature of the classification seeks to stress that this definition pertains to primary legislation internal to the state. To illustrate this point, take for example the UK's Climate Change Act 2008: even where the legislation opens up or otherwise facilitates trading scheme capacities that can interact with EU and international-level carbon schemes, the framework itself emanates from within the UK and remains indigenous to it.[29] This can be contrasted with the UK's Greenhouse Gas Emissions Trading Scheme Regulations 2012: this instrument was created in the UK, but was issued for the express purpose of transposing EU Emissions Trading Scheme law into the UK legal order.[30] Thus, it cannot be construed as legislation internal to the state in the same manner, given these external transpositional drivers. It is also notable that the words 'set in place by a state legislature as an Act of Parliament' in the definition above both assume and require the existence of a national legislative parliament or equivalent national assembly that can create legislation.

Thus, where the present author or others use the term 'Climate Change Act(s)' throughout this book, unless otherwise indicated, the default assumption is that the intended meaning points to *national framework climate legislation* as defined above: the term should be interpreted in these relatively clear and precise technical terms.

In setting out this definition, the author is influenced by the main existing definition available in the literature at the time of writing, which has been provided by Nash and Steurer. It is quoted in Nash's contribution to this book as follows:

> A Climate Change Act (CCA) can be defined as:
>
> > [F]ramework legislation adopted by parliament that lays down general principles and obligations for climate change policymaking in a nation-state (or sub-state entity),

---

[28] Author's definition.
[29] Macrory and Muinzer, ch 3 in this volume.
[30] Greenhouse Gas Emissions Trading Scheme Regulations 2012, SI 2012/3038.

with the explicit aim of reducing greenhouse gas (GHG) emissions in relevant sectors through specific measures to be implemented at a later stage.[31]

This helpful, concise definition broadly harmonises with the definition set out by the present author above, although there are two pronounced differing emphases of form:

(1) the author's definition does not focus as narrowly on mitigation (described in the Nash-Steurer definition as 'the explicit aim of reducing greenhouse gas emissions'), but rather stays more general (in particular to incorporate the issue of adaptation in addition to mitigation);[32]

(2) the author's definition is expressly concerned with *national* framework climate legislation, which forms the primary analytical focus and overall thematic content of this book, whereas the Nash-Steurer definition implicitly evokes sub-state Climate Change Acts as well (evoked by the term 'sub-state entities').[33] However, note that sub-state entities will no doubt be engaged by national legislation of the kind pertinent to the author's definition in most if not all cases, in spite of the fact that the definition itself places its definitional emphasis on the national dimension inherent in *national framework climate legislation*.

III. Climate Law Matters

The issue of anthropogenic climate change amounts to one of the great challenges of our time. In the context of mainstream cultural concerns, renowned UK television documentary-maker and natural historian Sir David Attenborough has described it as 'our greatest threat in thousands of years'.[34] In the narrower world of scholarly print, it has been appropriately characterised as a 'catastrophe in slow motion', where the slow-moving intensification of the problem (relative to the more immediate appearance of other major natural catastrophes such as earthquakes and asteroid impacts) tends to belie the fact that climate change 'is a catastrophe equal to nearly any other in our planet's history'.[35]

---

[31] Sarah Louise Nash, 'Denmark's Climate Change Act(s)', ch 5 in this volume. See also Sarah Louise Nash and Reinhard Steurer, 'Taking Stock of Climate Change Acts in Europe: Living Policy Processes or Symbolic Gestures?' (2019) 19 *Climate Policy* 1.

[32] See further, eg, Muinzer, ch 10 in this volume, where it is stressed that adaptation in addition to mitigation is a major thematic component that one can expect to find in fully developed national framework climate legislation.

[33] The Climate Change (Scotland) Act 2009, operational within the UK in Scotland, provides a cutting-edge example of a sub-state Climate Change Act.

[34] Sir David Attenborough, quoted in Rebecca Nicholson, 'Climate Change: The Facts Review – Our Greatest Threat, Laid Bare' (*The Guardian*, 18 April 2019), https://www.theguardian.com/tv-and-radio/2019/apr/18/climate-change-the-facts-review-our-greatest-threat-laid-bare-david-attenborough.

[35] Raymond T Pierrehumbert, 'Climate Change: A Catastrophe in Slow Motion' (2005) 6 *Chicago Journal of International Law* 573, 573.

Currently, the international scientific community continues to force political action around the issue by stressing the severity of the problem, most notably through the work of the most developed international scientific body monitoring climate change, the Intergovernmental Panel on Climate Change (IPCC).[36] Progressive action is also being stimulated at present by the emergence of increasingly prevalent climate protests across the world,[37] including those being led by Extinction Rebellion and others, and by changing dynamics within the mainstream news media, which is becoming gradually more inclined to afford climate change the level of coverage it deserves.[38] With these and other complex factors impacting, shaping and moderating political and social thinking and responsiveness pertaining to the climate change challenge, it is also necessary and important to take stock of the sorts of contributions that *law* is making to the current crisis.

Law, of course, really *matters*,[39] not least in the context of humanity's response to climate change, given that law provides a system of rules tailored – it is hoped – to suitably managing problems and permitting society to function appropriately. Where law engages with a social problem effectively, it functions usefully in contributing to improving the problematic matter at issue.[40] However, where law does not engage with a problem effectively, it might unhelpfully neglect or overlook that problem, or – perhaps worse – it might serve to actively impede a capacity to deal with a given problem effectively, not merely through applying unsuitable solutions but also insofar as existing legal constraints can function to prevent appropriate remedial action from being taken in a particular area.[41] While such concerns are not specific to climate law, given that they pervade 'law' in a general sense, from criminal law to contract law, to constitutional law and so on, it is submitted that one must tread especially carefully where the express matter of climate change is at issue, for a number of particular reasons:

- First, as emphasised above, climate change is one of the great problems of our times and therefore the stakes are unusually (and extremely) high in terms of finding appropriate solutions, meaning in turn that the stakes are abnormally high for climate law itself.

---

[36] See further Thomas Stocker et al (eds) *Climate Change 2013: The Physical Science Basis* (Cambridge, Cambridge University Press, 2014); and the many other major assessment outputs from the IPCC.

[37] See, eg, the discussion in Sarah Pickard, *Politics, Protest and Young People: Political Participation and Dissent in 21st Century Britain* (Dordrecht, Springer, 2019) 423–24.

[38] Benedetta Brevini and Justin Lewis (eds), *Climate Change and the Media* (Bern, Peter Lang, 2018).

[39] As notably acknowledged in the title of Alon Harel's exploration of law's intrinsic value in *Why Law Matters* (Oxford, Oxford University Press, 2014).

[40] See, eg, Denis Galligan, 'The Social Value of Law' in *Law in Modern Society* (Oxford, Oxford University Press, 2006).

[41] Martin Luther King Jr eloquently put this point as follows: 'Law and order exist for the purpose of establishing justice and … when they fail in this purpose they become the dangerously structured dams that block the flow of social progress.' Quoted in Abraham A Singer, *The Form of the Firm: A Normative Political Theory of the Corporation* (New York, Oxford University Press, 2018) 246.

- Second, climate law is compelled unavoidably to engage with very complex headline issues, due to the fact that anthropogenic climate change is highly complex in its own right and also due to the fact that its resolution involves (amongst other things) complex economy-wide decarbonisation transitions. These complexities, which are to some extent in-built into the issue, mean that climate law has very substantial challenges that it must inherently rise to.

- Third, climate change poses novel problems for technical/doctrinal law, insofar as it is a unique problem that law has comparatively little experience in grappling with in direct terms.[42] For example, one might contrast the newly emerging sphere of 'climate law' that is crystallising in order to tackle the problem[43] with conventional English criminal law; English criminal law, while being as current and contemporary as any other branch of law one may seek to identify in practice, stretches back in its direct and conscious development over hundreds of years.[44] The novel character of the climate change problem, combined with law's inexperience in managing it directly, leads to newly identifiable practical legal problems that the law must endeavour to cope with effectively.[45]

As noted at the outset, this chapter, in keeping with this book in general, is concerned to examine and investigate crucial aspects of climate law with reference to a fledgling legislative innovation that has emerged recently within that field, namely national framework climate legislation/'Climate Change Acts'. This form of climate law regime has been defined above, such that the conceptual concern here is with a broad national legislative framework that has been set in place by a state legislature as an Act of Parliament for the purpose of redressing specific problems posed by climate change in an overarching or otherwise broadly strategic manner within that particular country.[46]

---

[42] Note, however, that the law has effective experience of governing problems posed by the ozone layer since the latter half of the twentieth century (see the Montreal Protocol 1987) and a tradition of engaging with air pollution under the terms of developed legal regimes stretching back to the 1800s. These sorts of matters synergise with problems posed by climate change and, indeed, these areas of law and aspects of climate law will frequently overlap. Thus, for example, chlorofluorocarbons (CFCs) are ozone gases that national and international law endeavours to reduce in order to protect the ozone layer, and they are also greenhouse gases, such that their mitigation also assists in greenhouse gas emissions reductions within the purview of 'climate law'.

[43] See further Part I ('Climate Law as an Emerging Discipline') of Hollo, Kulovesi and Mehling (n 24).

[44] See further James Fitzjames Stephen, *A History of the Criminal Law of England, Volume 1* (London, Macmillan and Co, 1883).

[45] For example, such technical problems can include questions concerning the following: the extent to which human rights law is to be interpreted as being applicable to particular climate law problems (*State of the Netherlands v Urgenda* ECLI:NL:GHDHA:2018:2591); the extent of the enforceability of legally binding mitigation targets and the remedies that courts might apply in the event of a breach (Colin Reid, 'A New Sort of Duty? The Significance of 'Outcome' Duties in the Climate Change and Child Poverty Acts' [2012] *Public Law* 749); and the relationship between climate law and constitutional law and principles (*Friends of the Irish Environment v Government of Ireland* [2017 No 793 JR]; Thomas L Muinzer, 'Is the Climate Change Act 2008 a Constitutional Statute?' (2018) 24(4) *European Public Law* 733).

[46] Per section II.A above.

In investigating and elucidating certain key reasons behind why these regimes are of relevance and importance in the context of modern climate law and governance, *international* law rather than national law provides an optimum starting point for the purposes of the present chapter, for a number of reasons.[47] First, climate change is an international problem: it is global in scale, its repercussions impact the entire planet, and the greenhouse gas that the international community continues to release into the air accumulates together as one in the shared atmosphere. Second, it is reasonably assumed that international solutions are required in order to tackle a shared international challenge of this nature: the international reaction to the hole in the ozone layer provides a major climate-oriented precedent for this position[48] and further evidence shows that international developments are profoundly bound up with domestic legislative responses to climate change in complex ways.[49] Third, the first and second assumptions outlined above have contributed to driving important developments in international law and a substantial ICL Regime ('International Climate Law Regime') has emerged as a result. This bespoke international regime has acted as a driver that has both contributed to inspiring the creation of Climate Change Acts within various countries at the national level and continues to operate as a functional, important international backdrop as national developments evolve on an ongoing basis across the world.[50]

IV. Emergence and Strengthening of the ICL Regime

Although a first World Climate Conference took place as early as 1979 and the IPCC itself was established in 1988, issuing its first Assessment Report in 1990,[51] it was not until 1992 that international law manifested its first landmark contribution to the problem of climate change: the United Nations Framework Convention on Climate Change (UNFCCC).[52] Agreed in 1992 and entering into force in 1994, the UNFCCC accomplished a great deal. It drew the international community together for the first time under the terms of a common agreed framework

---

[47] See also ch 2 in this volume, which provides further investigation of Climate Change Acts in the international-national setting, taking the Paris Agreement as a targeted focal point, and ch 10, which explores the conceptual content of Climate Change Acts.

[48] See Stuart Bell, Donald McGillivray, Ole W Pedersen, Emma Lees and Elen Stokes, 'Climate Change, Ozone Depletion and Air Quality' in *Environmental Law*, 9th edn (Oxford, Oxford University Press, 2017).

[49] Fankhauser, Gennaioli and Collins, 'Do International Factors Influence the Passage of Climate Change Legislation?' (n 1).

[50] The delineation of the ICL Regime in this study focuses chiefly on general milestones in the regime's development rather than on granular detail. This is for two reasons: first, limitations of space constrain the scope of the analysis; and, second, it is more useful analytically to first acquire a broad view of the ICL Regime rather than getting lost at the outset in a degree of granular detail that would serve to prevent some overall headline sense of the regime's broader development being sketched out.

[51] IPPC, 'First Assessment Report', *Volumes I–III* (1990).

[52] United Nations Framework Convention on Climate Change 1992.

predicated on mutual objectives and principles.[53] It also established international emissions monitoring and reporting processes, and set in place various supporting bodies, including a UNFCCC Secretariat.[54] Further, it provided for regular 'Conference of the Parties' meetings to take place on an ongoing basis, that is, large-scale meetings focused on the climate change challenge where signatory parties to the UNFCCC could come together in a productive conference format. In practice, these events involve senior international leaders and diplomats, and they also typically attract numerous others, including from the media, the NGO sector, think tanks and research institutes.

Certain elements of the UNFCCC's legal text are somewhat curious or imprecise. This includes Article 7, which establishes the Conference of the Parties mentioned above. In doing so, Article 7 describes it as the 'supreme body of this Convention';[55] this seems an unusual way to refer to the regular gatherings or conferences of the signatory states. Article 7(2)(m) asserts that: 'The Conference of the Parties … shall: [e]xercise such other functions as are required for the achievement of the objective of the [UNFCCC] as well as all other functions assigned to it under the [UNFCCC].'[56] The 'objective' noted here requires one to refer to Article 2, 'Objective'.[57] Here the UNFCCC's objective is defined as follows:

> The ultimate objective of this Convention … is to achieve … stabilization of greenhouse gas concentrations in the atmosphere at a level that would prevent dangerous anthropogenic interference with the climate system. Such a level should be achieved within a time-frame sufficient to allow ecosystems to adapt naturally to climate change, to ensure that food production is not threatened and to enable economic development to proceed in a sustainable manner.[58]

The general delineation of the Conference of the Parties' scope and remit under Article 7, and particularly the honing of that delineation by Article 7(2)(m) to the stipulation that it can '[e]xercise such … functions as are required for the achievement of' the sort of sweeping objective noted above, amounts to a dramatic over-statement of the Conference's powers. In practice, the principle of state sovereignty means that the Conference has no licence to intrude on individual state responses to climate change beyond what autonomous individual states

---

[53] See, eg, Kilaparti Ramakrishna, 'The UNFCCC: History and Evolution of the Climate Change Negotiations' in *Climate Change and Development: A Collaborative Project of the UNDP Regional Bureau for Latin America and the Caribbean and the Yale School of Forestry & Environmental Studies* (New Haven, UNDP) 47–62 (in particular 'The Unique Nature of the United Nations Framework Convention on Climate Change', 51–53).

[54] On these and the rest of the UNFCCC's components, see further the treaty itself. Rich commentary is also provided by Daniel Bodansky, Jutta Brunnée and Lavanya Rajamani, 'The Framework Convention on Climate Change' in *International Climate Change Law* (Oxford, Oxford University Press, 2017).

[55] UNFCCC, art 7(2).

[56] ibid art 7(2)(m).

[57] ibid art 2.

[58] ibid.

themselves may expressly permit.[59] Moreover, as noted above, the Conference of the Parties as presently configured is primarily a diplomatic gathering rather than some form of constituted institution (a 'supreme body') that can truly 'exercise functions' in the way described.

Setting the narrower issue of slightly uneven textual content aside, the 1992 UNFCCC taken in a broader general sense is largely devoid of precise, specific measures that can be applied to deal with climate change in meaningful practical terms within states.[60] Thus, the international community further developed the ICL Regime, building on these 1992 landmark foundations in an effort to respond to this type of problem. Article 17 of the UNFCCC permits the parties to the agreement to create and adopt 'protocols' together, that is to say, legally binding agreements linked to the UNFCCC that operate within its broad-brush parameters.[61] This creates opportunities to innovate going forward and, in particular, to improve existing weaknesses and generalities underpinning the existing ICL Regime. This mechanism was employed in 1997 to enact the Kyoto Protocol.[62] The Kyoto Protocol, so called because it was adopted on 11 December 1997 in Kyoto, Japan, embedded a range of innovations into the ICL Regime; most importantly, it entrenched legally binding greenhouse gas emissions reduction targets for the first time, applying them to a large cohort of developed world UNFCCC signatory nations.[63]

The Kyoto Protocol advanced the ICL Regime substantially. Entering into force on 16 February 2005, its reduction targets centred on developed countries because these nations were economically robust and could thus cope with the imposition of significant emissions reductions obligations.[64] They were also responsible historically for the majority of greenhouse gas emissions since the inauguration of the Industrial Revolution.[65] Implementation rules for the emissions reductions obligations were set in place after much international debate at Marrakesh, Morocco,

---

[59] A counter-argument would be that in signing the UNFCCC, states have agreed to grant to the Conference of the Parties the sort of sweeping powers noted here by virtue of the fact that they have signed the agreement and are thus bound by it under the terms of international law. However, the Conference of the Parties insists that state sovereignty must be respected (see UNFCCC Decision 2/CP.17), as does the preamble of the UNFCCC: 'Reaffirming the principle of sovereignty of States in international cooperation to address climate change' (etc).

[60] The UNFCCC's substance has been elucidated in detail by Bodansky: Daniel Bodansky, 'The United Nations Framework Convention on Climate Change: A Commentary' (1993) 18 *Yale Journal of International Law* 451.

[61] UNFCCC, art 17.

[62] Kyoto Protocol to the United Nations Framework Convention on Climate Change.

[63] ibid Annex B; this sets out reduction targets applicable to UNFCCC, Annex I parties.

[64] On both the Kyoto Protocol's background and content, see further Sebastian Oberthür and Hermann Ott, *The Kyoto Protocol: International Climate Policy for the 21st Century* (Dordrecht, Springer, 1999).

[65] The overall approach was pursuant to art 3(1) of the UNFCCC, which asserts that: 'The Parties should protect the climate system ... in accordance with their common but differentiated responsibilities and respective capabilities. Accordingly, the developed country Parties should take the lead.'

in 2001, entitled the 'Marrakesh Accords'.[66] The binding reduction targets were required to be achieved over the period 2008–12,[67] pursuant to Article 3 of the Kyoto Protocol:

> The Parties included ... shall ... individually or jointly, ensure that their aggregate anthropogenic carbon dioxide equivalent emissions of the greenhouse gases listed in Annex A do not exceed their assigned amounts ... in accordance with the provisions of this Article, with a view to reducing their overall emissions of such gases by at least 5 per cent below 1990 levels in the commitment period 2008 to 2012.[68]

As this provision states, the overall obligation on developed nations was to reduce greenhouse gas emissions by 5 per cent based on 1990 emissions levels. This figure was disaggregated out so that different nations received different reduction targets within the 5 per cent bubble.[69] For example, the EU (at that time named the European Community) received an 8 per cent reduction figure overall.[70] The UK received a 12.5 per cent reduction within that 8 per cent bubble, Germany received 21 per cent etc and some Member States were permitted increases, such as Ireland, which was allowed a 13 per cent increase.[71] The Protocol also created or expanded special market mechanisms in the context of the UNFCCC in order to assist with achieving reductions.[72]

Here, the ICL Regime as initially delineated under the terms of the UNFCCC and then developed by the Kyoto Protocol can be seen to have increased in strength:

---

[66] 'The Marrakesh Accords & the Marrakesh Declaration'; this is the collective title for a bundle of agreements reached at COP 7.

[67] The emissions reduction implementation period ran over 2008–12 insofar as this constituted the formal implementation period under the agreement; however, states were free to proceed with pursuing emissions reductions objectives within the parameters of the Kyoto Protocol prior to 2008 if they chose to do so. The agreement itself came into force in 2005.

[68] Kyoto Protocol, art 3(1). Although this is a relatively robust example of law in the express context of international climate law, where the legal framing is characteristically 'soft', taken in isolation on its merits, this legally binding provision is expressed in soft language in its own right. Precise, tight legal drafting would replace the words 'with a view to reducing their overall emissions of such gases by at least 5 per cent' with the words 'will reduce their overall emissions of such gases by at least 5 per cent', or equivalent.

[69] ibid Annex B.

[70] ibid.

[71] These emissions levels were set out in EU law in Decision 2006/944/EC: Commission Decision of 14 December 2006 determining the respective emission levels allocated to the Community and each of its Member States under the Kyoto Protocol pursuant to Council Decision 2002/358/EC (notified under document number C(2006) 6468). Again, the framing of climate law at the international level is somewhat unhelpful here. The Kyoto Protocol set all the EU Member States' targets at an 8 per cent reduction (see Annex B); however, the EU as a whole was given an 8 per cent bubble in that same Annex. This bubble permitted the EU, in a legally legitimate manner, to assign differing targets to its Member States within the 8 per cent target. As a result, in the case of Ireland (for example), the lawyer referring only to the Kyoto Protocol would find that an 8 per cent reduction was applied to the Member State (Annex B), whereas the lawyer referring only to EU law would find that a permissible 13 per cent increase was applied (Decision 2006/994/EC). If the first lawyer ceased inquiries there, he or she would be subject to a misleading interpretation of Ireland's headline obligation.

[72] See in particular art 17 of the Kyoto Protocol concerning international emissions trading, art 6 on joint implementation and art 12 on the clean development mechanism.

most importantly, the Kyoto Protocol fleshed out legally binding reduction targets and applied them to states in the context of a sophisticated formal implementation phase. Granted, the 5 per cent overall reduction level for 2008–12 did not go remotely far enough towards securing appropriate levels of mitigation suitable for holding the earth's rising global temperature average to safe levels. Nevertheless, it added a significant building block to the unfolding ICL Regime that the international community was well placed to bulk out and further develop over subsequent Kyoto-style phases, which were anticipated to follow on from this initial starting phase. This momentum towards continuation was built into the Kyoto Protocol itself, per Article 3(9):

> Commitments for subsequent periods for Parties included in Annex I [to the UNFCCC] shall be established in amendments to Annex B to this Protocol, which shall be adopted in accordance with the provisions of Article 21, paragraph 7. The Conference of the Parties serving as the meeting of the Parties to this Protocol shall initiate the consideration of such commitments at least seven years before the end of the first commitment period referred to in paragraph 1 above.[73]

Another legitimate criticism of the initial Kyoto arrangements concerns the fact that only 37 industrialised countries and the EU agreed to be legally bound and participate in the 2008–12 Kyoto I phase, with the US excluding itself. China and India also excluded themselves; these two countries, along with the US and the EU, were the world's four largest greenhouse gas emitters at the time, meaning that three out of four of the world's major emitters were outside of Kyoto's 2008–12 purview. But, again, there remained something meaningful to build on over future phases, such that hope was held out that these parties and indeed other states could be persuaded to join in due course.[74]

Some analysts were incorrectly concluding as early as 2001 that the Kyoto Protocol had failed already.[75] In reality, the 2008–12 phase proceeded with a degree of success in practice, notwithstanding the neglect of certain key obligations by a minority of parties, perhaps most dramatically Canada, where the government did not take appropriate steps to curb Canadian emissions and then exited the agreement in 2011 in the midst of the compliance period.[76] On the face of it, this action appeared to amount to the first major breach of international climate law in its short history to date, given that Canada failed consistently to constrain its emissions in line with the reduction period it was subject to, then withdrew from the arrangement that it had agreed formally to be bound to. The Canadian government's response was that Canada had a 'legal right to formally

---

[73] ibid art 3(9).

[74] For an insight into the negotiation, adoption and content of the Kyoto Protocol, see further Oberthür and Ott (n 64).

[75] See David Victor, *The Collapse of the Kyoto Protocol and the Struggle to Slow Global Warming* (Princeton, Princeton University Press, 2001).

[76] 'Canada Pulls out of Kyoto Protocol (*The Guardian*, 13 December 2011), https://www.theguardian.com/environment/2011/dec/13/canada-pulls-out-kyoto-protocol.

withdraw'[77] and, subject to certain timing and notification conditions set down in the Protocol for the purpose, this indeed appears to be the case.[78] In the present writer's view, it appears that Canada met the withdrawal conditions set down at Article 27 of the Kyoto Protocol and so the likelihood is that no breach of the law technically occurred.[79] Added to this, breaches of law require a cause of action and it is difficult to see what occurred that equates to an actionable breach; in leaving in the midst of a compliance period, Canada had not yet committed a breach of the target for the compliance period, as it was not yet over. At any rate, due to a lack of significant compliance and enforcement mechanisms present in the ICL Regime, no meaningful negative legal consequences did, nor would have, followed for Canada either way, and no remedies existed to be applied for this type of breach – if indeed it had amounted to a breach – under the terms of the ICL Regime.

V. Weakening of the ICL Regime

Imperfect as it may have been, significant progress had been made under 'Kyoto I' (2008–12), where the Kyoto Protocol built usefully on the UNFCCC by developing and strengthening the ICL Regime in certain respects. This occurred most conspicuously via the introduction of meaningful binding emissions reduction targets that were passed down from the international level to a significant cohort of developed nations. Presently, however, the ICL Regime's development became stalled as state negotiators struggled to construct a broadly accepted 'Kyoto II' phase (2013–?) that could follow on from Kyoto I.[80] This logjam occurred chiefly as a consequence of an inability amongst state leaders, national ministers and senior state diplomats to achieve a commonly accepted agreement on a way forward, in spite of the fact that the UNFCCC applies an obligation to secure 'stabilization of greenhouse gas concentrations in the atmosphere at a level that would prevent dangerous anthropogenic interference with the climate system … within a time-frame sufficient to allow ecosystems to adapt naturally to climate change'.[81] With time running out on Kyoto I in the approach to 2012, the UNFCCC parties

---

[77] The quotation comes from then Canadian Environment Minister Peter Kent, quoted here: Adam Vaughan, 'What Does Canada's Withdrawal from Kyoto Protocol Mean?' (*The Guardian*, 13 December 2011), https://www.theguardian.com/environment/2011/dec/13/canada-withdrawal-kyoto-protocol.

[78] Kyoto Protocol, art 27.

[79] See further ibid. On 15 December 2011, Canada informed the Depositary that it had decided to withdraw from the Kyoto Protocol. In accordance with art 27(2) of the Protocol, Canada's withdrawal took effect on 15 December 2012. See Depositary Notification C.N.796.2011.TREATIES-1 dated 16 December 2011, available in English at: https://treaties.un.org/doc/Publication/CN/2011/CN.796.2011-Eng.pdf.

[80] See further the special issue of the International Institute for Sustainable Development's *Earth Negotiations Bulletin* (12(567)) entitled 'Summary of the Doha Climate Change Conference: 26 November–8 December 2012'. This includes detailed coverage of both the Doha conference negotiations and the background lead-up to it.

[81] UNFCCC, art 2.

finally agreed and adopted a new legal text at the eleventh hour on 8 December 2012, just before the Kyoto I phase concluded at the end of the month without a regime to succeed it. The agreement was named the Doha Amendment to the Kyoto Protocol, because it was adopted at Doha, Qatar.[82]

The Doha Amendment legally amended the Kyoto Protocol, introducing a new commitment period.[83] This second commitment period was designed to span the period from 1 January 2013 to 31 December 2020, and the timeframe has not yet elapsed at the time of writing. Its primary purpose has been to apply new emissions reduction obligations to Annex I Parties to the UNFCCC by virtue of amending the targets at Annex B to the Kyoto Protocol,[84] thus serving to extend the progress made on the implementation of progressive emissions reduction targets under the Kyoto I phase into the new period for 2013. It ramps the original 5 per cent reduction figure up to a minimum of 18 per cent for 2013–20 based on 1990 emissions levels.[85]

On the face of it, the Doha extension appeared to develop the ICL Regime in a very encouraging direction, most particularly by extending Kyoto I and augmenting its headline reduction target. However, this is not to say that problems did not continue to persist from the outset, even where such apparently beneficial dimensions are considered in isolation. The 18 per cent figure was a substantial improvement on the preceding 5 per cent, but was still too low to hold increasing average global temperatures to anything approaching safe levels.[86] Further headline problems included a persisting need for more developed countries to join the reductions drive in order to achieve improved mitigation outcomes, not least the US. Moreover, such difficulties were exacerbated by a minority of developed countries that *had* participated initially in the first Kyoto compliance period, but that subsequently refused to receive Kyoto II emissions reductions.[87] In this respect, the Kyoto Protocol received a particularly resonant blow on a symbolic level when Japan, which had been party to the Kyoto I period, refused to adopt Kyoto reductions beyond this.[88] In addition to Japan's position as a developed economy that emits substantial quantities of greenhouse gas, the Protocol itself was named after Kyoto in Japan and was facilitated and signed there. Thus, Japan's withdrawal amounted to a heavy loss both in terms of actual emissions reductions

---

[82] Decision 1/CMP.8 Amendment to the Kyoto Protocol pursuant to its Article 3, paragraph 9 (hereinafter the Doha Amendment).

[83] ibid Annex 1, art 1.

[84] ibid Annex 1, art 1.A.

[85] ibid Annex 1, art 1.C, amending Kyoto Protocol, art 3(1).

[86] As stressed by the *Earth Negotiations Bulletin* in its summary commentary on the Doha negotiations and the Doha Agreement: 'it is well-known that the average 18% emission reduction by Annex I parties from 1990 levels in 2013–2020 is not nearly enough to put the world on track to avoid the 2°C temperature increase limit'. *Earth Negotiations Bulletin* (n 80) 26.

[87] Note also the case of Canada discussed above, which withdrew during the first Kyoto phase (it also refused to adopt emissions reductions in the second Kyoto phase).

[88] Thomas L Muinzer, *Climate and Energy Governance for the UK Low Carbon Transition: The Climate Change Act 2008* (Dordrecht, Springer, 2018) 90–91.

contributions under the ICL Regime and in terms of the broader undermining signals that the Japanese withdrawal sent. In addition to Japan, New Zealand and the Russian Federation also participated in Kyoto I and withdrew from Kyoto II. These circumstances have increased a lack of legal coherence that troubles the ICL Regime, insofar as it is unclear as to how an Annex I UNFCCC state can be party to the Kyoto Protocol without adopting the Kyoto II emissions limits.[89]

Such difficulties and apparent inconsistencies notwithstanding, in principle the Doha Amendment nevertheless provided for the meaningful extension of the Kyoto regime over a significant period of time, improved on its overall reduction figure from 5 per cent to 18 per cent, and created conditions where other countries could be brought within the compliance period's parameters going forward if they could be so persuaded. There was much to build on.

However, one over-riding problem emanating from the domain of law has served to undermine much of this positive potential: the Kyoto II period is not yet in legal force.[90] Article 2 of the Doha Amendment asserts that: 'This amendment shall enter into force in accordance with Articles 20 and 21 of the Kyoto Protocol.'[91] Articles 20 and 21 of the Kyoto Protocol establish amending criteria, with Article 20(3)–(4) stating as follows:

> (3) The Parties shall make every effort to reach agreement on any proposed amendment to this Protocol by consensus. If all efforts at consensus have been exhausted, and no agreement reached, the amendment shall as a last resort be adopted by a three-fourths majority vote of the Parties present and voting at the meeting. The adopted amendment shall be communicated by the secretariat to the Depositary, who shall circulate it to all Parties for their acceptance.

> (4) Instruments of acceptance in respect of an amendment shall be deposited with the Depositary. An amendment adopted in accordance with paragraph 3 above shall *enter into force for those Parties having accepted it on the nineteeth day after the date of receipt by the Depositary of an instrument of acceptance by at least three fourths of the Parties to this Protocol.* (Emphasis added)[92]

Thus, against a backdrop of disagreement as Kyoto I came close to timing out, the 'agreement … by consensus' over the most appropriate way forward outlined in Article 20(3) could not be reached by diplomats, and consequently the law requires a minimum of three-quarters of the signatory parties to deposit instruments of

---

[89] Thus, Bothe notes that: 'From a legal and technical point of view, the way in which the Doha conference responded to the refusal of the three states [ie, Japan, New Zealand and Russia] is peculiar. One has to wonder whether it is legally possible for an Annex I state to be a party to the KP [Kyoto Protocol] without accepting any [quantified emission limitation and reduction commitments]. New Zealand expressly declared that it would remain a party to the KP, but that it would only accept reduction obligations in accordance with the UNFCCC. Whether this approach is legally tenable is a question of interpretation of the KP.' See further Michael Bothe, 'Doha and Warsaw: Reflections on Climate Law and Policy' (2014) 4(1–2) *Climate Law* 5.

[90] This is the case at the time of writing in May 2020.

[91] Doha Amendment, art 2.

[92] Kyoto Protocol, art 20(3)–20(4).

acceptance to permit the Doha Amendment to 'enter into force' (Article 20(4)); three-quarters or more have not yet done so.[93]

Some encouraging diplomatic consequences have flowed from Kyoto II in spite of these circumstances, such as some states being inspired or encouraged by it in various ways and, indeed, certain nations pursuing its obligations in spite of its lack of legal force because they have chosen to do so.[94] Nevertheless, this particular evaluation of headline trends in the ICL Regime is concerned with the condition of *law*, as opposed to diplomacy, inspiration or otherwise. The late Justice Louis Brandeis of the US Supreme Court points out that: 'If we desire respect for the law we must first make the law respectable.'[95] The fact that this hard-fought framework, engaging with the crucial issue of climate change, has not yet been brought into law is about as serious a problem as one can encounter in the context of international climate law in purist lawyerly terms. Kyoto II was 20 years in the making, insofar as one can trace its outworking from the emergent ICL Regime seeded in 1992 by the UNFCCC. Kyoto II's persistent lack of ratification serves to reduce and undermine the momentum and force that had been building at the international level of governance 'above' states under the terms of the ICL Regime.

One finds little deep critical evaluation of the implications of Kyoto II's lack of legal force in existing legal and other serious commentary.[96] This is all the more surprising given that leading authorities, including Bodansky, Brunnée and Rajamani, pointed out insightfully back in 2017 that 'the Doha Amendment is yet to (*and may never*) enter into force' (emphasis added).[97] Instead, they noted, the

---

[93] As of 1 May 2020, 137 parties have deposited instruments of acceptance with the UNFCCC Depositary out of a required minimum total of 144 (author's inquiry).

[94] For example, the EU completed ratification of the Doha Amendment on 21 December 2017. Internally, this required 30 ratifications in total by the then 28 EU Member States, Iceland and an overall EU ratification. The EU has been working towards its overall 2020 target under the Doha Amendment through its 20–20–20 Climate and Energy Package. As Böhringer and Keller noted in 2011: 'The main driving force behind the Climate and Energy Package was the EU's ambition to play a leading role in the battle against anthropogenic climate change. More specifically, the EU had hoped to push an international greenhouse gas emission reduction agreement during the Copenhagen climate change conference in December 2009 as a follow-up to Kyoto which is to expire in 2012.' Christophe Böhringer and Andreas Keller, 'Energy Security: An Impact assessment of the EU Climate and Energy Package' (2011) 335(11) *Wirtschaftswissenschaftliche Diskussionspapiere* 4.

[95] Joseph Baron (ed), *A Treasury of Jewish Quotations*, (Lanham, MD, Rowman and Littlefield, 1996) 269, quoting Brandeis in the *Cleveland Plain Dealer* (15 October 1912).

[96] Unless one turns to the frequently neglected voices of those in the developed world who are on the frontline of the negative consequences to be suffered as a result of the shortcomings. For example, Nagmeldin El Hassan, Chair of the African Group of negotiators at the Lima, Peru COP in December 2014, has stated: 'We would like to point out that slow ratification of Commitment Period Two of Kyoto by developed countries does not build confidence. In our view, the developed countries are reneging, abandoning and weakening the Kyoto Protocol.' Wambi Michael, 'Africa Laments as Kyoto Protocol Hangs in Limbo' (*Our World*, 12 April 2014. unpaginated *Inter Press Service* release). In scholarly analysis, see further Robert Keohane and Michael Oppenheimer. 'Paris: Beyond the Climate Dead End through Pledge and Review?' (2016) 4(3) *Politics and Governance* 142.

[97] Daniel Bodansky, Jutta Brunnée and Lavanya Rajamani, *International Climate Change Law* (Oxford, Oxford University Press, 2017) 206.

Paris Agreement seems 'set to take over from the Kyoto Protocol', meaning that a 'significant departure from the protocol' appears to be under way.[98] Zahar put matters somewhat more bluntly in 2014 in noting that:

> The [UN]FCCC's offshoot treaty, the Kyoto Protocol, is more concrete and prescriptive than the [UN]FCCC about mitigation targets for individual states ... While it still has some life in it, it is already considered doomed. It will limp on until 2020, after which it will be retired.[99]

These important observations concerning profound changes to the form and emphasis of the ICL Regime indicate that detailed targeted research is required in order to better understand and assess the impact that these major likely developments are due to exert in this crucial area of global governance.

VI. Strength and Weakness Trends in the ICL Regime So Far

The present analysis has placed an analytical focus on international law and has isolated for the purposes of investigation an important thread of emergent law within the international legal order. This thread has been summarised for analytical convenience and utility as the ICL Regime, encapsulating a specific and important international climate law regime that has been unfolding and evolving at the international level over recent decades. This novel regime has acted as an international-level driver that has served to establish 'top-down' conditions favourable to the construction and passage of Climate Change Acts within certain states at the national level.[100] It continues to influence conditions in the context of state-level climate law substantially.[101] Furthermore, it will be argued below on the evidence that the present condition of the ICL Regime also serves to validate the intrinsic utility and importance of Climate Change Acts in their own right going forward.

Thus far, the analysis has traced the first major roots of the ICL Regime to the 1992 UNFCCC treaty. It has been seen that these roots were first set down in the form of an important, unifying framework, replete with objectives, common

---

[98] ibid.

[99] Alexander Zahar, *International Climate Change Law and State Compliance* (Abingdon, Routledge, 2014), 2.

[100] On this point, see also Matthias Duwe and Ralph Bodle, ch 2 in this volume.

[101] In noting that national climate legislation exists in a global context in spite of its more overtly 'national' character, Brewster points out that '[u]nlike international arenas where recalcitrant countries can be cut out of the benefits of cooperation (such as international trade), the global commons is nonexcludable' and therefore 'a solution to the climate change crisis requires multilateral cooperation'. Rachel Brewster, 'Stepping Stone or Stumbling Block: Incrementalism and National Climate Change Legislation' (2009) 28 *Yale Law & Policy Review* 245, 311. Thus, a 'two-level game' can be interpreted as playing out between the national and international arenas; see further Brewster (ibid), drawing on the work of Putnam.

procedures and mechanisms that the international community could usefully build on. The UNFCCC was not a robust, practical regime, but merely an important starting point. Thus, for example, it did not embed in law specific substantial measures designed to drive down emissions that were to be applied 'downwards' to states in a legally binding manner. Nor did it contain legally binding emissions reduction targets. It has been concluded above that the ICL Regime was in a weak condition at this time.

It has also been established that the 1997 Kyoto Protocol presently strengthened the ICL Regime. It did so chiefly through employing the tools of international law as a means of applying the latter of the two toughening approaches mentioned above: that is, it applied legally binding emissions reduction targets 'downwards' from the international level to (at that time) a limited pool of developed countries. Certain broad international-level mechanisms were also opened or expanded, such as emissions trading and joint implementation, albeit that each state with a binding reduction commitment retained the legal freedom to follow its own course as to how best to meet its target in practice. It has been concluded above that the ICL Regime was in a stronger condition over the 2008–12 Kyoto I compliance period than it had been previously.

The investigation above then considered the 2013–20 Kyoto II period, pointing out that the underlying legal amendments to the Kyoto Protocol pertinent to this timeframe have not been brought into legal force yet. While this phase exhibits a capacity to strengthen the ICL Regime in principle, albeit to a limited degree, this potential has not been realised substantially due to the Doha Amendment's lack of ratification. The momentum driving the Kyoto developments forward since 1997 has been constrained as a result. In particular, the ICL Regime's capacity to apply commonly agreed legally binding emissions reduction targets downwards to particular states has been obstructed. It has been concluded above that the ICL Regime has regressed to a weaker condition once more.

Here, then, a basic picture of the milestone features of the ICL Regime has emerged: a weak but auspicious beginning (UNFCCC, 1992); significant strengthening and development (Kyoto, 1997, 2008–12); and partial deconstruction and regressive weakening (unratified Kyoto II, 2013–2020). However, this reductive picture of the ICL Regime's milestones and headline trends is incomplete in its own right. As noted in the previous section, Bodansky, Brunnée and Rajamani have commented that the Paris Agreement seems 'set to take over from the Kyoto Protocol', with a 'significant departure from the protocol' appearing to be well under way.[102] The Paris Agreement thus requires to be accounted for in the context of the ICL Regime paradigm that has just been outlined. It will be interpreted below that the introduction of the Paris Agreement has had the effect of dividing the ICL Regime into two parallel tracks.

---

[102] Bodansky, Brunnée and Rajamani (n 97) 206.

VII. Splitting of the ICL Regime into Two Parallel Tracks

A. Ratification of the Paris Agreement

The Paris Agreement was reached by the parties to the UNFCCC in December 2015, meeting in Paris at the 21st Conference of the Parties.[103] This amounts to another important breakthrough in international diplomacy and can be justly recognised as a new milestone in the evolution of the ICL Regime.[104] The Agreement enriches the ICL Regime not only through its substantive content, but also insofar as it is a legal agreement that has actually been ratified, unlike Kyoto II. It can thus be interpreted as legally binding, having entered into force on 4 November 2016.[105] In this regard, even before one comes to consider the Agreement's substance, a significant question is seen to arise in the context of the ICL Regime, namely: how was it that the parties to the UNFCCC could successfully bring the Paris Agreement into legal force, while Kyoto II has continued to be legally frozen alongside it?

An answer to this question on purely diplomatic grounds is that there was ultimately a reasonably strong overall appetite amongst the UNFCCC parties for the key proposals that would form the basis of the Paris Agreement to succeed, in particular after the US and China both sent favourable signals by entering into a climate accord in advance in November 2014.[106] This diplomatic momentum was then facilitated in legal terms by an expedited path towards the ratification of the Agreement. Here, the UNFCCC parties simplified ratification by circumventing the 'three-quarters ratification' lock that continued to stall Kyoto II.[107] Part of the key to this process lies in the name of the Paris Agreement itself: this document is an *Agreement* rather than a Protocol, thus placing it outside the specific Protocol rules set down under the UNFCCC.[108] Unlike the Kyoto II arrangements, the Paris Agreement was agreed by consensus by the Conference of the Parties. This basis of consensual agreement on a non-protocol text permitted the parties to write

---

[103] UNFCCC, *Adoption of the Paris Agreement*, Report No FCCC/CP/2015/L.9/Rev.1.

[104] See, eg, the praise noted in Radoslav Dimitrov, 'The Paris Agreement on Climate Change: Behind Closed Doors' (2016) 16(3) *Global Environmental Politics* 1, 1–2.

[105] For an excellent granular treatment of legality and the Paris Agreement, see Daniel Bodansky, 'The Legal Character of the Paris Agreement' (2016) 25(2) *Review of European, Comparative & International Environmental Law* 142. Amongst many other observations, Bodansky highlights that not all the provisions create a legal obligation and not all of them are mandatory. Although the present discussion is sketching out broad trends in international climate *law*, he also persuasively emphasises that the Paris Agreement's overall importance cannot be limited to the issue of its legal character alone.

[106] On the background to the Paris Agreement, see further Daniel Klein, Maria Pia Carazo, Meinhard Doelle, Jane Bulmer and Andrew Higham (eds), *The Paris Agreement on Climate Change: Analysis and Commentary* (Oxford, Oxford University Press, 2017), which includes significant coverage of the background at various stages, notably at ch 3 ('Negotiating History of the Paris Agreement').

[107] As discussed above.

[108] See further UNFCCC, art 17, 'Protocols'.

bespoke articles into the Paris Agreement's legal provisions that assisted in expediting its ratification:[109]

Article 20

This Agreement shall be open for signature and subject to ratification … at the United Nations Headquarters in New York from 22 April 2016 to 21 April 2017. Thereafter, this Agreement shall be open for accession from the day following the date on which it is closed for signature. Instruments of ratification … shall be deposited with the Depositary.[110]

Article 21

This Agreement shall enter into force on the thirtieth day after the date on which at least 55 Parties to the Convention accounting in total for at least an estimated 55 percent of the total global greenhouse gas emissions have deposited their instruments of ratification, acceptance, approval or accession.[111]

In sum, the agreement was to come into force 30 days[112] after 55 parties to the Convention or more ratified it, provided that those parties accounted for a minimum of 55 per cent of total global greenhouse gas emissions. In contrast to Kyoto II, this softer threshold of ratification, combined with the prevailing diplomatic consensus that sketched out the Agreement itself, meant that ratification could be successfully achieved as intended by the international community, whereas Kyoto II remained stalled.

A further major driver serving to galvanise the Paris Agreement's ratification in the evolving context of the ICL Regime – indeed, the most crucial driver – pertains to the general substance of the Agreement itself. The Paris Agreement is profoundly different in character from the Kyoto II regime.

B. The Substance of the Paris Agreement and its Impact on the ICL Regime

Substantively, the Paris Agreement endeavours to do a number of useful things in the area of climate change. Under its terms, governments have agreed to: sustain

---

[109] The UNFCCC follows the Vienna Convention on the Law of Treaties 1969 in using the terms 'ratification', 'acceptance', 'approval' and 'accession'. In relation to their legal effect, the terms are largely similar (indeed, often identical), see further Vienna Convention on the Law of Treaties 1969, arts 2(1)(b), 14(1) and 16 ('ratification'), 2(1)(b) and 14(2) ('acceptance and approval') and (1)(b) and 15 ('accession').

[110] Paris Agreement, art 20(1).

[111] ibid art 21(1).

[112] Article 21(3) provides that: 'For each State or regional economic integration organization that ratifies, accepts or approves this Agreement or accedes thereto after the conditions set out in paragraph 1 of this Article for entry into force have been fulfilled, this Agreement shall enter into force on the thirtieth day after the date of deposit by such State or regional economic integration organization of its instrument of ratification, acceptance, approval or accession.'

and expand international financial and diplomatic support for developing countries; broaden green finance flows at the international level; improve on efforts to manage climate change adaptation; and develop a more sophisticated technology framework.[113] A broad intention prior to the Agreement had been to strive to hold the rise in global average temperature this century to within an absolute limit of 2°C above pre-industrial levels. The Paris Agreement cements this objective, but it also goes further, stating that signatories should actively 'pursue efforts' to hold the global average temperature increase beneath the substantially lower figure of 1.5°C.[114] The language here, as with most of the Agreement throughout, is soft and aspirational ('pursue efforts'), and these soft qualities are echoed by the Agreement's lack of a meaningful compliance mechanism. On the compliance point, one finds undemanding language mandating a need to 'promote compliance', which will involve an 'expert … facilitative' committee that is 'non-adversarial and non-punitive'.[115] Soft and aspirational as much of the Agreement's character may be, all this is nevertheless progress of a kind.[116]

In practical terms, one of the most significant elements of the Paris Agreement concerns a major ongoing emissions reduction reporting process in which states are required to participate; this feeds into global monitoring via a 'global stocktake' of emissions that is to occur every five years.[117] Countries are required to sketch out and deposit a statement of their reduction intentions and plans in the form of 'Nationally Determined Contributions' (NDCs), which are to be lodged formally with the UNFCCC institutions. The Agreement benchmarks the ambition of these important NDCs as follows:

> As nationally determined contributions to the global response to climate change, all Parties are to undertake and communicate ambitious efforts as defined in Articles 4, 7, 9, 10, 11 and 13 with the view to achieving the purpose of this Agreement as set out in Article 2. The efforts of all Parties will represent a progression over time, while recognizing the need to support developing country Parties for the effective implementation of this Agreement.[118]

The intention is that states will intensify their NDCs over time; much faith is placed in this gradual 'ratchetting' process.[119] In the years ahead, the NDC mechanism will play a crucial role in assisting the Paris parties in meeting or missing

---

[113] See generally the Paris Agreement. A concise summary of the headline elements of the Agreement is provided by the Welsh Assembly's research services: Chloe Corbyn, *The Paris Agreement on Climate Change: A Summary* (Cardiff, National Assembly for Wales, Senned Research, 2016).

[114] Paris Agreement, art 2(1)(a).

[115] ibid art 15(1)–(2).

[116] But it is a separate question as to whether or not the Paris Agreement amounts to an improvement on Kyoto II in the overall context of the ICL Regime (which is considered below).

[117] Paris Agreement, art 14(1)–(2).

[118] ibid art 3. Further, parties to the Agreement 'should strive to formulate and communicate long-term low greenhouse gas emission development strategies': art 4(19).

[119] Robert Falkner, 'The Paris Agreement and the New Logic of International Climate Politics' (2016) 92(5) *International Affairs* 1107.

their overall intention of keeping average global temperature to within a maximum of 1.5–2°C above pre-industrial levels.[120] While the mechanism might prove highly effective if suitable political will is demonstrated by the parties, the Paris Agreement does not impose set reduction levels or target requirements on the signatories, and its soft, aspirational framing leaves individual countries with pronounced autonomy to establish their own particular NDC reduction levels. Thus, Climate Focus has captured the key element where the Paris Agreement parts company with the Kyoto Protocol in the broader context of the ICL Regime as follows: 'The Paris Agreement puts emphasis on processes rather than on defined mitigation goals. *Unlike the Kyoto Protocol, the Paris Agreement does not formulate country specific emissions targets.* Instead, the Paris Agreement *depends on voluntary mitigation contributions*' (emphasis added).[121]

As of 2015–16, therefore, over the period where the Paris Agreement was established by consensus (2015) and ratified (2016), two major tracks can be interpreted as having opened up within the parameters of the ICL Regime. Here, a substantial Paris Agreement track begins to run in parallel alongside the presently unratified but still important Kyoto II track, with the Paris track assuming the mantle of the more dominant track in legal terms by virtue of ratification. In assessing whether the development of this binary-track ICL Regime is to be interpreted as amounting to either an overall *weakening* or *strengthening* of the ICL Regime in some general sense, the point raised above by Climate Focus is crucial. As noted, the Paris Agreement is '[u]nlike the Kyoto Protocol' in that it 'does not formulate country specific emissions targets'.[122] On the Paris track, one encounters an absence of top-down international emissions reduction targets; in contrast, this headline mechanism is present within the Kyoto track, having been introduced under the terms of Kyoto I and extended to Kyoto II in a ratchetted, intensifying short-term progressive pattern that was due to be ongoing over time. Instead of relying on binding targets, the Paris Agreement depends on voluntary mitigation contributions, doing so in a period where states have tended to be, and continue collectively to be, both far too slow and far too reluctant in committing to robust greenhouse gas mitigation levels appropriate to managing the climate crisis.[123] Thus, this development can be seen to significantly weaken the ICL Regime overall. It does so chiefly by affording states more rather than less opportunity to declare inadequate mitigation levels (ie, inadequate 'voluntary contributions') and imbues this circumstance with an authoritative capacity under the actual terms of the Paris Agreement itself. While the top-down targets mechanism that was being developed under the terms of the Kyoto track continues to persist in the design of

---

[120] Paris Agreement, art 2(1)(a).
[121] Climate Focus, *The Paris Agreement – Summary* (Amsterdam, Climate Focus (Briefing Note), 2015) 1.
[122] ibid.
[123] Jan Burck, Ursula Hagen, Franziska Marten, Niklas Höhne and Christoph Bals, *The Climate Change Performance Index: Results 2019* (Bonn, Germanwatch, 2018).

Kyoto II, the Kyoto track's diminished position in relation to the Paris track, most notably evidenced in lawyerly terms by a lack of ratification, serves to weaken the mandated actions required by states in the overall context of the ICL Regime in a significant manner.

VIII. The ICL Regime Now and Going Forward

In spite of its weaknesses, the Paris Agreement does provide meaningful cause for hope. For example, a cohort of scientists working at the University of Maryland have considered the content of the Paris Agreement in detail, projecting antici-pated global warming trends against its intended temperature goals and associated requirements (where it is assumed that requirements including progressively intensified NDC contributions will match the Agreement's stated temperature objective over time).[124] They find that if the Agreement is adhered to appropriately up to 2060 and beyond, it provides a substantial 'beacon of hope' in the effort to successfully manage global warming over the rest of the century.[125] Nevertheless, Radoslav, while acknowledging the Paris Agreement's positive dimensions, points out that it 'is a laissez-faire accord among nations that leaves the content of domes-tic policy to governments … The policy agreement has considerable weaknesses and, obviously, it is still too early to assess its effectiveness'.[126] With the Kyoto II track apparently running out of steam as international diplomats turn their attention and enthusiasm towards Paris, the Paris Agreement itself appears to be structured in effect to block off the Kyoto track once the Kyoto II 2020 end point times out. Thus, for example, Article 14(2) delays the Agreement's first crucial 'global stocktake' until well into the post-Kyoto II period:

> The Conference of the Parties serving as the meeting of the Parties to the Paris Agreement shall undertake its first global stocktake in 2023.[127]

The terms of the Paris Agreement also serve to help move the Paris track's ambi-tions to the top of the Conference of the Parties' agenda going forward, thereby likely diminishing prioritisation of the Kyoto track in the immediate years ahead:

> The first session of the Conference of the Parties serving as the meeting of the Parties to the Paris Agreement shall be convened by the secretariat in conjunction with the first session of the Conference of the Parties that is scheduled after the date of entry into force of this Agreement. Subsequent ordinary sessions of the Conference of the Parties serving as the meeting of the Parties to the Paris Agreement shall be held in conjunction with ordinary sessions of the Conference of the Parties.[128]

---

[124] Ross Salawitch, Timothy Canty, Austin Hope, Walter Tribett and Brian Bennett, *Paris Climate Agreement: Beacon of Hope* (Cham, Springer, 2017).
[125] See ibid.
[126] Dimitrov (n 104) 2.
[127] Paris Agreement, art 14(2).
[128] ibid art 16(6).

Thus, it is very possible – indeed, arguably likely – that the presently diminished, unratified Kyoto track may be terminated and superseded altogether by the dominant Paris Agreement track in the immediate post-2020 period, such that the top-down targets-oriented approach embedded in the Kyoto track is likely due to fall away altogether. In this respect, a protracted weakening of the ICL Regime arising as a result of the impact of the present Paris track on the Kyoto track will likely become entrenched over the course of the next decade.

In her essay on the Paris Agreement entitled 'Politics, Economics, and Society', Ivanova begins by noting that climate change 'was accepted as a major global concern in 1992, when 166 governments adopted the [UNFCCC]' and suggests that, after that point, '[t]hree milestones stand out in the subsequent twenty-year history of the international climate regime'.[129] The milestones she identifies are: the Kyoto Protocol of 1997; COP 15 at Copenhagen in 2009, where the Copenhagen Accord that was agreed was broadly considered to amount to an inadequate achievement;[130] and the Paris Agreement of 2015. She points out that her third milestone (Paris) has 'been hailed as a monumental achievement and a game changer'.[131] This interpretation of headline international milestones contrasts with the delineation of the ICL Regime above, where it has been advanced that the Paris Agreement does not stand as an isolated milestone. Rather, the analysis above indicates that Paris embodies the creation of a divergent governance track that must be accounted for in a broader two-track context. On this type of reading, while the Paris Agreement remains important and meaningful, it is interpreted as running alongside a parallel Kyoto track, with this latter track being embodied presently by Kyoto II.[132] The analysis above has found that indicators suggest that Paris is on course, in effect, to actively supersede the Kyoto track once the Kyoto II period times out (2013–20).

On this interpretation, the Paris Agreement, for all its importance, also exerts a subversive influence on the parallel Kyoto track. It partially serves to disincentivise ratification of the Doha Amendment due to attention and efforts being transferred to the Paris track. Moreover, in substantive terms, Paris's headline effect is to transfer power attaching to hard-won international targets back down to states via the capacity that this track allows states to produce and implement their own NDCs. On this view, then, where one seeks to track overall *strengthening/weakening* trends in the broader context of the ICL Regime's development over time, a summary trend characterised by an initial rising and subsequent falling in the ICL Regime's overall degree of strength is detectable over the course of the regime's major inauguration in 1992 up to the present.

[129] Maria Ivanova, 'Politics, Economics, and Society' in Klein et al (n 106) 17.

[130] Copenhagen Accord, Decision 2/CP.15. On the context and weaknesses underpinning the agreement, see further Veerabhadran Ramanatahn and Yangyang Xu, 'The Copenhagen Accord for Limiting Global Warming: Criteria, Constraints, and Available Avenues' (2010) 107(18) *Proceedings of the National Academy of Sciences* 8055.

[131] Ivanova (n 129) 18.

[132] At the time of writing (Kyoto II's 2013–20 bracket is currently set to time out after 2020).

IX. Conclusions: The Utility of National Framework Climate Legislation

Based on the ICL Regime trends that have been identified above, it can be argued strongly on a credible basis that national framework climate legislation can play a crucial role going forward, given the condition of this broader international setting. Such legislation, if appropriately designed,[133] has a capacity to act as a national-level 'holding force' in the face of potential standards slippage that could persist or intensify under the terms of the Paris track. Here, it has been noted that Paris's NDC regime is both unsupported in international law by significant compliance mechanisms and affords a relatively radical degree of autonomy to states to determine their own emissions reduction commitments. This has implications for the relationship between the international and national spheres of governance, with an onus falling on national climate legislation and other forms of nationally led political and legal action in order to drive the Paris Agreement's objectives in practice.[134] Where states internally lock substantial emissions reduction targets and associated long-term decarbonisation pathways into binding national framework climate legislation at the national level, this can serve to provide a greater degree of certainty, rigour and long-term stability within states, acting in turn as a partial remedy to problems arising in an ICL Regime that has been subject to Paris-track weakening.

Once a target and its decarbonisation trajectory are locked into national framework climate legislation, this legislative architecture can assist in entrenching and preserving those obligations in a robust and meaningful way over time. Furthermore, a Climate Change Act can also act as an indication to both a country's national community (including business and industry) and to the international community more broadly that the state in question is *serious* about tackling climate change in the context of its unique national setting over time:

> Each country's approach to climate change reflects its unique institutional context, capacities, economic characteristics and current level of political engagement with the issue … Nevertheless, legislative action is a helpful indicator of how serious a country is about climate change.[135]

Climate change is an area of governance where most developed states have exhibited a tendency thus far to avoid committing to the necessary substantial levels of national action required in order to manage the problem.[136] Moreover, in instances

---

[133] On the substantive design of national framework climate legislation, see ch 10.

[134] Navroz Dubash, Markus Hagemann, Niklas Höhne and Prabhat Upadhyaya, 'Developments in National Climate Change Mitigation Legislation and Strategy' (2013) 13(6) *Climate Policy* 649.

[135] Townshend, Fankhauser et al (n 1).

[136] Kieran Mulvaney, 'Climate Change Report Card: These Countries are Reaching Targets' (*National Geographic*, 24 September 2019). Mulvaney summarises the condition of knowledge based on the work of *Climate Action Tracker*, which monitors countries' climate performance.

where relatively substantial reduction commitments have been made by states, it is sometimes the case that those commitments are not ultimately achieved.[137] National framework climate legislation has a capacity to assist in improving these circumstances. At the present time, top-down pressures created by the evolution of the ICL Regime since 1992, combined with greater levels of scientific understanding pertaining to climate change and an associated sense of rising social urgency emerging globally around the issue, have come to place states under a greater burden to improve their responses to the problem. Against this backdrop, where newly emerging targets and decarbonisation trajectories can be locked into national framework climate legislation, this serves to put states' decarbonisation intentions on a more robust, stable and predictable footing appropriate to the challenge by anchoring them in hard law rather than positioning them in, for example, soft policy.[138]

This type of approach also helps to attend to some of the negative consequences of ICL Regime-weakening. Where, for example, a state seeks to translate an emissions reduction level that it has set out in an NDC under the terms of the ICL Regime into an actual emissions reduction target(s) that is to be embedded in national framework climate legislation, this assists in circumventing weaknesses inherent in the ICL Regime's Paris track. In particular, it echoes a stronger Kyoto track style of approach by locking a target level and its associated decarbonisation trajectory into law, this time in robust legislative terms at the national level rather than under the less stringent, aspirational terms of international law. Further, in employing the force of law at the internal state level, capacities are also opened up to integrate significant compliance mechanisms and other components into the national legislative regime, thus creating opportunities to mitigate the impacts of the compliance vacuum detected above under the Paris track (and indeed the Kyoto track).[139] Taken cumulatively, an approach grounded in national framework climate legislation that entrenches and legislatively reinforces requirements to meet specific emissions reduction obligations in a legally binding manner assists in guarding against emissions reduction target objectives being semi-ignored or directly departed from within a given state. Similarly, the legally binding nature of the objectives also assists with the general prevention of emissions reduction

---

[137] Climate Action Network, "Off Target: Ranking of EU Countries' Ambition and Progress in Fighting Climate Chang." (Climate Action Network Europe, 2018), www.caneurope.org/publications/reports-and-briefings/1621-off-target-ranking-of-eu-countries-ambition-and-progress-in-fighting-climate-change.

[138] Townshend and Matthews convincingly suggest that this type of practice may also create a positive feedback loop where the implementation of substantial national climate legislation within states may feed upward into the international experience in a collective manner prompting the tightening or progressive development of the international regime itself: Terry Townshend and Adam Matthews, 'National Climate Change Legislation: The Key to More Ambitious International Agreements' (CDKN/Globe International, 2013), https://assets.publishing.service.gov.uk/media/57a08a4eed915d3cfd0006ce/CDKN_Globe_International_final_web.pdf.

[139] See further Zahar's excellent study of compliance (Zahar (n 99)).

performance slippage, while also offering a sense of long-term financial and investment certainty to business and industry.

In these respects, national framework climate legislation has a capacity to function within states both as an antidote to ICL Regime-weakening and as a means of holding states to their NDC commitments in a meaningful way, given the substantial degree of autonomy and wriggle-room permitted under the NDC scheme as currently configured. With countries doing much less than is necessary to respond to climate change in practice, the relatively broad capacity for response provided by the NDC regime creates the space and opportunity for states to perpetuate aspects of this problem. Once locked in by national parliaments, national framework climate legislation, if appropriately designed and implemented, creates conditions wherein these problematic circumstances can be significantly improved.

*

The 'appropriate design' just alluded to that might usefully underpin optimal national framework climate legislation is examined elsewhere across this book. It is explored in a narrow, context-specific manner in Chapters 3–9, through deep-dive case studies engaging a range of major national Climate Change Acts in states that have pioneered the form to date, and it is explored directly in general conceptual terms in Chapter 10, which investigates what the optimum design and substance of an appropriately formed Climate Change Act might look like in principle. In doing so, Chapter 10 draws in part on evidence from Chapters 3–9, which inform its analysis and findings.

Chapter 2 is read most usefully in conjunction with this present chapter, as it assists in exploring, evaluating and better understanding the importance of national framework climate legislation in our broader global context. In doing so, it partially develops the species of message derived from ICL Regime analysis in the present chapter (from a different analytical angle), namely that national framework climate legislation has a crucial role to play in the context of climate change governance, both at the present time and going forward.

2

'Paris Compatible' Climate Change Acts?

National Framework Legislation in an International World

MATTHIAS DUWE AND RALPH BODLE*

I. Introduction

Climate governance is a topic of growing interest for academic study. National framework laws represent the most concrete form in which climate governance systems are being established. Globally, the number of such framework laws is growing, with the majority arising around the time of the adoption of the Paris Agreement or shortly thereafter – especially those that include a long-term time horizon (eg, 2050; see Table 2.1 below). Even without a detailed empirical analysis, arguably there has been an evident 'Paris momentum' behind the spread of these national climate laws.[1] National climate policy is at least partially determined by obligations at the supranational level, in particular the European Union (EU), and at the international level, eg, through United Nations (UN) treaties. These levels influence *why* states take climate action as well as *how* they act, ie, which measures they take.

This chapter looks specifically at the question of whether and to what extent the Paris Agreement requires, promotes or steers its parties towards not only national climate policy generally, but, more specifically, the adoption of national framework climate legislation. We approach this question in three distinct analytical steps:

(1) we describe the fundamental elements of the Paris Agreement and identify how these determine or influence national climate policy-making;

* The authors are grateful for the support with background research and editorial work given by Selma Clara Kreibich and Nick Evans.

[1] Matthias Duwe et al, '"Paris Compatible" Governance: Long-Term Policy Frameworks to Drive Transformational Change' (Ecologic Institute, 2017) 4.

(2)   we identify which of these elements have a bearing on or can be linked to the establishment of national climate change laws;
(3)   we look at the influence of the Paris Agreement on EU climate governance and analyse the extent to which the agreement has incorporated and extended or diverted connections between international aims and national climate change laws in EU Member States.

We conclude that there is a clear connection between the Paris Agreement and the establishment of national climate legislation. While the Paris Agreement clearly does not require its parties to adopt legal climate change frameworks, we argue that parties who take the collective temperature goal of the Paris Agreement seriously will want to direct their national policies towards this goal. This suggests establishing corresponding governance procedures that facilitate goal-directed action – and overarching climate change laws are the most robust way of doing so.

Table 2.1 Chronological list of national climate laws with an explicit long-term perspective

Country	Status	Date of original adoption	Time horizon	Official title
1. The UK	Adopted (revised 2019)	26 November 2008	2050	Climate Change Act
2. Mexico	Adopted (revised twice)	6 June 2012	2020, 2050	Ley General de Cambio Climático
3. Denmark	Adopted, revision planned	25 June 2014	2030, 2050	Lov om Klimarådet, klimapolitisk redegørelse og fastsættelse af nationale klimamålsætninger
4. Finland	Adopted, revision planned	1 June 2015	2050	Kansallinen ilmastolaki
5. France	Adopted (revised 2019)	17 August 2015	2030, 2050	Loi de transition énergétique pour la croissance verte
6. Ireland	Adopted, revision planned (2020)	10 December 2015	2050	Climate Action and Low Carbon Development Act 2015
7. Norway	Adopted	16 June 2017	2030, 2050	Lov om klimamål (klimaloven)

(continued)

Table 2.1 *(Continued)*

Country	Status	Date of original adoption	Time horizon	Official title
8. Sweden	Adopted	22 June 2017	2030, 2040, 2045	Klimat Lag
9. The Netherlands	Adopted	2 July 2019	2030, 2050	Klimaatwet
10. New Zealand	Adopted	7 November 2019	2030, 2050	Climate Change Response (Zero Carbon) Amendment Act 2019 (amending the Climate Change Response Act 2002)
11. Germany	Adopted	12 December 2019	2030 (2050)	Bundes-Klimaschutzgesetz (KSG)
12. Fiji	In preparation	Expected 2020	2050	Climate Change Act
13. Chile	In preparation	Expected 2020	2050	Ley Marco de Cambio Climatico
14. Spain	In preparation	Expected 2020	2050	Ley de Cambio Climático y Transición Energética

Note: Several other countries have adopted laws with no specific long-term dimension.[2]

II. What Does the Paris Agreement Say and Require Parties to Do?

A. Key Obligations Stemming from the UN Climate Treaty

This section provides an overview of the Paris Agreement and thus serves as contextual background to our argument regarding its relevance for national climate laws.[3]

---

[2] In addition to insights from previous publications and interviews, complemented by desk research, including news coverage, this figure draws information from the Climate Change Laws of the World database, Grantham Research Institute on Climate Change and the Environment and Sabin Centre for Climate Change Law, available at: www.lse.ac.uk/GranthamInstitute/legislation.

[3] This overview is based on Ralph Bodle, Lena Donat and Matthias Duwe, 'The Paris Agreement: Analysis, Assessment and Outlook' (2016) 5 *Carbon & Climate Law Review* 5; Ralph Bodle and Sebastian Oberthür, 'Legal Form of the Paris Agreement and Nature of Obligations' in Daniel Klein et al (eds), *The Paris Agreement on Climate Change: Analysis and Commentary* (Oxford, Oxford University Press, 2017).

The Paris Agreement is a treaty under international law that was adopted in December 2015 and entered into force in November 2016. In less than four years, it attracted almost universal ratification around the world and now has 189 parties[4] to it, including the largest greenhouse gas (GHG) emitters such as China, the US[5] and India, as well as the EU and each individual EU Member State.[6] Importantly, the Agreement does not replace but supplements the existing 1992 UN Convention on Climate Change (UNFCCC) and its 1997 Kyoto Protocol, incorporating existing elements of the climate regime.

In a nutshell, the Paris Agreement is structured around collective overarching goals for mitigation, adaptation and finance flows. With regard to mitigation, parties have to submit climate plans every five years and report on their implementation. The Conference of the Parties (COP) to the Paris Agreement,[7] which meets once a year, is mandated to adopt more detailed rules on specific modalities, procedures etc. Also, every five years, the COP to the Paris Agreement takes stock of collective progress towards the overarching goals. Parties must take this 'global stocktake' into account in their subsequent climate plans, which are then by design supposed to be more ambitious, starting the cycle anew.

Naturally, implementation of the Paris Agreement's primary objectives is more detailed. The document's overarching purpose, stated in Article 2(1), lists three specific, non-exclusive elements: (a) a long-term temperature goal of staying 'well below' 2°C above pre-industrial levels, while also pursuing efforts to stay below 1.5°C; (b) increasing parties' abilities to adapt to climate change; and (c) making financial flows consistent with low emission and climate-resilient development.[8] All parties are required to undertake individual 'ambitious efforts' towards

---

[4] The Paris Agreement is open to states and regional economic integration organisations (such as the EU) that are parties to the UNFCCC. For ease of reference, any mention of 'states' in this chapter also includes the EU, unless otherwise stated.

[5] In August 2017, the US announced its intention to withdraw from the Paris Agreement and submitted a notification of withdrawal on 4 November 2019. The withdrawal goes into effect on 4 November 2020, in accordance with art 28 of the Agreement.

[6] The EU is a party to, and therefore bound by, the Paris Agreement as a legal entity that is separate from its individual Member States. In addition, each EU Member State is also a party to the Paris Agreement.

[7] The COP is a regular meeting of all parties to a treaty, such as the Paris Agreement. Many international agreements – environmental or otherwise – establish these meetings and mandate them to discuss and adopt details on implementation, review progress and address new issues. The annual climate conferences formally comprise three COPs that are held simultaneously: the COP to the UNFCCC, to the Kyoto Protocol and to the Paris Agreement. A COP typically acts by adopting 'decisions'.

[8] Article 2(1) of the Paris Agreement reads: 'This Agreement, in enhancing the implementation of the Convention, including its objective, aims to strengthen the global response to the threat of climate change, in the context of sustainable development and efforts to eradicate poverty, including by: (a) Holding the increase in the global average temperature to well below 2°C above pre-industrial levels and pursuing efforts to limit the temperature increase to 1.5°C above pre-industrial levels, recognizing that this would significantly reduce the risks and impacts of climate change; (b) Increasing the ability to adapt to the adverse impacts of climate change and foster climate resilience and low greenhouse gas emissions development, in a manner that does not threaten food production; and (c) Making finance flows consistent with a pathway towards low greenhouse gas emissions and climate-resilient development.'

reaching these collective goals, as defined in the other articles of the Agreement.[9] Each article of the Agreement covers one of the UNFCCC's traditional thematic areas: mitigation, adaptation, support and finance, technology capacity-building, accounting and reporting, and also other issues, such as loss and damage. They define thematic objectives and what parties are to do to achieve them. While the treaty as a whole is binding under international law, its individual provisions are not equally prescriptive or precise. To different degrees, some are quite vague, leave room for flexibility or are subject to qualifiers.[10]

In this chapter, we focus particularly on the elements relevant to mitigation. In order to reach the long-term temperature goal, the Paris Agreement further specifies the aim of reaching a global peak in GHG emissions as soon as possible and to rapidly reduce GHG emissions to net zero by the second half of the century.[11] Essentially, this sets out a global emissions trajectory. There are no quantified emission reduction obligations for individual parties, but the efforts to be undertaken by each party are embedded in a structure that is designed to make parties raise their ambition over time. Parties are required to prepare and present individual climate plans every five years, so-called nationally determined contributions (NDCs), which detail how the party intends to contribute to the collective goals. Parties are not obliged to implement or achieve their NDCs exactly as submitted, but they have to take measures with the aim of achieving them.[12] They also have to account for their emissions and removals corresponding to their NDCs in accordance with rules and modalities set by the IPCC and the COP.[13] The Paris Agreement also explicitly envisages that the NDCs reflect each party's 'highest possible ambition'.[14]

In addition, starting in 2023 and then every five years thereafter, a 'global stock-take' by the COP to the Paris Agreement will regularly assess the sum total efforts of parties towards the collective purpose and long-term goals. Parties then have to take this into account when they update their actions and develop their next NDC[15] in a way that represents a 'progression beyond previous efforts', thereby starting a new cycle of NDCs.[16]

Nevertheless, the Paris Agreement gives very limited guidance on the content of NDCs. Developed countries 'should' include economy-wide absolute emission reduction targets, and other countries are encouraged to move towards such targets.[17] Beyond these parameters, there are no specific rules in the Paris Agreement as to the content or ambition level of NDCs. Such specific issues are

---

[9] Paris Agreement, art 3.
[10] For an analysis of the legal form and nature of the obligations, see Bodle and Oberthür (n 3).
[11] Paris Agreement, art 4(1).
[12] ibid art 4(3); Bodle and Oberthür (n 3) 99.
[13] Paris Agreement, art 4(13).
[14] ibid art 4(3).
[15] ibid arts 4(9) and 14(3).
[16] Bodle, Donat and Duwe (n 3) 7.
[17] ibid.

left to parties to define independently unless the COP adopts guidance in this respect.[18] For instance, the Paris Agreement does not indicate whether NDCs should cover a five-year or 10-year period. Neither energy in general nor renewable energy in particular is explicitly addressed, except for a small reference in the preamble to the non-binding Paris Decision that accompanied the adoption of the treaty.[19]

In addition to the NDCs, the Agreement stipulates that parties 'should strive to formulate and communicate long-term low greenhouse gas emission development strategies'. However, the wording falls short of a clear legal requirement to prepare such a strategy.[20] These strategies are commonly referred to as long-term strategies (LTSs).[21]

The Paris Agreement thus leaves a lot of leeway for countries when it comes to their approach to reducing GHG emissions and which sectors to focus on. But it establishes a transparency framework under which parties have to account for their NDCs and regularly report on their GHG emissions 'inventories' and on their progress in implementing their NDCs.[22] These core obligations are accompanied by institutional provisions and an implementation and compliance mechanism.[23]

B. The Specific Nature of the 'Paris System'

The design of the Paris Agreement has been called a 'pledge and review' structure.[24] It is often juxtaposed with the quantified emission reduction targets for individual developed country parties established under the Kyoto Protocol.[25] Overall, the Paris Agreement represents a shift to a collective approach that is based on national planning and policies (NDCs, national adaptation plans and 2050 climate strategies) and international transparency obligations, and that relies

---

[18] ibid 22.

[19] COP Decision 1/CP.21 2015. On the nature of COP decisions, see n 7. COP Decision 1/CP.21 specifies further details: a work programme with mandates for elaborating modalities, procedures and guidelines, as well as political processes. By default, COP decisions are not binding as such, but can be if the treaty so provides or implies. The Paris Agreement makes the content of certain existing and future decisions binding in international law; see Bodle and Oberthür (n 3) 47; Sebastian Oberthür and Ralph Bodle, 'Legal Form and Nature of the Paris Outcome' (2016) 6 *Climate Law* 40, 92–93.

[20] Paris Agreement, art 4(19); Bodle and Oberthür (n 3) 98.

[21] See, eg, the UNFCCC website repository of submitted strategies: https://unfccc.int/process/the-paris-agreement/long-term-strategies.

[22] For an overview, see European Capacity Building Initiative (ECBI), 'Pocket Guide to Transparency under the UNFCCC' (2019), https://ecbi.org/news/2019-edition-pocket-guide-transparency-under-unfccc.

[23] On the mechanism under art 15 of the Paris Agreement, see Gu Zihua, Christina Voigt and Jacob Werksman, 'Facilitating Implementation and Promoting Compliance with the Paris Agreement under Article 15: Conceptual Challenges and Pragmatic Choices' (2019) 9 *Climate Law* 65, 65.

[24] Robert O Keohane and Michael Oppenheimer, 'Paris: Beyond the Climate Dead End through Pledge and Review?' (2016) 4 *Politics and Governance* 142; Maria Jernnäs et al, 'Cross-national Patterns of Governance Mechanisms in Nationally Determined Contributions (NDCs) under the Paris Agreement' (2019) 19 *Climate Policy* 1239.

[25] See, eg, Jernnäs et al (n 24) 15.

on peer pressure and public pressure to safeguard ambition. This was the trade-off for getting developing states on board to take on binding obligations on a par with developed country parties. In this sense, the Paris Agreement breaks new ground by supplementing the principle of common but differentiated responsibilities with core obligations for *all* parties and a range of techniques to express differentiation.[26]

For virtually all provisions, the Paris Agreement and the accompanying Paris Decision[27] contain mandates for elaborating on how to implement them. At COP24 in 2018, parties to the Paris Agreement adopted more detailed rules regarding modalities, procedures and rules for implementation of many issues. However, this so-called 'Paris rulebook' left some issues unresolved.[28] With regard to NDCs, the parties did not come to an agreement on the question of which 'features' each NDC should have. They basically realised that they would not agree on elements beyond those already stated in the Paris Agreement, and therefore postponed the issue until 2024.[29] Likewise, the rulebook postponed the issue of common timeframes for NDCs until 2031.[30]

The structural core of the Paris Agreement is a binding iterative procedure for each individual party guided by overarching, collective global goals. The Paris Agreement has been called an experiment,[31] but it could also be called a gamble, both in the sense of 'game' and 'risk'. The way in which the Paris Agreement is designed can be understood through the lens of game theory as a two-level *game*, where each party makes strategic choices in defining and implementing their NDCs.[32] At the same time, setting up this strategic game is also a risky *gamble* because global climate change does not allow time for second chances.

III. Why is Paris Relevant for Governance and Climate Laws at the National Level?

We argue that while the Paris Agreement does not *require* its parties to have climate laws, the way it and its obligations are structured strongly implies that parties need to have a compass that directs their climate policies towards the Paris Agreement's long-term temperature goal and associated emissions trajectory. National framework climate legislation can serve as this compass by connecting individual parties' actions with the collective global goals.

---

[26] Bodle, Donat and Duwe (n 3) 7.
[27] See nn 7 and 19.
[28] Earth Negotiations Bulletin (ENB), 'No 747' 12.
[29] Decision 4/CMA.1 2018, paras 19 and 20.
[30] Decision 6/CMA.1 2018; currently, those parties with an NDC covering five years are requested to communicate a new NDC by 2020 and those parties with an NDC covering 10 years are requested to communicate or update their NDC by 2020. Article 4(10) of the Paris Agreement requires common timeframes for NDCs to be considered; see Earth Negotiations Bulletin (n 28).
[31] Bodle, Donat and Duwe (n 3) 21.
[32] Keohane and Oppenheimer (n 24) 146, 147–50.

A. The Paris Agreement Does Not Require its Parties to have Climate Laws

We have shown that there are only a few prescriptive and precise obligations in the Paris Agreement. Parties are clearly required to regularly prepare and submit NDCs, to account for them and to report on emissions and NDC implementation. But the Paris Agreement says very little about *how* parties are to define and direct their national policy in terms of individual goals and measures. It requires each party to take 'domestic mitigation measures, with the aim of achieving the objectives of its NDC', but it does not specify *which* measures.[33] This reflects the political rationale for obtaining political support for the Paris Agreement. The term 'measures' is not defined and comprises anything a party does at the domestic level to achieve its NDC, including domestic policies, actions, plans, strategies, laws, information, investments etc. Neither the few provisions in the Paris Agreement that provide some guidance on which action parties should take at the national level nor the more detailed rules in the subsequent decisions comprising the 'Paris rulebook' stipulate that parties *have to* adopt an overarching climate law.

Yet notwithstanding the Paris Agreement's largely procedural nature, states are not *completely* free in relation to their climate policies. The less prescriptive and precise elements of the Paris Agreement contribute to providing legal and political direction for parties towards the long-term temperature goal. For instance, developed country parties should undertake economy-wide absolute emission reduction targets.[34]

In addition, the legal character, though important, is only one factor in assessing the significance of the Paris outcome.[35] The Paris Agreement also represents a high degree of *political* commitment by governments at the international level vis-a-vis other parties and at the domestic level through the ratification process.[36] Furthermore, the drafting of the Paris Agreement describes a clear political narrative of what parties are expected to do towards which aims.[37]

B. No Long-Term Tools for Individual Parties to Achieve the Collective Long-Term Goal

Taken together, the elements of the Paris Agreement (described above) and most importantly the long-term temperature goal imply transformational change and continuous action towards this change over a long period of time. While the

---

[33] Paris Agreement, art 4(2).
[34] ibid art 4(4).
[35] Daniel Bodansky, 'The Legal Character of the Paris Agreement' (2016) 25 *Review of European, Comparative & International Environmental Law* 142, 150.
[36] Bodle, Donat and Duwe (n 3) 19.
[37] ibid 22.

Paris Agreement sets the long-term temperature goal as an overarching *collective* objective, it requires parties to make *individual* efforts towards it. These efforts are reflected in the NDC cycle, with the global stocktake providing an impetus for adjustments and change. However, there is an inherent conceptual misalignment in the Paris Agreement between the long-term temperature goal it sets and the tools it legally prescribes to achieve this. The long-term temperature goal and the necessary transformational change require long-term policy action at the national level. But the main tool the Paris Agreement requires parties to use – ie, parties' individual NDCs – is a short-term to mid-term timeframe of five or 10 years, and the Paris Agreement is weak in asking parties to direct these plans towards the long-term temperature goal. In particular, the long-term strategies are not mandatory.[38] Therefore, simply fulfilling the letter of the Paris Agreement by merely implementing the procedural obligation to have an NDC every five years runs the risk of only addressing short-term and medium-term action from one NDC to the next. On its own, this is unlikely to be sufficient to reach the long-term temperature goal.

Parties that take the Paris Agreement seriously will seek to design their national policy not only along the legal obligations from one NDC to the next; it is essential to also consider the Paris Agreement's political narrative[39] and design national policy more generally with a long-term perspective. This also includes the less prescriptive elements, overall structure and long-term goals of the Paris Agreement. For a party that takes the Paris Agreement seriously, the way in which the Agreement is structured arguably requires the party to ensure that its short-term to medium-term efforts in the NDCs are aligned with the long-term direction. In order to manage the transformation implied by the Paris goals in the short timeframe of only two to three decades, an effective governance system is certainly advisable.

C. National Climate Laws Can Link Short-Term and Long-Term Goals and Thus Connect Individual Action with the Collective Objective

We have seen that the Paris Agreement mainly sets collective goals and procedures by which parties have to show their intended actions and progress. It does not prescribe specific individual targets and actions for its parties. There is also another level of governance that the Paris Agreement does not address, which is between an overarching collective target and concrete mitigation actions by individual states. This 'between' level is necessary because there is a myriad of potential mitigation measures that a party can take. These actions have to be directed,

---

[38] See n 20 above.
[39] Bodle, Donat and Duwe (n 3) 20.

coordinated and aligned towards the collective long-term goal. At that level, a party defines the intermediate steps it intends to take and thereby consolidates and specifies its climate policy. The Paris Agreement implies a specific future, but it is up to national governments to provide their respective stakeholders with at least a degree of policy certainty about the manner and speed of getting there. This is a frequent particular demand from the business sector, which requires above all clarity for its business strategies and related investments.

It is at this critical gap in the Paris system that national governance frameworks have their most important role to play: they can help ensure that the promised national action (ie, NDCs) is delivered in a coherent manner and in a way that aligns short-term policies with the long-term objectives. They provide a degree of policy certainty beyond the short term and function as a compass to guide policy actions and investments.

Arguably the most effective way of providing policy certainty is enshrining the governance framework into law.[40] A law usually represents the highest level of commitment a government can engage in and the strongest signal it can send. Moreover, enshrining institutional responsibilities and hierarchies in a law compels all relevant actors to participate accordingly, ensuring a coordinated and comprehensive government response – a prerequisite for successful long-term climate action. A dedicated system to organise governmental action towards not only five-year NDCs but also long-term goals can provide stability across electoral cycles and create a shock-resistant climate policy. Adopting such a system in the form of a law can thus create a safeguard against policy rollback.[41]

Long-term climate governance frameworks – in particular, dedicated climate laws – thus fulfil an important bridging function between the collective goals of the Paris Agreement and the many actions countries need to put in place over time to realise their short-term contribution towards these goals. The growing number of examples of existing national framework climate legislation with a long-term component suggests that many parties to the Paris Agreement regard this bridging function as necessary and useful.

D. Paris Inputs Towards Core Elements Found in Climate Change Laws

The existing literature on climate governance frameworks and climate laws has identified a set of core elements, which include, inter alia: short-term and long-term

---

[40] Duwe et al (n 1); Thomas L Muinzer, *Climate and Energy Governance for the UK Low Carbon Transition: The Climate Change Act 2008* (London, Palgrave Macmillan, 2019).

[41] eg, in the case of Brexit, see Sam Fankhauser, Alina Averchenkova and Jared Finnegan, '10 Years of the UK Climate Change Act' (Grantham Research Institute on Climate Change and the Environment, Centre for Climate Change Economics and Policy, 2018).

targets, long-term *planning*, identification and adoption of specific *measures* (ie, policy instruments), monitoring and reporting procedures to measure *progress*, and independent *institutions* to support transparency and scientific underpinnings, plus opportunities for *public participation*.[42] We conclude our assessment of the Paris Agreement's relevance for establishing climate laws by evaluating what it provides with regard to these core elements.

i. Targets

With regard to targets, it should be distinguished whether parties are required to have targets generally, for which timeframe, and to what extent the Paris Agreement sets or determines the content of such targets. The Paris Agreement does not strictly require parties to have targets. For developed countries, it states that they 'should' set themselves 'economy-wide quantified emissions reduction objectives', while developing country parties are encouraged to do so over time.[43] Since the wording does not define the timeframe, it could be argued that it is sufficient for a party to define targets from NDC to NDC and that no long-term target is needed. However, the link that the Paris Agreement makes between individual NDCs and the long-term temperature goal is a strong argument for parties to set themselves long-term targets. The Paris Agreement establishes a collective long-term temperature goal and defines a rough emissions trajectory to achieve it. The latter expresses the shape of global emissions patterns. Since collective global emissions are supposed to be net zero by the second half of the century, at some stage, emissions from individual parties will have to be directed towards net zero as well. Several provisions emphasise that parties have to direct their individual efforts towards the collective long-term temperature goal.[44] In addition, each new NDC is subject to the principle of progression in Article 4(3) and has to be informed by the outcome of the global stocktake, which assesses progress towards the long-term goal. These provisions suggest that parties should define specific long-term objectives as part of their respective contributions. The growing list of countries establishing net-zero emissions objectives at least to some extent indicates that many countries acknowledge this.[45]

The Paris Agreement requires the communication of NDCs every five years, but does not provide further specification for these (interim) targets. The regular frequency of NDC submission creates a strong expectation that such targets be defined in line with the long-term goal, and the 'principle of progression' further underlines the downward emission trajectory that can be anticipated for most

---

[42] Matthias Duwe and Nicholas Evans, 'Climate Laws in Europe: Good Practices in Net-Zero Management' (Ecologic Institute, European Climate Foundation, 2020).

[43] Paris Agreement, art 4(4).

[44] ibid art 3 states that 'with a view to achieving the purpose of this Agreement'. Article 4(1) states that: 'In order to achieve the long-term temperature goal set out in Article 2.'

[45] See ECIU overview on net-zero commitments: https://eciu.net/netzerotracker.

parties. This principle and the five-year cycle could be integrated directly into governance frameworks at the regional and national levels – and, indeed, several existing laws have included review procedures in some form, and recent ones specifically reference the Paris Agreement cycle (see also section IV below).[46]

ii. Planning

LTSs are an important instrument for effective long-term climate governance, as they are a vehicle for connecting the objective of long-term transformation with present-day action. They can help inform short-term target setting and decisions on necessary measures.[47] The Paris Agreement merely invites all parties to develop long-term strategies under Article 4(19) and the Paris Decision suggests that these should be submitted by 2020.[48] The Paris Decision further specifies that they should point towards 2050 ('mid century'). The Paris Agreement says parties should be 'mindful' of the long-term goals in this context,[49] but it is silent on whether and how the strategies are linked to the NDCs.[50] There are thus few specifications other than the fact that there is a dedicated explicit expectation that each party delivers its own LTS. At the time of writing (June 2020), 17 countries have submitted their strategies to the UNFCCC.[51]

iii. Measures

The Paris Agreement offers hardly any specific requirements regarding the means through which parties are meant to achieve their NDCs. This fits well into the overall logic of the treaty's structure, which is to leave the setting of national targets to individual countries – and, by implication, the measures through which these can be met. Article 4(2) only specifies that 'Parties shall pursue domestic mitigation measures, with the aim of achieving' their NDCs, so the development of measures as such is an obligation.[52]

iv. Progress Monitoring

Several provisions of the Paris Agreement relate to monitoring and reporting for the purpose of measuring progress. The Paris Agreement establishes an

---

[46] Duwe et al (n 1) 23.

[47] Matthias Duwe and Ewa Iwaszuk, 'LTS in Europe: Experience from National and EU-Wide 2050 Climate Planning' (Ecologic Institute, 2019).

[48] Paris Agreement, art 4(19).

[49] ibid.

[50] Bodle, Donat and Duwe (n 3) 8–9.

[51] The UNFCCC website contains a registry for all submissions of long-term strategies as per art 4(19) of the Paris Agreement; see https://unfccc.int/process/the-paris-agreement/long-term-strategies.

[52] Paris Agreement, art 4(2).

'Enhanced Transparency Framework' in Article 13 and requires transparency on action (NDC implementation) and support (eg, finance, technology transfer and capacity-building).[53] It explicitly builds upon the existing system of data provision and the transparency arrangements under the UNFCCC, and is supposed to enhance and eventually supersede it.[54] It contains specific reporting requirements (such as national inventory reports and Biennial Transparency Reports) and also provides for reviews to ensure the quality of the information provided. With the adoption of the Paris Rulebook, these obligations have been substantiated and more precisely defined through detailed modalities, procedures and guidelines, some specific features of which still need to be elaborated (such as templates).[55] The reporting rules now specify inter alia that countries have to provide progress indicators to show their NDC is being implemented and achieved, and 'Parties are also required to provide information on the actions, policies, and measures' that are adopted towards this purpose.[56]

Moreover, with the global stocktake, the Paris Agreement has established a regular mechanism for measuring progress towards the global goals. Its conclusions inform the submission of the next round of NDCs by parties. Several existing national climate laws also include such triggers for additional action as a result of a lack of progress towards targets.[57]

v. Science-Based Institutions

The Paris Agreement does not establish new institutions specifically for the purpose of supporting science-based implementation and transparent progress monitoring. However, the Paris Decision calls upon the Intergovernmental Panel on Climate Change (IPCC) as a global authority on the state of climate science to establish the implications of limiting warming to 1.5°C over pre-industrial levels.[58] The IPCC is also referenced in the Paris Agreement in the context of common reporting requirements.[59] Furthermore, the UNFCCC, the Kyoto Protocol and the Paris Agreement have subsidiary bodies to call upon (including the Subsidiary Body for Scientific and Technological Advice (SBSTA)) for input.[60]

---

[53] ibid art 13.
[54] ibid art 13(3); COP Decision 1/CP.21, para 98.
[55] European Capacity Building Initiative (n 22) 17–18.
[56] ibid 21.
[57] Duwe and Evans (n 42) ch 5.3.
[58] COP Decision 1/CP.21, para 21.
[59] Paris Agreement, art 13.7.
[60] The SBSTA and the Subsidiary Body for Implementation (SBI) are work-level negotiation bodies that serve the COP and the other UNFCCC treaties' meetings. The SBSTA supports the COP on technical matters related to, inter alia, the impacts of climate change, guidelines for the reporting of GHG emission inventories and the proliferation of low-carbon technologies. It also plays a key role in delivering and communicating the scientific work of the IPCC to negotiators and policy-makers. The work of the SBI is focused on implementing the central pillars of the UNFCCC as operationalised in

There is also the UNFCCC Secretariat, which supports the implementation of the Paris Agreement in many ways, including synthesising information, such as on the aggregate effect of NDCs and acting as a repository for information (eg, on NDCs, LTSs and reported emissions data). Having these bodies and their resources available enhances the transparency of the process and helps provide an independent basis of information to guide the negotiations.

Overall, the global stocktake as the Paris Agreement's mechanism for measuring progress towards the global goals could thus be argued to serve one of the functions (transparent progress monitoring and adequacy) that independent scientific advisory bodies are asked to provide in some existing national climate laws.

vi. Public Participation

The Paris Agreement does not include specific requirements regarding public participation. The preambular text of the treaty notes the importance of public participation (in a list of similar topics) 'at all levels on the matters addressed in this Agreement'. Furthermore, the importance of engaging public and private actors in implementation is recognised in Article 6(8) (on non-market approaches), while Article 12 (on cooperation) lists public participation as a goal for parties. However, no actual article establishes an obligation to involve the public, be it for the definition, implementation or monitoring of NDCs or any other key requirement under the Paris Agreement.

In sum, the Paris Agreement contains a number of provisions that are directly relevant to key elements found in many national climate law frameworks: regular target-setting (through the NDCs), the adoption of specific measures to reach them and reporting on progress are all obligatory under the Paris Agreement. The development of long-term strategies is not directly binding, but an expectation is created. There is no requirement to involve the public, but its importance is generally recognised, which can be interpreted as support for inclusion of this dimension in national legislation. And while no dedicated new institutions for scientific inputs and progress monitoring are established, a mechanism for review and improvement is built into the system, and the IPCC continues to provide the best available inputs on the underlying state of climate science.

The Paris Agreement thus legally requires that parties address several of the elements captured in existing long-term governance frameworks and requests others. This further strengthens the case for the establishment of national frameworks – specifically in the form of legislation – to ensure that parties to the Paris Agreement meet their obligations.

the various treaties: transparency, mitigation, adaptation, finance, technology and capacity-building, including guidance on each element. For more on this, see the UNFCCC Secretariat's website at www. unfccc.int.

IV. The Special Case of the EU

A. The EU as a Supportive Actor in the UN Climate Treaties with its Own Interests

The EU has supported international collaboration on climate action and tried to be a frontrunner in advancing the regime, often trying to drive progress in the talks by putting forward new targets for itself early in the process (in 1996 for the 1997 Kyoto Conference, in 2007 for the 2009 Copenhagen Conference and in 2014 for the 2015 Paris Conference).[61] It also invested significant political capital in the negotiations on the Paris Agreement and thus has high stakes in it becoming a success.

Figure 2.1 Main historic and current climate and energy policy goals in the EU

	Pre-Kyoto	European Climate Change Programme	Climate and Energy Package	Climate and Energy Framework	Clean Planet for All
	Target year: 2000	Target year: 2010 (2008–2012 – Kyoto Protocol)	Target year: 2020 (2013–2020 period)	Target year: 2030 (2021–2030 period)	Target year: 2050
GHG	Return to 1990 levels	- 8% compared to 1990 levels	- 20% compared to 1990 levels	- 40% compared to 1990 levels (EU NDC) (revision underway)	Climate neutrality
RES		12% of energy consumption	20% of energy consumption	32% of energy consumption	
EE		12% improvement	20% improvement	32.5% improvement	
1990					2050

Key: GHG = Greenhouse Gases; RES = Renewable Energy Systems; EE = Energy Efficiency

The EU has been setting EU-wide targets for GHG emissions since the late 1980s and also developed instruments to achieve these targets. There now exists a veritable toolbox of measures, from a binding cap-and-trade scheme with broad coverage of large point sources (the EU Emissions Trading System (ETS)) to specific CO_2 standards for new vehicles, energy performance standards for a range of white goods, minimum standards for energy taxation across the EU and rules concerning fluorinated gases and landfills. A plethora of different types of policies have been adopted to guide national action – plus a set of laws that establish framework conditions and (binding and non-binding) national targets, but leave Member States to decide on the best way to implement these in their

---

[61] Benjamin Görlach, Matthias Duwe and Nicholas Evans, 'Frameworks for Regional Co-operation: The EU' in Robert Looney (ed), *Handbook of Transitions to Energy and Climate Security* (Abingdon, Routledge, 2016).

respective national contexts. GHG targets have always been combined with support for renewable energy and energy efficiency, and for the milestone target years 2010, 2020 and 2030, there are quantitative targets for all three dimensions (see Figure 2.1).

The EU's outlook on the UN climate negotiations is thus determined by a combination of factors. On the one hand, it wants to advance the international regime, is willing to compromise to get more countries on board and tries to act as a pioneer to show its credibility. On the other hand, the EU tries to influence the negotiations on certain matters in a way that ensures that decisions made at the UN level are consistent with the systems and policies that the EU has already established in order to limit interference and strengthen compatibility. In sum, by way of what has been referred to as a 'tandem' or co-evolution in policy-making, the EU does not only take inputs from the UNFCCC negotiations, but has historically also tried to shape and steer them for the global good, but also to serve the EU's interests.[62]

B. How Has the EU Implemented the Paris Agreement Since its Adoption in Late 2015?

The EU is presently a unique entity in legal terms. In addition to each individual Member State, the EU as an entity is also a party to the UNFCCC and the Paris Agreement, and is thus bound by the legal requirements of these treaties. With regard to NDCs, the EU makes a joint submission for the EU and its Member States – the individual Member States do not have separate NDCs. Under EU law, the EU can adopt laws and create new and additional legal requirements for all its Member States and for its institutions. The legislative process in most cases consists of proposals by the European Commission that have to be adopted by the European Parliament, which is directly elected, as well as the Council, which is composed of representatives of the Member States.

With regard to the implementation of the Paris Agreement, the EU's internal processes essentially started with the preparation of the substantive inputs from the EU to the UN negotiations. This took the form of a political decision on new headline targets for the EU for 2030 (on GHG emissions, renewable energy share and energy efficiency improvements) taken by heads of state and government in October 2014, more than a year before the Paris Conference.[63] Building on these internal decisions, the European Commission already started preparing updates to existing laws to adjust them to the new targets and published the

---

[62] Sebastian Oberthür and Marc Pallemaerts, 'The EU's Internal and External Climate Policies: An Historical Overview' in *The New Climate Policies of the European Union: International Legislation and Climate Diplomacy* (Brussels, VUB Press and Brussels University Press, 2010) 27.

[63] Council Conclusions EUCO 169/14 of 23 and 24 October 2014.

first of these in July 2015 (the review of the EU ETS Directive), still half a year before the Paris Conference. The ETS covers around half the EU's GHG emissions (mainly from the power sector and industry). The other half, defined simply as 'non-ETS' emissions (mainly buildings, transport, waste and agriculture), are split up via binding national targets among Member States defined in the Climate Action Regulation.[64] Together, these two pieces of legislation are the overarching frameworks through which the EU seeks to ensure that it can deliver on its NDC, which is a 40 per cent reduction in GHGs from 1990 levels by 2030.

Following the adoption of the Paris Agreement, a whole series of further proposals for revised and new legislation was prepared. A number of these laws were bundled together as the 'Clean Energy for All Europeans' package which was put forward by the European Commission in November 2016. The last of these laws was adopted in 2019. The Clean Energy package also includes the proposal for a new Regulation on the Governance of the Energy Union (hereinafter the 'Governance Regulation'), which incorporated planning and reporting obligations from several existing laws and combined them into a new integrated process across several policy areas, connecting in particular energy and climate policy.[65] Due to the split between targets for the ETS and non-ETS sectors, the Governance Regulation is the only law that actually covers the EU NDC as a whole.

The new governance system has slightly different rules for the GHG target and for the energy targets, based on differences in the extent to which these are broken down into specific individual national targets and the differences in how binding they are, and this chapter only considers the GHG side of the governance system.

The key vehicles for the implementation of the new governance system are so-called integrated national energy and climate plans (NECPs) produced by Member States, which are meant to cover the whole energy system and all related policy areas. They have to include the respective national objectives for these policy areas until 2030, including national climate targets, and list all relevant policies and their expected impacts (on achieving those targets) towards 2030 and beyond. The Governance Regulation prescribes an iterative process by which Member States were required to submit draft NECPs by the end of 2018 and, following an analysis and recommendations from the European Commission, final plans by the end

---

[64] Regulation (EU) 2018/842 of the European Parliament and of the Council of 30 May 2018 on binding annual greenhouse gas emission reductions by Member States from 2021 to 2030 contributing to climate action to meet commitments under the Paris Agreement and amending Regulation (EU) No 525/2013 [2018] OJ L156, 19 June 2018 (hereinafter 'Climate Action Regulation').

[65] Regulation (EU) 2018/1999 of the European Parliament and of the Council of 11 December 2018 on the Governance of the Energy Union and Climate Action, amending Regulations (EC) No 663/2009 and (EC) No 715/2009 of the European Parliament and of the Council, Directives 94/22/EC, 98/70/EC, 2009/31/EC, 2009/73/EC, 2010/31/EU, 2012/27/EU and 2013/30/EU of the European Parliament and of the Council, Council Directives 2009/119/EC and (EU) 2015/652 and repealing Regulation (EU) No 525/2013 of the European Parliament and of the Council [2018] OJ L328, 21 December 2018 (hereinafter 'Governance Regulation').

of 2019, which will then be subject to regular progress monitoring with reports from Member States and assessment by the European Commission. The NECPs are updated after five years and new ones are drafted every 10 years.

In addition to the NECPs, the Governance Regulation also takes up the call from the Paris Agreement on the development of long-term strategies. It legally requires each Member State to prepare an LTS with a 2050 time horizon by 1 January 2020 and update it every five years, 'where necessary'.[66] While the NECPs focus on the next 10 years and provide detail on specific policies, the LTSs are supposed to look further into the future and are expected to provide analytical results of projections towards 2050, but without the policy detail required for the NECPs. The Governance Regulation specifically states that the NECPs should be coherent (and thus aligned) with the LTSs.[67] It also tasks the European Commission to prepare a proposal for an EU-wide LTS, which it delivered at the end of November 2018.[68] The European Commission spelled out in its proposal a vision for a climate-neutral EU by 2050. This was a change from the existing EU 2050 target of 80–95 per cent GHG reduction from 1990 levels, adopted almost a decade earlier. Whether to adopt this as a formal objective was debated in a variety of EU fora, including by heads of state and government. After several rounds of negotiations, they were finally able to agree joint language endorsing 'the objective of achieving a climate-neutral EU by 2050' at their meeting in December 2019.[69]

In early March 2020, the European Commission presented a proposal for a European Climate Law.[70] This proposal was a priority for Ursula von der Leyen, the President of the European Commission, which she had promised to present within the first 100 days of her time in office. She had been under considerable political pressure to support stronger climate action around the time of her election in July 2019. She made the climate-neutrality objective for 2050 a central pillar of her political guidelines and wanted to enshrine it in a European Climate Law.[71] If adopted as presented, the law would strengthen the long-term dimension of EU climate policy in several ways. It would allow the Commission to adopt a

---

[66] ibid art 15.1.

[67] ibid art 15.6.

[68] Commission Communication COM/2018/773 to the European Parliament, the European Council, the Council, the European Economic and Social Committee, the Committee of the Regions and the European Investment Bank, 'A Clean Planet for All, A European strategic long-term vision for a prosperous, modern, competitive and climate neutral economy' (hereinafter 'EU 2050 Strategy').

[69] Council Conclusions EUCO 29/19 of 12 December 2019. This overall endorsement came with a disclaimer from Poland ('One Member State, at this stage, cannot commit to implement this objective as far as it is concerned'), which prompted further discussion on the matter.

[70] Commission Proposal COM/2020/80 for a Regulation of the European Parliament and of the Council establishing the framework for achieving climate neutrality and amending Regulation (EU) 2018/1999 (hereinafter 'European Climate Law Proposal').

[71] Ursula von der Leyen, 'A Union That Strives for More: My Agenda for Europe. Political Guidelines for the Next European Commission 2019–2024' (2019), https://op.europa.eu/en/publication-detail/-/publication/43a17056-ebf1-11e9-9c4e-01aa75ed71a1.

trajectory towards the EU's climate-neutrality goal (in five-year increments), with five-yearly reviews. It would also add more specific climate-neutrality progress measurement processes and a check on new policy initiatives for consistency with the climate-neutrality goal.[72] Already in December 2019, von der Leyen had presented a proposal for a so-called European Green Deal as an overarching strategy to make the EU climate-neutral.[73]

C. Assessment against the Paris Agreement

The rules laid down in the revised and new laws governing the EU's 2030 targets and policies implement several aspects of the Paris Agreement. Here we focus on those related to mitigation.

i. Targets

The EU has made its own 40 per cent GHG reduction target (which is the EU's NDC) legally binding, albeit indirectly, as responsibility for its delivery is split in two (see the explanation above on ETS and non-ETS targets). The Governance Regulation specifically covers the EU's overall climate (and energy) goals, but does not specify the respective figures in a formal article of the Regulation. The European Climate Law Proposal could be an opportunity to provide an overarching legislative roof for the EU climate target, but the proposal presented only includes a process to consider raising it and does not set the target per se. If implemented as proposed, the law would also give the long-term dimension more visibility and elevate climate-neutrality to a guiding principle for all future policy-making.

ii. Review Process

The five-year cycle from the Paris Agreement is referenced in review clauses of several relevant existing laws and is partially emulated in governance procedures (eg, updates to NECPs and LTSs), but there is no dedicated review process for the NDC itself. This appears to reflect how the 2020 and 2030 targets were set: it was a political consensus negotiated and adopted solely by the European Council, ie, EU heads of state and government. This political decision de facto pre-determined the subsequent EU legislation, despite the fact that the European Council does

---

[72] See also forthcoming analysis in Nils Meyer-Ohlendorf, 'A European Climate Law: An Analysis of the European Commission Proposal' (Ecologic Institute & Umweltbundesamt, 2020).

[73] Commission Communication COM/2019/640 to the European Parliament, the European Council, the Council, the European Economic and Social Committee and the Committee of the Regions, the European Green Deal (hereinafter 'European Green Deal').

not have the mandate to be involved in legislation.[74] The lack of a pre-defined and agreed procedure for the NDC review is evident in the discussion on the level of the EU NDC for 2030 and creates uncertainty for EU actors and external partners alike. The President of the Commission has announced her intention to propose at least 50 per cent as a revised EU NDC and will consider raising it to 55 per cent.[75] The European Climate Law Proposal includes a process to adopt a post-2030 trajectory towards 2050, to be reviewed every five years. This could act as a direct implementation of the Paris cycle and could effectively create a new legal 'home' for the EU NDC.[76]

iii. Long-Term Strategy

Alongside the endorsement of the climate-neutrality objective at the European Council in December 2019, EU heads of state and government invited 'the Commission to prepare a proposal for the EU's long-term strategy as early as possible in 2020'.[77] As a result, EU Environment Ministers adopted a two-page document (drafted by the European Commission) at their March 2020 meeting, which was then transmitted to the UNFCCC as the formal submission by the EU under Article 4(19) of the Paris Agreement.[78] The text cites the adoption of the climate-neutrality goal and references the Commission's 2018 communication that had put forward this objective. Furthermore, it contains the December 2019 Council conclusions as an annex. It is thus not itself a strategy document, but rather a summary of the EU specific process and a statement of the new long-term target. The European Climate Law Proposal does not make any reference to the EU long-term strategy or a possible update of it. There is thus no actual strategy document other than the Commission's 2018 analysis and the respective summary communication, and no process for a repeat or updating.

At the national level, the NECPs (with a focus on 2030) have been the more dominant planning instrument, and the connection to the long-term objective and the need for transformative policies may have been lost to some extent, as an assessment of the draft plans suggests.[79]

---

[74] See section IV.B above; see also Nils Meyer-Ohlendorf, 'EU Climate Policies after 2020: Robust Review and Ratcheting up Targets' (Ecologic Institute, 2017).

[75] Ursula von der Leyen, 'Mission Letter to Frans Timmermans, Executive Vice-President-Designate for the European Green Deal' (2019), https://ec.europa.eu/commission/sites/beta-political/files/mission-letter-frans-timmermans-2019_en.pdf.

[76] Nils Meyer-Ohlendorf and Lisa Meinecke, 'A Climate Law for Europe: Making the Paris Agreement Real' (Ecologic Institute, 2018).

[77] EUCO 29/19.

[78] Council of the European Union, 'Press Release: Climate Change – Council Adopts EU Long-Term Strategy for Submission to the UNFCCC' (5 March 2020), https://www.consilium.europa.eu/en/press/press-releases/2020/03/05/climate-change-council-adopts-eu-long-term-strategy-for-submission-to-the-unfccc.

[79] Matthias Duwe et al, 'Planning for Net-Zero: Assessing the Draft National Energy and Climate Plans' (Ecologic Institute, Climact, European Climate Foundation, 2019).

In sum, the EU has already adjusted its legal framework to prepare for the implementation of the 2030 targets for energy and climate action (and thus the delivery of its NDC) and has incorporated other aspects of the Paris Agreement, at least partially, including the five-year review cycle. It has also made it legally binding on its Member States to produce LTSs, opting for a stronger degree of binding power than the Paris Agreement itself. However, a dedicated review mechanism for the EU NDC is missing. Nevertheless, at the time of writing, the political debate is moving towards an increase in the EU 2030 target regardless. With the 2050 dimension more prominent in the debate now, the European Climate Law Proposal could make climate-neutrality by 2050 a guiding principle for EU and national policy. If this were to become an effective mechanism, it would have fulfilled the core function of climate governance frameworks identified above: to connect short-term and medium-term policy-making to long-term goals.

D. What Does this Mean for National Climate Laws in the EU?

The EU's climate and energy policy provides an additional layer of guidance and obligations to the Paris Agreement. This also has an effect on the extent to which Member States can or have to implement national framework laws and the respective functions covered by them. To analyse the influence of EU legislation, we assess the impact on each of the core elements identified from the range of existing framework climate legislation discussed above.

i. Targets (and the Review System)

EU Member States do not have their own NDCs under the Paris Agreement as they are represented by the EU as a whole in this regard. The Climate Action Regulation establishes binding national targets for each Member State for the sectors not covered by the EU ETS. They are defined as annual emission allocations with some built-in flexibilities between years and potential trading between Member States. This system has largely already been in operation for the period 2013–20 and has been extended and slightly adjusted for the period 2021–30. Action plans need to be drawn up by Member States in case a lack of progress is evident. Failure to comply with the targets triggers an automatic emissions penalty. The EU system thus creates a binding system with strong pressure to enact national policies to achieve the reductions.

If the EU NDC is increased, as is being discussed, national non-ETS targets may have to be changed accordingly and with them the respective NECPs. The lack of a clear and transparent NDC review process thus creates uncertainty about the national targets. This subsequently produces uncertainty for the respective national climate governance systems, which have to define what measures are necessary to reach their respective targets. Some individual Member States (Spain, Sweden and Luxembourg) have already indicated in their NECPs that they want to go beyond their mandatory targets.[80]

ii. Planning

Strategic planning for future climate policy is a strong element in the post-Paris EU governance system in place since 2018, with the new integrated NECPs and the mandatory LTSs. Member States and the European Commission have been investing in additional capacity to establish procedures and an analytical basis for these planning exercises. Thus, the provisions go significantly beyond the requirements under the Paris Agreement and establish the main tools, some detail on content and also evaluation procedures (at least for the NECPs), which individual Member States do not have to reinvent in their national governance systems. However, updates to both NECPs and LTSs after five years are foreseen only in principle and are not prescriptive. That being said, changes to the EU's overall targets could require updates to all NECPs even before the timeline currently in the legislation for the NECP reviews (2023–24).

iii. Measures

The EU already has a toolbox of climate and energy policy instruments; these are still being applied and expanded, and others may be adopted in addition. However, there is also significant leeway for EU Member States to choose their own approaches and design policies befitting their national contexts. For the non-ETS sectors, there is a strong impetus for such measures to be enacted, and the mandatory submission of NECPs requires that each country provide details on intended policies and their expected impacts. EU legislation thus exercises pressure on governments to develop measures that far exceed the requirements under the Paris Agreement, without telling Member States what these measures should be. With the adoption of a concrete and periodic process, EU laws already prescribe significant detail for this element of a national climate governance framework. The European Climate Law Proposal would add an additional consistency check to assess whether measures proposed in the NECPs are in line with the climate-neutrality objective.[81]

iv. Reporting and Progress Monitoring

A detailed system for progress monitoring has been in place in the EU for many years. The Governance Regulation retains this system and includes updates to fit

---

[80] ibid.
[81] European Climate Law Proposal, art 6.

the new arrangements (using NECPs, for example).[82] It incorporates the reporting duties under the UNFCCC and the Paris Agreement, and expands these to fit with the procedures on targets and planning established in the EU specifically. In addition to annual data submissions, Member States need to provide detailed progress reports every two years that contain information on their implementation of the NECPs.[83] The European Commission has its own reporting duties for the EU as a whole and also issues annual 'State of the Energy Union' reports, which summarise progress for years in which Member States have not submitted their own detailed reports.[84] The Commission is also mandated to provide recommendations to Member States on the basis of their national reports. EU requirements thus ensure that detailed information is gathered and made public at regular intervals, beyond the requirements under the Paris Agreement. The European Climate Law Proposal would add to this reporting system the policy consistency check mentioned above, which could also result in recommendations from the Commission to Member States to make changes to their policies. These reporting requirements for Member States and the assessments by the Commission could be used as inputs to national progress monitoring processes. However, separate provisions in a national governance system may also be necessary to create windows for political debate and to draw public attention to relevant information.

v. Institutions

The EU governance system does not establish new institutions to provide external advice on science or carry out additional analysis. The proposal for an EU climate law is similarly silent on the matter. The European Environment Agency (EEA) is and will be tasked with quality control and providing summaries of reporting by Member States and thus provides some transparency functionality. The European Commission also issues reports and data, and can take on the role of providing analysis. It has also on occasion established temporary high-level expert groups and stakeholder commissions, but there is no separate entity like a 'Paris Agreement Observatory' to oversee progress and issue independent advice. The lack of a dedicated NDC review process is evident here again, as a dedicated entity at the EU level could provide an independent targeted input to inform a target review.[85] The EU institutions thus do provide additional institutional capacity beyond the Paris Agreement, but they do not create the specific functionality of external scientific advisory bodies seen in several examples of national climate laws.[86]

---

[82] Governance Regulation, ch 4, arts 17–28.
[83] ibid art 17.
[84] ibid art 35.
[85] Meyer-Ohlendorf (n 74).
[86] Duwe and Evans (n 42) ch 6.

vi. Public Participation

A variety of EU laws and also international treaties such as the Aarhus Convention govern public participation in the EU. In addition, and more concretely, the Governance Regulation specifies that Member States have to carry out public consultations on NECPs and LTSs, but assessments show that the current practice is weak for draft NECPs.[87] It is also mandatory to have (or establish) so-called multilevel stakeholder dialogues, but there are no specifications on the frequency or format of these fora.[88] The European Climate Law Proposal contains a separate article on public participation that obliges the Commission to 'facilitate an inclusive and accessible process at all levels' and references the dialogues mentioned above as a source to draw on, as well as extending their mandate to the climate-neutrality objective.[89] Compared to the Paris Agreement, EU legislation thus includes specific obligations to involve the public in national climate policy-making, but there is significant flexibility for Member States and EU institutions in terms of how to meet them.

In sum, it is clear that EU legislation adds a considerable level of specification to the provisions of the Paris Agreement with significant impact for the establishment of national climate laws. EU law does not require Member States to establish national framework legislation. However, it creates more and more specific obligations, defines additional governance elements (such as national non-ETS targets and mandatory development of NECPs) and thus already provides greater specificity for core elements often included in national climate governance systems. One could argue that this lowers the need for Member States to implement their own overarching governance frameworks.

At the same time, the opposite could also be true. For one thing, the EU still leaves room for Member States to define their own approaches, both in terms of policies and also internal institutional arrangements. EU laws do specify the overall outcome (targets) and establish a means of communication (NECPs). They do not prescribe how Member States organise themselves and what individual measures they adopt, and thus national governments need to define their own governance arrangements. Furthermore, the fact that the national targets are directly legally binding at the EU level creates a much stronger pressure on Member States to enact policies that have an effect on emissions. We would argue that this emphasises and strengthens the impetus from the Paris Agreement to establish 'management tools' to ensure that the government can produce these policies.

There is a third specific argument, which is the conundrum faced by essentially all governments aiming for emissions reductions: how to involve all sectors.

---

[87] Governance Regulation, art 10; Duwe et al (n 80); David Donnerer, 'Main Findings in Good Practice Governance: Summary of Main Findings in Good Practices in Energy and Climate Governance in EU Member States' (Plan up, 2019).

[88] Governance Regulation, art 11.

[89] European Climate Law Proposal, ss 8 and 10.

In the EU, existing emission reductions from 1990 levels are the result of sector specific changes in some areas (eg, industrial production patterns), changes in practice in others (eg, waste) and most notably structural change towards renewable energy and away from coal combustion in the energy sector. Other sectors, such as transport, have not undergone similar changes yet, in part due to more effective resistance by incumbent economic actors. But for the next set of more ambitious milestone emissions reduction goals and the overarching achievement of the long-term targets, all sectors have to contribute. One way of addressing this could be realised in national framework climate laws. The obligation for all ministries involved to deliver policies is included in more than one existing climate framework law (see, eg, the laws in Mexico and Finland). Moreover, the framework climate law in Germany is particularly innovative; it establishes sector specific targets for 2030 and annual allocations for each of the respective ministries in charge of policies for each sector.[90] The French Low Carbon Strategy also includes sector-specific budget breakdowns. Specifically, for EU Member States that need to meet their binding 2030 non-ETS targets, finding a way to ensure that all sectors contribute will be a key challenge going forward – a challenge that may be best addressed using a national framework law.

V. Summary and Conclusions

While the Paris Agreement does not demand that its parties enact national framework climate legislation, its objectives evidently require transformational change from every party that takes the Agreement seriously. Managing this global transition towards climate-neutrality is a task that also needs to happen at the national level. Most governments are not equipped to organise such broad changes over periods of time that are both short compared to the magnitude of the challenge and long considering electoral cycles.

The Paris Agreement contains obligations on parties that have a bearing on some of the essential elements found in many national climate governance frameworks, including the need to define targets (NDCs), monitoring procedures and a review process. However, it cannot enforce the setting of adequate targets or the adoption of specific measures. It cannot even enforce compliance with the NDCs that countries have set for themselves. The entire system relies on countries delivering (voluntarily) on their pledged actions and on these being increased steadily in line with the transformation required in the long run. The focus on collective long-term targets combined with binding procedural elements for individual parties is both the core strength of the Paris Agreement and its greatest weakness.

---

[90] Duwe and Evans (n 42) ch 5.5.

Achieving the Paris Agreement's targets and making the system a success – winning the 'gamble' – is thus an onus on all parties. It is evident that this requires establishing the management tools, a governance framework, in order to organise the necessary transformation. Achieving climate-neutrality requires smart policies and broad political support and buy-in, and a socially inclusive approach to proactively address the implications of the changes required. Framework climate legislation can serve these functions as a compass that guides the implementation of the procedural elements of the Paris Agreement at the national level with a view towards achieving the collective long-term goals.

The EU has already set requirements for its Member States in addition to those stemming from the UNFCCC regime. It has further refined and adjusted its internal laws concerning the targets beyond 2020, and included requirements from the Paris Agreement, strengthening and specifying essential aspects (such as binding national targets) that determine national climate policy.

Several EU Member States already have adopted national framework climate legislation, and they are starting to reflect certain design elements specific to the EU context. This is anecdotal evidence for the thesis that the Paris Agreement has created an impetus for the establishment of national governance systems in the form of laws, and that the specifications provided by EU laws do not reduce the need for such arrangements, but strengthen it.

The European Climate Law Proposal would make the 2050 climate-neutrality goal legally binding for the EU and its Member States. The proposal can be taken as support for the argument that the long-term goals of the Paris Agreement need to be anchored in law to become benchmarks for policy-making. This could create a more reliable compass towards 2050 and fill gaps in the current EU governance system, such as a dedicated process for future NDC reviews, an independent advisory body as well as improved public participation and progress monitoring. This would provide the EU – and its Member States – with a better chance of making an adequate contribution to fulfilling the objectives of the Paris Agreement.

3

The UK's Climate Change Act

RICHARD MACRORY AND THOMAS L MUINZER

I. Introduction

In passing the Climate Change Act (CCA) 2008, the UK became the first country to place national long-term legally binding emissions reduction targets on the government in law, doing so in the context of a specially constructed legislative regime designed to drive a national low carbon transition. The CCA 2008 is an ambitious, extensive and pioneering Act, which addresses a pressing area of governance, climate change. At the time of the Act's creation, Friends of the Earth appropriately summed it up as a 'huge step in the fight against climate change,'[1] though it has also attracted criticism in addition to praise from legal experts and political scientists.[2]

While substantial work on the Act had been reasonably slow in coming, attention, analyses and assessments of the framework have finally built up a head of steam. The framework's tenth anniversary year in particular (2018) saw the release of the first detailed book-length exploration and evaluation of the Act,[3] and an important 10-year review document was published by the Grantham Institute and the London School of Economics (LSE).[4] Elements of the interesting academic and other commentary to emerge around the Act will be raised in due course below. The following text will provide a concise summary of the Act's background and emergence, and will convey a clear sense of the framework's key features, in

---

[1] Public statement released by Friends of the Earth UK's climate team in 2008. Friends of the Earth was largely instrumental in initiating the idea of a new Climate Change Act, which was then promoted by the government with support from all political parties. See section II below.

[2] For a largely positive assessment, see, eg, Harriet Townsend, 'The Climate Change Act 2008: Something to Be Proud of after All?' (2009) 7(8) *Journal of Planning and Environmental Law* 842. For a more negative assessment, see Peter McMaster, 'Climate Change: Statutory Duty or Pious Hope?' (2008) 20(1) *Journal of Environmental Law* 115.

[3] Thomas L Muinzer, *Climate and Energy Governance for the UK Low Carbon Transition: The Climate Change Act 2008* (London, Palgrave Macmillan, 2018).

[4] Sam Fankhauser, Alina Averchenkova and Jared Finnegan, *10 Years of the UK Climate Change Act* (London, Grantham Research Institute and London School of Economics, 2018).

conjunction with drawing on the extant commentary on the regime as and where appropriate.

Muinzer's monograph *The Climate Change Act 2008*[5] posits a basic conceptual scheme that can be used in order to frame analysis of the regime:

- Two major thematic elements underlying the framework as a whole can be usefully identified: *mitigation* and *adaptation*. Mitigation, pertaining to the mitigation of greenhouse gases, can be summarised in basic terms as concerning the 'reduction of emissions'[6] or their 'removal' from the atmosphere.[7] Adaptation pertains to the need to 'adapt to the tangible problems and severities arising as a consequence of climate change',[8] and the practices and processes surrounding this issue.

- The framework can be usefully viewed as being founded on two major categories of duties, *substantive* duties and *procedural* duties.[9] '[S]ubstantive duties should be understood to refer to the active goals and concrete outcomes that are required to be achieved under the terms of the Act', including most importantly, but not limited to, the requirement to meet the Act's milestone 2020 and 2050 reduction targets (these are outlined below).[10] '[P]rocedural duties should be understood to refer to the automatic processes that are set down by the CCA [2008] in order to allow the machinery of the framework to operate',[11] most particularly the framework's major reporting and advisory duties.[12]

- A basic binary conceptual framework for expressing and interpreting certain aspects of the means by which the CCA 2008 might be improved going forward can be usefully articulated.[13] This is described as involving *strengthening* and *deepening*. Strengthening 'should be taken to indicate most particularly the ramping up of target percentages and the tightening of other associated quantifiably measurable decarbonisation objectives generated by the framework, particularly the carbon budget thresholds'.[14] Deepening 'indicate[s] a greater socio-economic depth of reach that could be accorded to the CCA [2008]'s processes', which means 'in essence' that the generation of heat and electricity must 'no longer be treated as the low-hanging fruit that can bear the lion's share

---

[5] Muinzer (n 3).
[6] ibid 68.
[7] ibid 4.
[8] ibid.
[9] ibid 20.
[10] ibid.
[11] ibid.
[12] ibid.
[13] See ibid 123–27 ('Conclusions').
[14] ibid 124.

of emissions reductions'.[15] In other words, pressure and innovation must be expanded much more broadly across all of the UK's socio-economic sectors in as pervasive a fashion as possible.

These elements will be returned to at certain points below.

II. Background to the Act

The CCA 2008 was passed in late 2008 and came into force over 2008–09.[16] A national climate change programme had been adopted by the UK in 2000[17] and an important White Paper[18] concerning energy was issued by the UK government in 2003.[19] The national climate change programme was revised in 2006[20] and a further significant White Paper on energy appeared in 2007.[21] These programmes and strategies were underpinned by an intention to mitigate national greenhouse gas emissions, most particularly from the energy sector, which was both the most abundant national sectoral emitter and where its emissions levels were seen to be interconnected with concerns ranging beyond climate change to intersect with problems around UK energy security and affordability. The climate regime in this pre-CCA 2008 stage was relatively weak and partial in nature, and was characterised by a soft policy approach.

In June 2000, the Royal Commission on Environmental Pollution, an independent and highly respected advisory body, had published its 22nd Report, *Energy – The Changing Climate.*[22] The Report received enormous publicity. It accepted that the government's then policy of reducing the UK's annual CO_2 emissions by 20 per cent from their 1990 levels by 2010 was a step in the right direction, but argued that a longer-term, more ambitious strategy was necessary. It proposed that the government should adopt a strategy of reducing emissions by 60 per cent from current levels by 2050.[23] The Report contained many recommendations for the types of policies needed to secure such a goal, but did not argue for new climate change legislation as such. Following the publication of the Report,

---

[15] ibid.

[16] See further CCA 2008, s 100.

[17] DETR, *Climate Change: The UK Programme* (London, HM Government, 2000).

[18] White Papers are important policy documents issued by the UK government that contain information on proposed future legislation.

[19] DTI, *Our Energy Future – Creating a Low Carbon Economy* (London, HM Government, 2003).

[20] DEFRA, *Climate Change: The UK Programme 2006* (London, HM Government, 2006).

[21] DTI, *Meeting the Challenge: A White Paper on Energy* (London, HM Government, 2007).

[22] Royal Commission on Environmental Pollution, *Energy – The Changing Climate*, 22nd Report, Cm 4749 (London, HMSO, 2000).

[23] The figure was based on the concept of contract and convergence setting an upper global limit of 550 ppmv by 2050. In the light of developments in the scientific understanding of climate change, the figure was increased to 80 per cent by the time that the CCA 2008 was passed.

the Prime Minister immediately accepted the need for the longer-term reduction target identified by the Commission.

Against this backdrop, Friends of the Earth UK played an important role in pressing for improvements, pushing strategically for the creation of a Climate Change Bill in April 2005 and launching 'The Big Ask' campaign in the following month to champion the issue.[24] A Stop Climate Chaos coalition was formed in July 2005 to draw a range of non-governmental organisations (NGOs) together, serving to pool resources around this issue and associated climate concerns.[25] At this time, the Labour Party under Tony Blair, which was in government after having achieved its third successive general election victory in May 2005, was emphasising climate change as an important issue and ensured that it was treated as a foregrounded matter at the G8 summit that took place in the UK at Gleneagles shortly after this re-election in July 2005. The Conservative Party under David Cameron was also endeavouring to redefine itself in the public mindset in this period, including by 'bas[ing] a renewal of British conservativism on a partly green platform'.[26] This included an inclination towards taking on the problem of climate change more directly than had previously been the case.

The Stern Report, published in October 2006, contributed further momentum towards the Act's creation.[27] This extensive review examined climate change issues from an economic perspective, finding that inadequate action in the sphere of climate change mitigation and adaptation would exert substantial, negative and persistent economic impacts on the UK over time; the extent of these problems could be economically limited by taking appropriate measures as soon as possible.[28] These and other signals like them from the research and policy community were increasingly convincing elements of the more normally obstructive and resistant corporate and business lobby that the sort of locked-in, long-term design that the CCA 2008 would ultimately come to embody could be to some extent highly desirable. This was due in major part to the manner in which that form of approach would lock decarbonisation obligations in over time and provide investors, markets and industries with a degree of market

---

[24] The key role played by Friends of the Earth has been explored insightfully in Neil Carter and Mike Childs, 'Friends of the Earth as a Policy Entrepreneur: "The Big Ask" Campaign for a UK Climate Change Act' (2018) 27(6) *Environmental Politics* 994. See also Bryony Worthington, *What the Government Should Do to Tackle Climate Change* (London, Friends of the Earth, 2005); this report was an influential response to the UK government's review of the Climate Change Programme.

[25] Neil Carter, 'The Party Politicization of Climate and Energy Policy in Britain' in Giles Leydier and Alexia Martin (eds), *Environmental Issues in Political Discourse in Britain and Ireland* (Newcastle, Cambridge Scholars, 2013) 74.

[26] Noel Castree, 'The Future of Environmentalism' (2006) 34 *Soundings* 11.

[27] Nicolas Stern et al, *Stern Review: The Economics of Climate Change* (London, HM Government, 2006).

[28] See also Nicolas Stern, 'What is the Economics of Climate Change?' (2006) (7) 2 *World Economics* 1.

clarity and certainty in the face of the uncertainty that was then confronting them.[29]

In April 2005, three MPs came together[30] in a rare display of progressive cross-party unity and presented a model Climate Bill to the UK Parliament.[31] The Bill's progress was interrupted by a general election, but subsequently a parliamentary motion was put forward in favour of the adoption of climate legislation, receiving support by a substantial majority of MPs,[32] and presently the UK government published a draft Climate Change Bill (March 2007).[33] A public consultation on the Bill was published on 13 March 2007 and ran until 12 June 2007, garnering a huge response of almost 17,000 submissions from individuals and organisations, which the UK government described as 'overwhelming[ly] ... supportive of the Bill's aim to set and enable the achievement of ambitious emissions reduction targets'.[34] The Bill was introduced to Parliament in November 2007, received Royal Assent on 26 November 2008 and its key legal components were all in force by the end of January 2009.

III. The Form and Content of the Act

The CCA 2008 is a large and substantial item of legislation (contrast, for example, the Swedish Climate Change Act, which Romson and Forsbacka[35] describe in this volume as consisting of one page and five paragraphs).[36] Some of its provisions pertain to major mechanisms and features, whereas other elements are comparatively minor in nature.[37] The main body of the legislation is arranged in a number of parts, and these are followed by a series of schedules at the end

---

[29] Mark Stallworthy, 'New Forms of Carbon Accounting: The Significance of a Climate Change Act for Economic Activity in the UK' (2007) 18(10) *International Company & Commercial Law Review* 331; Neil Carter, 'Combating Climate Change in the UK: Challenges and Obstacles' (2008) 79(2) *Political Quarterly* 194.

[30] John Gummer (Conservative Party), Michael Meacher (Labour Party) and Norman Baker (Liberal Democrats).

[31] Prime Minister Tony Blair's Labour government was in power at this time.

[32] See further Karla Hill, *The UK Climate Change Act 2008: Lessons for National Climate Laws* (London, ClientEarth 2009) 9 ('Background').

[33] Draft Climate Change Bill, Cm 7040, March 2007.

[34] DEFRA, *Taking Forward the UK Climate Change Bill: The Government Response to Pre-Legislative Scrutiny and Public Consultation* (London, HM Government, 2007) 6. A detailed analysis of the consultation phase, with reference to broader theories around consultation processes in general, can be found in Adela Maciejewski Scheer and Corina Höppner, 'The Public Consultation to the UK Climate Change Act 2008: A Critical Analysis' (2010) 10(3) *Climate Policy* 261.

[35] See further Åsa Romson and Kristina Forsbacka, ch 7 in this volume.

[36] Richard B Macrory, 'The UK Climate Change Act: Towards a Brave New Legal World?' in Inge Lorange Backer, Ole Kristian Fauchald and Christina Voigt (eds), *Pro Natura* (Oslo, Universitetsforlaget, 2012) 306–22.

[37] On distinguishing between *major* and *minor* elements, see Muinzer (n 3) 41 and ch 2 generally.

of the Act. There are six parts and eight schedules in all, which are arranged and titled as follows.

Table 3.1 Structure of the Climate Change Act

CLIMATE CHANGE ACT	
PARTS AND SCHEDULES	**TITLES**
Part 1	'Carbon Target and Budgeting'
Part 2	'The Committee on Climate Change'
Part 3	'Trading Schemes'
Part 4	'Impact of and Adaptation to Climate Change'
Part 5	'Other Provisions'
Part 6	'General Supplementary Provisions'
Schedule 1	'The Committee on Climate Change'
Schedule 2	'Trading Schemes'
Schedule 3	'Trading Schemes Regulations: Further Provisions'
Schedule 4	'Trading Schemes: Powers to Require Information'
Schedule 5	'Waste Reduction Schemes'
Schedule 6	'Charges for Carrier Bags'
Schedule 7	'Renewable Transport Fuel Obligations'
Schedule 8	'Carbon Emissions Reduction Targets'

The framework is designed to drive an economy-wide decarbonisation transition, predicated in significant part upon driving down particular greenhouse gases.[38] Thus, the legislation carefully sketches out the specific greenhouse gases that it seeks to control, describing these as 'targeted greenhouse gases'.[39] 'Greenhouse gas' under the terms of the framework refers to the following cohort of gases:

(a)   carbon dioxide (CO_2);
(b)   methane (CH_4);
(c)   nitrous oxide (N_2O);
(d)   hydrofluorocarbons (HFCs);
(e)   perfluorocarbons (PFCs);
(f)   sulphur hexafluoride (SF6).[40]

---

[38] The expression 'in significant part' is used here because the framework is concerned importantly with climate change *adaptation* in addition to the process of driving down greenhouse gas emissions (ie, *mitigation*).

[39] CCA 2008, s 24(1).

[40] ibid s 92(1)(a)–(f).

It is these specific greenhouse gases that are covered by the CCA 2008's decarbonisation regime.[41] The Secretary of State can amend this definition in certain instances,[42] 'add[ing] to the gases listed in that definition' if it becomes internationally understood at the 'European' or 'international' level that it is appropriate to recognise an additional gas as a pertinent climate change contributor that ought to be brought within this sort of definition.[43] 'Emissions' of a targeted greenhouse gas refers to 'emissions of that gas into the atmosphere that are *attributable to human activity*' (emphasis added).[44] Here one witnesses an emergent principle of well-crafted climate law: the 'climate' is so broad, complex and pervasive as to tend towards something approaching meaninglessness where one simply talks loosely of 'climate law'; the UK regime, like the United Nations Framework Convention on Climate Change (UNFCCC),[45] fences in the parameters so that the legal issues can be seen to engage emissions *attributable to human activity*, thus narrowing the frame of the legal concerns so that they can be made a little more concrete and meaningful in a lawyerly sense, mapping directly onto the issue of anthropogenic climate change.

As is common practice in UK legislation, the CCA 2008 uses the term 'Secretary of State', giving him or her important powers and duties for achieving the regime's major outcomes, as well as powers to amend the targets and definitions of greenhouse gases. It is a deliberately flexible term, designed to accommodate future changes in government departmental structures. In practice, the Secretary of State is a Cabinet Minister from the UK government who is in charge of the relevant government department dealing with climate change.[46] Bearing in mind that UK government departments are often subject to closure or restructuring,[47] as of 2016 lead climate and energy responsibilities have been allocated to the UK government's Department for Business, Energy and Industrial Strategy (BEIS). The result is that the Secretary of State, imbued with primary duties and powers under the CCA 2008, is currently the Secretary of State for BEIS, who has overall responsibility for leading that department.[48]

---

[41] See ibid ss 24–25; s 1, s 27(1).

[42] ibid s 24(1)(g), 24(2).

[43] ibid s 92.

[44] ibid s 97. Greenhouse gas emissions are 'measured or calculated in tonnes of carbon dioxide equivalent' (s 93(1)).

[45] UNFCCC, art 1(2).

[46] In UK legislation, 'Secretary of State' means 'one of Her Majesty's Principal Secretaries of State': Interpretation Act 1978, sched 1.

[47] At the time of the Act's creation, the pertinent Secretary of State was the Cabinet Minister leading the Department of Energy and Climate Change (DECC), but this Department has since been abolished.

[48] However, it should also be noted that the Department for Environment, Food and Rural Affairs (DEFRA) takes a lead role on adaptation.

IV. Carbon Targets and Carbon Budgeting

The greatest headline innovation under the terms of Part 1 of the Act concerns its imposition on the UK of long-term legally binding emissions reduction targets, which are pegged to the dates of 2020 and 2050. These have been described as the framework's 'milestone' targets.[49] An 80 per cent greenhouse gas emissions reduction target is applied for 2050 and this has since been adjusted upwards to 100 per cent ('net zero') at the time of writing,[50] and a 34 per cent emissions reduction target is applied for 2020.[51] The 100 per cent and 34 per cent reductions are measured from 1990 baseline emissions levels.[52] This '1990 baseline' level has a slightly convoluted definition: it does refer to net UK carbon dioxide emissions for 1990, but it also refers to the base year for the UK's other targeted greenhouse gases, and only two of these have an actual 1990 base year. The breakdown is as follows:

- methane (1990);
- nitrous oxide (1990);
- hydrofluorocarbons (1995);
- perfluorocarbons (1995);
- sulphur hexafluoride (1995).[53]

So, in the case of hydrofluorocarbons, for example, the '1990 baseline' means the 'net UK emissions ... for the year that is the base year for that gas', namely 1995.[54] Thus, it has been summarised that 'the 1990 baseline nominally refers to the general baseline emissions marker for the targeted gases, [however] section 25(1) indicates that the base years for some of the other targeted greenhouse gases differ in practice'.[55] The Secretary of State is imbued with the power to issue orders altering the base years, but under limited circumstances, namely where there are 'developments in European or international law or policy that make it appropriate to do so'.[56] The 1990 baseline is intended to assist the CCA 2008 in marrying up with international practice, where 1990 has been pegged as a baseline marker in the international setting by the UNFCCC.[57]

Long-term target duties placed on the government are not unknown in UK legislation, but have usually been qualified with phrases such as 'as far as reasonably

---

[49] Muinzer (n 21) 103 and 113.
[50] CCA 2008, s 1(1).
[51] ibid s 5(1)(a).
[52] The interim reduction target initially sat at 26 per cent, but the Secretary of State swiftly revised it upwards to 34 per cent after receiving parliamentary approval, issuing the Climate Change Act 2008 (2020 Target, Credit Limit and Definitions) Order 2009 to make the change.
[53] CCA 2008, s 25(1).
[54] ibid s 1(2)(b).
[55] Muinzer (n 3) 56.
[56] CCA 2008, s 25(4).
[57] See UNFCCC, art 4(2)(b).

practicable', giving governments considerable wriggle room from a legal perspective. The 2050 duty in the CCA 2008 is unusual in that it is expressed in absolute terms with no qualifications.[58] It is true that the Secretary of State can amend these targets by secondary legislation, but he or she can only do so where there have been significant developments in scientific knowledge on climate change or European or international law or policy. Economic challenges, for example, would not be a legal justification for amending the targets.

Part 1 of the Act sketches out and applies to the UK a sophisticated carbon accounting scheme rooted in environmental economics. Here, the regime establishes a 'net UK emissions' level, which represents the total amount of targeted greenhouse gases released by the UK over a particular period of time after the deduction of targeted greenhouse gas removals over that timespan.[59] The Act defines 'removals' of a greenhouse gas as 'removals of that gas from the atmosphere due to land use, land-use change or forestry activities in the United Kingdom'.[60]

A UK 'carbon budgeting' scheme is set in place and a 'net UK carbon account'[61] is opened. The underlying purpose of the mechanisms of regular carbon budgeting is to enable a smooth trajectory towards the long-term reduction targets, and to send the appropriate signals for industry and others planning investment strategies. The carbon budget mechanism in the Act employs fixed five-year budgetary periods, and the practical accounting process involves quantities of 'carbon units', with each unit representing a fixed measure of greenhouse gas.[62] Current 'net UK emissions' levels and future desirable levels can be used in order to calculate a UK carbon budget for the present and future five-year carbon budget cycles. Each five-year carbon budget cycle can be capped at a set level for the cycles to come, and an appropriate quantity of carbon units can be credited and debited to the UK's carbon account over the fixed periods in order to stimulate change in accordance with the limit caps. Thus, desirable future net UK emissions levels can be projected forward in time, with the UK carbon budget cap being steadily reduced over time in conjunction with requisite reductions in carbon units. This complex, sophisticated system, including the budget levels and the crediting and debiting process, is overseen by the Secretary of State, but with continuing input and advice from the Committee on Climate Change established under the Act, which is discussed further below. The milestone reduction targets of 34 per cent and 100 per cent for 2020 and 2050, respectively, serve to sketch out a minimum reductions-level pathway that the carbon budgets are required to reflect so that the targets can be met.

---

[58] 'It is the duty of the Secretary of State to ensure that the net UK carbon account for the year 2050 is at least 100% lower than the 1990 baseline' (CCA 2008, s 1(1)). For a discussion of the challenges in actually enforcing this duty before the courts, see Macrory (n 36); and see further section VII below.

[59] CCA 2008, s 29(1)(a)–(c).

[60] ibid s 29(1)(b).

[61] ibid ss 4–10, ss 26–28, s 1(1), s 4(1)(a).

[62] See ibid s 26(1).

Table 3.2 UK carbon budget levels and reduction targets

Budget	Carbon budget level	Reduction below 1990 levels
1st carbon budget (2008–12)	3,018 MtCO2e	25 per cent
2nd carbon budget (2013–17)	2,782 MtCO2e	31 per cent
3rd carbon budget (2018–22)	2,544 MtCO2e	37 per cent by 2020
4th carbon budget (2023–27)	1,950 MtCO2e	51 per cent by 2025
5th carbon budget (2028–32)	1,725 MtCO2e	57 per cent by 2030

Source: Committee on Climate Change.

The Secretary of State must set subsequent carbon budgets that are not yet in place at least 12 years in advance,[63] while also keeping Parliament appraised of progress under the scheme through reporting obligations imposed by the Act.[64] It is asserted that '[t]he amount of UK emissions and UK removals of a greenhouse gas' for a given period is to be 'determined consistently with international carbon reporting practice',[65] such that the scheme operates in the tradition established at the international level by the UNFCCC. The legislation affords the Secretary of State some flexibility in meeting the five-year budgetary limits, since amounts from one budget period can be carried over into another period in certain circumstances. Rules on this are stated at section 17 of the Act,[66] and though the legislation itself does not employ the rhetoric, this is the process described as the 'banking' and 'borrowing' of emissions in the jargon of environmental economists.[67] In the event that a set carbon budget is exceeded over the course of one of the mandatory budgeting periods, the Secretary of State is required to lay a report before Parliament that contains proposals designed to compensate over the future period(s) for the excesses; this report must be produced as 'soon as is reasonably practicable'.[68] Once a carbon budget has been set, the Secretary of State then has a duty to prepare proposals and policies for meeting the budget in question and to lay before Parliament a report setting these out. This is the critical step in relating the

---

[63] ibid s 4(2)(a)–(b).

[64] See ibid s 16 ('Annual statement of UK emissions').

[65] ibid s 29(2).

[66] ibid s 17.

[67] For example, it is stated that the 'Secretary of State may decide to carry back part of the carbon budget for a budgetary period to the preceding budgetary period', with the result that the 'carbon budget for the later period is reduced, and that for the earlier period increased, by the amount carried back'; however, the 'amount carried back … must not exceed 1% of the carbon budget for the later period' (CCA 2008, s 17(1)–(2)). See further Julien Chevallier, 'Banking and Borrowing in the EU ETS: A Review of Economic Modelling, Current Provisions and Prospects for Future Design' (2012) 26(1) *Journal of Economic Surveys* 157.

[68] CCA 2008, s 19(1).

fairly abstract budget figures to the detailed policies and practical steps needed to achieve them.[69]

The UK has been meeting these requirements successfully to date, with the first carbon budget having been achieved and with the third budget having already been outperformed by the close of the second carbon budget; the second budget concluded in 2017 and UK emissions were 43 per cent below the 1990 baseline for that year.[70] Thus, the framework has been very successful to date and there is cause for substantial positivity. However, it is also possible to project forward in the context of these indicators, and here matters are highly concerning. The government's expert advisory body, the Committee on Climate Change, has found that current approaches and efforts will not be sufficient to meet the required pending targets for the post-third carbon budget period.[71] The UK government has also evaluated the issue and reported that these targets will not be achieved as things stand.[72] Thus, a detailed assessment of the CCA 2008 published by the Grantham Institute in 2018 has emphasised that the 'UK is currently not on track to meet its statutory carbon targets for the mid-2020s and early 2030s (4th and 5th carbon budgets)'.[73]

V. The Committee on Climate Change

At Part 2, the CCA 2008 established a Committee on Climate Change (CCC).[74] While it does not have any active authority to set policy or to over-rule the Secretary of State, it is an influential and important public body. Sitting at an independent remove from the UK government,[75] it provides scrutiny of the national decarbonisation process and has been described appropriately as the 'custodian of UK climate policy'.[76] The Committee itself consists of a chair and up to eight members, and is supported by a substantial secretariat to assist it in

[69] ibid ss 14–15. The report on proposals and policies must be laid before Parliament 'as soon as reasonably practicable after making an order setting the carbon budget for a budgetary period'. There has been concern that this wording gives too much discretion to the government to determine the timing for producing the report. It took some nine months following the agreement of the Fifth Carbon Budget in July 2016 (covering 2028–32) for the government's proposals and policies to be published.

[70] See further *2017 Provisional UK Greenhouse Gas Emissions Statistical Summary* (London, BEIS, March 2018).

[71] CCC, *An Independent Assessment of the UK's Clean Growth Strategy* (London, CCC, 2018).

[72] Department for BEIS, *Updated Energy and Emissions Projections 2017* (London, BEIS, 2018).

[73] Fankhauser et al (n 4) 34.

[74] Although the CCC was formally created by the CCA 2008 itself, the body was in fact set up in 'shadow form' in advance of the Climate Change Bill's passage into an Act. This permitted this rudimentary version of the CCC to feed into the pre-CCA 2008 planning stage somewhat, with its most pronounced influence coming through in its advice on the fixing of the framework's 2050 target.

[75] CCA 2008, sched 1, para 27.

[76] Fankhauser et al (n 4) 2.

its functions.[77] In addition to supporting the UK government and the national Parliament at the state level, its reporting and advisory duties are also designed to serve and support the UK's devolved administrations of Northern Ireland, Wales and Scotland. McGregor et al have characterised the CCC as a type of 'Rolling Stern' body insofar as it undertakes a similar brief to the Stern Report (discussed above), but carries the functions out on a rolling basis over time.[78] This is an appealing analogy, but an over-generalisation, as the CCC is a statutory expert body that interacts in complex ways with the requirements of its broader CCA 2008 parent framework.

As to the CCC's specific advisory responsibilities, these include, inter alia, a duty to advise the Secretary of State where he or she may be intending to initiate substantive changes or otherwise take major decisions relating to key aspects of the CCA 2008 regime. This might involve a procedurally automatic sort of advisory obligation, such as where a carbon budget level is being set,[79] or a less pre-determined advisory obligation, such as where the government may decide for various reasons to review the 2050 milestone target with a view to potentially amending it.[80] The CCC cannot require the government to comply with its recommendations, but many of the statutory provisions concerning its advice in essence oblige the Secretary of State to justify a decision not to agree with the Committee, increasing his or her political and public accountability for doing so. For example, if the government proposes a carbon budget before Parliament which differs from that recommended by the CCC, the Secretary of State must 'publish a statement setting out the reasons for that decision'.[81] Advisory support can also be sought on request by national authorities.[82] The CCC's advisory (and other) roles can be subject to expansion or alteration, as evidenced by the passage of the Infrastructure Act 2015, which has conferred further obligations on the CCC to provide advice on the potential impact of onshore petroleum policy choices on the UK's decarbonisation trajectory.[83] In terms of its role as a reporting body, the CCC has issued a substantial range of influential reports and information papers. But arguably the most important function in this context is an annual report that the CCC is required to lay before Parliament (and the UK's devolved Parliaments) each year detailing the progress made under the terms of the Act to date and the further progress

---

[77] The more detailed structure and constitution of the CCC is contained in sched I to the Act. At the time of writing, the CCC has an annual budget of around £3.5 million funded by BEIS, DEFRA and the devolved administrations, and with around 40 staff assigned to the Secretariat: CCC, *Annual Reports and Accounts 2017–2018* (London, CCC, 2018).

[78] Peter G McGregor, Kim Swales and Matthew A Winning, 'The Committee on Climate Change: A Policy Analysis' (2010) Discussion Paper, University of Strathclyde, 1–74.

[79] CCA 2008, s 34.

[80] ibid s 33.

[81] ibid s 7(6).

[82] ibid s 38(1)(a)–(d).

[83] Infrastructure Act 2015, s 49.

required going forward.[84] It is thus an influential information gathering institution, an independent scrutiny body, and an advisory and reporting facility rolled into one overall unit.

VI. Further Major Components of the Framework

A. Trading Schemes

The CCA 2008 also opens up capacities for trading schemes to be created under secondary legislation.[85] Again, the powers fall chiefly to the Secretary of State, although the devolved Northern Irish, Welsh and Scottish governments also have some capacity to issue these sorts of regulations in their areas of devolved competence.[86] The powers permit these national authorities to appoint special administrators that can administrate a given scheme in practice.[87] Enforcement powers are also opened up:[88] civil financial penalties for non-compliance can be applied;[89] and criminal offences can also be applied, including the imposition of either a maximum of a one-year term of imprisonment, a fine of up to £50,000 or both.[90]

A 'trading scheme' is a scheme that either 'limit[s] or encourage[s] the limitation of activities that consist of the emission of greenhouse gas or that cause or contribute, directly or indirectly to such emissions'[91] or that encourages activities that 'consist of, or that cause or contribute, directly or indirectly, to reductions in greenhouse gas emissions or the removal of greenhouse gas from the atmosphere'.[92] The schedules to the Act contain substantial guidance and detail on the regulatory criteria pertinent to the schemes, their administrative elements and so on.[93] These sorts of trading schemes include the important cap and trade schemes that normally apply a 'cap'/limit on permissible greenhouse gas emissions from particular installations and issue carbon allowances that have a market value up to the level of the cap. This creates a market, such that participating installations can trade allowances/credits within the cap limit.[94]

---

[84] CCA 2008, s 36.
[85] ibid pt 3.
[86] ibid s 47.
[87] See ibid sched 2, para 21.3.e.
[88] ibid sched 2, para 28.
[89] ibid sched 2 para 29.
[90] ibid sched 2, para 30.
[91] ibid s 44(2)(a).
[92] ibid s 44(2)(b).
[93] ibid scheds 2–3.
[94] UK trading schemes under this part can be blended with European and international schemes (see eg, ibid sched 2, para 11), including the EU's emissions trading system; see further Directive 2003/87/EC (as amended) (hereinafter the EU ETS Directive).

B. Adaptation

There is a trend in climate law and policy analysis to focus on treatment of *mitigation* to the detriment of *adaptation*, with the latter dimension indeed having been viewed unhelpfully and not infrequently as '*a distraction* from the more urgent issue of … taking mitigating actions' (emphasis added).[95] In contrast, the CCA 2008 gives specific attention to the issue of adaptation, epitomised by the fact that it requires the CCC to establish a distinct sub-committee called the Adaptation Sub-Committee (ASC). While the legislation gives the CCC the option to create additional sub-committees,[96] the ASC's creation was explicitly required under the terms of the Act.[97] Parts 1–3 of the Act are largely focussed on mitigation, but Part 4 devotes explicit and extended attention to climate change *adaptation*. The ASC is required to furnish the CCC with 'advice, analysis, information or other assistance' pertaining to climate change adaptation.[98] Thus, the creation of a bespoke committee within the CCC is a useful means of preventing neglect or/and backsliding on this issue. The broader legislative approach to the issue of adaptation can be usefully interpreted through the twin lenses of *reporting* on the problem and providing *programmes* that actively respond to the issues identified by the reporting. Coming first to the *reporting* mechanism, the framework's basic approach here is to initiate a cycle of action that commences with the production of a major assessment report that sets out the current and projected impacts of climate change on the UK.[99] One cannot deal in certainty where climate impacts are being projected forward in this way, and so the primary purpose of the report is to sketch out a concrete sense of the 'risks' facing the UK.[100] The first report appeared in accordance with the Act's time procedures in early 2012, entitled *UK Climate Change Risk Assessment: Government Report*,[101] and was laid before Parliament by the Secretary of State, per the Act's requirements.[102] This triggered a pattern where new subsequent reports of this kind are to be published no later than every five years after the preceding risk report.[103]

Coming now to the *programmes* that endeavour to respond to challenges in the area of adaptation, the Secretary of State is obliged to produce climate change

---

[95] Robbert Biesbroek and Alexandra Lesnikowski, 'Adaptation: The Neglected Dimension of Polycentric Climate Governance?' in Andrew Jordan, Dave Huitema, Harro van Asselt and Johanna Forester (eds), *Governing Climate Change* (Cambridge, Cambridge University Press, 2018) 303.

[96] CCA 2008, sched 1, para 15.

[97] See ibid sched 1, para 16, 'The Adaptation Sub-Committee'.

[98] ibid sched 1, para 16(10).

[99] ibid s 56.

[100] ibid s 56(1).

[101] DEFRA, *UK Climate Change Risk Assessment: Government Report* (London, HM Government, 2012).

[102] CCA, s 56(1).

[103] ibid s 56(3). If a delay in publishing a report arises, the Secretary of State must explain why and state when the report will be provided to Parliament (s 56(4)).

adaptation programmes that are to include 'the objectives of Her Majesty's Government in the United Kingdom in relation to adaptation to climate change, the Government's proposals and policies for meeting those objectives, and the time-scales for introducing those proposals and policies'.[104] These programmes are locked into a cycle so that they naturally follow on from the risk assessment reports.[105] Thus, the first adaptation programme was required to address the risks identified in the most recent risk report preceding it.[106] It appeared in 2013 under the title 'National Adaptation Programme', covering 2013–18.[107] It is sometimes said that the *programme* must appear a year after the *report*,[108] but technically it is required to be produced by the Secretary of State and laid before Parliament 'as soon as is reasonably practicable after the laying of the' risk report before Parliament.[109]

C. Minor Components of the Framework

Some powers are also opened up that permit the Secretary of State to apply narrower, bespoke targets and obligations to electricity generators, distributors and suppliers, and certain other related parties, so that carbon emissions savings can be required of them in order to support the CCA 2008 objectives.[110] Other relatively modest measures include the following: the Secretary of State has a power under section 85 to introduce mandatory emissions reporting by companies;[111] UK government buildings are subject to annual reporting obligations to explain how

---

[104] ibid s 58(1)(a)–(c).

[105] The risk reports are UK-wide in orientation, whereas *The National Adaptation Programme* is 'primarily for England but also covers reserved, excepted and non-devolved matters', with the devolved jurisdictions of Northern Ireland, Wales and Scotland creating *programme* strategies in their own areas of devolved competence; DEFRA, *The National Adaptation Programme* (London, HM Government, 2013) 10.

[106] CCA 2008, s 58(1).

[107] DEFRA (n 101).

[108] Fankhauser et al (n 4) 11.

[109] CCA 2008, 58(3).

[110] ibid s 79, sched 8.

[111] ibid s 85. Since 2013, all Quoted Companies in the UK have been required to measure and publish details of their Scope 1 and 2 Emissions in their Annual Report to demonstrate a commitment towards reducing their energy use and emissions in line with a government plan to improve business energy efficiency by 20 per cent by 2030; see further the Companies Act 2006 (Strategic Report and Directors' Reports) Regulations 2013, amending the Large and Medium-Sized Companies and Groups (Accounts and Reports) Regulations 2008. A Quoted Company is defined in s 385(2) of the Companies Act 2006. More recent rules announced by BEIS mean that from April 2019, large UK companies are to publicly disclose and report on their energy use, energy efficiency actions and carbon emissions. The definition of large companies will now include all Quoted Companies regardless of their size and turnover, and unquoted companies (with at least 250 employees or an annual turnover greater than £36 million and an annual balance sheet total greater than £18 million). See the Companies (Directors' Report) and Limited Liability Partnerships (Energy and Carbon Report) Regulations 2018, which came into force on 1 April 2019 and apply to financial years starting on or after 1 April 2019.

their energy efficiency and sustainability standards are improving each year;[112] powers are created allowing for charges to be applied for single use carrier bags, ie, the type of bags that shops commonly provide to shoppers in the UK in order to permit them to carry their shopping.[113] A charge-per-bag was set initially at 5p in the UK. The scheme is not a tax that is fed back to the government, and so retailers have choices as to what they do with the additional monies.[114] The scheme is intended to reduce the public's perceived over-abundant usage of single-use plastic bags, which take a long time to degrade and can be environmentally damaging. This has had some positive effect to date in driving usage down.[115] On further granular changes made by the CCA 2008 to broader areas of UK law, including small tweaks to Waste Reduction Schemes and the UK's Renewable Transport Fuel Obligation, see Muinzer.[116]

VII. Treatment in the Courts

At the time of writing, the CCA 2008 has not found itself at the centre of many significant court cases in the UK to date, but certain important features of the framework have been raised in the courts at times in interesting and creative ways. An example is *Preston New Road Action Group v Secretary of State for Communities and Local Government* (2018), which involved an appeal against planning permission that had been granted for exploratory fracking (ie, 'hydraulic fracturing') works at two sites in Lancashire, England.[117] The Court of Appeal explicitly rejected the argument that, were such exploratory works to be permitted, this would likely lead to the commercial production of shale gas, thus increasing the consumption of gas in the UK, raising greenhouse gas emissions and therefore ultimately conflicting unacceptably with the objectives of the CCA 2008, where emissions are required to be driven down.[118] This line of argument exhibits a degree of imaginative flair on the part of the legal team that constructed it, but it is unsurprising that it was rejected, not least given that, for better or worse, the CCA 2008 does nothing to explicitly lock out fracking per se.

---

[112] CCA 2008, s 86.

[113] ibid s 77, sched 6.

[114] It is the case in Wales, Scotland and England that many retailers choose to send this money to 'green'/'environmental' charities. In Northern Ireland, the net proceeds of the levy go to the devolved Northern Irish Department of Agriculture, Environment and Rural Affairs (DAERA) at the end of each quarter, and DAERA uses the proceeds to deliver local projects that enhance and improve the environment.

[115] See, eg, DEFRA *Single-Use Plastic Carrier Bags Charge: Data in England for 2017 to 2018* (London, HM Government, 2018).

[116] Muinzer (n 3) 43–48 and 76–80.

[117] *Preston New Road Action Group v Secretary of State for Communities and Local Government Court of Appeal* (Civil Division) [2018] EWCA Civ 9.

[118] On the court's rejection of this position, see in particular ibid [72] (Lord Justice Lindblom).

The CCA 2008 played a more determinative role in *R (on the Application of London Borough of Hillingdon and Others) v Secretary of State for Transport.*[119] This case to some extent foreshadows aspects of the *Plan B* Heathrow runway case (discussed below), insofar as it involved a legal challenge to the UK government's support for the development of a third runway at Heathrow Airport. The government had stipulated in 2003 that it could support a third runway development if particular conditions were satisfactorily met, including in relation to climate change obligations. It went on to declare in 2009 that the stated conditions could be met and that support for the runway development was therefore appropriate; however, the CCA 2008 had been passed since this conclusion was reached and Lord Justice Carnwath (as he then was) held that 'common sense demanded that a policy established in 2003, before the important developments in climate change policy, symbolised by the Climate Change Act 2008, should be subject to review in the light of those developments'.[120] In other words, the UK government had erred, as the CCA 2008 had been passed since its 2003 strategy was set down, and so it would need to be reviewed in order to assess the extent to which the CCA 2008 developments had impacted its pertinent conditions, especially in relation to advice issued to the government by the CCC that the Act had created.[121]

The case that has centralised the CCA 2008 as its core legal touchstone to the greatest extent to date has probably been *R (Plan B Earth and others) v Secretary of State for Business, Energy and Industrial Strategy.*[122] Here, a number of claimants led by the charity Plan B sought permission from the Administrative Court to bring a judicial review action against the Secretary of State for his failure to revise the (then) 80 per cent reduction target for 2050 in the CCA to a more stringent figure.[123] Reduced to its essentials, the crux of the argument was that the 80 per cent reduction target for 2050 chosen at the time of the passing of the Act had been consistent with the then scientific advice to limit average global warming to 2°C above pre-industrial levels. But since then, there had been substantial developments in the science of climate change. More particularly, the UK had by this point ratified the 2015 Paris Agreement, which stipulates that the necessary intention is to now pursue efforts to keep average global warming to 1.5°C above pre-industrial levels, which goes some way further than the initial

---

[119] *R (on the Application of London Borough of Hillingdon and Others) v Secretary of State for Transport* [2010] EWHC 626 (Admin).

[120] ibid [52] (Lord Justice Carnwath).

[121] For more detail on this ruling, see Richard Macrory, *Regulation, Enforcement and Governance in Environmental Law*, 2nd edn (Oxford, Hart Publishing, 2014) 270–71.

[122] *R (Plan B Earth and Others) v Secretary of State for Business, Energy and Industrial Strategy* [2018] EWHC 1892 (Admin). Permission to appeal the decision was refused by the Court of Appeal on 25 January 2019: Ref C1/2018/1750. The CCC was ordered by the court to be represented in the case as an 'interested party'.

[123] In judicial review proceedings, permission of the court to bring proceedings must first be sought. At this stage, the court is concerned with whether the case is legally arguable.

2°C goal.[124] Although the power to amend the target in the CCA 2008 is expressed in discretionary terms, the claimants argued that these developments in international law and scientific understanding essentially turned the discretionary power into a duty on the Secretary of State to revise the 2050 80 per cent reduction target. Permission to proceed to judicial review was refused by Supperstone J, who rejected this line of reasoning, deeming each of five specific technical grounds for challenge that were put forward by the claimants to be unarguable in the process.[125] However, a critical factor was the fact that since the proceedings had started, it became clear that the Secretary of State (and the Scottish and Welsh governments) was in the process of seeking formal advice from the CCC as to whether the 80 per cent target should be reduced to a net zero carbon target.[126] The judge clearly felt it would be inappropriate and premature for the courts to intervene on the issue until these processes had been completed. As noted earlier, the figure now sits at 100 per cent ('net zero'), having since been amended from 80 per cent.

This case in turn has partially galvanised a subsequent case involving Plan B and others, including Friends of the Earth and Greenpeace; here, the claimants have lodged a challenge to the Secretary of State for Transport's decision to support an expansion of Heathrow Airport, as set out in an *Airports National Policy Statement*.[127] It is argued that a violation of sections 5(8) and 10(3) of the Planning Act 2008 has occurred and that that governmental support for the extension has not appropriately considered the impact of the airport expansion on climate change obligations under the terms of the CCA 2008 and the Paris Agreement.[128] The case is ongoing at the time of writing.[129]

---

[124] Paris Agreement, art 2(1)(a). The requirement under this provision is to 'pursue efforts' to limit the temperature increase to the 1.5°C level.

[125] The five points of challenge argued that the Secretary of State's failure to revise the milestone target was: ultra vires; based on an error of law pertaining to the Paris Agreement; irrational; in violation of elements of human rights law; and in breach of s 149 of the Equality Act 2010. See further the outcome court judgment: *R (Plan B Earth and Others)* (n 122).

[126] The formal request was made by letter, dated 15 October 2018. The CCC carried out extensive consultation on the issue and its advice was published on 2 May 2019: CCC, *Net Zero – The UK's Contribution to Stopping Global Warming* (London, CCC, 2019). The report advised an increase in the CCA 2008 2050 target to net zero.

[127] Department for Transport, *Airports National Policy Statement* (London, HM Government, 2018).

[128] *Plan B Earth and Others v Secretary of State for Transport: Statement of Facts and Grounds*, Claim No.CO/3149/2018.

[129] For a further case making (relatively minor) reference at the time of writing to a planning policy's failure to address targets under the CCA 2008, see: *Friends of the Earth Ltd v Secretary of State for Housing, Communities and Local Government* [2019] EWHC 518 (Admin); and *Stephenson v Secretary of State for Housing, Communities and Local Government* [2019] EWHC 519 (Admin), 6 March 2019. Editor's note: ultimately the case at ibid (n 128) reached the Court of Appeal, where it was ruled that the Secretary of State for Transport had acted unlawfully in producing the *Airports National Policy Statement* because climate change policy had not been adequately taken into account. Although it was found that the CCA 2008 *had* been taken into account suitably, a breach nevertheless arose on climate grounds due to infringement of the Planning Act 2008 and the Paris Agreement. See further *R (Friends of the Earth) v Secretary of State for Transport and Others* [2020] EWCA Civ 213. Permission to appeal to the Supreme Court has since been granted at the time of writing.

VIII. Discussion

The CCA 2008 has been recognised internationally for its 'innovative policy making ... due to its pioneering role in adopting a long-term legislative commitment to a low-carbon future'.[130] Discussing the CCA 2008 with reference to the 2050 milestone target, Laes, Gorissen and Nevens have pointed out that: 'This long-term goal does include ... a moral judgement on the "right" amount of responsibility (i.e., a burden-sharing obligation based on the principle of common but differentiated responsibilities) to be taken by an industrialized country'.[131] In other words, the framework cannot be disconnected from moral underpinnings that, reduced to their essentials, recognise that emissions reduction is a just action where individual state responsibilities are situated in the context of international responsibilities (here the responsibility to redress climate change in the common interest).

Clearly, one valuable feature of the CCA 2008's legal design is its locked-in, long-term nature. But one must not over-estimate its sense of permanence simply because it is expressed in law. Legislation is by its very nature impermanent, and the principle of *parliamentary sovereignty* in the UK means that current and subsequent parliaments are always at liberty to repeal it.[132] Nevertheless, it is also the case at present in the UK that the widely acknowledged importance of redressing climate change on objective scientific grounds, interpreted in concert with the substantial levels of concern around the issue predominating in both the UK's public and elite political arenas, indicate that the Act appears to remain safely and securely in place in the immediate years ahead.[133]

Yet this sense of 'legislative stability' is only one dimension of the framework's foundations. Thus, sophisticated analysis of the Act by Lockwood has served to emphasise that while the CCA 2008 itself has a degree of long-term legal stability in a way that is quite different from mere policy commitments made by the government, which are more readily subject to change than provisions in primary legislation, it also exists in a tumultuous political environment where political conflicts, uncertainties and tensions subject the practical operation of the framework to a protracted, ongoing degree of risk in their own right.[134] Muinzer has used the metaphor of a skeleton and flesh to describe the

---

[130] Erik Laes, Leen Gorissen and Frank Nevens, 'A Comparison of Energy Transition Governance in Germany, the Netherlands and the United Kingdom' (2014) 6(3) *Sustainability* 1130.

[131] ibid 1142.

[132] Jeffrey Goldsworthy, *Parliamentary Sovereignty: Contemporary Debates* (Cambridge, Cambridge University Press, 2010).

[133] See further Carter's important study revealing significant engagement and support for action on the issue of climate change across the left-right political spectrum in the UK: Neil Carter, 'Party Politicization of the Environment in Britain' (2006) 12(6) *Party Politics* 747. See also, eg, the points raised in relation to the discussion of interview data and documentary analysis in Fay Farstad, Neil Carter and Charlotte Burns, 'What Does Brexit Mean for the UK's Climate Change Act?' (2018) 89(2) *Political Quarterly* 291, 296.

[134] Matthew Lockwood, 'The Political Sustainability of Climate Policy: The Case of the UK Climate Change Act' (2013) 23(5) *Global Environmental Change* 1339.

relationship between the CCA 2008 framework (the skeleton) and the policies and secondary legislation that are stimulated to spring from it (the flesh added to the bones).[135] He has suggested with reference to the carbon budgeting and mitigation target governance architecture that the CCA 2008's 'blanket-style approach can be construed as a "skeleton" framework that facilitates a potentially broad range of targeted and/or pragmatic political-legal action'; thus, through 'realising and employing' the 'capacities for innovative action' actively enabled by the CCA 2008, which must be realised 'within the framework's permitted parameters' – parameters that both enable action and simultaneously impose constraints upon it – such 'action serves to put flesh on the bones of the skeleton framework and contributes towards the achievement of practical outcomes'.[136] Much of the form and nature of the 'flesh' that is added to the bones arises through capacities for secondary legislation, policy innovation and so on, created by and operating within the acceptable parameters of the skeleton framework. Importantly, then, and as Lockwood puts it, legal lock-in 'does not guarantee political lock-in'.[137]

Thus, in spite of the Act's legislative regime persisting, 'the politics of implementation of climate policy' do not guarantee adequate implementation in the contested policy arena itself.[138] In other words, the form and nature of implementation in its own right is a contested policy process, and 'the problem of securing politically sustainable policy change in the case of public interest reform is particularly difficult'.[139] One headline factor pushing back on progressive climate governance under the terms of the CCA 2008 in this contested political setting has been the impact of austerity imposed by the UK government as a consequence of the 2008 financial crisis, which amongst other things saw it endeavour to reduce the national deficit by reducing public spending, thus making it harder to sustain a robust economic case for decarbonisation over time.[140]

In terms of the framework's technical legal content, Reid has underscored the novel nature of the CCA 2008's substantive emissions reduction duties, highlighting that 2020/2050-style milestone targets resemble to some extent the goal-led duties often applied to EU Member States under the terms of

---

[135] Muinzer (n 3) 3–4 and 115.

[136] ibid 3–4.

[137] Lockwood (n 134) 1339 ('Abstract').

[138] ibid 1340.

[139] ibid 1341. Lockwood's analysis also usefully draws attention to the frequently overlooked negative impact of the media in various instances on confidence in the framework's longevity, including a damaging call in print from the widely read *Telegraph* newspaper to repeal the Act: 'it is time for [the UK government] to tear up its energy policy … The first priority must be to repeal the Climate Change Act of 2008, with its brutal, punishing targets' ('Too Much Green Energy is Bad for Britain' (*The Telegraph*, 23 March 2013). See ibid 1340.

[140] Ross Gillard, 'Unravelling the United Kingdom's Climate Policy Consensus: The Power of ideas, Discourse and Institutions' (2016) 40 *Global Environmental* Change 26. See also the further elucidation of this matter and associated important issues in Ross Gillard and Kathryn Lock, 'Blowing Policy Bubbles: Rethinking Emissions Targets and Low-Carbon Energy Policies in the UK' (2017) 19(6) *Journal of Environmental Policy & Planning* 638.

EU directives.[141] In the internal UK setting, the 'outcome' orientation here is unusual, in that it goes beyond conventional parameters to insist that the outcome must be met, even though significant things will have to be done by a broad range of public authorities that are not directly subject to the duty.[142]

It is also notable that the CCA 2008 does not contain explicit sanctions for breach of its major duties, eg, where the milestone reduction targets for 2020 and 2050 have been missed. Thus, analysts such as Stallworthy[143] and Townsend[144] have stressed that there are uncertainties concerning the extent to which the duties can be meaningfully enforced. Nevertheless, while emphasising the significance of this problem in his own right, Muinzer has also suggested that the practical impact of this issue should be 'kept in perspective':[145] most particularly, the framework *is* legally binding, and so the Secretary of State, the government, civil servants and so on must work on the assumption that their activities are subject to an overall obligation to secure the targets.

Developing effective policies to secure climate change goals will inevitably involve many different departments of government (including, for example, transport, housing and planning) to a greater extent than in many areas of environmental protection. Here the existence of long-term and clear legal duties concerning outcomes as contained in the CCA 2008 serves to empower those in government committed to the challenge of climate change to persuade less enthusiastic colleagues of the need to take action.

The existence of legal duties inevitably raises the question of their enforceability in the courts. In principle, judicial review is available in the UK as a legal mechanism for allowing the courts to enforce duties on government and other public authorities.[146] Whether the long-term duties such as the 2050 target would be susceptible in practice to effective judicial review raises problematic issues, not least due to the timing of any such action.[147] In any event, it is probably the case that a court's approach would be limited to awarding 'declaratory relief', declaring that there has been a breach of the obligation in question.[148] Because a duty like the 2050 target is owed to the UK public in general, it is unlikely

---

[141] Colin Reid, 'A New Sort of Duty? The Significance of "Outcome" Duties in the Climate Change and Child Poverty Acts' (2012) 4 *Public Law* 749, 752–53.

[142] ibid 749–50.

[143] Mark Stallworthy, 'Legislating against Climate Change: A UK Perspective on a Sisyphean Challenge' (2009) 72(3) *Modern Law Review* 412.

[144] Townsend (n 2) 842.

[145] Muinzer (n 3) 21.

[146] Reid (n 141) 757 ('Judicial [I]ntervention').

[147] See further Macrory (n 36). It is perhaps important to note that the CCA provides that the Secretary of State must provide Parliament with a statement in respect of the year 2050 and that 'if the target has not been met, the statement must explain why it has not been met'; CCA 2008, s 20(6). A court might argue that this provision implies that a Secretary of State is politically responsible to Parliament for a failure to meet the target rather than to the courts.

[148] Aileen McHarg, 'Climate Change Constitutionalism? Lessons from the United Kingdom' (2011) 2(4) *Climate Law* 469, 477.

that specific individuals could successfully claim compensation in this context. Indeed, McMaster goes beyond construing this as a duty owed to the general UK public to suggest that, viewed in the context of climate change, the 'class would include every person in the world'.[149] While *substantive* duties of this sort may be difficult to enforce in the courts in a conventional way, the CCA contains many important procedural duties imposed on government, and here legal action – or simply the prospective threat of such action – is likely to achieve more concrete outcomes; for example, if a reporting duty has been ignored, in determining the breach a court is unlikely to feel inhibited in ordering that the reporting obligation is carried out.

Accountability has also surfaced as a significant concern in commentary and analysis of the CCA 2008. Where a *substantive* target has been breached, courts will take practical realities into account in this sort of scenario,[150] including financial constraints and limits on the capacity of the Secretary of State for BEIS to innovate and dictate behaviour to other governmental actors. Thus, for example, it is salient that Carter, over the course of analysis of UK climate governance, has underscored the Treasury as amounting to arguably the most powerful division in the UK government's administration.[151] The courts will take account of the steering capacity of an actor like the Treasury to some extent when it comes to assessing the Secretary of State's facility to meet the relevant duty – for example, where the Treasury may have used its controls over taxation and subsidy to limit low carbon incentives, thereby constricting the Secretary of State's ability to work towards securing the CCA 2008 duties.[152] Such factors militate in their own right against courts intervening against the Secretary of State.[153] Moreover, a variety of secretaries of state may have held the post over a particular period and, as such, it may be unethical in the view of some to direct a punishment at one particular office holder.[154]

Another feature that has been investigated and evaluated in considerable detail pertains to the CCA 2008's relationship to its constitutional environment. Here, in the context of a given state, 'constitution' indicates the body of rules that govern the political system, the exercise of public authority, and the relations between the citizen and the state.[155] Unlike most countries, the UK does not have a codified constitution, that is to say, a written constitutional document that draws

---

[149] McMaster (n 2) 117.

[150] See Catherine Callaghan, 'What is a "Target Duty"?' (2000) 5(3) *Judicial Review* 186.

[151] Carter (n 25) 201.

[152] See Thomas L Muinzer, '"To PV or Not to PV": An Analysis of the High Court's Recent Treatment of Solar Energy' (2015) 17(2) *Environmental Law Review* 128. The analysis addresses two major judicial reviews where the Treasury's budgetary control was factored into the courts' assessment of the Secretary of State's decisions relating to aspects of large-scale and small-scale solar energy incentives; on the relevance of the CCA 2008, see fn 41 and the accompanying text in that article.

[153] Callaghan (n 150) 185–86.

[154] Noted by McMaster (n 2) 118.

[155] Colin Turpin and Adam Tomkins, *British Government and the Constitution*, 6th edn (Cambridge, Cambridge University Press, 2007) 3.

together the UK's core constitutional fundamentals and principles;[156] rather, a range of sources are commonly linked together in the UK that add up to convey a concrete sense of the national constitution. In this context, the courts have in recent years characterised some Acts of Parliament as having such fundamental and wide-ranging importance concerning fundamental constitutional rights or the relationship of the citizen and the state that they should be termed 'constitutional statutes'.[157] The general rule of statutory interpretation by the courts is that where provisions of a later Act of Parliament are in conflict with those in an earlier Act, the more recent provisions must prevail. But this doctrine of 'implied repeal' does not apply to so-called constitutional statutes whose provisions can only be repealed subsequently by express legislation.

McHarg has explored the CCA 2008's relationship to constitutionality[158] and Muinzer has developed this discussion in order to test whether the CCA 2008 could be construed as a 'constitutional statute'.[159] The conclusions are that the matter is up for debate, with it being possible to credibly categorise the CCA 2008 (or parts of it) as 'constitutional'.[160] If it is assumed that the CCA 2008 *is* a constitutional statute, the study demonstrates that: it will likely be subject to a greater degree of entrenchment than an 'ordinary' statute, ie, it will be harder in all likelihood to repeal or replace it in certain respects in comparison to ordinary Acts; and courts may consider adopting more robust remedial approaches in relation to breaches of the Act if it is clear they are dealing with breaches of a 'constitutional statute'.[161] This position gathers further momentum where one bears in mind that the UK government apparently anticipated during the parliamentary discussion on the CCA 2008 that the courts would ultimately play a robust role.[162]

IX. Conclusions: Closing Remarks on an Uncertain Future

In addition to key points just raised in the previous section, it is also notable that the CCA 2008's political-legal environment has been impacted by Brexit, that is, the UK's exiting of the EU. The UK had been a member of the EU since 1 January 1973,

---

[156] See further Neil Parpworth, *Constitutional and Administrative Law*, 8th edn (Oxford, Oxford University Press, 2014) 11.

[157] See in particular the judgment of Lord Justice Laws in *Thorburn v Sunderland City Council* [2002] EWHC 195, where the term was first proposed. Lord Justice Laws suggested that Magna Carta, the Bill of Rights Act 1689, the European Communities Act 1972, the Human Rights Act 1998 and the Devolution Acts would fall into this category. See also Parpworth (n 156) 12 ('Sources of the UK Constitution').

[158] McHarg (n 148).

[159] Thomas L Muinzer, 'Is the Climate Change Act 2008 a Constitutional Statute? (2018) 24(4) *European Public Law* 733.

[160] ibid.

[161] See generally ibid.

[162] See McMaster (n 2) 118–19.

with the UK Parliament giving effect to EU law in the UK under the terms of the European Communities Act 1972. After the UK voted by a majority to leave the EU in a referendum on 23 June 2016, Article 50 of the Treaty on European Union was triggered and a negotiated exiting process commenced. Interpreting the CCA 2008 and its future in the context of the UK's exit from the EU, it should be noted that the CCA 2008 was originally a national rather than an EU initiative, and therefore Brexit does not affect its core provisions. Some adjustments to the framework may be required, eg, the reference to developments in European legislation as a ground for changing the framework's targets,[163] or reference made to ministerial functions under the European Communities Act 1972;[164] however, such changes are fairly modest in character. Brexit has also caused the UK to drop out of the EU Emissions Trading Scheme, although according to understanding at the time of writing, in the post-Brexit period, the UK is to retain a 'linked' emissions trading system with the EU.[165] The UK will also continue to be bound by the Paris Agreement and any other international climate change agreements, and in future discussions on international provisions the UK will be acting in its own right as an independent state rather than as part of the EU bloc.

Shortly before the UK's departure from the EU, Nigel Haigh of the Institute for European Environmental Policy suggested that:

> Brexit will weaken the EU in its ability to act internationally. Not only is the UK one of the most populous and economically most powerful Member States ... but it also has a greater global reach than any other Member State. Only France has a comparable diplomatic service. Both France and the UK, acting in concert with EU officials, played a major role in getting so many countries to agree to the Paris Climate Change Agreement.[166]

The EU has been a powerful player on the international stage in the area of climate change in recent years and, in terms of the UK's contribution to that process, it may be that the absence of a major economy and a government committed to climate change could weaken the EU's negotiating strength. On the other hand, it remains to be seen whether the UK might tend towards joining forces in supporting the EU's negotiated stance rather than endeavouring to stand alone. Only time will tell.

---

[163] See, eg, CCA 2008, s 2(2)(ii).

[164] See ibid s 70(5)(a)(i).

[165] UK Government (Consultation), *The Future of UK Carbon Pricing* (May 2019).

[166] Nigel Haigh, 'What Could Brexit Mean for the Next 40 Years of EU Environmental Policy?', Institute for European Environmental Policy, 4 October 2018, https://ieep.eu/news/what-could-brexit-mean-for-the-next-40-years-of-eu-environmental-policy.

4

Mexico's Framework Legislation on Climate Change

Key Features, Achievements and Challenges Ahead

ALINA AVERCHENKOVA

I. Introduction

The experience of Mexico with legislating on climate change is interesting from multiple perspectives. Mexico is currently the world's tenth largest greenhouse gas (GHG) emitter and is expected to become the world's seventh largest economy by 2050.[1] It became the first large oil-producing emerging economy to adopt climate legislation when in April 2012 its Parliament passed the General Law on Climate Change (Ley General de Cambio Climático or LGCC).[2] Its climate change legislation provides an example of a comprehensive legislative framework adopted in an emerging economy, the first of its kind at the time. The evolution of Mexico's climate legislation over time towards a greater level of ambition in response to international developments and the enabling impact of the framework climate law on other national legislation, in particular in the energy sector, offer important learnings.

While lacking in stringency in terms of emission reduction objectives in its original form in 2012 compared to other cases reviewed in this volume, this climate change law has been an important achievement for Mexico politically. Despite strong opposition from fossil fuel-intensive industries during a two-year period of negotiations, the passage of the law has set the direction of travel for

---

[1] PWC, 'The Long View: How Will the Global Economic Order Change by 2050?', 2017, https://www.pwc.com/gx/en/world-2050/assets/pwc-the-world-in-2050-full-report-feb-2017.pdf.

[2] Ley General de Cambio Climatico. Nueva Ley publicada en el Diario Oficial de la Federación el 6 de junio de 2012. Texto Vigente. Camara de Diputados Del H, Congreso de la Union. Secretaría General. Secretaría de Servicios Parlamentarios. Últimas Reformas DOF 13 May 2015.

domestic climate policy in the country and has laid the foundation for a subsequent ratcheting of ambition. The law outlined long-term objectives for emissions reduction and clean energy targets, and set up the institutional infrastructure required to deal with climate change.

In 2015, building on the objectives set in its climate change legislation, Mexico adopted the Energy Transition Law, which advances decarbonisation of energy production and consumption.[3] In the same year Mexico became the first developing economy to submit an intended Nationally Determined Contribution (NDC) ahead of the adoption of the Paris Agreement.[4] Guided by its NDC and the lessons learnt from the implementation of the climate change law in April 2018, Mexico passed a decree amending the law to bring it into greater consistency with the Paris Agreement.[5]

This chapter provides a brief overview of the pathway towards the adoption of the LGCC and of the key provisions of the law in its original reading in 2012. It then outlines the main features of the amendments of 2018 and discusses the challenges and lessons learnt from the implementation of the legislation.

II. Background to the Act

Mexico is one of the largest economies of Latin America with a high potential for renewable energy, in particular, solar, wind, bioenergy, hydropower and geothermal energy. It is also vulnerable to the impacts of climate change. Drought and desertification threaten food production and livelihoods in the northern and central regions of the country, while coastal areas are affected by rising sea levels and increased tropical storms.[6] These impacts are also of concern to the oil-producing region in the Gulf of Mexico.[7] While being vulnerable to the impacts of climate change, Mexico is also among the largest GHG emitters, ranking tenth

---

[3] Ley de Transición Energética, Nueva Ley publicada en el Diario Oficial de la Federación el 24 de diciembre de 20. Texto Vigente. Camara de Diputados Del H, Congreso de la Union. Secretaría General. Secretaría de Servicios Parlamentarios. Nueva Ley. DOF 24 December 2015. Available at: www.diputados.gob.mx/LeyesBiblio/pdf/LTE.pdf.

[4] EDF and IETA (Environmental Defense Fund and International Emissions Trading Association), 'Mexico: A Market Based Climate Policy Case Study' (2018), www.ieta.org/resources/Resources/Case_Studies_Worlds_Carbon_Markets/2018/Mexico-Case-Study-Jan2018.pdf%20.

[5] DOF (Cámara de Diputados del H Congreso de la Unión, 'Ley General de Cambio Climático' (2018), modified version available at: www.diputados.gob.mx/LeyesBiblio/pdf/LGCC_130718.pdf.

[6] Simone Pulver and Jaime Sainz-Santamaría, 'Characterizing the Climate Issue Context in Mexico: Reporting on Climate Change in Mexican Newspapers, 1996–2009' (2018) 10(6) *Climate and Development* 538.

[7] Patricia Romero-Lankao, Joel Smith, Debra Davidson, Noah Diffenbaugh, Patrick Kinney, Paul Kirshen, Paul Kovacs and Lourdes Villers Ruiz, 'North America' in Vincent Barros et al (eds), *Climate Change 2014: Impacts, Adaptation, and Vulnerability* (Cambridge, Cambridge University Press, 2014) 1439–98.

globally and fifth among developing countries in 2016.[8] In 2014, Mexico's per capita GHG emissions were 6.16 t CO_2e, compared to 20 CO_2e for the US and 8.5 CO_2e for China.[9]

The country is a federal republic composed of 32 federal entities (31 states and Mexico City) and 2,457 municipalities, whose autonomy was recognised by constitutional reforms in 1983.[10] Mexico has a two-tier system of subnational governance. According to the Constitution, the powers that are not expressly given to the Federation are understood as reserved to the states. States' joint responsibilities with the federal government include primary education, healthcare, poverty alleviation, social protection and water. Municipalities are responsible for urban planning and development, utilities, local roads and public transport, street lighting, markets, parks and public safety, and can delegate some responsibilities to the state by agreement.[11]

Mexico's climate change policy leading up to the adoption of the law had gone through periods of alternating levels of attention and priority being given to climate change within the government. These fluctuations were influenced by the efforts of environmental non-governmental organisations (NGOs), the relationship between energy and environmental agencies, developments in international climate change negotiations and overall changes in political leadership in Mexico.[12] Pulver outlines five phases in climate policy in Mexico:[13]

- The early years (1990–92) with climate change being mainly an issue of diplomatic interest.

- The emergence of the epistemic community, mainly in the scientific circles, concerned about climate change (1992–96).

- The politicisation of climate change as a contested topic between Mexico's environmental and energy ministries, including during the debate on the ratification of the Kyoto Protocol (1996–2000).

- The reactive phase in Mexico's climate politics, when it was driven by international developments (2001–05), including the withdrawal by the US from the Kyoto Protocol in 2001 and the ratification of the Protocol by the European Union (EU) in 2005.

---

[8] World Resources Institute, 'CAIT Climate Data Explorer', 2016, http://cait.wri.org.

[9] Climate Watch, https://www.climatewatchdata.org.

[10] 'Mexico: OECD Country Profile', https://www.oecd.org/regional/regional-policy/profile-Mexico.pdf.

[11] ibid.

[12] Pulver and Sainz-Santamaría (n 6).

[13] Simone Pulver, 'Climate Change Politics in Mexico' in Henrik Selin and Stacy VanDeveer (eds), *Changing Climates in North American Politics* (Cambridge, MA, MIT Press, 2009) 25–46; and Simone Pulver, 'A Climate Leader? The Politics and Practice of Climate Governance in Mexico' in David Held, Charles Roger and Eva-Maria Nag (eds), *Climate Governance in the Developing World* (Cambridge, Polity Press, 2013) 174–95.

- Renewed momentum at the domestic and international levels (2006–12) under the leadership of President Felipe Calderón, which was marked by announcements of multiple domestic climate change strategies and Mexico's strong leadership in international climate change negotiations.[14]

A drive for a national climate change framework started to emerge in Mexico in around 2005, when the government started to develop structural clean energy and climate change policies. In the National Development Plan 2007–2012, the government stated that climate change must become an important consideration for all sectors.[15] It also took the decision to develop the 2007 National Strategy on Climate Change (Estrategia Nacional de Cambio Climático or ENCC) and a Special Programme on Climate Change (Programa Especial de Cambio Climático or PECC) to achieve this goal. The first programme was published in 2009 and outlined the long-term climate change agenda and medium-term goals for adaptation and mitigation.[16] It included a long-term GHG emissions reduction target for Mexico, which the government formally announced at the fifteenth round of the UN climate negotiations in Copenhagen in December 2009.

However, there was no legal instrument that embedded climate change objectives and could protect them from future political change. In 2010, under the initiative of the Congress of Mexico, the government started work on the development of a legal instrument to deal with climate change. According to a recent study, one of the main objectives for these efforts was to protect long-term climate policy objectives against future political change, so that they are mandatory for the government regardless of the political orientation of those who are in power in the future.[17]

Politically, the adoption of the LGCC has been enabled by Mexico's strong international leadership on climate change since the early 1990s[18] and by the personal commitment of President Calderón to the issue of climate change during his time in office in 2006–12. In 2010, under the leadership of Mexico, the international climate change negotiations held in Cancun reached an important milestone and resulted in the adoption of the Cancun Agreements, which laid the foundation for action on climate change up to 2020. The Cancun Agreements created a

---

[14] Pulver (n 13).

[15] 'Mexico: Plan nacional de desarrollo 2007–2012', Poder Ejecutivo Federal 2007, CEFP/096/2007, www.paot.org.mx/centro/programas/federal/07/pnd07-12.pdf.

[16] Marlene Vinluan and Hilen Meirovich, 'GGBP Case Study Series: Development of the Special Climate Change Program in Mexico' (2014), www.greengrowthknowledge.org/sites/default/files/downloads/best-practices/GGBP%20Case%20Study%20Series_Mexico_Development%20of%20the%20Special%20Climate%20Change%20Program_0.pdf.

[17] Alina Averchenkova and Sandra Guzman Luna, *Mexico's General Law on Climate Change: Key Achievements and Challenges Ahead* (London, Grantham Research Institute on Climate Change and the Environment and Centre for Climate Change Economics and Policy, London School of Economics and Political Science, 2018).

[18] Guy Edwards and J Timmons Roberts, *A Fragmented Continent: Latin America and the Global Politics of Climate Change* (Cambridge, MA, MIT Press, 2015).

registry for developing countries to officially list their pledges to reduce GHGs, a Green Climate Fund to finance climate adaptation and mitigation by developing countries, and a new technology mechanism intended to facilitate technology cooperation and transfer.[19] In the same period, Mexico also held the presidency of the G20, which strengthened its global leadership on the climate agenda. Its hosting of the international climate negotiations in 2010 was a major incentive for the engagement of many stakeholders who were later involved in the design, negotiation and approval of the law.

Economically, Mexico was at that time going through reforms in the energy sector towards greater decentralisation. There was also recognition of the need to decarbonise energy and reduce the country's oil dependence. Petrochemicals and oil-derivative products until the mid-2000s accounted for about 13 per cent of gross domestic product (GDP).[20] Around 80 per cent of Mexico's energy generation is based on fossil fuels, making decarbonisation of energy one of the priorities for the country's climate policy. Around half of its emissions come from transport and electricity generation, with industry responsible for a further 18 per cent.[21] While there is an alignment between the strategic objectives of energy and climate policy in Mexico, fossil fuel dependency has posed significant challenges both on the way to adopting the law and subsequently in its implementation, due to strong opposition to climate change policy and legislation from carbon-intensive industries, which are influential in national politics.

III. The Path to the Adoption of the Law

Debate on the draft climate change legislation was launched in 2010 with extensive stakeholder participation, during the course of which several legislative initiatives were started by different parties. At the time, Mexico was also holding presidential elections, which meant the debate took political rather than technical direction early on. According to experts who were directly involved in the process, the development of Mexico's climate legislation benefited from close examination of and learning from the UK's Climate Change Act of 2008.[22] At the end of 2011, the proponents of different legislative initiatives reached an agreement that only one draft would go forward as the basis for further negotiations.[23]

---

[19] Jennifer Morgan, *Reflections on the Cancun Agreements* (Washington DC, World Resources Institute, 2010).

[20] Organisation for Economic Co-operation and Development, *Economic Surveys: Mexico* (Paris: OECD, 2017).

[21] INECC, 'Inventario Nacional de Emisiones de Gases y Compuestos de Efecto Invernadero' (2018), https://www.gob.mx/inecc/acciones-y-programas/inventario-nacional-de-emisiones-de-gases-y-compuestos-de-efecto-invernadero.

[22] Thomas L Muinzer, *Climate and Energy Governance for the UK Low Carbon Transition: The Climate Change Act 2008* (London, Palgrave Macmillan, 2019) 98.

[23] Averchenkova and Guzman Luna (n 17).

Thanks to Mexico's active international stance and to its hosting of the international negotiations, there was an overall consensus on the importance of climate change as a policy issue among key stakeholders. The major disagreements were on the necessary level of ambition and the timeframes for action, as well as the policy instruments needed to reach the objectives.[24] Environmental NGOs pushed for the law to contain concrete emission reduction targets and adaptation goals and an implementation roadmap for 2020–50 for the key sectors. Some NGOs also proposed including a long-term financing strategy and a budget, indicating a minimum percentage of GDP spending on climate change. At the same time, the private sector, in particular the petroleum, steel and energy sectors, strongly opposed the elements of the draft law dealing with emission reduction objectives. Significant efforts were also devoted to building capacity of the legislators on climate change in order to enable them to deal with more the technical aspects of the legislation.[25]

After two years of work and negotiations, the LGCC was approved by all parties in the Chamber of Deputies of the national Parliament, with 280 votes in favour, 11 against and one abstention, and unanimously in the Senate.[26] An agreement with the private sector led to the weakening of some provisions in the final draft of the law. The decision taken by legislators was that the law should not carry mandatory quantitative objectives, but rather aspirational goals on mitigation and no goals on adaptation. Furthermore, provisions for the carbon market were changed, making participation for the private sector voluntary.

Despite the weakening of some of the key provisions in the final draft of the law, its approval was a major political step for Mexico's climate change policy. The law outlined the longer-term objectives for climate policy, established the key elements of the institutional infrastructure required to deal with climate change and enabled a further increase of ambition in subsequent years in the energy sector, and most recently for climate policy overall (as will be discussed in more detail below).

IV. The Form and Content of the 2012 Law

The objective of the LGCC is to guarantee the right to a healthy environment and establish the concurrence of powers of Mexico's federal government, states and municipalities in the elaboration and implementation of public policies on climate change. Effectively, the LGCC embedded into law the mandates of the relevant institutions that existed prior to its adoption and gave them new mandates putting

---

[24] ibid.
[25] ibid.
[26] Sandra Guzman Luna, 'La importancia de la nueva Ley de Cambio Climático en México' (2012), www.ambienteycomercio.org/la-importancia-de-la-nueva-ley-de-cambio-climatico-en-Mexico.

in place an overarching institutional mechanism for dealing with climate change in Mexico – the 'National System on Climate Change' (abbreviated to SINACC in Spanish).[27] The SINACC's primary objective is to operate as the permanent mechanism of communication, collaboration and coordination for national climate policy. It includes the Inter-ministerial Commission on Climate Change (CICC), the permanent coordination mechanism on climate change among the federal ministries (Secretaries of State in Mexico). It also includes the Consultative Council on Climate Change (C3), which is the permanent consultative body of the CICC composed of members from the social, private and academic sectors, and the National Institute of Ecology and Climate Change (INECC in Spanish). The SINACC provides for the participation of the representatives of the state governments, the associations of municipal governments and the representatives of the Mexican Congress. It also mandates Mexico's 32 states and 2,475 municipalities to develop local mitigation and adaptation programmes. The LGCC also defines the key policy instruments to be employed, with its initial regime having been subsequently enhanced via a decree in 2018 (see Figure 4.1 below) and by the addition of quantitative objectives for emission reductions for the medium and long term, as will be discussed in more detail later.

The LGCC in its original reading consists of nine titles and 116 articles. Title One focuses on general provisions of the law, such as the framework's nature, objectives and definitions. Title Two defines powers for the federal government, the states and municipalities. Title Three contains provisions setting up the National Institute of Ecology and Climate Change (INECC), establishing it as the entity entrusted with the coordination and carrying out of scientific research on climate change and the provision of technical and scientific assistance to the Secretariat for the Environment or SEMARNAT (in Mexico the equivalent to the Ministry of the Environment). It outlines the INECC's objectives, mandate, governance arrangements and powers. As part of these key institutional provisions, the LGCC establishes the so-called Coordination for Evaluation, comprised of the head of INECC and six civil society advisors, which has the function of evaluating national climate change policy. However, the provisions do not indicate when and with what frequency such evaluations should be undertaken, leaving a possibility for the evaluation to be carried out by other institutions. More specific guidance on coordination of evaluation comes later in Title Six of the law, as will be discussed below.

Title Four of the LGCC is devoted to the National Policy on Climate Change, including the general principles that are to be followed in the formulation of the national policy, as well as the specific objectives and key provisions for adaptation and mitigation policy. In the articles relating to adaptation, the LGCC states that federal, state and municipal authorities, to the extent of their

---

[27] Averchenkova and Guzman Luna (n 17).

own powers, shall include adaptation actions in the design of public policies, the national strategy and programmes, and the state programmes. It then goes on to define the provisions for the implementation of adaptation actions by the federal agencies, states and municipalities.[28] However, these provisions are general and do not outline specific responsibilities or timelines for particular agencies.

On mitigation, the LGCC determines that mitigation policy shall include the diagnosis, planning, measuring, monitoring, reporting, verification and evaluation of national emissions.[29] Mitigation policy should also establish plans, programmes and regulatory instruments for gradually achieving emission reductions for specific sectors and activities. Policies and activities imposing or transferring costs to the private sector or to society should be implemented in two phases: the strengthening of capacities of the regulated sectors with policies and activities to be implemented first on a voluntary basis; and then the establishment of specific emission reduction goals.[30]

The subsequent articles of the LGCC define the overall objectives of mitigation policies[31] and the specific principles or types of mitigation actions that should be considered for the major sectors, including: emissions reductions in the generation and use of energy, in transportation and in the waste sector; emissions reductions and carbon capture in the agricultural, forest, land use and preservation of ecosystems sectors; and education and behaviour, consumption, and production patterns changes.[32] The LGCC allocates specific mandates to the Secretariat of Energy to establish policies and incentives to promote the use of low-carbon emissions technologies.[33] It also mandates the SEMARNAT, in coordination with the Secretariat of Finance and Public Credit and the Secretariat of Energy, to promote programmes that create fiscal and financial incentives for the voluntary implementation of emissions reduction activities.[34]

Title Five establishes the SINACC, including general principles for coordination between the federal, state and municipal levels on climate change, as well as the specific objectives and mode of operation for the system. It then goes on to outline the nature, composition and the mandates of CICC and the C3. In addition to the provisions setting up and outlining mandates for the key coordinating mechanisms, Title Five also defines the key planning instruments for climate change policy in Mexico and outlines their key elements, responsible institutions and frequency of preparation. These instruments include the following:

- The National Strategy, which should govern national policy to combat the effects of climate change and to transition to a competitive, sustainable low

---

[28] LGCC, arts 27–30.
[29] ibid arts 31–37.
[30] ibid art 32.
[31] ibid art 33.
[32] ibid art 34.
[33] ibid art 36.
[34] ibid art 37.

carbon emissions economy in the medium and long term. The national strategy is to be prepared by the SEMARNAT with the participation of the INECC and the advice of the C3, and should be reviewed at least once every 10 years for mitigation and once every six years for adaptation.

- The National Climate Change Programme, which would establish objectives, strategies and actions, and would define priorities on adaptation, mitigation and research, allocate responsibilities, and would define implementation timeframes, in accordance with the National Development Plan and the National Strategy.

- The programmes of the states, which would establish the strategies, policies and actions to be implemented and accomplished during the corresponding term of the administration, in accordance with the National Strategy and the programme.

Furthermore, Title Five contains provisions for the inventory of emissions and sinks to be developed by the INECC with the state and municipal authorities providing relevant data,[35] and the Climate Change Information System to be developed by the National Institute of Statistics and Geography.[36] The latter would contain a set of key indicators related to emissions, emission reduction projects, climate change impacts and key vulnerabilities, estimated climate change-related costs of adaptation and management of biodiversity.

A Climate Change Fund is established through the LGCC with the purpose of attracting and channelling public, private, national and international financial resources to support the implementation of actions to combat climate change. The provisions related to the fund outline the major sources of its assets (domestic budget, donations, international finance, tax and other charges) and the general destination of its resources.[37] The Fund should operate through a public trust created by the Secretariat of Finance and Public Credit guided by the technical committee composed of representatives from several key ministries.

The LGCC mandates the SEMARNAT to create a registry of emissions for stationary and mobile sources and to develop regulation determining what sources would need to report to the registry, the thresholds beyond which the facilities subject to federal reporting shall report their direct and indirect emissions, the methodologies for calculating emissions and the system for the monitoring, reporting and verification of emissions, as well as guidance on the linking to other federal or state emissions registries.[38] It explicitly states that individuals and legal entities responsible for emissions subject to reporting shall provide the necessary information for incorporation into the Registry.

---

[35] ibid arts 74 and 75.
[36] ibid arts 76–79.
[37] ibid arts 80–86.
[38] ibid arts 87–90.

Interestingly, a number of articles in the LGCC are devoted to economic instruments.[39] They state that the federal government, the states and the federal districts, within their respective authority should develop and apply economic instruments to provide incentives for meeting the objectives of national climate change policy. The LGCC then lists several types of instruments that could be used for this purpose and in particular mentions that the government may establish a voluntary emissions trading system. However, there are no specific details on when such instruments should be developed. Finally, the LGCC mandates the SEMARNAT with the participation of other agencies where appropriate to issue Mexican official standards (*normas oficiales mexicanas*) for mitigation and adaptation measures.[40]

In order to determine and recommend any necessary policy amendments Title Six outlines provisions for the periodic and systematic evaluation of the national climate change policy to be carried out by the Coordination for Evaluation.[41] As was noted earlier, the coordination comprises the head of the INECC and six civil society advisors. The evaluations should be carried out every two years; however, the Coordination for Evaluation could take a decision to apply longer periods. Beyond that, the provisions outline objectives for the evaluation specifically for adaptation and mitigation.

Figure 4.1 Key policy instruments established or amended by the LGCC in 2012 and through the decree amending it in 2018

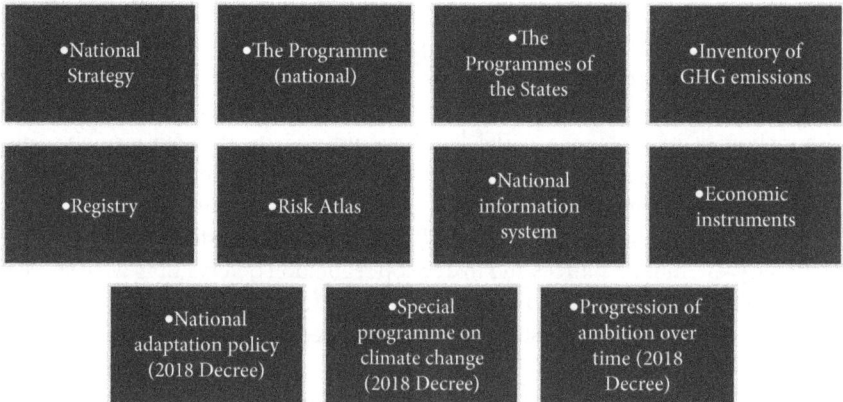

Provisions on Transparency and Access to Information as well as on Participation of Society (Titles Seven and Eight, respectively) mandate the CICC in collaboration with other relevant government agencies to elaborate and make available on

---

[39] ibid arts 91–95.
[40] ibid.
[41] ibid arts 90–105.

the Web a detailed annual report on the general state of the climate. It should also make available the results of the evaluations of the National Climate Change Policy and promote the participation of society in the planning, implementation and oversight of the policy.[42]

Several articles address inspection and surveillance, security measures and sanctions.[43] In particular, these give powers to the SEMARNAT through the Federal Prosecutor for Environmental Protection to carry out inspection and surveillance of individuals and legal entities that are subject to emissions reporting and to impose fines on such individuals or legal entities that do not provide information or documents required within the established timeframe. The size of the fine can vary from 500 to 3,000 days of the minimum wage in force in the federal district.[44]

There are a further 10 'transitory articles', which in Mexico refer to a provision that is added after the matter to be legislated has been dealt with in the core articles.[45] Transitory articles have a temporary validity and are viewed as secondary or auxiliary to the main articles. They may be used to specify the entry into force of the new legal text or determine other conditions under which the new legislation will begin to take legal effect. Transitory articles are viewed as complementary legislation to existing legislation and they cannot stand on their own. They can be amended or replaced over time or as soon as the condition they specify is present. When it comes to the enactment of a new law, articles of a permanent nature and transitory articles are separated. The latter are organised under the title of 'transitory' and are assigned their own and independent numbering.[46]

The transitory articles in the 2012 LGCC contained the framework's aspirational emission targets and defined the timelines for the federal agencies, states and municipalities to develop the key programmes and strategies on adaptation and mitigation that the law requires. Specifically, in the original reading in 2012, these provisions stated that the country adopted the aspirational goal of reducing its emissions by 30 per cent by 2020 below the baseline scenario (which is not specified by the LGCC) and by 50 per cent by 2050 below the emissions level in 2000. It was envisioned that these goals would be reviewed in the next national strategy, which was due to be published during the first half of 2013.[47] The federal government, states and municipalities were mandated to establish programmes on adaptation before the end of 2013, as well as to develop a national risk atlas, and state and local risk atlases for the most vulnerable areas.

---

[42] ibid arts 106–10.

[43] ibid arts 111–16.

[44] ibid art 114.

[45] Francisco Avalos and Elisa Donnadieu, 'Update: An Electronic Guide to Mexican Law', Hauser Global Law School Program, New York University School of Law (2014), www.nyulawglobal.org/globalex/Mexico1.html; and Mexico, 'Artículo Transitorio', *Enciclopedia Jurídica Online*, https://mexico.leyderecho.org/articulo-transitorio.

[46] ibid.

[47] LGCC, transitory art 6.

On mitigation, this included, among other things, a goal for the municipalities, in coordination with the states and all other institutions, to develop and build by 2018 infrastructure for the management of solid waste that does not emit methane in urban centres with over 50,000 inhabitants, and to generate electricity utilising methane emissions. It also included a mandate to several agencies to gradually develop by 2020 a system of subsidies to promote non-fossil fuels, energy efficiency measures and sustainable public transportation. Furthermore, the LGCC mandated the establishment by 2020 of an incentive-based system for renewable energy and the obligation to ensure that electricity generation from clean energy sources reaches at least 35 per cent by 2024.[48]

V. Enabling Energy Transition Legislation

On 10 December 2015, the Mexican Congress approved the Energy Transition Law (Ley de Transición Energética or LTE). This law aims to operationalise the energy transition initiated with the constitutional energy reform in 2013. It establishes a legal framework for the efficient use of energy and gradual increase of clean energy in electricity production to achieve established GHG emissions reduction goals. The LTE explicitly links to the objective of the LGCC for the reduction of emissions and clean energy targets that were set as aspirational in 2012.

Averchenkova and Guzman find that the LGCC was an important precursor to the LTE and enabled its adoption, providing justification for the measures to decarbonise energy.[49] Furthermore, coalitions of stakeholders that support the climate change agenda and the decarbonisation of the economy that were formed during the discussions on the LGCC were helpful in attracting support for the LTE. This has made the negotiation of the LTE easier.[50]

Effectively, the LTE surpasses any other previously enacted piece of legislation on energy transition and sustainable electric production in Mexico, and articulates the electric industry's obligations to comply with standards established in the LGCC.[51] Specifically, the LTE legislated for the aspirational clean energy target set in the LGCC of 35 per cent electricity generation from clean energy by 2024 and set new intermediate goals: 25 per cent by 2018 and 30 per cent by 2021. It also mandates the government to establish energy efficiency targets. While the LTE itself has not specified a long-term clean energy goal, Mexico has subsequently

---

[48] ibid transitory art 3.

[49] Averchenkova and Guzman Luna (n 17).

[50] ibid.

[51] Alejandra Elizondo, Vanessa Pérez-Cirera, Alexandre Strapasson, José Carlos Fernández and Diego Cruz-Cano, 'Mexico's Low Carbon Futures: An Integrated Assessment for Energy Planning and Climate Change Mitigation by 2050' (2017) 93 *Futures* 14.

set a goal to generate 37.7 per cent by 2030 and 50 per cent by 2050 from clean electricity in addition to the original legislated mid-term target of 35 per cent electricity generation from clean energy by 2024 through the Energy Transition Strategy to Promote the Use of Cleaner Technologies and Fuels, which stems from the LTE.[52]

The implementation of the LTE is based on three main policy mechanisms:

- The Energy Transition Strategy to Promote the Use of Cleaner Technologies and Fuels, with 15- and 30-year planning horizons containing the clean energy and energy efficiency goals and assessment of compliance.

- The Special Programme for Energy Transition, which supports the implementation of the Strategy, with clean energy targets, actions, instruments, and financial and regulatory mechanisms.

- The National Programme for the Sustainable Use of Energy (PRONASE), which focuses on actions and projects on energy efficiency and energy conservation to meet the goals set in the LTE and is mandated to set an indicative energy efficiency goal. The PRONASE states that energy intensity in Mexico in 2018 must be at least equal to that in 2012 and that an additional 5 per cent of final energy consumption must meet energy efficiency regulations (from 46 per cent in 2012 to 51 per cent in 2018). It also mandates the creation of Energy Commissions in the states by 2018.[53]

The LTE also outlined several specific policy instruments, which included flexible compensation that can be used to comply with emission standards and clean energy certificates, as well as the intelligent electrical networks programme to support the modernisation of the national transmission and general distribution networks. It also created an Excellence in Energy Efficiency device, that is a voluntary process of certification and recognition for products, equipment and buildings created with sustainable and efficient use of energy.[54]

VI. The 2018 Amendment to the LGCC

In April 2018, Mexico's Parliament passed a decree amending the LGCC.[55] This decree made Mexico one of the first countries to modify its domestic legislation to make it more consistent with the Paris Agreement. The 2018 decree was motivated by bringing emission targets in line with the NDC. It recognised

---

[52] CNUEE México, 'Estrategia de Transición para Promover el Uso de Tecnología y Combustibles más Limpios' (2016), https://www.gob.mx/cms/uploads/attachment/file/182202/20161110_1300h_Estrategia_CCTE-1.pdf.

[53] Elizondo et al (n 51) 14–26.

[54] Alina Averchenkova, 'Legislating for a Low Carbon and Climate Resilient Transition: Learning from International Experiences', Elcano Policy Paper, March 2019.

[55] DOF (n 5).

the need to keep global temperature rise to within 2ºC above pre-industrial levels and to undertake efforts to keep this increase below 1.5ºC. These objectives translated into a range of unconditional and conditional mid-term targets for 2030 for greenhouse gas and black carbon emissions, and are supported by clean energy and sectoral targets, while keeping the original long-term goal of a 50 per cent reduction below the baseline level of greenhouse gas emissions in 2000 by 2050. While no explicit provisions for the ratcheting up of ambition are envisioned in the LGCC, the decree passed in 2018 mention the need to increase the ambition over time.

As noted earlier, in 2012 the LGCC set a mid-term target of reducing greenhouse gas emissions by 30 per cent below business-as-usual levels by 2020. These objectives were conditional on international support. The decree of 2018 amended the targets in accordance with the NDC, including an unconditional commitment to reduce greenhouse gas emissions by 22 per cent and black carbon emissions by 51 per cent below business-as-usual levels by 2030. The 2018 decree also indicated that emissions would peak by 2026 and that the intensity of greenhouse gas emissions per unit of GDP should be reduced by about 40 per cent between 2013 and 2030.[56] Furthermore, the decree set a conditional target of a 36 per cent reduction in greenhouse gas emissions and a 70 per cent reduction in black carbon emissions below business-as-usual levels by 2030 if international support is provided.

Another important change to the LGCC introduced by the 2018 decree is the definition of a set of sectoral targets for reducing greenhouse gas emissions in order to meet the national objective of reducing emissions by 22 per cent below business-as-usual levels by 2030. Specifically, these include reductions in emissions below business-as-usual levels by 2030 by 18 per cent in transportation; by 31 per cent in power generation; by 18 per cent in residential and commercial sectors; by 14 per cent in oil and gas; by 5 per cent in industry; by 8 per cent in agriculture and livestock; and by 28 per cent in waste.[57]

While the LGCC in its original reading of 2012 was heavily focused on mitigation, the revision of 2018 mandates the development of a national adaptation plan at the national level and a requirement for the states and municipalities to address adaptation. The decree also makes provisions for new mechanisms, including the reformed emissions trading system and further mandates regarding the transparency framework through which to observe the development and implementation of NDCs.

The aim of the emissions trading system is to promote emission reductions that can be made with the lowest possible cost in a measurable, reportable and verifiable way, without harming the international competitiveness of the participating sectors.[58] The system would be developed gradually with a 36-month trial period, starting in May 2018. The amended provisions on the transparency framework

[56] ibid.
[57] ibid.
[58] LGCC, art 94.

mandate the government to provide an annual report on climate change online that includes: an account of actions carried out with resources from the Climate Change Fund; the resources that are annually allocated in the Expenditure Budget of the Federation to comply with the obligations of the LGCC and the way in which they were implemented, and the results of evaluations of the National Policy on Climate Change. Individuals can also review the inventory and registry online.

VII. The Implementation of the LGCC and its Impact

The adoption of the LGCC has been an important step in advancing Mexico's efforts on climate change and in strengthening its reputation globally in this area in the face of political changes, a strong fossil fuel lobby and other governance challenges typical in emerging economies. While for the Calderón government, climate change was a priority issue, the administration of Enrique Peña Nieto that took over in 2012 did not treat it as being of the same importance. Yet the existence of the LGCC enabled policy continuation towards the objectives enshrined in the legislation, requiring the government to comply with the mandates of the law. The LGCC has had a major impact on Mexican climate change policy, having laid the institutional foundations for developing, mainstreaming and implementing the climate change agenda at the national, state and municipal levels. According to a recent assessment, its major achievement included the establishment of key institutions to deal with climate change at the federal level, the definition of responsibilities for the states and municipalities, and the definition of long-term objectives effectively setting the basis for long-term climate policy in Mexico.[59] According to expert assessments, the LGCC has also strengthened political continuity and improved the quality of the political debate on climate change. Most importantly, it has enabled advances in the low carbon energy transition by providing guidance on long-term climate change and clean energy objectives for energy reform.[60]

The amendment to the legislation through the 2018 decree that maintains its relevance in evolving circumstances and consistent with Mexico's international commitments highlights its continued role as the main vehicle for domestic climate policy. The timing of the amendments to the LGCC, which occurred in April 2018 before the presidential elections of July 2018, is also significant: it signalled the desire of the outgoing government and legislature to maintain their commitment to the Paris Agreement and ensure that the next government would follow the path that had been set in motion.

---

[59] Averchenkova and Guzman Luna (n 17).
[60] ibid.

At the same time, the LGCC has faced a number of challenges in its implementation. For example, the Special Programme on Climate Change for 2014–18 included 30 mitigation-related measures estimating an abatement of 83.2 MtCO$_2$eq per year by 2018.[61] The Programme reflected a balance in its sectoral policy focus, except for waste, where most of the initiatives were centred on the sustainable management and use of agricultural waste.[62] However, a strategic assessment of the progress made in implementing the Programme showed that during the period 2014–18, only 43 per cent of the goals it set were achieved.[63]

Subsequently, Mexico's performance on reducing greenhouse gas emissions is still below the set objectives. In 2015 the country emitted 683 million tons of carbon dioxide-equivalent (MtCO$_2$e), two-thirds of which came from electricity generation, transport and industry. This represents an increase in emissions of 54 per cent compared to the 1990 level of 445 MtCO$_2$e, or 1.7 per cent annually, although from 2010 to 2015, the rate of increase reduced to 0.8 per cent per year.[64] According to Climate Action Tracker, Mexico's unconditional target to reduce greenhouse gas emissions by 22 per cent below business-as-usual levels in 2030 is equivalent to 72 per cent above 1990 levels and 9 per cent above 2010 levels, excluding land use and land use change and forestry (LULUCF), by 2030. The conditional target of a 36 per cent reduction below business-as-usual levels by 2030 translates as 40 per cent above 1990 levels and 11 per cent below 2010 levels, excluding LULUCF, by 2030.[65] However, while the current policies in Mexico will likely lead to an overall decrease in emissions below the 2015 levels, Mexico is likely to miss its 2020 and 2030 emissions targets.[66]

According to the analysis by Averchenkova and Guzman,[67] some of the implementation challenges can be traced back to the design of the LGCC and, in particular, to the lack of timelines and precision in the mandates, although most of them relate to the ways in which the law is being executed. In particular, challenges are presented in relation to institutional and financial capacity and political will, which is typical in many emerging economies.[68] Going forward, Mexico needs to close the gap between what is set out in the LGCC and the actual policy arrangements, processes and practices. Specifically, the LGCC does not set sufficiently clear mandates or implementation guidelines for the responsible institutions and

---

[61] 'Programma Especial de Cambio Climatico 2014–2018', Gobierno de la Republica, 2014. Available at: www.semarnat.gob.mx/sites/default/files/documentos/transparencia/programa_especial_de_cambio_climatico_2014-2018.pdf.

[62] Elizondo et al (n 51) 14–26.

[63] INECC, 'Evaluación Estratégica del Programa Especial de Cambio Climático 2014–2018' (2017), https://www.gob.mx/cms/uploads/attachment/file/261388/Informe__evaluacion_PECC_final_limpio_1_.pdf.

[64] INECC (n 21).

[65] Climate Action Tracker, 2018, https://climateactiontracker.org.

[66] ibid.

[67] Averchenkova and Guzman Luna (n 17).

[68] ibid.

lacks strong accountability mechanisms, with no independent body entrusted with accountability and enforcement. The independent advisory body lacks strategy and allocated funding, and is highly ineffective. The general mandate on the allocation of public funding is not sufficiently strong, resulting in low levels of finance raised for climate change policy in recent years.[69]

Mexico's performance is more positive in relation to the transition towards clean energy. In 2006–16 the installed capacity for renewable energy generation in Mexico grew by 4.3 per cent on average per year, with solar and wind energy growing by 33.6 per cent and 110.3 per cent, respectively.[70] In a statement made in 2018, Leonardo Beltrán, Mexico's Deputy Minister for Planning and Energy Transition, said that based on the growth rate at the time, Mexico could reach its goal of generating half of its power from clean energy by 2034, 16 years sooner than the target set in the Energy Transition Strategy.[71]

Going forward, in order to be effective, implementation of the LGCC will require that the mid- and long-term goals are backed up by intermediate steps to achieve them, and by strong planning and implementation mechanisms and timelines. Strong mechanisms for coordination beyond the environmental sector are needed to ensure adequate implementation. Ambiguities in institutional mandates can impede coordination, policy development and implementation. Effective implementation also requires a clear financing strategy and the backing of sufficient financial resources. Mexico needs to develop such a strategy and improve budgeting processes on climate change.

Furthermore, the independent and adequately resourced monitoring and evaluation mechanism will be crucial for the effective implementation of the LGCC and Mexico's NDC. Currently, the lack of dedicated financial resources impedes the effectiveness of the C3 in this respect. Capacity needs to be strengthened, and the participation of the state and municipal governments and sectoral agencies incentivised, including by targeted guidance on how to develop climate change plans and improving resource allocation.

The government under López Obrador, who took office in December 2018, has not at the time of writing adopted the third Special Programme on Climate Change for 2019–24 mandated under the LGCC. Similarly, the government's National Development Plan for 2019–24 did not mention climate mitigation goals or implementation strategies.[72] The government has taken several backward steps on climate action, including the construction of a new oil refinery and allocating funds to the 'modernisation' of fossil-fuelled power plants (some of which had

---

[69] ibid.

[70] SENER (Ministry of Energy), 'Prospectiva de Energía Renovable 2017–2031' (2017), https://www.gob.mx/cms/uploads/attachment/file/325642/Prospectica_de_Energ_as_Renovables_2017-2031.pdf.

[71] Platts News, 'SENER Official Expects Half of Mexico's Power to Come from Clean Energy by 2034', 6 June 2018, https://www.spglobal.com/platts/en/market-insights/latest-news/electric-power/043018-sener-official-expects-half-of-mexicos-power-to-come-from-clean-energy-by-2034.

[72] Climate Action Tracker, 2020, https://climateactiontracker.org.

been previously scheduled for retirement), at the expense of the renewable energy programme.[73] The cancellation of the 2018 'long-term electricity auctioning' round (part of Mexico's main instruments for achieving its clean energy targets) further endangered the country's ability to implement the objectives set in the LGCC and to increase the uptake of new renewable energy investment.

Adoption of the legislation increases political awareness of climate change, improves the quality of the political debate and helps maintain political consensus over time. The LGCC has guided the low-carbon transition in the energy sector, providing long-term climate change and clean energy objectives for energy reform. However, the challenge for the future is to close the gap between what is set out in the LGCC and its implementation, which will require renewed political leadership.

Climate change laws alone do not substitute for political leadership. Sustained commitment is required for their successful implementation, particularly given the continued strong opposition to climate change policies in Mexico from fossil fuel-dependent industries.

---

[73] ibid.

5

Denmark's Climate Change Act(s)

SARAH LOUISE NASH

Author's Note

Since this chapter went to print, the 2020 'Law on Climate' (Lov om klima, LOV nr 965 af 26/06/2020) has been passed by the Danish Parliament. As expected, the law includes binding targets to reduce GHG emissions 70 per cent by 2030 and for Denmark to become climate neutral by 2050, drawing on the Paris Agreement's 1.5°C target. A system of interim targets to be set every five years is also introduced with the new law. As such, two central building blocks that were missing from the 2014 legislation and were central to the proposals of the Borgerforslag have now been introduced into Danish law.

I. Introduction

In 2014, Denmark became the third European Union (EU) Member State to pass a Climate Change Act (CCA) with its 'Act on the Climate Council, climate policy statements and determination of national climate objectives',[1] which entered into force on 1 January 2015. By passing this law, Denmark followed in the footsteps of both the UK and Austria, which passed their own laws in 2008[2] and 2011,[3] respectively.

A CCA can be defined as:

> [F]ramework legislation adopted by parliament that lays down general principles and obligations for climate change policymaking in a nation-state (or sub-state entity),

---

[1] 'Klimalov', Lov Om Klimarådet, Klimapolitisk Redegørelse Og Fastsættelse Af Nationale Klimamålsætninger (Act on the Climate Council, Climate Policy Statements and Determination of National Climate Objectives), LOV nr 716 af 25/06/2014 (Denmark, 2014).

[2] Climate Change Act, c 27 vols (UK, 2008).

[3] Klimaschutzgesetz (Climate Protection Law), GPXXIVRV1255AB1456S.124.BR:AB8596S.801. vols. (Austria, 2011).

with the explicit aim of reducing greenhouse gas (GHG) emissions in relevant sectors through specific measures to be implemented at a later stage.[4]

As the third EU Member State to introduce a CCA, Denmark is an early adopter of this kind of legislation. In 2019, the main political parties in Denmark also agreed the main aspects of a new stronger CCA to be passed in early 2020. Denmark is therefore an unusual case as both an early adopter of a CCA and as having a legislature that is in the process of legislating for a new, stronger CCA five years on from its first CCA entering into force.

As the international framework for climate change mitigation continues to be centred around the GHG emissions reductions of individual nation-states, for example, through the Nationally Determined Contributions (NDCs) that are a cornerstone of the Paris Agreement,[5] the strategies employed by states to lower their GHG emissions are going to be important not only on the national level, but also on the global level.

Denmark is both a party to the United Nations Framework Convention on Climate Change (UNFCCC) and a Member State of the EU and, as such, its climate change policy consists not only of Danish legislation, but also provisions stemming from the UNFCCC and the EU. Denmark has ratified the 2015 Paris Agreement of the UNFCCC, which sets the objective of 'holding the increase in the global average temperature to well below 2°C above pre-industrial levels and pursuing efforts to limit the temperature increase to 1.5°C above pre-industrial levels'.[6] Denmark's climate policies should therefore be aligned with achieving this global target.

As an EU Member State, Denmark is also part of the EU Emissions Trading System (EU ETS) and is covered by binding targets that have been set for non-ETS sectors. EU-wide targets for non-ETS sectors have been set for reducing GHG emissions 20 per cent by 2020[7] and at least 40 per cent by 2030.[8] These EU-wide targets have been translated into individual targets for each Member State, which for Denmark have been set at 20 per cent reduction in GHG emissions for the

---

[4] Sarah Louise Nash and Reinhard Steurer, 'Taking Stock of Climate Change Acts in Europe: Living Policy Processes or Symbolic Gestures?' (2019) 19(8) *Climate Policy* 1052.

[5] Paris Agreement (UNFCCC, 2015).

[6] Ibid, art 2(1)(a).

[7] Directive 2009/29/EC of the European Parliament and of the Council of 23 April 2009 Amending Directive 2003/87/EC so as to Improve and Extend the Greenhouse Gas Emission Allowance Trading Scheme of the Community (Official Journal of the European Union, 2009), http://eur-lex.europa.eu/legal-content/EN/TXT/PDF/?uri=CELEX:32009L0029&from=EN; Official Journal of the European Union, Directive 2009/31/EC of the European Parliament and of the Council of 23 April 2009 on the Geological Storage of Carbon Dioxide and Amending Council Directive 85/337/EEC, European Parliament and Council Directives 2000/60/EC, 2001/80/EC, 2004/35/EC, 2006/12/EC, 2008/1/EC and Regulation (EC) No 1013/2006 (2009), http://eur-lex.europa.eu/legal-content/EN/TXT/PDF/?uri=CELEX:32009L0031&from=EN.

[8] Communication from the Commission to the European Parliament, the Council, the European Economic and Social Committee and the Committee of the Regions. A Policy Framework for Climate and Energy in the Period from 2020 to 2030 (European Commission, 2014), http://eur-lex.europa.eu/legal-content/EN/TXT/PDF/?uri=CELEX:52014DC0015&from=EN.

2013–20 period[9] and 39 per cent for the 2021–30 period[10] compared to 2005 levels. The targets for Denmark are thus some of the most stringent amongst all EU Member States.

This chapter provides an overview of the Danish CCA of 2014, as well an introduction to the building blocks that have been agreed for the new CCA that is timetabled to be passed in early 2020. Section II outlines the building blocks of the CCA 2014, section III focuses on the process of negotiating the legislation and section IV deals with its implementation. Section V outlines a 'citizens' initiative' proposal for a new CCA before section VI provides an overview of the multi-party agreement on a new CCA due to be legislated in early 2020.

II. Content of the CCA 2014

The 2014 legislation consists of two documents. First, the 'Act on the Climate Council, Climate Policy Statements and Determination of National Climate Objectives'[11] is the core legal text of the CCA setting out provisions that are binding on the government. Second, additional provisions are added by a subsidiary document, 'Comments on the Bill' ('Bemærkninger til lovforslaget'), which is a non-binding policy decision made between a number of political parties before the act had passed. Due to the different legal character of these documents, only the provisions contained in the Act are interpreted as provisions of the CCA here.

The CCA is made up of three main building blocks. First, the law sets out its purpose, which is to establish:

[A]n overarching strategic framework for Denmark's climate policy with regard to transitioning to a low-emissions society in 2050, i.e. a resource efficient society with an energy supply based on renewable energy and markedly lower emissions of greenhouse gases from sectors, which at the same time supports growth and development.[12]

---

[9] Decision No 406/2009/EC of the European Parliament and of the Council of 23 April 2009 on the Effort of Member States to Reduce Their Greenhouse Gas Emissions to Meet the Community's Greenhouse Gas Emission Reduction Commitments up to 2020 (Official Journal of the European Union, 2009), http://eur-lex.europa.eu/legal-content/EN/TXT/PDF/?uri=CELEX:32009D0406&from=EN.

[10] Regulation (EU) 2018/842 of the European Parliament and of the Council of 30 May 2018 on Binding Annual Greenhouse Gas Emissions Reductions by Member States from 2021 to 2030 Contributing to Climate Action to Meet Commitments under the Paris Agreement and Amending Regulation (EU) No 525/2013 (Official Journal of the European Union, 2018), https://eur-lex.europa.eu/legal-content/EN/TXT/PDF/?uri=CELEX:32018R0842&from=EN.

[11] 'Klimalov', Lov Om Klimarådet, Klimapolitisk Redegørelse Og Fastsættelse Af Nationale Klimamålsætninger (n 1).

[12] ibid para 1. Author's translation. In original Danish: 'Loven har formal at etablere en overordnet strategisk ramme for Danmarks klimapolitik med henblik på at overgå til et lavemissionssamfund i 2050, dvs. et ressourceeffektivt samfund med en energiforsyning baseret på vedvarende energi og markant lavere udledninger af drivhusgasser fra øvrige sektorer, som samtidig understøtter vækst og udvikling. Loven skal derudover fremme gennemsigtighed og offentlighed om status, retning og fremdrift for Danmarks klimapolitik.'

The purpose of the law is also to 'promote transparency and openness about the status, direction and progress of Denmark's climate policy'.[13] The second building block of the law establishes a Climate Council (Klimarådet) that is constituted as an independent advisory expert body by the relevant government minister.[14] The Climate Council is allocated the following four tasks: 'estimating the status of Denmark's compliance with national climate objectives and international climate commitments'; 'analysing possible ways for readjustment to a low-emissions society'; elaborating 'recommendations on the design of climate policies'; and contributing 'to the public debate'.[15] The Council is made up of one chairperson and six other members, who are all 'experts with broad expertise and a high climate-relevant expert level including in energy, buildings, transport, land-use, environment or nature and economy, including socio-economic and business-economic expertise'.[16] The Climate Council chairperson is appointed by the relevant government minister and the other members are appointed by this minster in consultation with other government ministers.[17] The final building block of the 2014 CCA is a government reporting mechanism in the form of a climate policy statement (*Klimapolitisk redegørelse*) that is to be presented annually to Parliament.[18] The statement includes historical GHG emissions broken down by sector, projections for GHG emissions, planned climate actions and instruments and their anticipated effects, status of performance in line with national climate objectives and international climate commitments, the Climate Council's recommendations to the government minister, and the minister's position on these recommendations.[19]

With its sparse procedures and lack of quantified targets for GHG emissions reductions, the Danish CCA is at the weaker end of the spectrum of CCAs that have entered into force in EU Member States.[20]

The subsidiary document 'Comments on the Bill' is the product of a political agreement between the coalition Social Democrat (Socialdemokraterne) and Social Liberal Party (Det Radikale Venstre) government, as well as the Socialist People's Party (Socialistisk Folkeparti), the Red-Green Alliance (Endhedslisten)

---

[13] ibid para 1. Author's translation. In original Danish: 'Loven skal derudover fremme gennemsigtighed og offentlighed om status, retning og fremdrift for Danmarks klimapolitik.'

[14] ibid para 2.

[15] ibid paras 2.1, 2.2, 2.3 and 2.4. Author's translation. In original Danish: 'Vurdere status for Danmarks opfyldelse af nationale klimamålsætninger og internationale klimaforpligtelser'; 'Analysere mulige omstillingsveje mod et lavemissionssamfund i 2050 og mulige virkemidler for at opnå drivhusgasreduktioner'; 'Udarbejde anbefalinger om udformning af klimapolitikken'; 'Bidrage til den offentlige debate'.

[16] ibid para 3.2 Author's translation. In original Danish: 'Klimarådet sammensættes af eksperter med bred ekspertise og et højt klimarelevant fagligt niveau inden for energi, bygninger, transport, landbrug, miljø eller natur og økonomi, herunder bred samfundsøkonomisk og erhvervsøkonomisk ekspertise.'

[17] ibid para 3.2.

[18] ibid para 5.

[19] ibid para 5.

[20] Nash and Steurer (n 4).

and the Conservative People's Party (Det Konservative Folkeparti). The agreement added a third procedural element alongside the Climate Council and the climate policy statements in the form of national climate objectives (*Nationale klimamålsættninger*) that are to be set by the relevant minister on behalf of the government and presented to Parliament at least every five years. The objectives must have a 10-year perspective.[21]

The Comments on the Bill also include more detail on the aim in the CCA of 'transitioning to a low-emissions society in 2050'.[22] In the political agreement, a more specific interim objective of a 40 per cent reduction in GHG emissions by 2020 compared to 1990 levels is included.[23] The important difference between these two provisions contained in the Comments on the Bill and the CCA itself is that the Comments on the Bill is not part of the legislation, but rather is an adjacent political agreement. This means that changes can be made to these provisions without having to legislate for it in Parliament.

III. Negotiating the 2014 CCA

The negotiations towards the 2014 CCA commenced with a change in government following Denmark's 2011 elections. Prior to the 2011 election, a centre-right two-party coalition of the Liberal Party (Venstre) and the Conservative People's Party had been in government. After the election, a three-party centre-left coalition was formed consisting of the Social Democrats, Social Liberal Party and the Socialist People's Party.[24] In establishing the coalition government, the three parties negotiated a 'Platform for Government', a policy document outlining the agreement between the coalition partners of what would be pursued during their government. The 'Platform for Government' included seven goals on climate and energy:

(1) all of Denmark's energy supply will come from renewable energy by 2050, electricity and heat supply will be generated completely from renewable energy by 2035, and coal in Danish power plants and oil furnaces will be phased out by 2030;

(2) GHG emissions will be reduced by 40 per cent by 2020 compared to 1990 levels;

---

[21] Bemærkninger Til Lovforslaget (Lov Om Klimarådet, Klimapolitisk Redegørelse Og Fastsættelse Af Nationale Klimamålsætninger) (Comments on the Bill (Act on the Climate Council, Climate Policy Statements and Determination of National Climate Objectives)), LOV nr 716 af 25/06/2014 (Denmark, 2014) 3.

[22] 'Klimalov', Lov Om Klimarådet, Klimapolitisk Redegørelse Og Fastsættelse Af Nationale Klimamålsætninger (n 1) para 1.

[23] Bemærkninger Til Lovforslaget (Lov Om Klimarådet, Klimapolitisk Redegørelse Og Fastsættelse Af Nationale Klimamålsætninger) (n 21) 4.

[24] The Socialist People's Party left the government in early 2014 and a coalition government of the Social Democrats and the Social Liberal Party continued until the 2015 elections.

(3) half of Denmark's electricity consumption will come from wind energy by 2020;

(4) an overall strategy will be prepared for the establishment of a smart grid in Denmark;

(5) research and development funds for climate and green energy technologies will be prioritised;

(6) Denmark will work within the EU to establish binding targets for energy saving and renewable energy for after 2020 and work to increase the EU objective for reducing CO_2 emissions to 30 per cent rather than 20 per cent by 2020;

(7) Denmark will work actively for an ambitious and binding international climate agreement.[25]

The 'Platform for Government' sets up these goals as the foundation for a CCA, specifying that 'the goals will be written into a climate law – inspired by the British and Scottish laws'.[26] However, it does not contain any more details as to the proposed contents of this law or the timeframe in which the legislative process was planned.

Based on the 'Platform for Government', the government parties started cross-party negotiations on the content of the proposed law following a Danish tradition of consensual policy-making, especially in the area of energy policy.[27] In 2012, one of these energy agreements was finalised between the government (the Social Democrats, the Social Liberal Party and the Socialist People's Party) as well as the Liberal Party, the Danish People's Party (Dansk Folkeparti), the Red-Green Alliance and the Conservative People's Party. The opening passage of the agreement states that:

> The parties agree that the transition to a Denmark with an energy supply covered by renewable energy rests on a credible, stable and long-term framework for Danish energy policy. This agreement establishes concrete energy policy initiatives for the period 2012–2020.[28]

---

[25] Danish Government, *Et Danmark, Der Står Sammen. Regeringsgrundlag Oktober 2011* (Copenhagen, Danish Government, 2011), www.stm.dk/publikationer/Et_Danmark_der_staar_sammen_11/Regeringsgrundlag_okt_2011.pdf, 28.

[26] ibid 28. Author's translation. In original Danish: 'Målene skrives ind I en klimalov – inspireret af den britiske og den skotske klimalov.'

[27] Franziska Ehnert, 'Governance-Formen und die Entstehung der Dänischen Energievereinbarung von 2012: "We are Doing Things the Danish Way"' in Jana Rückert-John and Martina Schäfer (eds), *Governance Für Eine Gesellschaftstransformation: Herausforderungen des Wandels in Richtung Nachhaltige Entwicklung* (Wiesbaden, Springer Fachmedien Wiesbaden, 2017).

[28] Danish Government, 'Aftale Mellem Regeringen (Socialdemokraterne, Det Radikale Venstre, Socialistisk Folkeparti) Og Venstre, Dansk Folkeparti, Enhedslisten Og Det Konservative Folkeparti Om Den Danske Energipolitik 2012–2020' (2012), https://ens.dk/sites/ens.dk/files/EnergiKlimapolitik/aftale_22-03-2012_final_ren.doc.pdf. Author's translation. In original Danish: 'Parterne er enige om, at omstillingen til et Danmark med en energiforsyning dækket af vedvarende energi hviler på troværdige, stabile og langsigtede rammer om den danske energipolitik. Med denne aftale fastlægges konkrete energipolitiske initiativer for perioden 2012–2020.'

The cross-party consensus surrounding the Energy Agreement, as well as its long timeframe crossing over multiple parliamentary terms, is important for providing consistency and predictability in energy policy. This means that changes in government that might arise after elections do not cause changes in policy.

A similar negotiation process took place in the lead-up to agreeing the CCA. However, in contrast to the Energy Agreement, only the parties that already supported the government and the Conservative People's Party supported the CCA.[29] Although this did not provide the same level of predictability as the broad consensus around the Energy Agreement, the participation of the Conservative People's Party in the CCA was very important. The Conservative People's Party is a party located on the centre-right of the political spectrum, meaning that the CCA is not only legislation of the centre-left, increasing the chances of the legislation surviving a change in government.

Although the 'Platform for Government' stated that the Danish CCA would be inspired by the British and Scottish laws, the content of the law does not strongly resemble UK and Scottish legislation,[30] which are both based on a complex system of long-term and interim targets for 2050 and 2020, carbon budgets (UK) or annual targets (Scotland), planning frameworks, independent advice from the Committee on Climate Change (CCC), as well as government reporting. Therefore, in Denmark initial inspiration has been taken from the UK and Scottish CCAs, but specific provisions that are key to these CCAs have failed to diffuse.

IV. Implementing the 2014 CCA

In June 2015, shortly after the CCA was agreed (June 2014) and entered into force (January 2015), Danish parliamentary elections resulted in a change of government away from the centre-left governing coalition, which was replaced by a minority Liberal Party government supported by the Danish People's Party, the Liberal Alliance and the Conservative People's Party. In 2016, the Liberal Alliance and the Conservative People's Party also entered the government to form a three-party coalition with the Liberal Party. For the implementation of the CCA, the participation of the Conservative People's Party supporting the Liberal Party government was very important because it meant that one of the key parties supporting the CCA was thus close to government.

At least in part because of the support of the Conservative People's Party, the CCA was not repealed when the government changed, despite the governing party itself not being a supporter of the Act. However, the political agreement that was contained in the Comments on the Bill did not have the same longevity.

---

[29] Bemærkninger Til Lovforslaget (Lov Om Klimarådet, Klimapolitisk Redegørelse Og Fastsættelse Af Nationale Klimamålsætninger) (n 21).
[30] Climate Change (Scotland) Act 2009.

The target for a 40 per cent reduction in GHG emissions by 2020 that was contained in the Comments on the Bill[31] and the previous government's 'Platform for Government'[32] was disputed by the incoming Liberal Party government. Lars Christian Lillehold, the government minister who was responsible for the CCA, argued that a 37 per cent emissions reduction target for 2020 would be more realistic, following a policy of 'green realism'.[33] This was consistent with the climate politics of the Liberal Party government more broadly, which were generally less ambitious than those of the preceding government, with the result that 'overall, the environment seems to have lost in the 2015 election'.[34]

Despite the change in priority for climate policy and although the provisions included in the Comments on the Bill were not valid after the change in government, the procedural elements contained in the CCA continued to be implemented. As discussed above, this included both government reporting in climate policy statements, and reporting and advice by the newly constituted Climate Council.

The constitution of the Climate Council was the central, longest section of the CCA 2014,[35] which has been identified as the most promising aspect of the law.[36] As appointments to the Climate Council are for four years,[37] with the first council being appointed prior to the general election in 2015, a Climate Council will work across at least two parliamentary terms. The appointees sitting as the Climate Council at any one time therefore have not necessarily been appointed by the particular government under which they are working. This was the case with the 2015–18 Climate Council, which was appointed by the centre-left government, but carried out the majority of its work under the Liberal Party and centre-right coalition governments.

The Climate Council has published annual reports as provided for in the CCA.[38] The Climate Council used its first report in 2015 to paint 'a broad picture

---

[31] Bemærkninger Til Lovforslaget (Lov Om Klimarådet, Klimapolitisk Redegørelse Og Fastsættelse Af Nationale Klimamålsætninger) (n 21).

[32] Danish Government (n 28).

[33] 'Klima- Og Energiminister Vil Sænke Klimaambition' (*Politiken*, 19 August 2015), https://politiken. dk/oekonomi/2050/klima/art5592792/Klima-og-energiminister-vil-s%C3%A6nke-klimaambition.

[34] Karina Kosiara-Pedersen and Conor Little, 'Environmental Politics in the 2015 Danish General Election' (2016) 25(3) *Environmental Politics* 561.

[35] 'Klimalov', Lov Om Klimarådet, Klimapolitisk Redegørelse Og Fastsættelse Af Nationale Klimamålsætninger' (n 1) para 2.

[36] Ellen Margrethe Basse, 'Klimaloven Uden Betydning for De Danske Klimamål' (*Klimadebat. dk*, 2015), www.klimadebat.dk/ellen-margrethe-basse-klimaloven-uden-betydning-for-de-danske-klimamaal-r631.php.

[37] 'Klimalov', Lov Om Klimarådet, Klimapolitisk Redegørelse Og Fastsættelse Af Nationale Klimamålsætninger' (n 1) para 3.3.

[38] Klimarådet (Danish Council on Climate Change), 'Transition towards 2030. Building Blocks for a Low-Carbon Society. Main Conclusions' (2017), https://klimaraadet.dk/en/rapporter/transition-towards-2030; Klimarådet, 'Converting with Care: Status and Challenges for Danish Climate Policy' (2015), https://klimaraadet.dk/en/rapporter/converting-care; Klimarådet, 'Charges Which Transform: A Proposal for Climate-Friendly Tax Restructuring' (2016), https://klimaraadet.dk/sites/default/files/downloads/klimaraadet_rapport2_online_03.pdf; Klimarådet, 'The Role of Biomass in the Green Transition. Climate Perspectives and Recommendations for Regulation of Solid Biomass Used for Energy Production' (2018), https://klimaraadet.dk/en/rapporter/role-biomass-green-transition.

of the challenges of transition in order to pave the way for the Council's future work'.[39] The report sets out 'the long-term climate change targets' as the starting point for the Climate Council's work.[40] According to the Climate Council's interpretation of the CCA, the overarching target is 'making Denmark a low-carbon society by 2050', but it also draws on the 40 per cent target for 2020.[41] Four fundamental principles for Danish climate policy moving forward are stated as follows: 'reach unequivocal agreement on the climate policy framework', 'stay focused on achieving a balanced transition', 'maintain a steady transition' and 'employ technology-neutral means – taking into account the interaction between sectors'.[42] In this report, the Climate Council developed two packages of measures that could be used to achieve 40 per cent GHG emission reductions for 2020, with the differentiating factor being whether to implement measures in the agricultural sector. The most cost-effective package of measures is mostly related to the agricultural sector; however, the Climate Council also identifies a package of measures that does not involve the agricultural sector, recognising the pressure that the sector is under.

Five particular long-term challenges to be overcome have been identified. First, the electricity and heat sectors will have to be overhauled so that 'future heat and electricity will come from wind, solar and biomass'. Second, transport 'must be powered by renewable energy', as the transport sector accounts for about a quarter of GHG emissions. Third, the way in which agricultural emissions are estimated and reported will need to change, as emissions are currently not calculated for individual farms and as such there is no incentive for individual farms to reduce emissions. Fourth, buildings will play a large role with a large proportion of energy consumption coming from both private households and businesses. Fifth, the future role of waste will need to be clarified, with a significant proportion of Danish waste being combusted for electricity and heat generation.[43] Immediate action is recommended to address problematic preferential tax breaks for biomass, to increase the pace of development of renewable energy, to reduce energy taxes that are standing in the way of electrification and to reduce the role of combined heating and power plants.[44]

A series of eight recommendations are put forward by the Climate Council, which are as follows: (1) maintain the GHG emissions reduction target for 2020 at 40 per cent; (2) ensure steady expansion of supply infrastructure such as electric vehicle charging points; (3) thoroughly examine the taxation system to support changes that need to be made in the transport sector; (4) clarify the climate impacts of different types of biomass and ensure that this is reflected in reporting;

---

[39] Klimarådet, 'Converting with Care' (n 38) 4.
[40] ibid 9.
[41] ibid.
[42] ibid.
[43] ibid 12–13.
[44] ibid 15–16.

(5) change the tax and subsidy system so that it ceases to favour biomass; (6) modify levies so that they do not distort electricity consumption; (7) deliver base payment for district heating so that it encourages an increase in electric heating; and (8) expand renewable energy in the electricity and district heating sectors.[45]

In 2016, the Climate Council published a thematic report on the tax system, making a proposal for climate-friendly restructuring of the tax system that removes some of the perverse incentives that favour climate-damaging behaviour that were identified in the 2015 report.[46] In 2017, the report focused on building blocks for a low-carbon society in the lead-up to 2030. This followed the new 'Platform for Government' that was published when the Liberal Alliance and the Conservative People's Party joined the Liberal Party in government in 2016, which stated that:

> Greenhouse gas emissions must continue to decrease. Denmark is ready to under-take an ambitious 2030 target for non-ETS sector reductions. Before the end of 2017 the government will draw up a cost-effective strategy for meeting Denmark's 2030 reduction target. Among others, the government will draw on recommendations from the Danish Council on Climate Change.[47]

In 2018, the Climate Council focused in particular on the biomass industry in Denmark and the regulation of biomass used for energy production.[48]

The impact of the Climate Council is difficult to measure as it is hard to ascertain to what extent Climate Council reports have impacted the thinking of government parties and policy decisions that the various governments in power since 2015 have taken. However, one clear point where the Climate Council has influenced policy is the renewable energy target that was set in the 2018 Energy Agreement. According to the Climate Council's analysis published in advance of the Energy Agreement, the government's goal was 'that at least 50% of Danish energy consumption in 2030 must come from renewable energy'.[49] The goal that was finally set in the Energy Agreement was 55 per cent,[50] which was the recommendation made by the Climate Council.[51]

---

[45] ibid 17.

[46] Klimarådet, 'Charges Which Transform' (n 38).

[47] Danish Government, *Regeringsgrundlag Marienborgaftalen 2016. For Et Friere, Rigere Og Mere Trygt Danmark* (Copenhagen, 2016), https://www.regeringen.dk/publikationer-og-aftaletekster/regeringsgrundlag-marienborgaftalen-2016. Quoted (in English translation) in Klimarådet, 'Transition towards 2030' (n 38).

[48] Klimarådet, 'The Role of Biomass in the Green Transition' (n 38).

[49] Klimarådet, 'Fremtidens Vedvarende Energi. 5 Centrale Pointer Om Mål, Udbygning Og Støtte I En Kommende Energiaftale' (2017), https://klimaraadet.dk/da/analyser/fremtidens-vedvarende-energi, 8. Author's translation. In original Danish: 'Regeringens mål er, at mindst 50 pct. af det danske energiforbrug i 2030 skal komme fra vedvarende energi.'

[50] Danish Government, Energiaftale Af 29. Juni 2018 (Energy Agreement of 29th June 2018) (2018), https://efkm.dk/media/12222/energiaftale2018.pdf, 2.

[51] Klimarådet, 'Fremtidens Vedvarende Energi' (n 49) 11.

V. A Citizens' Initiative Proposal for a New CCA

In January 2018, a new scheme for direct democracy was launched in Denmark, in the form of the 'Citizens' Initiative' (Borgerforslag). According to this scheme, any person entitled to vote in Denmark can submit a proposal to be put forward as a motion for a resolution that will be voted on in the Danish Parliament. In order to qualify, a proposal has to be co-sponsored by three people and gain signatures of support from 50,000 citizens who are entitled to vote in parliamentary elections.[52] Proposals have to be submitted in Danish, conform with the Danish Constitution and may not be offensive or discriminatory.[53] The 'Danish Climate Law Now' ('Dansk klimalov nu') proposal, which opened for signatures on 16 January 2019 and reached the required 50,000 signatures within 13 days, was only the fifteenth proposal under the scheme to fit the qualifying criteria and be opened for signatures.[54] Although this did not automatically guarantee a new climate law, it did mean that the Parliament had to discuss the proposal.

The proposal, put forward by Danish citizens working for 11 non-governmental organisations (NGOs), set out six elements that should be contained in the new law: (1) 'Denmark must contribute to achieving the objectives of the Paris Agreement'; (2) 'Five-year interim goals must be set at least 15 years in advance'; (3) 'Climate considerations must be integrated into other policies'; (4) 'The Climate Council must be strengthened and ensured independence'; (5) 'Denmark must focus on developing green solutions'; and (6) 'Denmark must be a driving force in international climate policy'.[55]

The content of the new law as proposed by the NGO campaigners therefore differs greatly from the 2014 CCA and is more aligned with provisions from the 2008 UK Climate Change Act that was identified as inspiration in 2014 without individual provisions being included in the Danish Act. The proposal for a new Danish law along the lines of the Citizens' Initiative proposal would see Denmark legislate targets for GHG emission reductions in line with the objectives of the Paris Agreement: 'The law must commit Denmark to set national climate targets that live up to the Paris Agreement in the short, medium, and long term.'[56] In contrast to the 2014 law that set the vague goal of making Denmark a 'low-emissions society

---

[52] Folketinget, 'Om Borgerforslag', https://www.borgerforslag.dk/om-borgerforslag.

[53] ibid.

[54] Morten Øyen, 'Borgerforslag Om Ny Klimalov Skal Behandles I Folketinget' (*Altinget*, 30 January 2019), https://www.altinget.dk/energi/artikel/borgerforslag-om-ny-klimalov-skal-behandles-i-folketinget.

[55] Troels Christensen, 'Dansk Klimalov Nu' (2019), https://www.borgerforslag.dk/se-og-stoet-forslag/?Id=FT-02233. Author's translation. In original Danish: '1: Danmark skal yde sit bidrag til at nå Paris-aftalens mål. 2: Der skal sættes femårige delmål mindst 15 år frem. 3: Klimahensyn skal integreres i andre politikker. 4: Klimarådet skal styrkes og sikres uafhængighed. 5: Danmark skal satse på udvikling af grønne løsninger. 6: Danmark skal være drivkraft i international klimapolitik.'

[56] Christensen (n 55). Author's translation. In original Danish: 'Loven skal forpligte Danmark til at sætte nationale klimamål, der lever op til Paris-aftalen på kort, mellemlangt og langt sigt.'

in 2050',[57] the proposal for a new law puts forward the case for a 'precisely defined and ambitious long-term goal'.[58] The proposal suggests the Climate Council as the body best placed to set this goal, with the Climate Council also being suggested as the body that should 'assess when Denmark must achieve a net-zero emissions target'.[59]

The second point set out in the proposal for a new law, the idea of five-year interim goals set at least 15 years in advance, is particularly reminiscent of the system of carbon budgets created in the UK Act, which are given as follows:

Carbon budgets

(1)   It is the duty of the Secretary of State –

    (a)   to set for each succeeding period of five years beginning with the period 2008–2012 ('budgetary periods') an amount for the net UK carbon account (the 'carbon budget'), and

    (b)   to ensure that the net UK carbon account for a budgetary period does not exceed the carbon budget.

(2)   The carbon budget for a budgetary period may be set at any time after this Part comes into force, and must be set –

    (a)   for the periods 2008–2012, 2013–2017 and 2018–2022, before 1st June 2009,

    (b)   for any later period, not later than 30th June in the 12th year before the beginning of the period in question.[60]

None of the CCAs currently in force at the nation-state level in Europe other than the UK has introduced such a system of carbon budgets,[61] despite their centrality in the UK Act. However, they are a central component of the 'Citizens' Initiative' proposal, which argued that sub-goals 'will ensure clarity for politicians, companies, municipalities and citizens about the necessary direction and speed of the transition', as well as ensuring that 'there is a constant focus on climate action among all actors'.[62]

Another major difference between the 2014 law and the proposal is that the proposal is rhetorically very closely tied to the Paris Agreement. It argues that:

[T]he Paris Agreement of 2015 commits the world's countries to keeping the global temperature rise well below 2 degrees and striving for 1.5 degrees. The IPCC's latest

---

[57] 'Klimalov', Lov Om Klimarådet, Klimapolitisk Redegørelse Og Fastsættelse Af Nationale Klimamålsætninger (n 1) para 1.

[58] Christensen (n 55). Author's translation. In original Danish: 'et præcist defineret og ambitiøst langsigtet mål'.

[59] ibid. Author's translation. In original Danish: 'Samtidig skal rådet vurdere, hvornår Danmark skal nå et mål om netto nuludslip.'

[60] Climate Change Act 2008, s 4(1)–(2).

[61] Nash and Steurer (n 4).

[62] Christensen (n 55). Author's translation. In original Danish: 'Delmålene skal sikre klarhed for politikere, virksomheder, kommuner og borgere om den nødvendige retning og hastighed i omstillingen og dermed, at der er et konstant fokus på klimahandling blandt alle aktører.'

report shows that even a 2 degree increase will have serious consequences, so it is important that we seek to keep the increase down to 1.5 degrees.[63]

Anchoring new legislation in the Paris Agreement provides a level of specificity in the normative framing of the law that did not exist when the CCA was being negotiated in 2014. It is therefore conceivable that this normative framing will provide a stronger basis for negotiating both a long-term quantified target and strong planning mechanisms such as carbon budgets.

After the rapid collection of the 50,000 signatures required for the Citizens' Initiative, the proposal was debated in the Danish Parliament on 26 February 2019. In his opening speech, Lars Christian Lilleholt, the then Minister for Energy, Utilities and Climate, praised the Citizens' Initiative, emphasising its alignment with government policy:

> The citizens' initiative ... fits well with the government's plan that we will present proposals for a new climate law in the next session. Here, of course, it goes without saying that the 2050 climate neutrality target from the [2018] energy agreement must be written into the law – a target that is fully in line with the Paris Agreement.[64]

During the debate, opposition politicians pushed the Minister on three points in particular. First, the actual level of alignment between the proposal and government policy was questioned. The political party The Alternative (Alternativet) pointed to government figures that suggested a rate of GHG emission reductions that would see net-zero emissions achieved in 2101, a long time after 2050.

Second, with the government only signalling vague support for the proposal, opposition politicians pushed the Minister to clarify whether the government supported all elements of the proposal, with the Social Democrats asking directly: 'Can the government agree with all six principles in the law – yes or no?'[65] In answering, the Minister signalled support for the direction and attitude of all six elements, although relying on the caveat that 'it is clear that it [the proposal] must be translated into concrete action and into a bill, and then we will of course discuss the individual elements'.[66]

---

[63] ibid. Author's translation. In original Danish: 'Paris-aftalen fra 2015 forpligter verdens lande til at holde stigningen i den globale temperatur et godt stykke under 2 grader og stræbe efter 1,5 grader. Klimapanelets seneste rapport viser, at selv en 2 graders stigning vil have alvorlige konsekvenser, så det er vigtigt, at vi søger at holde stigningen nede på 1,5 grader.'

[64] Lars Christian Lilleholt in Folketinget, *Dokumenter Samling 2018–19 (1. Samling) Beslutningsforslag B96 Forhandling (1. Behandling). B96 Forslag Til Folketingsbeslutning Om En Dansk Klimalov Nu (Borgerforslag)* (Copenhagen, Danish Parliament, 2019), https://www.ft.dk/samling/20181/ beslutningsforslag/B96/BEH1-65/forhandling.htm#t68924C542233449782137DDB3807CA3A tab1. Author's translation. In original Danish: 'Borgerforslaget passer samtidig rigtig godt sammen med regeringens plan om, at vi i næste samling vil fremsætte forslag til en ny klimalov. Her giver det selvfølgelig sig selv, at 2050-målet om klimaneutralitet fra energiaftalen skal skrives ind i loven – et mål, som er helt i overensstemmelse med Parisaftalen.'

[65] Jens Joel in ibid. Author's translation. In original Danish: 'Kan regeringen stemme ja til de seks prinsipper – ja eller nej?'

[66] Lars Christian Lilleholt in ibid. Author's translation. In original Danish: 'at det skal omsættes i konkret handling og i lovforslag, og så kommer vi selvfølgelig til at drøfte de enkelte elementer'.

Third, the opposition challenged the government's reluctance to show support for the 2014 CCA, which it did not support in the consensus agreement made between the Social Democrats, the Social Liberal Party, the Socialist People's Party, the Red-Green Alliance and the Conservative People's Party. In the debate, the Socialist People's Party asked whether the government now acknowledged the law,[67] with the Minister responding: 'Yes, we acknowledge it and we believe that there is a need to strengthen the climate law, that is, make it even more ambitious'.[68] This was met with some incredulity from the opposition, who pointed out that 'both the Social Liberals, the Socialist People's Party and other parties have again and again called for the government to acknowledge the first climate law – which has been rejected again and again'.[69]

In April 2019, shortly before the planned date for a second debate and vote on the proposal, in a meeting of the Energy, Utilities and Climate Committee, the government announced that it had been unable to complete work on the proposal and indefinitely postponed its adoption.[70] This was criticised by both opposition parties and green NGOs as tactical manoeuvring in order to avoid a vote on the proposal before elections that were due were called.[71] In the aftermath of delay, the left and centre-left opposition parties – the Social Democrats, the Red-Green Alliance, The Alternative, the Social Liberals and the Socialist People's Party – published a minority opinion emphasising their support for the proposal. They supported not only the principle of a new CCA but were also in favour of closely aligning it with the content of the proposal:

> [T]he climate law must be based on the citizens' initiative, including that: Denmark must make its contribution to reaching the Paris Agreement's target to limit global temperature risk to 1.5 degrees above pre-industrial levels, 5-year interim targets must be set for CO_2 reductions at least 15 years in advance in climate pollution budgets, climate considerations must be integrated into other policies, the Climate Council must be strengthened, have independence guaranteed and continually assess whether Denmark is on the way to reach the stipulated target, Denmark must invest in developing green solutions, and Denmark must strengthen its role as a driving force in international climate policy.[72]

---

[67] Pia Olsen Dyhr in ibid.

[68] Lars Christian Lilleholt in ibid. Author's translation. In original Danish: 'Ja, den anerkender vi, og vi mener, at der er behov for at styrke den klimalov, der er, gøre den endnu mere ambitiøs.'

[69] Pia Olsen Dyhr in ibid. Author's translation. In original Danish: 'har bade Radikale Venstre, SF og andre partier jo igen og igen efterlyst, at regeringen ville anerkende den første klimalov – som jo er blevet afvist igen og igen'.

[70] Jørgen Steen Nielsen, 'Venstre Vælter Tidsplan for Borgerforslag Om Klimalov' (*Information*, 27 April 2019), https://www.information.dk/indland/2019/04/venstre-vaelter-tidsplan-borgerforslag-klimalov.

[71] ibid.

[72] Socialdemokratiet et al, 'Betænkning Til Borgerforslag Om Klimalov Fra S, El, Alt, Rv Og Sf' (Unpublished document, shared by Jens Joel (Member of Parliament for the Social Democrats) on Twitter on 26 June 2019), https://twitter.com/Jens_Joel/status/1121802443157835776. Text also on file with the author. Author's translation. In original Danish: 'Klimaloven skal baseres på borgerforslaget, herunder at: Danmark skal yde sit bidrag til at nå Parisaftalens mål om at begrænse den globale temperaturstigning til 1,5 grader over førindustrielt niveau, der skal sættes 5-årige delmål for

However, a vote was not held and when Parliament was suspended on 7 May 2019 following the announcement of elections for 5 June 2019, the proposal for a new CCA had not progressed any further.

VI. The 2019 Agreement on a Climate Law

The 2019 parliamentary elections in Denmark resulted in a change of government away from the three-party Liberal Party, Liberal Alliance and Conservative People's Party coalition to a Social Democrat minority government supported by the Socialist People's Party, the Red-Green Alliance and the Social Liberals.[73]

In the 'Platform for Government' published as part of the process of government formation, the 'climate crisis'[74] is extremely prominent, headlining the first page as well as being the topic of the first substantive section of the document. The headline amounts to a strong statement, reading:

> We must take the lead in the fight against the climate crisis. Denmark must significantly increase ambition on climate, environment and nature and assume international leadership for the green transition. The Danish parliament can become the greenest parliament in the world that doesn't just do something, but does that which is needed to live up to the Paris Agreement.[75]

The 'Platform for Government' also sets out the target of reducing GHG emissions by 70 per cent by 2030.[76] Furthermore, the Climate Council will be tasked with assisting the new government to decide on reduction targets and instruments that will be compliant with the Paris Agreement's goals.[77] The 'Platform for Government' also signals the intention to legislate on a CCA, stating that 'in the next parliamentary year, a new government will present a proposal for a climate law with binding interim targets and binding long-term targets'.[78]

CO2-reduktioner mindst 15 år frem med udgangspunkt i klimaforureningsbudgetter, klimahensyn skal integreres i andre politikker, Klimarådet skal styrkes, sikres uafhængighed og løbende vurdere om Danmark er på vej til at opdylde de fastsatte mål, Danmark skal satse på udvikling af grønne løsninger, og Danmark skal styrke sin rolle som drivkraft i international klimapolitik.'

[73] Emma Qvirin Holst, 'Nu Er Det Officielt: Mette Frederiksen Kan Danne En Ny Regering' (*Altinget*, 26 June 2019), https://www.altinget.dk/artikel/nu-er-det-officielt-mette-frederiksen-kan-danne-en-ny-regering.

[74] Socialdemokraterne et al, 'Politisk Forståelse Mellem Socialdemokratiet, Radikale Venstre, Sf Og Enhedslisten: Retfærdig Retning for Danmark' (2019), https://politiken.dk/incoming/static/7271359-Aftale.pdf. 1. Author's translation. In original Danish: 'klimakrisen'.

[75] ibid 1. Author's translation. In original Danish: 'Vi skal gå forrest i kampen mod klimakrisen. Danmark skal markant hæve ambitionerne for klima, miljø og natur og påtage sig det internationale lederskab for den grønne omstilling. Folketinget kan blive det grønnste parlament i verden, der ikke kun gør noget, men som gør det, der skal til for at leve op til Paris-aftalen.'

[76] ibid 3.

[77] ibid.

[78] ibid. Author's translation. In original Danish: 'I det førstkommende folketingsår vil en ny regering fremlægge et forslag til en klimalov med bindende delmål og bindende langsigtede mål.'

Following in the tradition of broad agreements on energy and climate, the Social Democrat government undertook negotiations with the other political parties in Denmark to secure a broad agreement on a new CCA. This agreement was published on 6 December 2019 supported by the Social Democrats, the Liberal Party, the Danish People's Party, the Social Liberals, the Socialist People's Party, the Red-Green Alliance, the Conservatives People's Party and The Alternative.[79] This is a much broader political consensus than was possible in 2014, straddling both the left and right of the political spectrum. The agreement sets out the central building blocks of a new CCA to be passed in 2020, organised under five headings:

I.   Interim targets and climate action plans.
II.   Annual climate programmes and a duty to act.
III. Organisation of the Climate Council.
IV.   Global reporting and strategy.
V.   Calculation methods.[80]

The first chapter on interim targets and climate action plans contains the provisions that garnered the most attention in the Citizens' Initiative proposal and during the election campaign. The parties to the agreement are agreed on a 'mechanism for setting interim targets',[81] which entails that 'every fifth year the sitting government must set a climate target with a ten-year perspective'.[82] The first interim target for 2030 will be set in 2020 and will be set at the level of a 70 per cent reduction in GHG emissions compared to 1990 levels. The long-term goal is to reach climate-neutrality in 2050 at the latest.[83] The interim targets must be set following consideration of the framework of the Paris Agreement, developments in climate science, the 2050 climate-neutrality goal and the objective of limiting global warming to 1.5°C and following the involvement of the Climate Council. Furthermore, to prevent backsliding, an interim target may not be less ambitious than the previous target.[84] The interim targets are complemented by climate action plans, which are also to be prepared by the government at least every fifth year and at a minimum in conjunction with the setting of the interim targets, with the plans

---

[79] Folketinget, 'Aftale Om Klimalov' (2019), https://kefm.dk/media/12965/aftale-om-klimalov-af-6-december-2019.pdf.

[80] ibid 2. Author's translation. In original Danish: 'I. Delmål & klimahandlingsplan II. Årligt klimaprogram & handlepligt III. Klimarådets organisering IV. Global afrapportering & strategi V. Opgørelsesmetoder.'

[81] ibid 3. Author's translation. In original Danish: 'en mekanisme for fastsættelse af delmål'.

[82] ibid. Author's translation. In original Danish: 'Mekanismen medfører, at den til enhver tid siddende regering, hvert femte år skal fastsættes klimamål med et tiårigt perspektiv.'

[83] ibid.

[84] ibid.

also having a 10-year perspective.[85] This mechanism is very much reminiscent of the UK's system of carbon budgets, which set targets and plans ahead of time for GHG emission reductions to be achieved over five-year periods leading up to the long-term targets.

The second chapter explicitly sets out a duty to act that is attached to the 70 per cent target for 2030 and the long-term goal of climate neutrality that falls on the Climate, Energy and Utilities Minister. Whether this duty is adhered to is the subject of parliamentary oversight, aided by regular reporting to Parliament by the minister.[86] In the third chapter, provisions are included to strengthen the independence of the Climate Council, in particular changing the appointment process so that the chairperson is selected by the members of the Climate Council rather than appointed by the minister, as well as adding an additional two members to the Climate Council.[87] The parties to the agreement have also agreed to establish a Climate Dialogue Forum (Klimadialogforum) in which stakeholders (for example, sectoral organisations, think tanks, green organisations, labour organisations and ministers) are represented and are able to give written comments to the Climate Council's recommendations and advice.[88]

In the fourth chapter, Denmark's envisaged role within global climate politics is set out. Denmark will work towards the 1.5°C goal included in the Paris Agreement and will play the role of a 'global driving force in international climate policy'.[89] There will also be a focus on cooperation, especially with large emitters and developing countries, and including a focus on the export of Danish energy technologies.[90] The final chapter deals with specificities regarding calculation methods. In particular, the 70 per cent target for 2030 will be measured as an average over the years 2029–31 in order to avoid fluctuation in individual years.[91]

The agreement on the climate law that is to be introduced in early 2020 is a great deal more substantial than the 2014 CCA and is much closer to the UK and Scottish CCAs, which provided only very loose inspiration in 2014. The new agreement contains provisions that are much more closely aligned to some of the specific provisions of the UK CCA (and that were not contained in the 2014 CCA), in particular the interim target mechanism, which is very similar to the UK's system of carbon budgets.

[85] ibid.
[86] ibid 4.
[87] ibid 6.
[88] ibid 7.
[89] ibid 8. Author's translation. In original Danish: 'global drivkraft i international klimapolitik'.
[90] ibid.
[91] ibid.

VII. Conclusion

With such a broad political agreement behind it, it is very likely that the new Danish CCA that is planned for early 2020 will broadly resemble the 2019 cross-party agreement and will not face many challenges in the legislative process. The 2020 CCA will therefore represent a significant strengthening of the Danish framework legislation on climate change, with both quantitatively higher targets and more stringent procedures at its core. In contrast to the 2014 CCA, which is pre-Paris Agreement legislation, the new CCA will also be able to draw on the context that the Paris Agreement provides, in particular the headline objective of limiting global warming to 1.5°C. This has provided on the one hand a guiding line for the political discussions surrounding new legislation and on the other hand a concrete global framework (which Denmark has ratified) that new legislation should be compliant with.

Going forward, it will be interesting to follow the process of translating the political agreement from late 2019 into concrete legislation and its implementation. In particular, it will be interesting to observe whether the future-oriented target-setting and planning processes that the new legislation will introduce will lead to increased stability in the implementation of climate policy in Denmark, even when changes of government occur. Finally, a new avenue for research will be the influence that new Danish legislation may have on climate policy beyond Denmark in both the EU and global arenas. Here, it will be interesting to observe whether the Danish legislation is used as a model for other legislation that is developed or whether the new targets that Denmark has set for GHG emission reductions are used to drive higher ambitions elsewhere.

6

Ireland's Climate Action and Low Carbon Development Act 2015

Symbolic Legislation, Trojan Horse, Stepping Stone?

ANDREW JACKSON

I. Introduction

'Serious planning and environmental law of a domestic variety are all but non-existent in Ireland' wrote Dillon in 1999.[1] While much has changed legally in Ireland since then,[2] domestic environmental law innovations remain relatively rare[3] and politically, strong vestiges of reluctance persist when it comes to environmental policy and law.[4] Addressing the European Parliament in 2018, the Taoiseach (head of government) Leo Varadkar described Ireland as a 'laggard' when it comes to climate change,[5] and this is confirmed by international rankings and by Ireland's high per capita emissions, the third highest in the EU.[6]

---

[1] Sara Dillon, 'The Mirage of EC Environmental Federalism in a Reluctant Member State Jurisdiction' (1999) 8 *New York University Environmental Law Journal* 1, 21.

[2] See, eg, Áine Ryall, 'Challenges and Opportunities for Irish Planning and Environmental Law' (2018) 25(3) *Irish Planning and Environmental Law Journal* 104; and Garrett Simons, 'The Increasing Influence of EU Law on Irish Planning Law' (2015) 22(2) *Irish Planning and Environmental Law Journal* 63. For a slightly different take, see Diarmuid Torney and Roderic O'Gorman, 'A Laggard in Good Times and Bad? The Limited Impact of EU Membership on Ireland's Climate Change and Environmental Policy' (2019) 34(4) *Irish Political Studies* 575.

[3] For a discussion of some important exceptions in the climate policy context, see Torney and O'Gorman (n 2) s 4.

[4] Torney and O'Gorman (n 2).

[5] Niall Sargent, 'Taoiseach Tells EU He is Not Proud of Ireland's Role as Europe's Climate "Laggard"' (*The Green News*, 18 January 2018).

[6] See Diarmuid Torney, 'Climate Laws in Small European States: Symbolic Legislation and Limits of Diffusion in Ireland and Finland' (2019) 28(6) *Environmental Politics* 1124, 1125–26.

Several interrelated factors are key to understanding Ireland's general approach to climate change and its specific approach to domestic climate legislation:

- First, there is the historical prominence of agriculture: as the state agency Teagasc wrote in 1991, 'the agricultural sector is of significant importance to the national economy in terms of food security, volume and value of output, employment and net foreign exchange earnings ... Agriculture is the dominant land-use activity in Ireland and claims about 82% of the surface area of the country'.[7]

- Second, while the agricultural sector's role in the national economy has in relative terms 'inexorably declined' over the past few decades,[8] Ireland's agricultural lobby remains disproportionately powerful. The main lobby group – the Irish Farmers' Association (IFA) – has more than 72,000 members,[9] about 70 staff,[10] an annual turnover of €16 million,[11] owns an influential newspaper (the *Irish Farmers' Journal*)[12] and maintains a Brussels office as well as a large headquarters and conference centre in Dublin. As Chubb explains, '[i]t is without doubt among the country's most effective pressure groups: it is also among the most vociferous'[13] and according to Murphy, it has 'retained its influence in the policy process despite the shrinking size of the agricultural sector'.[14]

- Third, agriculture remains the single largest contributor to Ireland's greenhouse gas (GHG) emissions, accounting for 34 per cent of the total.[15] This is anomalously high. The dominance of beef and dairy farming and the relative absence of heavy industry go some way towards explaining this high percentage contribution.

- Fourth, from the early days of Ireland's response to climate change, an official narrative developed, from state level down, that climate change would be *beneficial* for Irish agriculture. This perspective informed Ireland's first

---

[7] Teagasc, 'Agriculture' in Brendan McWilliams (ed), *Climate Change: Studies on the Implications for Ireland* (Dublin, Department of the Environment, 1991) 6.

[8] Brendan Kearney, 'The Past, Present and Future of Irish Agriculture' (IIEA Working Paper, Dublin, 2010).

[9] IFA, Annual Report 2018.

[10] Shane Phelan and Darragh McCullough, 'Former Farming Secretary Smith in Defamation Claim against IFA' (*Irish Independent*, 7 November 2019).

[11] IFA (n 9).

[12] Technically owned by the Agricultural Trust, but the IFA's President is automatically a Director of the Trust, and half the board of directors is nominated by the IFA: Constitution of the Agricultural Trust (adopted by special resolution passed on 8 June 2015).

[13] Basil Chubb, *The Government and Politics of Ireland*, 3rd edn (London, Addison Wesley Longman, 1992) 113.

[14] Gary Murphy, 'The Policy-Making Process' in John Coakley and Michael Gallagher (eds), *Politics in the Republic of Ireland*, 6th edn (Abingdon, Routledge, 2018) 280.

[15] EPA, 'Ireland's Provisional Greenhouse Gas Emissions 1990–2018' (October 2019).

national climate strategy in 1993, which listed as the first bullet point under the implications of climate change for Ireland: 'broadly beneficial effects for the agriculture sector'.[16] This view influenced and arguably continues to influence the views of prominent figures in Irish agriculture.[17]

- Fifth, Ireland's Climate Act was adopted under a coalition government in which Fine Gael was the senior partner. As Gallagher and Marsh explain: 'Farmers, especially larger farmers (those with more than 50 acres), have long been the backbone of Fine Gael support.'[18]

- Finally, it is worth noting that Ireland went abruptly from being permitted to increase its emissions to being required to rapidly reduce them, based on its transition during the Celtic Tiger years from a relatively poor to a relatively wealthy country in EU terms. Thus, under Ireland's 1993 climate strategy, the goal was to limit the growth in CO_2 emissions to a maximum *increase* of 20 per cent between 1990 and 2000;[19] similarly, under the EU's burden sharing agreement pursuant to the Kyoto Protocol, Ireland was entitled to *increase* its emissions by 13 per cent between 1990 and the 2008–12 reference period.[20] Ireland went from this to having one of the highest reduction targets in the EU under the Effort Sharing Decision of 2009, based on its relatively high per capita gross domestic product (GDP) at that time: a required reduction in non-Emissions Trading System (ETS) emissions of 20 per cent in 2020 compared to 2005 levels.[21] Thus, Ireland has been legally obliged (yet has failed) to perform a screeching emissions U-turn pursuant to EU law over the past decade.

Given these factors, it is perhaps surprising that it took only a decade from the launch of Friends of the Earth's 'The Big Ask' campaign in May 2005 – which first called for framework climate legislation in the UK before the campaign rolled out across Europe[22] – for Ireland to adopt its own climate law, entitled the Climate Action and Low Carbon Development Act 2015 (hereinafter the 'Climate Act').

[16] Department of the Environment, *Climate Change: CO2 Abatement Strategy* (Dublin, The Stationery Office, 1993). See also the scientific studies that informed this first strategy: 'Executive Summary' in McWilliams (n 7) v.

[17] See, eg, Paddy O'Keeffe, 'CO_2 Mania Spells Danger' (*Irish Farmers' Journal*, 2 February 2008); and John Gibbons, 'Farmers Journal is Undermined by Climate-Change Denial' (*The Village*, 17 July 2017).

[18] Michael Gallagher and Michael Marsh, 'Party Membership in Ireland: The Members of Fine Gael' (2005) 10(4) *Party Politics* 407, 412; and Kevin Cunningham and Michael Marsh, 'Voting Behaviour' in Coakley and Gallagher (n 14) 143.

[19] Department of the Environment (n 16).

[20] Council Decision of 25 April 2002 concerning the approval, on behalf of the European Community, of the Kyoto Protocol to the United Nations Framework Convention on Climate Change and the joint fulfilment of commitments thereunder, ELI, http://data.europa.eu/eli/dec/2002/358/oj.

[21] Decision No 406/2009/EC of the European Parliament and of the Council of 23 April 2009 on the effort of Member States to reduce their greenhouse gas emissions to meet the Community's greenhouse gas emission reduction commitments up to 2020, ELI, http://data.europa.eu/eli/dec/2009/406/oj.

[22] See Neil Carter and Mike Childs, 'Friends of the Earth as a Policy Entrepreneur: "The Big Ask" Campaign for a UK Climate Change Act' (2018) 27(6) *Environmental Politics* 994.

Diarmuid Torney has published on the development of Ireland's Climate Act[23] and this chapter does not propose to traverse identical ground. Rather, building on Torney's work, an historical narrative is provided here as a vital backdrop to the issues under consideration in this chapter, with the discussion taking as its starting point the following concluding remark from Torney: 'Whether [Ireland's] climate legislation is anything more than symbolic depends partly on one's point of view, but also depends on how it is implemented. As time passes it will be important to study not just the letter but also the practice of national climate laws.'[24] More than four years on from the Act's adoption, we now have some experience of the Act in practice to inform additional insights.

With this in mind, this chapter examines three potential characterisations of the Climate Act: the first views the Act as symbolic legislation; the second examines the Act as an alleged Trojan horse, subject to litigation despite the government's apparent intent to avoid this; and the third examines the Act as a stepping stone en route to more meaningful regulatory intervention.

II. The Circuitous Route to Ireland's Climate Act

A. Phase 1 (2005–11): Competing Legislative Proposals of Relative Ambition

In opposition from 2002 to 2007, Ireland's Green Party introduced a Climate Change Targets Bill in November 2005. The Bill included, inter alia, emissions reduction targets of 15–30 per cent by 2020 and 60–80 per cent by 2050 compared to 1990, with a view to contributing towards limiting the increase in global average temperature to less than 2°C above pre-industrial levels, then regarded as the threshold for dangerous anthropogenic interference with the climate system. The Bill did not have government support and was rapidly defeated.

Friends of the Earth's 'The Big Ask' campaign had launched in the UK in May 2005, several months before the Green Party's failed legislative attempt in Ireland, and Friends of the Earth Ireland (FOEI) and the Stop Climate Chaos coalition[25] (of which FOEI is a founding member) then took the lead in spearheading a campaign for national framework climate legislation in Ireland, beginning in 2006 with FOEI calling for a 'Climate Security Act' mandating 3 per cent year-on-year

---

[23] See, eg, Diarmuid Torney, 'If at First You Don't Succeed: The Development of Climate Change Legislation in Ireland' (2017) 32(2) *Irish Political Studies* 247; and n 6 above.

[24] Torney (n 23) 263.

[25] An Irish coalition of development, environmental, youth and faith-based NGOs that launched in April 2007 with the adoption of a climate law as one of its first asks: Stop Climate Chaos, 'Launch of Stop Climate Chaos' (25 April 2007).

cuts in emissions[26] and establishing an independent body to monitor progress. The campaign intensified in advance of Ireland's May 2007 general election;[27] to this end, in April 2007, FOEI proposed draft legislation (drafted by legal academic and Labour Party senator Ivana Bacik)[28] entitled the Climate Protection Bill 2007. This took Ireland's National Climate Change Strategy 2007–12 as its starting point[29] and mirrored many of the 'Big Asks' in the UK context. The Bill required, inter alia, the drawing up of a national GHG emissions budget for 2010–50, including an annual reduction of 3 per cent per annum from a mandated target figure in 2010 to ensure a reduction of at least 60 per cent in emissions by 2050 (compared to 1990);[30] annual GHG emissions budget reports were to be produced, including long-term and short-term strategies to achieve the targets; actions were to be taken if targets were not met, including required strategy revision to get back on course; and a Commission on Climate Change was to be established to oversee progress.

Ireland's May 2007 general election returned a coalition government, with the Green Party entering power for the first time, forming part of a three-way coalition with Fianna Fáil as the largest partner and the Progressive Democrats and the Green Party as the smaller coalition partners, plus support for the government from four independents. The Green Party secured two senior ministerial portfolios: communications, energy and natural resources; and the environment, community and local government. While the Programme for Government that emerged included a commitment to reduce emissions by 3 per cent per annum, it did not include a commitment to create a Climate Act, making the emissions reduction commitment a matter for (at best) political rather than legal accountability.[31]

Ireland's Labour Party – in opposition during the lifetime of this coalition – pursued a domestic climate law at this time, proposing draft legislation that did not make it on to the statute book: in 2007, Labour senator Ivana Bacik introduced her FOEI-backed Climate Protection Bill to the Seanad (the upper house) and in 2009, the Labour TD (Teachta Dála: member of Dáil Éireann) Eamon Gilmore introduced into the Dáil (the lower house) a Climate Change Bill that was clearly modelled on the UK's Climate Change Act 2008.

---

[26] An approach subsequently adopted in Scotland's Climate Change (Scotland) Act 2009 (s 3). This is discussed in Thomas L Muinzer, *Climate and Energy Governance for the UK Low Carbon Transition: The Climate Change Act 2008* (London, Palgrave Macmillan, 2018).

[27] See FOEI, 'A New National Climate Change Strategy for Ireland: Friends of the Earth's Submission to the Government's Review of Climate Change Policy' (October 2006); FOEI, 'Only a Law Can Ensure Ireland Acts on Climate Change' (6 November 2006); FOEI, 'Climate Strategy is Tinkering When We Need Transformation' (2 April 2007); FOEI, 'Friends of the Earth Publishes Climate Protection Bill' (12 April 2007); FOEI, 'Campaign Urges Candidates to Act for Climate' (14 May 2007).

[28] FOEI, 'Seanad to Debate Climate Protection Bill' (1 October 2007).

[29] ibid.

[30] Ireland's emissions had risen not fallen since 1990, such that the starting point for the 3 per cent per annum reduction was above 100 per cent in 2010.

[31] See Fianna Fáil, Green Party, Progressive Democrats, 'Programme for Government 2007–2012'.

These Labour Party initiatives and the UK's adoption of its Climate Act in 2008[32] served to keep up the pressure on the Green Party, which – following the onset of the global financial crisis – found its hand strengthened somewhat domestically, at least in the short term, by the reduction of the coalition government's majority by way of parliamentarians resigning from Fianna Fáil.[33] Delegates at the Green Party's annual convention in March 2009 adopted a motion calling for the introduction of a climate law as 'the best means of ensuring that Ireland meets its greenhouse gas reduction targets'.[34] When the coalition's Programme for Government fell to be renegotiated in October 2009 after the coalition parties' disastrous performance in Ireland's local elections in June, a commitment to introduce a climate law enshrining, inter alia, a 3 per cent annual reduction target and an annual carbon budget was then included.[35]

In the same month – October 2009 – a parliamentary committee (the Joint Committee on Climate Change and Energy Security),[36] with Labour's Liz McManus as rapporteur, published a report entitled 'The Case for Climate Change Law'.[37] The report reviewed climate legislation in various jurisdictions and contained a detailed statutory framework ('Heads of Bill') for climate legislation 'that has all party support'.[38] The Joint Committee's work maintained the pressure on the Green Party, whose leader John Gormley announced a framework of proposed government-backed climate legislation shortly before travelling to the COP15 meeting of the United Nations Framework Convention on Climate Change (UNFCCC) in Copenhagen in December 2009.[39] The dynamic between the Joint Committee's climate law work and the government's work in the same area is worth mentioning, and is captured well in this criticism from Fine Gael's Simon Coveney, then in opposition:

> [W]e [via the Joint Committee process] are trying to put together legislation which all parties will buy into and will support if in Government in the future. We are trying to put a new institutional framework in place that can survive different parties in Government with different agendas, priorities and ideology over the next 40 years. It is regrettable that the Government has decided to adopt the tactic that it will not accept a draft Bill from the all-party committee which it could change and amend but instead has decided

---

[32] FOEI, 'World's First Climate Law Should Spur Debate in the Oireachtas' (29 October 2008).

[33] Harry McGee, 'Coalition Majority Wiped out by Sligo TDs' Resignations' (*Irish Times*, 6 August 2009).

[34] FOEI, 'Green Party Calls for a Climate Law' (10 March 2009).

[35] Fianna Fáil and the Green Party, 'Renewed Programme for Government' (10 October 2009).

[36] A cross-party parliamentary committee, comprising members from both houses.

[37] Joint Committee on Climate Change and Energy Security, 'Second Report: The Case for Climate Change Law, Together with Heads of Bill: A Comparative Review of Existing and Planned Legislation in Other Jurisdictions' (October 2009).

[38] Joint Committee on Climate Change and Energy Security, 'Oireachtas Committee Publishes Climate Change Bill' (13 October 2010).

[39] Department of the Environment, Heritage and Local Government, 'Framework for Climate Change Bill 2010' (December 2009).

to produce its own Bill ... No political party and no Minister has a monopoly of wisdom on this issue. We should not try to play politics nor look for recognition or thanks for being the first to introduce a climate change Bill. For the first time in our history we should aim for Government and Opposition, collectively, putting together legislation which all future Governments will be able to implement.[40]

Unfortunately, this argument was not heeded and, as Torney highlights, the 'political and economic context continued to deteriorate over the course of 2010', with significant opposition within government and the civil service to the idea of a climate law: 'Among government departments, the Departments of Agriculture, Finance and Taoiseach were most strongly opposed to the idea of a climate law, but even civil servants within the Department of Environment did not support the proposal.'[41] Kennedy was therefore prescient to conclude in April 2010 that: 'Proposals for climate change legislation are becoming more concrete, but we are clearly some months, if not years, from seeing these passed by the Oireachtas [ie, the Irish legislature] and coming into force. The road ahead is murky, twisty and full of dead ends.'[42]

While the Green Party–Fianna Fáil coalition made slow progress with its Bill during 2010,[43] the Joint Committee produced its second report in October 2010, this time comprising a full draft bill that drew heavily on the UK's Climate Change Act 2008. However, 'a crucial distinction from other climate change legislation', per the rapporteur McManus, was that the Taoiseach as head of government would hold statutory responsibility for ensuring that climate targets were met.[44]

The Green Party welcomed the publication of the Joint Committee's Bill, commenting that: 'The Bill includes some good elements which we will take into consideration in the finalisation of our own Climate Change Bill ... [which is] ... very well advanced.'[45] At this time, of course, the financial crisis was reaching a crescendo in Ireland, with speculation building in late 2010 that Ireland would require an international bailout. On 21 November, the state formally applied for multibillion euro aid[46] and the political fallout was swift: the following day, the

---

[40] Simon Coveney, 'Fifth Report of the Joint Committee on Climate Change and Energy Security: Motion', Dáil Éireann debate (11 November 2010).

[41] Torney (n 23) 254.

[42] Rónán Kennedy, 'Climate Change Law and Policy after Copenhagen' (2010) 17(3) *Irish Planning and Environmental Law Journal* 101.

[43] FOEI, 'Have the Greens Delivered on Climate Change?' (26 November 2010). The Progressive Democrats were no longer part of the coalition, the party having formally dissolved in 2009. However, its two TDs continued to support the government as independents for most of the government's term.

[44] Liz McManus, 'Fifth Report of the Joint Committee on Climate Change and Energy Security: Motion', Dáil Éireann debate (11 November 2010). For a discussion of the advisability of this, see Conor Linehan, 'UK and Irish Domestic Greenhouse Gas Reduction Targets: Justiciability, Enforceability and Political Context' (2013) 21(2) *Environmental Liability* 45, 55–56.

[45] FOEI, 'Gormley and Cuffe Welcome Oireachtas Committee Bill' (13 October 2010).

[46] Harry McGee and Arthur Beesley, 'EU Approves Irish Request for Multibillion Euro Aid' (*Irish Times*, 22 November 2010).

Green Party announced that it wanted a general election in the second half of January 2011.[47] In the run-up to Christmas 2010, the Green Party then came under intense pressure[48] to publish its long-promised Climate Bill, finally doing so in the form of the Climate Change Response Bill 2010 on 23 December.[49] The Party sought to progress the legislation rapidly before the general election, but faced 'particularly strong opposition from both the business lobby group IBEC and the Irish Farmers' Association'.[50] The IFA claimed that the proposed measures went beyond what was required by EU law[51] and would decimate the national herd, citing Teagasc figures.[52] The IFA's intensive lobbying continued into early 2011,[53] assisted by IBEC, which claimed that the Bill's targets would be 'hugely damaging to Ireland's economic competitiveness unless they are revised'.[54]

Such opposition was matched within the apparatus of parliament[55] and government (as noted above), with the Attorney General's Office amongst the opposition.[56] A key sticking point was the question of whether the inclusion of targets could result in litigation against the state if the targets were not met.[57] The fudge adopted in the end was that targets would be included in the Bill, but they would be expressly non-justiciable.[58]

Politically, the government's Bill was criticised for failing to secure the sort of cross-party support that had been a feature of the Joint Committee's work,[59]

---

[47] Jennifer Wade, 'Greens Call for a General Election to Be Called in January' (*The Journal.ie*, 22 November 2010).

[48] See FOEI, 'Have the Greens Delivered on Climate Change?' (26 November 2010); FOEI, 'Greens' Legacy Hangs by a Thread, Depends on Delivering Climate Bill' (1 December 2010); FOEI, 'Snowmen Protest Demands Climate Bill as the Green Party's Legacy on Climate Hangs in the Balance' (4 December 2010); FOEI, 'Gormley's Carbon Budget Speech is Welcome But Where is the Climate Bill?' (16 December 2010); FOEI, 'What a Week, Broken Promises, Carbon Budgets and More Promises' (22 December 2010); plus the concerted public action 'All I want for Christmas is a Climate Bill' organised by FOEI, as mentioned in the last-mentioned press release.

[49] FOEI, 'Friends of the Earth Hail Landmark Publication of Climate Bill' (23 December 2010).

[50] Torney (n 23) 255.

[51] This point was disputed during the parliamentary debates, but was not helped by the Green Party's odd choice of 2008 as the baseline for its 2020 target and the complex calculation method for that target.

[52] Sean MacConnell, 'IFA Seeks to Delay Climate Change Bill' (*Irish Times*, 10 January 2011). Friends of the Earth accused the IFA of 'scaremongering': Sean MacConnell, 'Farmers Concerned over Climate Bill' (*Irish Times*, 23 December 2010). See also Tara Connolly, 'A Climate Bill Post-mortem' (*ThinkorSwim.ie*, 11 February 2011).

[53] Frank Farragher, 'Labour Stance on Climate Bill to Become Big Election Issue' (*Connacht Tribune*, 21 January 2011); and Frank McDonald, 'Opponents Turn up the Heat on Green Party's Climate Change Bill' (*Irish Times*, 17 January 2011).

[54] Frank McDonald and Deaglán de Bréadún, 'Greens Want to Enact Climate Bill before Election' (*Irish Times*, 24 December 2010).

[55] The Oireachtas Committee on Agriculture called for the Bill to be postponed: Deaglán de Bréadún, 'Future for Legislation on Climate in Serious Doubt' (*Irish Times*, 22 January 2011).

[56] See Torney (n 6); and Harry McGee, 'Climate Change Bill May Go to Seanad' (*Irish Times*, 3 January 2011).

[57] Torney (n 6).

[58] On which see Linehan (n 44).

[59] Paudie Coffey, Seanad Éireann debate, Climate Change Response Bill 2010: Second Stage (13 January 2011).

and having attempted to progress its Bill rapidly before the impending general election, which had been called for 11 March, the Green Party ultimately withdrew from government on 23 January 2011, leading to an earlier-than-planned general election.[60] The Green Party–Fianna Fáil coalition's Bill fell with the dissolution of the Oireachtas and with it vanished hopes for relatively ambitious climate legislation.

B. Phase 2 (2011–15): 'Realistic' Climate Legislation

The 2011 general election resulted in a Fine Gael (76 seats) and Labour (37 seats) coalition, with the Green Party losing all of its seats and Fianna Fáil losing 51 of its previous 71.[61] Both Fine Gael and Labour had committed in their manifestos to pass climate legislation, albeit that the coalition agreement fell short of their individual commitments to enshrine targets in law:[62] 'We will publish a Climate Change Bill which will provide certainty surrounding government policy and provide a clear pathway for emissions reductions, in line with negotiated EU 2020 targets.'[63]

Fine Gael 'fixer'[64] Phil Hogan was appointed Minister for the Environment, Community and Local Government by the new government. Many were sceptical of Hogan's commitment to environmental matters, and their fears were not assuaged by the revelation that Fine Gael's leading environmental policy adviser was a climate change sceptic.[65] In March 2011, Hogan stated: 'I will be implementing a Climate Change Act, which John Gormley [of the Green Party] failed to do. It will be a different type of Bill. We will meet our 2020 targets by working with our EU partners, not by isolating ourselves.'[66] Six months later, in September 2011, Hogan announced that a review (*another* review) of national policy on climate change was under way within his department with a view to charting 'an ambitious

---

[60] Green Party statement, (*Irish Times*, 24 January 2011).

[61] Diarmaid Ferriter, 'Recapturing Relevance a Huge Challenge for FF' (*Irish Times*, 1 March 2011).

[62] Fine Gael committed in its 2011 manifesto to 'legislate for a climate change law that sets the Kyoto and EU2020 targets in national legislation but only on the basis of all party agreement', while Labour said it would 'pass Labour's Climate Change Bill to set legally binding carbon reduction targets in line with EU targets'.

[63] Fine Gael and Labour, 'Government for National Recovery 2011–2016'.

[64] See Harry McGee, 'Career Politician Has Reputation as a Strategist: Kenny-Loyalist Credited with Helping Defeat Leadership Challenge' (*Irish Times*, 11 September 2014).

[65] See John Gibbons, 'The Viscount, the Architect and Phil Hogan' (*ThinkorSwim.ie*, 13 March 2011); and Frank McDonald, 'FG Adviser a Sceptic on Climate Change' (*Irish Times*, 12 March 2011). Northern Ireland of course faced the even worse situation of having a Minister for the Environment (2008–09), Sammy Wilson, who denied human-induced climate change; see Thomas L Muinzer, 'Warming up: Northern Ireland's Developing Response to Climate Change in the Context of UK Devolution' (2016) *UKELA E-Law*, September/October, 19–22.

[66] Mary Minihan, 'Hogan to Review 2010 Planning Legislation' (*Irish Times*, 23 March 2011).

but realistic way forward'.[67] At the beginning of October, he participated in a private seminar organised by the business lobby IBEC, which drew heavy criticism from environmentalists.[68] This intensified when, just one month later, on publishing the internal review of national climate policy he had announced in September, the Minister announced that a climate change bill was no longer a priority and that he 'wanted to concentrate on other initiatives and policies before turning to legislation'.[69] The move was welcomed by the IFA and IBEC.[70]

Appearing before a parliamentary committee in December 2011, Hogan clarified that he intended to fulfil the commitment in the Programme for Government to bring forward climate legislation within the lifetime of the government, but argued that 'we must develop policy first and underpin it with legislation as required'.[71] He therefore announced a three-pronged approach to policy development: first, he would ask the secretariat of the National Economic and Social Council (NESC) to carry out an analysis to inform policy development; second, he announced that a public consultation would run in early 2012; and, third, he would continue to pursue mitigation initiatives through a cabinet committee and relevant government departments.[72] This was the very epitome of 'go slow' on climate legislation – 'paralysis by analysis' as Tara Connolly put it.[73] Opposition politicians tried to keep the pressure on the government around this time by introducing as private members' bills the Energy Security and Climate Change Bill 2012[74] and a Climate Change Bill 2013,[75] the latter of which sought to resurrect the Joint Committee's Bill of 2010. Both Bills sought, inter alia, to enshrine emissions reduction targets in domestic law, but neither bill progressed far.

In a February 2013 debate, Minister Hogan softened people up for a government bill without targets, and this continued with a report in the *Irish Times* that broke the news officially, reporting that the Heads of Bill to be taken to cabinet would 'not provide for binding targets for emission reductions, nor a powerful independent commission to ensure Government compliance'.[76] The Bill, reported the *Irish Times*, would be based on the report Minister Hogan had commissioned

---

[67] Frank McDonald, 'Climate Change Policy Review Has Begun, Says Hogan' (*Irish Times*, 16 September 2011).

[68] Frank McDonald, 'Friends of the Earth Criticises Hogan over Climate Seminar' (*Irish Times*, 4 October 2011). Hogan offered a defence in a letter to the *Irish Times*: Phil Hogan, 'Climate Change Priority' (*Irish Times*, 8 November 2011).

[69] Harry McGee, 'Hogan Shifts Policy on Climate Change as Bill "Not a Priority"' (*Irish Times*, 3 November 2011).

[70] Harry McGee, 'Coalition's Climate Policy Shift Condemned' (*Irish Times*, 4 November 2011).

[71] Joint Committee on the Environment, Transport, Culture and the Gaeltacht, 'Climate Change Policy: Discussion with the Minister for the Environment, Community and Local Government' (15 December 2011).

[72] ibid.

[73] McGee (n 70).

[74] Promoted by independent TD Catherine Murphy.

[75] Promoted by Sinn Féin, working with FOEI and Stop Climate Chaos.

[76] Harry McGee, 'New Climate Bill to Set No Binding CO2 Targets' (*Irish Times*, 11 February 2013).

from the NESC Secretariat, which would be published at the same time as the Heads of Bill.[77] The NESC Secretariat's report argued 'for a marked departure from the type of legislation in the UK' and NESC was quoted as saying that it 'agreed strongly' with the government's argument that Ireland needed to move beyond a 'compliance-centric approach' in favour of 'innovative' bottom-up processes.[78] The NESC Secretariat's report recommended an experimental, exploratory approach to national climate policy development that shifted the emphasis away from targets: 'it is necessary to balance the policy emphasis on "how much" emissions reduction to target with more focus on "how to" achieve decarbonisation of the economy and society'.[79]

The NESC Secretariat cited with approval a 'thoughtful discussion' in a February 2012 report by Joe Curtin and Gina Hanrahan of the Institute of International & European Affairs (IIEA) – an Irish think tank – entitled 'Why Legislate? Designing a Climate Law for Ireland'.[80] The authors of the IIEA study argued in an accompanying opinion piece that:

> Onerous or complex target-setting is a key pitfall to be avoided. Ireland's 2020 target is already legally binding and is one of the most challenging of all the 27 EU member states. Additional targets, or annual reduction targets, could greatly increase the cost. Nevertheless, legislation that includes a target for 2050 would be useful to establish an overall goal ... A climate law is therefore not about setting challenging new targets ... Legislation could instead seek to address the problems of the past by creating a framework that results in effective policy implementation.[81]

The NESC Secretariat appeared to cherry-pick the IIEA's report in its own final report, citing with approval the need to 'avoid inclusion of vague or excessively onerous target setting, [and] weak reporting and accountability mechanisms', but without addressing the IIEA's reference to the usefulness of legislation including a 2050 target.[82] The NESC Secretariat also opined against the idea of a UK-style independent climate commission, claiming that this could 'militate against

---

[77] ibid.

[78] ibid.

[79] NESC Secretariat, 'Ireland and the Climate Change Challenge: Connecting "How Much" with "How To". Final Report of the NESC Secretariat to the Department of Environment, Community and Local Government' (December 2012).

[80] In 2012, Curtin worked 'full time as a climate policy consultant with NESC, advising the team of in-house analysts on Irish climate policy development' and in that capacity produced several background papers that were published alongside the NESC Secretariat's main report: Joe Curtin, 'Submission on the Outline Heads of the Climate Action and Low Carbon Development Bill' (2013). Curtin was later appointed to the Climate Change Advisory Council, the advisory body established under Ireland's Climate Act.

[81] Joe Curtin and Gina Hanrahan, 'A Poorly Designed Climate Law Will Cost Us Dearly' (*Irish Times*, 2 February 2012).

[82] NESC Secretariat (n 79) 41. One of the background papers that informed the NESC Secretariat's final report discusses the idea of including a 2050 target in legislation: Joe Curtin, 'A Vision for 2050: Evaluating the Options. Background Paper No 7' (December 2012).

achieving real commitment, technical engagement and action within government'
and instead favoured a 'government-led steering and oversight board'.[83]

The NESC Secretariat's report quickly drew heavy criticism. The head of the
Environmental Pillar (a coalition of Irish environmental non-governmental
organisations (NGOs)) emphasised that the report was produced by the secretariat alone and not the full NESC Council (on which the Pillar sat), and that
had the 'document been presented to the NESC Council for approval, we would
have vetoed it'.[84] The *Irish Times'* environment editor described the report as a
'dismal technocratic document that fails to specify any real targets or chart a clear
course for the future'.[85] Criticism in the media was matched by academic criticism,
including a strong critique by Peadar Kirby.[86]

As anticipated, the heads of the government's climate bill approved in February
2013 – entitled the Climate Action and Low Carbon Development Bill – did
not specify any targets for 2050 or before, opting instead for a vague reference
to 'pursu[ing] and achiev[ing] transition to a low carbon, climate resilient and
environmentally sustainable economy in the period up to and including the year
2050'.[87] Further, the envisaged National Expert Advisory Body was to consist of a
chair plus five to seven ordinary members, with four of these to be *ex officio* drawn
from state agencies or bodies reliant on state funding,[88] who could therefore form
a majority. The perceived lack of independence was reinforced by the fact that
the Heads of Bill envisaged the government's consent being required before the
Advisory Body could publish its reports.

The NESC Secretariat's report and the Heads of the Bill were referred to the
Joint Committee on Environment, Culture and the Gaeltacht for consideration,
and submissions were sought from the public. The Joint Committee then held a
series of hearings for this purpose, hearing evidence from stakeholders as well
as parliamentarians. Appearing before the Joint Committee on 10 July 2013,
Minister Hogan cited Ireland's emissions profile in defending his Bill, including the high proportion of emissions from agriculture: 'I have heard suggestions
that we should follow the policy or legislative approach taken in other countries,
particularly the United Kingdom. When I look at the latter's emissions profile,

---

[83] NESC Secretariat (n 79) 41 and 43. For his part, Joe Curtin favoured independence and argued that
NGOs should not be on the advisory body: 'An NGO is there to push a particular agenda, as are IBEC
and the IFA'. See Joseph Curtin, 'Heads of Climate Action and Low Carbon Development Bill 2013:
Discussion (Resumed)' Joint Committee on Environment, Culture and the Gaeltacht (12 July 2013).

[84] Michael Ewing, 'Preparing for the Climate Bill' (*Irish Times*, 16 February 2013).

[85] Frank McDonald, 'Climate Report is a Dismal Technocratic Document' (*Irish Times*, 22 February
2013). The head of the NESC secretariat offered a defence: Rory O'Donnell, 'Ireland Needs to Be
Ambitious on Climate Change' (*Irish Times*, 1 March 2013).

[86] Peadar Kirby, 'Policy Optimism: NESC, Climate Change, and Achieving Decarbonisation' (2013)
61(2) *Administration* 75.

[87] General Scheme of a Climate Action and Low Carbon Development Bill 2013.

[88] The Director General of the Environmental Protection Agency (EPA); the CEO of the Sustainable
Energy Authority of Ireland (SEAI); the Director of Teagasc (the State Agriculture and Food
Development Authority); and the Director of the Economic and Social Research Institute (ESRI).

however, I see little similarity with ours … it would be naive and potentially very harmful to assume that what works elsewhere provides an easy or appropriate solution for Ireland.'[89]

When the Joint Committee reported, its members were split on the question of the inclusion of emissions reduction targets in the legislation, and the report made no recommendations on the question.[90] However, the report did recommend that the Advisory Body should be fully independent and should have regular and robust reporting mechanisms.[91]

On 23 April 2014, Minister Hogan published revised (and final) heads of the Climate Bill together with a separate National Policy Position, which he said 'brings clarity and certainty to the national low-carbon transition objective for 2050'.[92] The National Policy Position, which would sit outside the legislation, set out a long-term vision based on 'an aggregate reduction in carbon dioxide emissions of at least 80% (compared to 1990 levels) by 2050 across the electricity generation, built environment and transport sectors; and, in parallel, an approach to carbon neutrality in the agriculture and land-use sector, including forestry, which does not compromise capacity for sustainable food production'.[93]

On 11 July 2014, a cabinet reshuffle took place: Labour's Alan Kelly[94] was made Minister for the Environment, Community and Local Government and Phil Hogan was nominated for a position in the European Commission.[95] Having criticised the 'unrealistic' nature of Ireland's 2020 target under EU law and having indicated his opposition to the adoption of 'unachievable' targets for 2030 with reference to Ireland's agricultural sector shortly after taking over the environment portfolio,[96] Kelly finally published the full text of the government's Climate Bill on 19 January 2015; it had changed little from the Heads of Bill presented by his predecessor a few months earlier.[97]

---

[89] Minister Phil Hogan, Joint Committee on Environment, Culture and the Gaeltacht debate (10 July 2013).

[90] Joint Committee on Environment, Culture and the Gaeltacht, 'Report on the Outline Heads of the Climate Action and Low Carbon Development Bill 2013' (November 2013). See also Harry McGee, 'No Targets in Report on Climate Legislation' (*Irish Times*, 19 November 2013); Harry McGee, 'Climate Change Watchdog Must Be Robust and Independent, Says Report' (*Irish Times*, 21 November 2013).

[91] ibid.

[92] Government press release, 'Minister Announces Government Agreement on National Climate Policy and Legislation' (23 April 2014).

[93] Government of Ireland, 'Climate Action and Low-Carbon Development: National Policy Position Ireland' (23 April 2014).

[94] A 'rurally based Minister, who was seen as unsympathetic to climate policy concerns; who had poor relations with NGOs (interviews 5, 9, 11); and who was involved in a standoff with the Energy Minister on planning guidelines for wind energy development': Conor Little, 'Intra-party Policy Entrepreneurship and Party Goals: The Case of Political Parties' Climate Policy Preferences in Ireland' (2017) 32(2) *Irish Political Studies* 199, 212.

[95] Cynthia Kroet, 'Phil Hogan Nominated as Ireland's European Commissioner' (*Politico*, 11 July 2014).

[96] John Gibbons, 'Another Fine (Gael) Mess on Climate Change' (*ThinkorSwim.ie*, 28 October 2014).

[97] Harry McGee, 'Climate Change Bill Gets Mixed Reaction: Bill Will Enable State to Make Transition to a "Low Carbon Economy" by 2050' (*Irish Times*, 20 January 2015).

The draft legislation did not contain targets, but required the National Mitigation Plans and National Adaptation Frameworks prepared under the legislation (see further below) to 'take into account' any existing obligations under EU law or any international agreement. Steps had been taken to bolster the independence of the Expert Advisory Council – eg, while the four *ex officio* members would remain, they could no longer form a majority on the Council, which would comprise 9–11 members. That said, the independence of the Council was not stated on the face of the legislation. FOEI said it was 'deeply disappointing that the Bill had ignored the proposals of the Oireachtas Committee', adding: 'The Bill does not include a definition of low carbon, it doesn't guarantee the independence of the council, and it doesn't include the principles of climate justice.'[98]

While the passage through the Oireachtas resulted in several changes to the draft legislation,[99] including the addition of a reference to the principle of climate justice and an explicit statement that the Advisory Council would be independent in the performance of its functions, it remained a weak piece of law, without targets. However, environmental NGOs had gradually abandoned their more ambitious policy requests such as the inclusion of targets and carbon budgets, and in the latter stages 'scaled back their lobbying efforts out of fear that the government might end before the bill would be passed'.[100]

Concluding the debate before the legislation was finally adopted, Senator Sean D Barrett had the final word: the process had been 'a very unsatisfactory way in which to make legislation regarding the environment as there are too many vested interests involved'.[101] For its part, FOEI welcomed the passage of the Bill, calling it a 'significant milestone', albeit 'weaker than it should be'.[102] The Green Party called the Act a 'charade' and a 'distraction', noting that: 'The Bill has no binding targets … and is purely aspirational.'[103] Agricultural and business lobby groups were 'broadly satisfied' with the legislation during its passage, with the IFA welcoming the exclusion of targets and the inclusion of Teagasc as a member of the Advisory Council.[104] The Act was signed into law by Ireland's President on 10 December 2015, two days before the Paris Agreement was adopted, and just

---

[98] ibid.

[99] See the useful summary of changes provided by Gerald Nash, Seanad Éireann debate, 'Climate Action and Low Carbon Development Bill 2015: Second Stage' (14 October 2015). In addition, references in the legislation to 'the Dáil' were amended to 'the Oireachtas' to ensure both Houses of the Oireachtas would be involved in scrutinising plans.

[100] Torney (n 23) 260.

[101] Seanad Éireann debate, 'Climate Action and Low Carbon Development Bill 2015: Report and Final Stages' (25 November 2015).

[102] FOEI, 'The Passing of the Climate Bill by the Dáil is a Significant Milestone, But a Concrete Plan to Actually Reduce Emissions is Long Overdue' (8 October 2015).

[103] Sarah Bardon and Harry McGee, 'Mixed Reaction as Climate Bill Passes' (*Irish Times*, 4 December 2015).

[104] See Torney (n 23) 259–60.

over a week after Taoiseach Enda Kenny briefed journalists at the UNFCCC COP21 that Ireland's EU targets for 2020 were 'unrealistic' and 'unreachable'.[105]

III. The Climate Act

The preambular words to the Climate Act[106] contain a neat summary of the final content. The Act provides for the adoption by the government of a National Mitigation Plan every five years[107] and a National Adaptation Framework (plus sectoral adaptation plans), to be reviewed and potentially replaced every five years,[108] for the purpose of pursuing the transition to a undefined 'low carbon, climate resilient and environmentally sustainable economy' by the end of 2050.[109] It establishes on a statutory footing a body known as the Climate Change Advisory Council[110] and it provides for matters connected therewith.[111] At base, then, the Act initiates a 'policy cycle'.[112]

The substantive content of the Act is further elaborated over the course of the analysis below, touching on the three parameters described by Nash and Steurer regarding Climate Acts in Europe:[113] GHG emissions reduction targets; planning mechanisms; and feedback and evaluation mechanisms.

A. Symbolic Legislation?

There is a consensus that Ireland's Climate Act does not measure up well against the UK's Climate Change Act 2008, which is widely regarded as the gold standard.[114] But is Ireland's Climate Act more than merely symbolic? This section applies

---

[105] Harry McGee and Lara Marlowe, 'Kenny Criticises "Unrealistic" Climate Targets' (*Irish Times*, 1 December 2015).

[106] For a more detailed summary of the content of the Act, see Rónán Kennedy, 'New Ideas or False Hopes?: International, European, and Irish Climate Change Law and Policy after the Paris Agreement' (2016) 23(3) *Irish Planning and Environmental Law Journal* 75.

[107] Climate Act, s 4.

[108] ibid ss 5 and 6.

[109] ibid s 3.

[110] ibid ss 8–13.

[111] ibid Preamble.

[112] Conor Linehan, 'An Initial Analysis of the "Scheme for a Climate Action and Low Carbon Development Bill 2013"' (2013), https://www.foe.ie/assets/files/doc/linehanconorsubmissionwordversion1.doc.

[113] Sarah Louise Nash and Reinhard Steurer, 'Taking Stock of Climate Change Acts in Europe: Living Policy Processes or Symbolic Gestures?' (2019) 19(8) *Climate Policy* 1052.

[114] See to this effect Peter Doran, 'Why Climate Targets are Critical in the Irish Climate Bill' (*Irish Environment*, 1 September 2013); and Peter Doran, 'The Climate Action and Low Carbon Development Bill (Draft Heads) – An Opinion: Part One' (2013) 20(3) *Irish Planning and Environmental Law Journal* 116.

Newig's 'symbolic legislation' framework to address this question, going beyond existing analyses[115] to consider the extent to which Ireland's Act is symbolic.

Newig distinguishes four prototypes of legislation, the fourth of which is 'symbolic legislation', which 'encompasses those pieces of legislation which are not intended and expected to be legally and substantively effective but which are enacted with certain political-strategic intentions'.[116] However, as Newig highlights, symbolic legislation is a graduated term, such that legislation may be more or less symbolic. Judged against Newig's indicators,[117] Ireland's Climate Act would seem to the present author to be at the 'very symbolic' end of the spectrum.

In terms of its substantive suitability, Ireland's Climate Act appears clearly unsuited to attaining its stated objective of pursuing the transition to a low-carbon, climate-resilient and environmentally sustainable economy by 2050.[118] While Ireland's Act is by no means alone in all the following regards,[119] the absence of targets and carbon budgets, the absence of meaningful sanctioning mechanisms, the Act's apparently weak 'have regard to' obligations when it comes to adopting National Mitigation Plans and National Adaptation Frameworks (for more on this, see below),[120] and the composition and functions of the Advisory Council[121] are all evident weaknesses. Discussion of these matters is divided between this section and section III.B below.

It is important to recognise that symbolic legislation is not necessarily without effects, as Newig makes clear. Ireland's Climate Act *has* led, for example, to the preparation of a National Mitigation Plan and a National Adaptation Framework, which must be made in accordance with the Act, and to the establishment of the Climate Change Advisory Council on a statutory footing.

Regarding the absence of sanctioning mechanisms and the composition/functions of the Advisory Council,[122] the limited accountability mechanisms that exist in the Act are to be found in the annual transition statements that must be presented by ministers to the Oireachtas[123] and in the reporting functions of the Advisory Council.[124] The Advisory Council of course set about its tasks against the backdrop of claims of a lack of independence owing to the presence of four *ex officio* members,[125] as discussed above. Interestingly, the Green Party–Fianna Fáil Bill of 2010 had proposed including only two *ex officio* members, from the

---

[115] Torney (n 6) applies this framework in assessing the limited diffusion to Ireland of the UK's Climate Change Act 2008.

[116] Jens Newig, 'Symbolic Environmental Legislation and Societal Self-deception' (2007) 16(2) *Environmental Politics* 276.

[117] ibid 280–81.

[118] Climate Act, s 3.

[119] See Nash and Steurer (n 113).

[120] See Climate Act, ss 3(2), 4(7) and 7(1).

[121] ibid ss 8–13.

[122] ibid.

[123] ibid s 14.

[124] ibid ss 12 and 13.

[125] ibid s 9(2).

EPA and the SEAI.[126] The addition of members from ESRI and Teagasc was a Fine Gael–Labour innovation.

The chair of the Advisory Council, Professor John FitzGerald, was at the time of appointment in 2015 a recently retired director of ESRI, making both the current and former directors of ESRI members of the Council. FitzGerald was something of a controversial choice for the role. Shortly before being selected, he wrote a strongly criticised[127] opinion piece for the *Irish Times* with the headline 'Solution to Global Warming is Technology'.[128] While the Council has repeatedly issued strong critiques of the government's failings on climate change,[129] the High Court held in 2019 that 'its conclusions and recommendations cannot be equated with the imposition of a legal obligation under the statutory framework'.[130] Moreover, the Advisory Council has been criticised for its lack of diversity and for its endorsement of continued gas exploration in Ireland.[131] Despite the Climate Act obliging the Minister to 'have regard to the range of qualifications, expertise and experience necessary for the proper and effective performance of the functions of the Advisory Council',[132] eight of the 11 members are primarily economists[133] and only two of the 11 are female. Here the Joint Committee's 2010 Bill would have made a difference, with its obligation on the proposed Climate Change Commission to 'have regard to the desirability of an equitable balance between men and women in the composition of the committee'.[134]

In addition to its composition, the Advisory Council has relatively limited functions.[135] Consider the UK's Committee on Climate Change, which is tasked with providing advice on, inter alia, the 2050 target and on the level of the carbon budget for each period.[136] However, there being no targets or carbon budgets in Ireland's Climate Act, naturally there are no related functions for the Advisory

---

[126] Climate Change Response Bill 2010, s 7(3).

[127] Letters by Professor John Sweeney and Professor Barry McMullin, 'Tackling Climate Change' (*Irish Times*, 30 March 2015); and John Gibbons, 'An Economic Analysis That Just Doesn't Add up' (*ThinkOrSwim.ie*, 26 March 2015).

[128] This was the headline in the print edition; the online edition went with John FitzGerald, 'Solution to Global Warming Will Be Found in New Technologies' (*Irish Times*, 24 March 2015).

[129] For example, its 2018 Annual Review states that 'Ireland's greenhouse gas emissions for 2016, and projections of emissions to 2035, are disturbing': Climate Change Advisory Council, 'Annual Review 2018' (July 2018).

[130] *Friends of the Irish Environment v Government of Ireland and Others* [2019] IEHC 747, judgment of the High Court of Ireland (19 September 2019), para 114.

[131] Climate Change Advisory Council, 'Letter: Advice on Future Offshore Oil and Gas Exploration and Recovery in Ireland' (20 September 2019).

[132] Climate Act, s 9(4). Contrast this with the obligations in para 1(3) of sched 1 to the UK's Climate Change Act 2008.

[133] See Climate Change Advisory Council, 'Council Members' (November 2019), www.climatecouncil.ie/aboutus/councilmembers.

[134] Joint Committee on Climate Change and Energy Security, 'Fifth Report of the Joint Committee on Climate Change and Energy Security. Second Report on Climate Change Law' (October 2010), at 38.

[135] Climate Act, ss 11–13.

[136] Climate Change Act 2008 (UK), ss 33 and 34.

Council. Again, had the Joint Committee's 2010 Bill been adopted in Ireland, things would have been different, since that Bill required the production of carbon budgets and proposed creating an Office of Climate Change and Renewable Energy to advise on the level of the carbon budget for each period.[137]

Regarding the political-strategic dimension of symbolic legislation, Newig highlights that legislators may wish to remove a contentious issue from the public agenda or simply boost their popularity. Certainly, Ireland's political parties competed to be able to claim responsibility for passing Ireland's first Climate Act. Thus, the Green Party–Fianna Fáil coalition ploughed on with its own government bill in 2010, notwithstanding the Joint Committee's further-advanced Climate Bill, which had cross-party support and was clearly superior in content to the government's bill across a range of measures. Equally, once in power from 2011, the Fine Gael–Labour coalition made much of the fact that it would succeed in passing a climate law where its predecessors failed.[138] In the end, the Climate Act 2015 was signed into law at the very end of the Fine Gael–Labour coalition's term, just two months before a general election; Newig cites precisely this sort of timing as an indicator of symbolic legislation.[139]

B. A Trojan Horse?

A recurring refrain during debates regarding climate legislation in Ireland has been a desire on the part of the government to avoid litigation. As discussed above, the Green Party–Fianna Fáil Climate Change Response Bill 2010 went as far as providing explicitly that targets in the Bill would be non-justiciable. As Linehan comments: 'It is difficult to think of any other prior legislative effort in Ireland – in any sphere – where such a direct ouster of the courts' jurisdiction was attempted.'[140]

Notwithstanding potential legal difficulties with enforcing via the courts any target enshrined in domestic climate legislation,[141] the Fine Gael–Labour government of course went one step further when it came to its Climate Act by omitting targets altogether. As Linehan records, 'a series of media stories reported that the office of the Attorney General (the government's chief legal adviser) held the view that the inclusion of targets might render the government vulnerable to legal action and/or to a constitutional challenge'.[142]

---

[137] Under s 6 of and sched 2 to that Bill, respectively.
[138] See, eg, Minihan (n 66); Phil Hogan, Energy Security and Climate Change Bill 2012: Second Stage (Private Members) Dáil Éireann debate (8 February 2013); Alan Kelly and Eoghan Murphy, Climate Action and Low Carbon Development Bill 2015: Second Stage, Dáil Éireann debate (11 February 2015).
[139] Newig (n 116) 281.
[140] Linehan (n 44) 59.
[141] ibid 54–60. See also Doran (both articles) (n 114).
[142] Linehan (n 44) 54.

A decision to omit targets to avoid being 'hauled into court'[143] in any event turned out to be a misplaced strategy, given that the government ended up in court in any case. The case in question – known as *Climate Case Ireland* and inspired by the *Urgenda* litigation in the Netherlands[144] – is an action for judicial review brought against the state by the NGO Friends of the Irish Environment (FIE),[145] alleging that the adoption of Ireland's first National Mitigation Plan in 2017:

(a) did not comply with Ireland's Climate Act;
(b) breached Ireland's Constitution (right to life; right to bodily integrity; right to an environment) and the European Convention on Human Rights (ECHR), via the ECHR Act 2003 (right to life (Article 2); right to respect for private and family life and home (Article 8)); and
(c) was manifestly unreasonable/disproportionate.

It is not proposed here to traverse all of the ground covered in the case and judgment, particularly in circumstances where the case is under appeal to the Supreme Court.[146] But by way of background, the alleged infringements of fundamental rights are based on the uncontested science of the Intergovernmental Panel on Climate Change (IPCC) and other authoritative, uncontested reports evidencing a vast array of risks of harm to humans and ecosystems, including but not limited to the risk of loss of life, severe ill-health, extreme weather events, coastal inundation, loss of biodiversity, and disrupted lives and livelihoods.

In its Fourth Assessment report (AR4), the IPCC in 2007 determined that in order to stand a reasonable (66 per cent) chance of staying below 2°C global average temperature increase above pre-industrial levels, the countries listed in Annex I to the UNFCCC (ie, developed countries, including Ireland) would need to follow an emissions trajectory that would reduce emissions by 25–40 per cent

---

[143] Victoria White, 'We Need to Put Climate Bill Back on Agenda before it's Too Late' (*Irish Examiner*, 13 December 2012).

[144] At the time *Climate Case Ireland* launched, only the District Court's judgment in *Urgenda v The Netherlands* (ECLI:NL:RBDHA:2015:7196) had been handed down; by the time *Climate Case Ireland* was heard in January 2019, the Court of Appeal had given its judgment in *Urgenda* (ECLI:NL:GHDHA:2018:2610). On this, see Laura Burgers and Tim Staal, 'Climate Action as Positive Human Rights Obligation: The Appeals Judgment in Urgenda v The Netherlands' in Janne Nijman and Wouter Werner (eds), *Netherlands Yearbook of International Law 2018* (Dordrecht, Springer, 2019). In December 2019, the Supreme Court of the Netherlands gave its judgment in *Urgenda* (ECLI:NL:HR:2019:2007), upholding the Court of Appeal's decision in favour of *Urgenda*; see André Nollkaemper and Laura Burgers, 'A New Classic in Climate Change Litigation: The Dutch Supreme Court Decision in the Urgenda Case' (*EJIL:Talk!*, 6 January 2020).

[145] See *Friends of the Irish Environment v Government of Ireland and* Others (n 130) for the judgment and https://www.climatecaseireland.ie.

[146] At the time of writing, FIE had received permission for a 'leapfrog' appeal directly from the High Court to the Supreme Court, with the hearing scheduled for 22/23 June 2020. See the Supreme Court's determination and associated application for leave: *Friends of the Irish Environment v Government of Ireland and Others* [2020] IESCDET 13.

by 2020 and by 80–95 per cent by 2050 (both compared to 1990).[147] This was recognised and endorsed by the parties to the UNFCCC and the Kyoto Protocol (including Ireland) in a series of decisions taken at the annual climate negotiations organised under the framework of the UNFCCC.[148] However, instead of falling by 25–40 per cent between 1990 and 2020, Ireland's emissions are projected to *increase* 11–12 per cent over that period,[149] and to increase over the life of the National Mitigation Plan itself (2017–22).[150]

In summary, the state has acknowledged that climate change poses a grave danger that must be avoided, and that the only way to do so is to significantly increase emissions reduction ambitions in the short term. However, FIE argued that the state had failed to explain why the pressing need to reduce short-term emissions at the global level did not apply to itself. The state's position appears to be that Ireland's emissions level in, say, 2020 does not really matter, so long as a reduction target for 2050 (eg, as set out in the National Policy Position, which sits outside the Act) is ultimately achieved. However, as FIE highlighted, this neglects the concept of the carbon budget and the strong, consistent, almost linear relationship between *cumulative emissions* (since the start of the Industrial Revolution) and temperature increase, as discussed by the IPCC in its Fifth Assessment Report.[151] In other words, the IPCC's 25–40 per cent reduction by 2020 and 80–95 per cent by 2050 (compared to 1990) describes an emissions *trajectory* that keeps temperature increase below 2°C at the lowest cost. But in order to achieve this temperature goal, emissions need to stay on or below the required trajectory. Merely meeting a 2050 target is not enough. To stay within the available carbon budget to help limit temperature rise to 2°C, the 2020 emissions target also needs to be met, since the 2020 and 2050 emissions reduction targets advised by the IPCC are two points on a required *trajectory* to stay within a particular carbon budget. Since the aim pursuant to the Paris Agreement is now to hold the increase in the global average temperature to 'well below' 2°C above pre-industrial levels and to pursue efforts to limit the temperature increase to 1.5°C, the required emissions reduction trajectory is now steeper than the one advised by the IPCC in AR4.[152]

---

[147] Sujata Gupta et al, 'Policies, Instruments and Co-operative Arrangements' in Bert Metz et al (eds), *Climate Change 2007: Mitigation. Contribution of Working Group III to the Fourth Assessment Report of the Intergovernmental Panel on Climate Change* (Cambridge, Cambridge University Press, 2007) ch 13, Box 13.7, 776.

[148] For a summary, see paras 6.1–6.19 of the Respondent's Notice on Appeal including Notice of Cross-Appeal in *Urgenda v The Netherlands*, Hague Court of Appeal, 18 April 2017, Case No 200.178.245, https://www.urgenda.nl/wp-content/uploads/Urgenda-notice-on-appeal-21112017.pdf.

[149] For the 1990 figure, see EPA, 'Ireland's Final Greenhouse Gas Emissions in 2015' (13 April 2017) 9; the 2020 range is given at 14.

[150] EPA, 'Ireland's Greenhouse Gas Emissions Projections 2017–2035' (May 2018), Figure 1, p 3.

[151] IPCC, 'Climate Change 2014: Synthesis Report. Summary for Policymakers. Contribution of Working Groups I, II and III to the Fifth Assessment Report of the Intergovernmental Panel on Climate Change' (2014).

[152] See art 2(1)(a) of the Paris Agreement; and IPCC, 'Summary for Policymakers. In: Global Warming of 1.5°C. An IPCC Special Report on the Impacts of Global Warming of 1.5°C' (2018).

FIE also argued that it was not open to the government to adopt a National Mitigation Plan allowing Ireland's emissions to rise over the life of the Plan and beyond rather than fall substantially in the short term. In such circumstances, FIE claimed that the state infringed fundamental rights, it acted manifestly unreasonably/disproportionately, the Plan was missing mandatory elements such as a specification of the manner in which it was proposed to achieve the national transition objective,[153] and the state could not be said to have had regard to the various matters referred to in sections 3(2) and 4(7) of the Climate Act, including, for example, the objective of the UNFCCC, climate justice, existing EU climate law obligations and obligations under international agreements such as the Paris Agreement.

The High Court held against FIE, ruling, inter alia, that even if the Plan is justiciable, the state must be given a broad margin of discretion in its adoption, with reference to the separation of powers and the nature, extent and wording of the statutory obligations in play. Two points from the judgment are particularly salient in the context of the Climate Act: first, the apparent weakness of the 'have regard to' obligations in the Act as interpreted by the High Court; and, second, the breadth of the mitigation plan-making power in the Act, according to the Court.

First, the High Court gave relatively brief treatment to the 'have regard to' obligations in the Act, simply quoting from an earlier High Court decision in the *Tristor* case to the effect that 'if the Oireachtas intended that there be an obligation to comply with a particular matter rather than simply have regard to it, it might be expected that the Oireachtas would have said so in the legislation concerned'.[154] Interestingly, there was a late attempt to make precisely this change to the Climate Bill – ie, seeking to replace the phrase 'have regard to' with the phrase 'comply with' in section 3(2), which deals with matters that must be considered when the government approves a National Mitigation Plan or National Adaptation Framework.[155] This was defeated in the Seanad in a narrow 14:12 vote.[156] In any event, the High Court in *Climate Case Ireland* does not appear to have addressed all of the section 3(2)/4(7) factors raised by FIE to which regard must be had, nor the specific point raised by FIE regarding *Tristor* and 'have regard to' obligations: that where a decision plainly flies in the face of a matter to which regard must be had (eg, climate justice), the state must establish that it had cogent reasons for such a departure.[157]

---

[153] See s 4(2) of Ireland's Climate Act 2015.

[154] *Tristor v Minister for the Environment, Heritage & Local Government and Others* [2010] IEHC 397, at 7.11. For a more detailed discussion of 'have regard to' in the Climate Act, see *Merriman and Others v Fingal County Council and Others; Friends of the Irish Environment Clg v Fingal County Council and Others* [2017] IEHC 695, at paras 217–20.

[155] Seanad Éireann debate, 'Climate Action and Low Carbon Development Bill 2015: Report and Final stages' (25 November 2015).

[156] ibid.

[157] *Tristor* (n 154) 7.14.

Second, per the High Court's decision, the mitigation plan-making power in the Climate Act is very broad, with reference to the broad objective of the Act ('transition to a low carbon, climate resilient and environmentally sustainable economy by the end of the year 2050'), the absence of intermediate targets and the requirement for the Plan to specify the policy measures that 'in the opinion of the Government' would be required to further the achievement of the transition objective. The Court held that it cannot be said that the Plan does not contain a proposal to achieve this 2050 objective or that the Plan does not specify policy measures which *in the opinion of the government* would be required in order to manage GHG emissions. On this basis, the Court concluded that the Plan was intra vires the Act. This being so, it held that it would be inconsistent for FIE to suggest that the Plan might be open to a freestanding challenge on the basis that it is in breach of fundamental rights. In other words, since the Plan was made (per the court) within the vires of legislation that is presumed constitutional, it cannot be impugned on the freestanding basis that the Plan itself is unconstitutional or in breach of human rights. The Court may potentially have been influenced in this regard by the state's argument that 'the Plan is essentially being employed as a vehicle'[158] – or Trojan horse, if you will – within which to maintain the fundamental rights challenges. FIE naturally did not share this characterisation of the case, and this aspect of the judgment is amongst the matters to be addressed by the Supreme Court on appeal.[159]

One might reflect on reading the *Climate Case Ireland* judgment that adopting symbolic legislation is not without consequence. As Newig explains, such legislation inter alia absorbs parliamentary time at the expense of the public purse, it violates the principle of proportionality that demands legislation be appropriate for its declared purpose and, in the case of litigation such as *Climate Case Ireland*, courts are arguably 'in the paradoxical situation of having to interpret laws which had never been intended to genuinely fulfil the purpose which they supposedly pursue'.[160] It remains to be seen, of course, whether FIE, via the Supreme Court, might manage to give the Act some sort of teeth.

C. A Stepping Stone?

Perhaps the most that can be said for Ireland's Climate Act is that it will ultimately be viewed as a stepping stone en route to more meaningful regulatory intervention. The government practically admitted as much during the passage of the Act.[161]

---

[158] *Friends of the Irish Environment v Government of Ireland and Others* (n 130) para 74.

[159] See the application for leave in *Friends of the Irish Environment v Government of Ireland and Others* (n 146).

[160] Newig (n 116) 277.

[161] See Eoghan Murphy, Climate Action and Low Carbon Development Bill 2015: Second Stage, Dáil Éireann debate (11 February 2015).

The inevitable review arose, in the end, via a process that began with Ireland's Citizens' Assembly, a body comprising a chairperson and 99 citizens randomly selected to be broadly representative of the Irish electorate, which was established to hear expert evidence and consider some of the most important issues facing Ireland's future. The Assembly produced its climate report and recommendations, entitled 'How the State Can Make Ireland a Leader in Tackling Climate Change', in April 2018.[162] The recommendations were far-reaching, with consensus around ambitious action.

The Citizens' Assembly's recommendations were considered by a parliamentary committee – the Joint Oireachtas Committee on Climate Action (JOCCA) – which in turn reported to the government in March 2019. In response to the JOCCA report, the government adopted an 'All of Government Plan to Tackle Climate Breakdown' (since renamed the Climate Action Plan 2019), which committed to introducing a new Climate Action (Amendment) Bill, which would:

- Make the adoption of carbon budgets a legal requirement
- Require the Government to set a decarbonisation target range for each sector, with the Minister with primary responsibility for the sector being accountable for delivering the relevant actions to meet the sectoral target
- Establish the Climate Action Council as a successor organisation to the Climate Change Advisory Council [and the new Council will 'recommend the Carbon Budget and evaluate policy']
- Establish that the Climate Action Plan shall be updated annually
- Establish that a Long-Term Climate Strategy, to match the period covered by the three five year carbon budgets, shall be published:
  - the first Strategy would be published for the period 2021 to 2035, and will also include a longer-term perspective to 2050
  - the Strategy will be updated at least every five years
- Ensure that the proposed governance arrangements retain sufficient flexibility to allow necessary reorientation of policy in the light of changing technologies, circumstances, challenges and opportunities over the period to 2030 and beyond
- Establish 2050 target in law

It is intended that the Long-term Climate Strategy will be a statutory successor to the National Mitigation Plan.[163]

While the relevant legislative changes had not been enacted by the time Ireland's general election was held in February 2020,[164] and while the JOCCA report and the government's Climate Action Plan 2019 did not embrace certain of the more

---

[162] Citizens' Assembly, 'Third Report and Recommendations of the Citizens' Assembly: How the State Can Make Ireland a Leader in Tackling Climate Change' (April 2018).

[163] Government of Ireland, 'Climate Action Plan 2019 to Tackle Climate Breakdown' (2019) 39–40.

[164] The General Scheme of the proposed Climate Action (Amendment) Bill 2019 was published in January 2020, but the Bill itself had not been introduced to the Oireachtas by the time of the election. At the time of writing, a new government has not yet been formed and it remains to be seen what attitude the next government will take to revising Ireland's Climate Act.

interesting ideas suggested by the Citizens' Assembly,[165] Ireland appeared close – before the general election – to embarking on the creation of meaningful (non-symbolic) climate legislation of the sort it could and should have created a decade ago, had support been offered to the cross-party initiative promoted by the Joint Committee, with Liz McManus as rapporteur, in 2010. Instead, the Green Party–Fianna Fáil coalition persisted with its own legislative proposal, and the rest is history.

While NGOs that campaigned to the bitter end to secure the adoption of the Climate Bill in 2015 might not share Clare Daly TD's sentiment that 'a bad [Climate] Bill [is] worse than no Bill',[166] the consequences of Ireland's legislative efforts up to and including the Climate Act 2015 include years of lost time, in circumstances where time is very much of the essence. This points to perhaps the Climate Act's greatest failing: it potentially stood in the way of more effective policy. As Newig notes, 'once a societal problem appears to have been tackled by symbolic legislation, the effort to deal with it in a substantive way will be considerably less intense, often leaving the problem at issue largely unresolved'.[167] This seems clearly to have happened in Ireland, until climate policy was jolted to life by a host of developments, including the IPCC's reports, the *Urgenda* case, the Citizens' Assembly, *Climate Case Ireland*, Greta Thunberg, the school strikes, Extinction Rebellion and other grassroots activism. While there is of course no counter-factual against which we can test the proposition that more effective policy might have emerged sooner in the absence of the Climate Act 2015, in pursuing a weak, symbolic climate law, Ireland's government embraced the politics of predatory delay[168] and for that history will not judge it kindly.

---

[165] eg, 'a new or existing independent body should be resourced appropriately, operate in an open and transparent manner, and be given a broad range of new functions and powers in legislation to urgently address climate change. Such functions and powers should include, but not be limited to those outlined below … 3. To pursue the State in legal proceedings to ensure that the State lives up to its legal obligations relating to climate change.' Citizens' Assembly (n 162) 19–20.

[166] Clare Daly, Dáil Éireann debate, 'Climate Action and Low Carbon Development Bill 2015: Report Stage (Resumed)' (8 October 2015). She added that 'many environmental groups contacted everyone and told us to get the Bill through, but something is not always better than nothing'.

[167] Newig (n 116) 277.

[168] Alex Steffen, 'Predatory Delay and the Rights of Future Generations' (*Medium*, 30 April 2016): while '"Policy should protect the future from the past, not the past from the future" … in every country on Earth, policies made at the top are still overwhelmingly designed not to meet our planetary crisis at the scale and speed it demands, but to protect the institutions, companies and systems causing that crisis from disruptive change'.

7

The Swedish Climate Policy Framework Including the Climate Act

ÅSA ROMSON AND KRISTINA FORSBACKA

I. Introduction

Sweden's ambition is to be a leader in the global work required to realise the ambitious targets in the Paris Agreement. The national goal is to be the first fossil fuel-free welfare society in the world and to reach zero net emissions of greenhouse gases by 2045 at the latest. When this goal was proposed in 2016, it was probably the world's most ambitious climate target. A few years later, it is notable that there are many countries that have ambitious national climate targets.

In June 2017, the Swedish Parliament (Swedish: Riksdag) decided on a Climate Policy Framework (CPF), which includes new ambitious climate targets, clarifies that the government is responsible for securing climate objectives, and sets out a structured process for the government's work to achieve the climate targets. This framework is the most comprehensive climate reform ever approved in Sweden, and it includes one of the world's most ambitious climate targets, as well as a Climate Act.[1] Sweden has a long tradition of broad political agreements in relation to questions of great and fundamental importance to society. It was considered important to also uphold this tradition regarding the policy area of climate change, which concerns issues of profound character and great importance for society as a whole. The CPF was prepared by the All-Party Committee on Environmental Objectives,[2] a committee open to all political parties, and was backed by a broad political majority. Forming the new CPF is a key component in the efforts to

---

[1] See Government Offices of Sweden, Ministry of the Environment and Energy, 'The Swedish Climate Policy Framework', https://www.government.se/495f60/contentassets/883ae8e123bc4e42aa8d 59296ebe0478/the-swedish-climate-policy-framework.pdf. 2.

[2] A committee, including representatives for all political parties at the time represented in Parliament, established by the government in 2010 to achieve broad agreement as regards important environmental issues.

comply with the Paris Agreement.[3] It should be noted that legislation regulating the climate work and climate targets is new to Swedish politics, as there has been a long-standing tradition of including climate targets in Orientational Bills (Swedish: inriktningsproposition) adopted by Parliament.[4]

The CPF adopted consists of three parts: (i) a Climate Act;[5] (ii) new ambitious interim and long-term climate targets; and (iii) a Climate Policy Council. The aim of the CPF is to provide long-term stability and transparency concerning the steps to mitigate all climate gas emissions in Sweden down to a globally sustainable level. By adopting the framework, Parliament highlights the need for societal transformation in order to reach the climate targets. It is underlined that the framework will work across sectors, aim to involve all actors, and ensure that Parliament and the public are given information on the progress of climate policies and on their impacts.

The climate policies in Sweden before the Climate Act stem from 2009, when the Swedish Parliament decided on a climate policy package including climate targets to 2020. These decisions did not include any major institutional arrangements and no legal act was adopted. The Swedish climate targets for 2020 were not long-term targets. In Parliament there was no agreement between a broader group of parties and thus the decisions on climate targets would vary as governments changed. This did not provide enough certainty for either the state planning authorities or non-state actors.

The Climate Act is a separate act instructing the government to develop and implement climate reforms in order to reach the national climate targets. It clarifies the purpose of the government's climate work and regulates how this work shall be carried out and monitored. The short Act, which consists of only one page with five paragraphs, does not in itself grant any legal rights or obligations to individual actors concerning their climate emissions and does not include specific policy measures. Thus, the Act is not placed to be part of the state's ordinary environmental legislation or part of its Environmental Code.[6] The Act's links to substantive environmental law are uncertain until further guidance is given by the legislator or by precedents in the courts.

---

[3] The Government Bill; Regeringens proposition 2016/17:146 Ett klimatpolitisk ramverk för Sverige (hereinafter 'the Government Bill'), 44 f.

[4] Orientational Bills are bills adopted by Parliament – and thus binding until changed – that include the direction of future policies, but are not legislative acts. Such bills have been commonly used when it comes to Swedish climate policy issues such as climate targets.

[5] Klimatlag SFS 2017:720.

[6] Since 1999, the major environmental acts in Swedish law are consolidated into the Environmental Code. The aim of the Code is to promote sustainable development. Apart from material provisions, the Code sets out the basic framework for implementing environmental protection through its provisions on procedure, supervision, sanctions and provisions on compensation and environmental damages. This includes provisions which set out a permit regime for environmentally hazardous activities as well as for certain water operations.

II. Background to the Act

A. The First Proposal for a Climate Act

The first proposal to create something like the UK Climate Change Act 2008 in Sweden was raised in 2012, when the Green Party put forward a motion in Parliament[7] which received support from the two other major opposition parties at the time during the parliamentary process: the Social Democrats and the Left Party. This proposal argued for a legal act, but its focus was to form a climate policy framework including long-term targets for mitigation of Swedish emissions and strict control of those emissions with the establishment of 'emission budgets' that must be kept. This initiative in the Swedish Parliament was not responding to any specific call from environmental non-governmental organisations (NGOs); rather, it stemmed from a will to have a greater focus on the political responsibility to form concrete climate actions in order to ensure the mitigation of Swedish emissions. Although Sweden had high climate ambitions, there was much uncertainty around the implementation of the climate targets.

The main problem in climate politics at the time was the lack of comprehensive, long-lasting and transformative mitigation actions ensuring that the climate emissions in Sweden continuously decreased. Political proposals for raising eco-taxes or introducing new climate regulation became a debate about the difficulties different stakeholders would have to cope with regarding such actions rather than their suitability to mitigate carbon emissions. The political debate seldom focused on how the climate targets, both nationally and internationally, were going to be met. Thus, there was a lack of coordinated action at the national level and the climate issue was regarded as a niche policy area, which was not in line with its importance for the welfare of society.[8] The proposal of a legal climate policy framework was made in order to clarify that the government has the responsibility for reaching the climate targets and to ensure that it would monitor Swedish greenhouse gas emissions and take measures required to reach necessary greenhouse gas reductions in an organised and systematic manner. It was also intended to provide increased transparency in the area of climate governance.

The intention was to use the UK Climate Change Act as a model, but to adapt it to the Swedish legislative tradition. In the proposal it was also suggested to use the structure of another policy framework in Sweden – the fiscal policy framework – as a model. This framework regulates how the state budget must keep deficits and debts within limits, and how the government must plan for the long

---

[7] Motion till Riksdagen 2012/2013 MJ481 av Åsa Romson m fl MP (hereinafter 'Motion in the Parliament').

[8] The IPCC Fourth Assessment Report in 2007 had announced huge impacts globally. IPCC, *Climate Change 2007: Synthesis Report. Contribution of Working Groups I, II and III to the Fourth Assessment Report of the Intergovernmental Panel on Climate Change* (Geneva, IPCC, 2007) 104.

term and be transparent on all budget issues.[9] The fiscal policy framework was agreed broadly among the Swedish parties to stabilise the shaky financial situation in Sweden during the financial crisis in the early 1990s, when the state's deficit escalated dramatically. This policy framework first formed a practice of strict budget control in 1996, an independent policy council for fiscal policies in 2007 and a legal act, the Budget Act, in 2011. In the proposal for the CPF, it was argued that combating climate change was of as much importance for the state as was securing financial stability, and that it would be feasible to control climate emissions with instruments paralleling those used in budgetary control.[10] The regulating challenge was similar in the sense that it was held that politicians with the perspective only of the short mandate period would not take the action required to secure the long-term climate goals. It was also argued that climate politics should be regarded as equally important to the politics of economics.[11]

B. How the Proposal was Taken Forward

The motion in Parliament from 2012 did not reach a majority and was voted down. But after general elections in September 2014 and the forming of a new coalition government comprising the Social Democrats and the Green Party, the proposal was taken forward within the government. In January 2015, the standing Committee on Environmental Objectives was issued with the task of preparing a governmental proposal of a CPF. The Committee included representatives from all political parties in Parliament, except the Swedish Democrats (right-wing nationalists), who were not in Parliament when the Committee was formed and did not express any wish to contribute to its work on climate issues. In addition to representatives from the political parties, key individuals from environmental NGOs, business organisations, science and public administration were appointed as experts to assist the Committee. A well-known and respected high-profile environmental figure, Anders Wijkman, former member of the European Parliament (European People's Party (EPP) group), was appointed to lead the Committee during this work. The government's instructions to the Committee also included building upon the work of previous governments on long-term climate targets in order to overcome diverging opinions between the parties and reach a common ground.

Already at the initial stage of preparing the proposal of a Swedish Climate Act, contact with UK experts and efforts to learn about the system in the UK played a significant role, both in forming the ultimate political framework and in building

---

[9] Swedish Fiscal Policy Framework, the Governments Communication to the Riksdag Skr 2017/18:207.
[10] Motion in the Parliament (n 7) 2.
[11] ibid 3.

trust in the system within the different political groups. The Committee met with British experts and politicians in order to learn about the experience of the UK Climate Change Act. It was important for the more sceptical politicians to hear from British party colleagues that their experiences of the UK Climate Change Act were positive.

Other fruitful learning arising from the British process of establishing the UK Climate Change Act included the importance of having the business community on-board. Businesses could embrace the idea of a stringent system on climate policies because that delivered better certainty for business and vitalisation of investments in sustainable solutions. In Sweden the main business organisation, Svenskt Näringsliv, was not particularly in favour of the proposal. However, a relatively new network of businesses from various sectors strongly engaged in climate mitigation, Swedish Hagainitiativet, had been established, and this network supported the work for a Swedish Climate Act.

The Committee worked over the course of one year to reach political agreement for the CPF and on the long-term targets to be set. During this time, it followed the ongoing climate negotiations at the international level that culminated in the global Paris Agreement. Almost all members of the Committee were present for some days of the COP21 in Paris. The strong and worldwide call for action raised during the Paris process from the science community, and the broad support for climate policies from cities and the business sector, equally inspired and pushed the work of the Swedish Committee forward.[12]

III. The Swedish CPF and the Climate Act

The Swedish CPF, consisting of the Climate Act, interim and long-term climate targets and a Climate Policy Council, is described below.

A. The Climate Act

i. Background to the Act

The Swedish Constitution (Swedish: Regeringsformen) states that the public authorities shall promote sustainable development, which leads to a good environment for present and future generations.[13] Furthermore, Sweden has obligations

---

[12] This conclusion is also drawn by researchers at the KTH Royal Institute of Technology who have surveyed the process within the committee though long interviews. See M Karlsson and E Alfredsson, 'Sweden's Climate Change Act – Conditions and Factors of Importance for the Emergence of a Common Political Ground', work in progress, abstract discussed at the Nordic Environmental Social Science conference 2019.

[13] See ch 1, s 2 of the Constitution.

under the United Nations (UN) Framework Convention on Climate Change. Based on these obligations, there is an obligation for the public authorities in Sweden to act in a way that ensures that the climate system is not changed in a harmful manner and that it protects citizens from dangerous changes in the climate system. The government has a responsibility to ensure that the climate policy is carried out in accordance with these obligations.[14]

The first pillar of the CPF is the Climate Act. According to the CPF adopted in June 2017, part of the government's climate policy work shall be regulated in law. The reasoning for this is explained in the Government Bill on a Climate Policy Framework for Sweden (Swedish: Regeringens proposition 2016/17:146 Ett klimatpolitisk ramverk för Sverige) (hereinafter 'the Government Bill').[15] The introduction of a legal act which describes the climate work means that the forms that the climate work will take will be accessible for everyone to scrutinise. This means there is an increased ability to examine part of the regulations and understand how the work develops and what measures need to be taken next. It was also argued that legal regulation will make it more difficult for the government to act in a manner which would counteract, or not sufficiently promote, reaching the national climate targets. The Climate Act is legally binding, as opposed to being a political agreement, and also increases the possibility that future climate work can be carried out in a long-term and continuous manner. By adopting the Climate Act, Parliament and the government also sent an important signal to the citizens, and to other states, that the Swedish state is committed to taking the climate work seriously.[16] The Climate Act was adopted as a piece of regular legislation rather than constitutional law, which would be more difficult to revoke or amend.

ii. General Overview of the Act

The Swedish Climate Act entered into force in January 2018. It establishes that each successive government has an obligation to pursue a climate policy based on the climate targets adopted by Parliament. It also contains general terms on how the Swedish government shall plan and monitor its climate work. The government shall provide reports on the progress of the work to achieve the targets set by Parliament. The Act does not include specific policy instruments, as these are to be decided in separate legislation.

The Climate Act establishes that the government's climate policy shall be based on the climate targets set by Parliament. It also describes how the government's work is to be carried out; the government is required to present a climate report

---

[14] Government Bill, 43 f.

[15] In Sweden, the Government Bill includes, in addition to the proposed Act, preparatory works that provide additional explanation of the act in question. The explanations and comments are a source of law often referred to when interpreting the act in question. This is the reason we repeatedly refer to the Government Bill below when we provide additional information and explanation of the Act.

[16] Government Bill, 44 f.

every year in the Budget Bill and to draw up a climate policy action plan describing how the climate targets are to be achieved every four years. Climate policy targets and budget policy targets shall be carried out so that the respective targets interact. It should be noted that the Climate Act does not include provisions on adaptation or enforcement provisions. An independent Climate Policy Council reviews how well the government's overall policy meets the climate targets. The Council constitutes one part of the CPF. However, it should be noted that the work of the Council is not regulated under the terms of the Climate Act, but via a separate ordinance issued by the government, as will be described below.

It is notable that in its opinion on the draft Climate Act, the Council on Legislation (Swedish: lagrådet)[17] expressed doubts as to whether the Act would fulfil the purpose expressed in the Bill. The Council inter alia referred to the fact that the Act does not include enforcement provisions and that the provisions of the Act are general in nature.[18] In response to this, the government pointed to the fact that Parliament has an obligation to control the work of the government according to Chapter 13 of the Constitution.[19] This control function is carried out through the review of the government's work by the Committee on the Constitution (Swedish: konstitutionsutskottet).[20] The Committee on the Constitution shall review the ministers' service and their handling of governmental matters, and there is a possibility for Parliament to adopt a motion of no confidence against a minister.[21]

As the Swedish Climate Act is general in nature and not extensive, it only includes five sections. In Sweden, the Government Bill includes, in addition to the proposed Act, preparatory works that provide additional explanations and comments to the Act. These explanations in the preparatory works are a source of law generally referred to when interpreting the legal act. We therefore refer to the Government Bill below for explanations to the Climate Act. We also comment below on the specific sections in the Act.

B. The Content and Purpose of the Climate Act

i. Section 1

The first section describes the content and purpose of the Climate Act and clarifies that it is addressing the government's obligations as regards its climate work.

---

[17] The Council of Constitution is an authority which reviews all important government bills before they are handled by Parliament. The members are Justices (or former Justices) of the Supreme Court and the Administrative Supreme Court.

[18] The Opinion of the Council of Legislation, attached to the Government Bill as Appendix 5, 68 f.

[19] See ch 13, s 1 of the Constitution.

[20] The Committee on the Constitution is one of 16 committees in Parliament. It consists of 17 members and reflects the composition of Parliament. It reviews the ministers' carrying out of their tasks and the handling of governmental matters, as regulated in ch 13, s 1 of the Constitution.

[21] See ch 13, s 4 of the Constitution.

It is established that the government as a collective – and ultimately the Prime Minister – is responsible for compliance with the Act.[22]

ii. Section 2

The second section includes provisions describing the purpose of the climate work to be carried out by the government and how that work shall be carried out. It states that the government shall implement a climate policy with the aim of preventing dangerous interference with the climate system. According to the Government Bill, the starting points of the provisions are: (i) the UN Convention on Climate Change; and (ii) Chapter 1, section 2 of the Constitution, which includes an obligation on public authorities to promote sustainable development, which shall ensure a good environment for present and future generations. In order to reach the climate targets, a radical adaptation by society will be required.[23]

The climate policy work of the government shall also contribute to protecting ecosystems, as well as present and future generations, against harmful effects of climate change. The government shall focus on reducing CO_2 and other greenhouse gas emissions, and maintaining and restoring environmental functions that mitigate climate change and its harmful effects. This includes the use of natural functions in the ecosystem. It is also established that the climate work shall be based on scientific research and on relevant technical, social, economic and environmental considerations.

C. A Long-Term Target, and Planning, Monitoring and Reporting

i. Section 3

In order to create the prerequisites for a long-term and stable climate policy, the third Section of the act establishes that the government's climate policy shall be designed to secure the long-term, timebound emission target adopted by Parliament (after being proposed by the government). In addition to this long-term target established by Parliament, the government shall set any other emission reduction targets needed to achieve the long-term target.

Furthermore, it is established in this section that climate policy shall be implemented in a manner that enables climate targets and budgetary targets to interact.

According to the Government Bill, the government shall decide in each specific case whether these targets shall be decided by itself or submitted to Parliament

---

[22] Government Bill, 51.
[23] ibid 51 f.

for a decision.[24] It is notable that the Swedish interim targets for 2020, 2030 and 2040 have all been decided by Parliament. The target for 2020 was decided in 2009 and the targets for 2030 and 2040 were decided when the CPF was adopted.

Planning, monitoring and reporting to Parliament on a regular basis can contribute to the clarity, continuity and the long-termism of climate policy. Section 3 also ensures that the CPF is therefore complemented with a planning and monitoring system, which takes the emission targets adopted by Parliament as its starting point. Based on this, the Climate Act states that an annual climate report, as well as a climate action plan for each government's term of office, shall be submitted to Parliament by the government.

In order to achieve the ambitious climate targets that have been set out, an efficient, credible and long-term climate policy is required. Regular action plans can contribute to creating continuity and predictability.[25] The basic parts of this system are set out under the terms of the Climate Act, but the Government Bill explains that each government shall have the possibility to decide in detail on how to draw up the plan.[26]

ii. Section 4

Section 4 states that each year, the government shall include a climate report to Parliament in the Budget Bill. The climate report shall contain: (1) an account of the progress towards emissions reduction; (2) an account of the most important decisions within the climate policy during the year and the impact these decisions will have on the mitigation of the greenhouse gas emissions; and (3) an assessment of whether there is need of additional measures and, if so, when and how such additional measures shall be decided. The purpose of this provision is to ensure continuity in the ongoing climate work.

According to the Government Bill, the climate report shall include emissions in both the Effort Sharing Regulation sector and the sector of the EU Emissions Trading Scheme (EU ETS).[27] As the information is made public in this manner, the need for and importance of taking measures within all policy areas is made visible, while at the same time, Parliament and the public are given access to information on how the climate work is carried out on a regular basis.[28]

iii. Section 5

Section 5 establishes that every four years, the government shall draw up a climate policy action plan. Thus, it will be the task of every government to draw up or

[24] ibid 47.
[25] ibid 39 f.
[26] ibid.
[27] ibid 40.
[28] ibid 53.

revise an existing action plan for how the climate targets shall be achieved.[29] The action plan should be turned over to Parliament the year after ordinary elections to Parliament, thus ensuring that the work to reach the interim targets and the long-term emissions target is integrated into the government's other policy areas from the outset.[30]

Section 5 includes eight points to be included in the climate action plan:

- Sweden's commitments within the EU framework and internationally;
- historical greenhouse gas emissions data, including the most recent emissions inventory;
- emissions reduction projections;
- an assessment of the effect of the measures taken to reduce emissions;
- the measures planned, including approximate information on when the measures will start;
- the extent to which the decided-upon and planned measures to reduce emissions will be expected to have an impact on reaching the national and global targets (which according to the Government Bill also includes measures taken or planned in relation to Sweden's international engagements, such as aid, technology transfer and international investments);[31]
- the extent to which the government's collective policy, in all relevant cost areas, contributes to reaching the national and global climate targets;
- any additional measures or decisions which may be required in order to reach national and global targets.[32]

IV. The Swedish CPF and Sweden's Climate Targets

The second pillar of the CPF includes the adoption of new ambitious climate targets. In order to reach the targets in the Paris Agreement, all states need to undertake tougher targets, and in this respect Sweden intends to take a leading role internationally.

The CPF introduces a tougher long-term target:

> By 2045, at the latest, Sweden shall have zero net emissions of greenhouse gas emissions into the atmosphere and shall thereafter achieve negative emissions.[33] Negative emissions mean that the overall amount of greenhouse gas emissions into the atmosphere

---

[29] The targets are outlined below.
[30] Government Bill, 40.
[31] ibid 53 f.
[32] ibid 53.
[33] ibid 25 f.

will be reduced. That is, the amount of greenhouse gases emitted by Sweden shall be less than the amount of greenhouse gases reduced through the natural eco-cycle, or through climate projects pursued by Sweden abroad.[34] The emissions from operations in Sweden shall also be at least 85 per cent lower than in 1990.[35]

In order to reach the long-term target, carbon capture and storage can be used where no other reasonable alternatives are available, as stated in the Government Bill.[36] The target also assumes that the rest of the world acts so that emissions are reduced in accordance with the Paris Agreement and that the EU adopts increased reduction levels under the EU ETS.[37] The government will monitor the climate undertakings and climate measures taken by other countries, and will assess how these contribute to the global climate transformation and affect the competition situation for Swedish corporations.[38]

Based on current population forecasts, the new target would mean that emissions in Sweden would be less than one tonne per person in 2045.

The CPF also includes the following interim targets for 2030 and 2040:

- By 2030, emissions from domestic transport, excluding domestic aviation, shall be reduced by at least 70 per cent compared to 2010.

- By 2030, emissions in Sweden in the sectors covered by the EU Effort Sharing Regulation (which means greenhouse gas emissions outside the EU ETS) shall be at least 63 per cent lower than in 1990.

- By 2040, emissions in Sweden in the sectors that will be covered by the EU Effort Sharing Regulation shall be at least 75 per cent lower than in 1990.

The targets above reflect the international leadership role that Sweden intends to take on and demonstrate that it will undertake to achieve emission reductions which far exceed its required emission reductions under the EU Effort Sharing Regulation, which states that emission reductions in Sweden shall be 40 per cent lower by 2030 than in 1990.

As regards the targets for 2030 and 2040, these can in part be achieved through supplementary measures, such as the increased uptake of CO_2 by forests or investments in climate projects abroad. Such measures may be used to achieve maximum reductions of 8 per cent and 2 per cent of the emission reduction targets for 2030 and 2040, respectively. In other words, by 2030 emissions from activities in Sweden should be at least 55 per cent lower than in 1990, and by 2040 at least 73 per cent lower than in 1990.

---

[34] ibid 33 f.
[35] ibid 25.
[36] ibid.
[37] ibid 27 f.
[38] ibid 25 f.

V. The Swedish CPF and the Climate Policy Council

The third pillar of the CPF is the establishment of a Climate Policy Council. The Climate Policy Council is an interdisciplinary expert body that supports the government by providing an independent assessment of the extent to which the overall policy presented by the government is compatible with the climate targets. The Council evaluates whether the direction of various policy areas will increase or reduce the likelihood of achieving the climate targets. The Council operates as an agency under the government, meaning that the independence of the Committee in relation to the government could be questioned, unlike in the case of the UK Committee on Climate Change, which is independent of the UK government and reports annually to the UK Parliament. The reason for the model chosen was that at the legislative stage comparison was made to the existing Swedish Fiscal Policy Council, which was established in 2007 and undertakes a similar role in that it reviews the government's fiscal policy.[39] The Swedish legislator preferred to choose an existing type of national legal model at the time when the Climate Policy Council was being established.

The work of the Climate Policy Council is not regulated in the Climate Act, but in a Government Ordinance with Instructions to the Climate Policy Council (Swedish: Förordning (2017:1268) med instruktion för Klimatpolitiska rådet) (hereinafter 'the Ordinance'). The Council is led by a committee, which consists of a chairman, a deputy chairman and no more than six other delegates. The delegates are appointed by the government following proposals by the Climate Policy Council. The Climate Policy Council shall make proposals which ensure that the committee includes delegates with high levels of scientific competence within climate, climate policy, political economics, social science and behavioural science and that there is an even allocation of the types of competence covered.[40]

The Swedish Climate Policy Council is required to:

- evaluate if the present policies contribute to or counteract the climate targets;
- review the effects of both existing and planned policies from a broad societal perspective;
- identify policy areas where additional measures need to be taken if the climate targets are to be achieved.

Besides evaluating government policy, the Climate Policy Council is also tasked with evaluating the analytical methods and models which are the basis for the government's climate policies, as well as contributing to the debate regarding climate policy.[41]

---

[39] ibid 41 f.
[40] Section 11 of the Ordinance.
[41] ibid s 2.

By the end of March each year, the Climate Policy Council is required to report to the government, and the report shall include: (i) an assessment of the climate work and the development of the emissions; (ii) an assessment of how the government's policy complies with the climate targets; and (iii) any other analyses and assessments that the Council has made. The Council is also required, within three months of the government's submission of its climate policy action plan, to submit a report to the government giving an assessment of the plan.[42]

VI. Adaptation and Capacity Building

In light of the Paris Agreement and its three pillars of mitigation, adaptation and capacity-building, it is worth noting that the Swedish CPF does not cover climate adaptation. This reflects the fact that domestic climate adaptation is considered to be part of another area of environmental policy, somewhat connected to water management and overall environmental protection. In this sense, the Swedish national framework stands apart from climate governance in many other countries, where capacity-building for adaptation is inter-related with the development of mitigating actions.

The CPF is also focused on domestic policies; assisting with mitigation or adaptation activities and capacity-building in developing countries is not covered. This does not mean that such reforms will not be carried out. Sweden has taken a very active role in global climate finance, assisting developing countries with climate policy issues. It has been part of the board for the UNFCCC Adaptation Fund and was one of the instrumental parties in the establishment of the UNFCCC Green Climate Fund. It has actively participated in the Clean Development Mechanism and capacity-building projects in developing countries, and has also actively contributed to World Bank Climate Funds addressing developing countries.

VII. Some Critical Views on the Climate Act

There was generally overwhelmingly positive feedback from different groups in society over the fact that there was a multi-party agreement on more ambitious climate policy targets for Sweden and on establishing a framework, including a law, to underpin the seriousness of reaching these targets.[43] Most of the disagreement that was raised concerned the climate targets. The views expressed were both that the climate targets were not stringent enough to fulfil the Paris Agreement and that

---

[42] Section 5 of the Ordinance.
[43] Compilation of the responses in the referral process, Ministry of Energy and Environment 2016-09-14 no M2016/00703/Kl.

they were too tough for Sweden's exporting economy.[44] These views came from the environmental NGOs and academia,[45] and some of the business sector organisations and economists, respectively.[46] However, criticism was also raised against the non-traditional approach to regulation and especially the proposed Climate Act. Academia and various Swedish actors regarded the Act not as a 'real' law, but rather as a piece of policy,[47] and it was considered that the Act should incentivise more stakeholders and place demands directly on actors.[48] These opinions were for the most part raised in the official referral process in which 130 bodies gave the government their responses.

There were opinions disagreeing on the legal character of the Climate Act, especially voiced by the legal community. Most important was the opinion of the Council of Legislation,[49] which suggested that the Climate Act be rejected on the basis that the legal form did not serve the purpose, since it contained no legal sanctions. The Swedish Administration for Public Management (Swedish: Statskontoret) expressed a similar view and was the only referral body (out of a total of 130) to completely reject the proposal on a CPF. In its opinion, it was inappropriate to put political ambitions into law in the way that the Climate Act did.[50] On the other hand, the Administrative Court in Sundsvall suggested the Climate Act should instead be part of the Swedish Constitution, as its aim was to limit the power of the government.[51]

Another opinion on the Climate Act concerned the lack of involvement and responsibilities placed on businesses and other climate actors, such as the municipalities.[52] Although the CPF recognises the importance of involving many actors in the transition of society, this is not reflected in the Climate Act, which has the government as its addressee. Some academic institutions raised the view that

---

[44] Compilation of the responses in the referral process, Ministry of Energy and Environment 2016-09-14 no M2016/00703/Kl, 4 and 5.

[45] Response in the referral process by Svenska Naturskyddsföreningen 2016-06-10; Response in the referral process by the Centre for Climate Science Policy Research at Linköping University 2016-06-08.

[46] Response in the referral process by Svenskt Näringsliv 2016-06-15 dnr 47/2016; and by The National Institute of Economic Research (Swedish: Konjunkturinstitutet) 2016-04-19 Dnr 2016-46.

[47] University of Uppsala suggested a more detailed legislation in their response in the referral process, 2016-06-07 UFV 2016/436; see also the response in the referral process by Statskontoret 2016-06-03 no 2016/57-4.

[48] Among these were the Climate Municipalities (Swedish: Klimatkommunerna), the University of Gothenburg Department for Environmental Economics and the Centre for Climate Science Policy Research at Linköping University.

[49] Protocol of opinion decided 2017-02-15. The Council on Legislation scrutinises draft bills which the government intends to submit to Parliament. The views are decided by a group of judges, including a justice of the Supreme Court or a justice of the Supreme Administrative Court; they are of an advisory nature and are not binding on the government or Parliament.

[50] Response in the referral process by Statskontoret 2016-06-03 no 2016/57-4.

[51] Response in the referral process by Kammarrätten i Sundsvall 2016-06-07 no 5-2016.

[52] Response in the referral process by the Climate Municipalities (Swedish: Klimatkommunerna) 2016-06-09.

by only addressing the government, the Climate Act would be weak in pushing for mitigating actions.[53]

So far, little has been said about the Swedish Climate Act in the legal literature: neither high-ranked environmental law scholars nor scholars in administrative or constitutional law have yet published any in-depth analysis or commentaries.[54] Looking at the Act alone using traditional legal dogmatic methodology, many would say that it is in itself weak, especially so as its provisions are very general and it does not include an enforcement mechanism or any other legal effects in case the government does not fulfil its obligations. However, more comprehensive scientific questions around the correlation between the new Act and the general environmental legislation, as well as the Act's impact on mitigating policies, need to be investigated. This new way to legislate on climate issues also raises new questions, such as what the inter-relationship between legal and political responsibility could be.

VIII. The CPF in Action

This section provides an analysis of the outcomes of the CPF in its first year in action. It covers the reporting from the Climate Policy Council and the indications this gives on the role taken by the new institution. It also gives an overview of the annual cycle of public reports on climate policies and climate emissions. Finally, it discusses how the Climate Act and its long-term climate goals have incentivised NGOs, authorities and the government to act in some cases regarding sources of carbon emissions.

A. The Climate Policy Council's First Recommendations

As the Climate Act entered into force in January 2018, the Swedish Climate Policy Council submitted its first report in March that year. With only a few months to set up the Council and prepare the report, the latter did not include a comprehensive evaluation of the government's climate policy actions, but rather a first declaration

---

[53] Response in the referral process by University of Gothenburg through the department for environmental economics 2016-05-31 no VR 2016/28 and the Centre for Climate Science Policy Research at Linköping University, 2016-06-08.

[54] A master's thesis in environmental law 2017 analysed how the Act establishes the responsibility of the government and whether there is recourse to legal review of the government's actions. As the Act does not have constitutional rank and does not include recourse to legal review, the thesis concludes that the Act is insufficient as a tool for mitigating climate change. See William Ellerström, 'Det klimatpolitiska ramverket – En analys av det klimatpolitiska ramverket i ljuset av Climate Change Act 2008' (master's thesis, University of Lund, 2017).

from the Council of its ambitions and line of work. In this report, the Council defined a broad scope for its task:

> The commission to review the government's comprehensive policy underscores the broad and interdisciplinary nature of the climate challenge. Achieving a fossil free society with zero net emissions of greenhouse gases in the next 25 years requires a transition of the society, with a complex interplay between factors, actors and driving forces. The climate issue thereby also spans over almost all scientific disciplines.[55]

The Council also pointed out the importance of evaluating the basis of the government's climate policies and scrutinising the models used for scenario analysis. It specified that it intended to cooperate with several national authorities as well as universities in this work.

The first full evaluation report was launched by the Council in March 2019, following the first 'record of climate policies' delivered together with the Budget Bill for 2019.[56] In this report, the Council set as its ambition to examine the government's policies related to climate actions and regarding policy targets, organisation and work procedures, as well as regarding all specific policy instruments.[57] The report concluded that progress is too slow and pointed out that transport and the EU ETS are critical areas for achieving the climate targets.[58]

The Council in particular scrutinised policies related to the transport sector, finding that progress is too slow and that more policies are needed to be able to meet the Swedish interim climate target for 2030. The report criticised the government for not presenting an analysis of the comprehensive policies effecting climate emissions, but rather limiting it to policies directed at climate mitigation. The Council also questioned the method of presenting the climate record as an annex to the environmental budget and proposed that it should be parallel to the fiscal plan, which is a central part of the Budget Bill.

The release of this first climate evaluation report was communicated quite broadly by the media.[59] The report was the basis for a special debate in Parliament two months after its release. However, what impact the report will have on political reforms cannot be analysed until the government's four-year climate policy is presented.[60] The council has made use of a new tool to visualise climate emissions and policy instruments pertaining to the mitigation of future emissions.[61]

---

[55] Climate Policy Council Report 2018, summary in English, 5.

[56] Annex to Budget Bill expenditures no 20 on the Environment; this was presented to Parliament in November 2018 by the 'caretaking' government, which awaited a new government to take office after the elections in September 2018 that resulted in an unclear situation in Parliament.

[57] Climate Policy Council Report 2019, summary in English, 10.

[58] ibid 2 f.

[59] All daily Swedish media referred to the release of the report, including Swedish Television.

[60] Section 5 of the Climate Act prescribes that this plan is presented to Parliament the year after a general election.

[61] The Climate View tool; the Swedish version is called 'Panorama'.

Together with the Swedish Environmental Protection Agency (EPA) (Swedish: Naturvårdsverket) and the Swedish Energy Agency (Swedish Energimyndigheten), the Climate Policy Council carries out the work to keep this tool updated. The intention is that the tool shall assist in building a better understanding for the challenges of the climate transition in various sectors.

The challenging Swedish goal for the transport sector of a 70 per cent reduction of emissions for 2030 means that the Climate Policy Council has devoted extra attention to reforms in that sector. One reform that gets much attention is the requirement to, little by little, substitute fossil fuels with renewables. The Council states that a robust decision to phase out all fossil fuels in the transport sector before 2040 is needed in order to fulfil the goal. This means that there is a need to substantially raise the level of renewable fuels, such as biodiesel and biogasoline, to be mixed into the fossil fuels in the ordinary fuel pumps. There is already a regulation in place demanding that companies selling fuels for transport should raise the content of renewables in both diesel and gasoline by more than the EU Directive RED II has set as a minimum. Policy actions to incentivise sustainable production of biofuels in Sweden have also been proposed by the Council.[62] Such proposals may be taken forward and launched in the government's climate policy action plan.

B. The Scheme to Monitor, Report and Evaluate Set by the Swedish CPF

The comprehensive monitor-reporting and evaluation scheme set by the climate policy framework can be summarised as follows:

Each year:

- March – the Climate Policy Council provides its policies evaluation report to the government;[63]
- September (unless it is an election year) – the government publishes its climate report to Parliament in the Budget Bill[64] on the results of the policies.

The year after general elections, by law every fourth year on the second Sunday in September (2018 was the most recent election year):

- the government provides a climate policy action plan to Parliament[65] on all climate measures planned and the projected impact of these; and

---

[62] Report of the Swedish Climate Policy Council 2019, 58.
[63] Section 4 of the Ordinance.
[64] Climate Act, s 4.
[65] ibid s 5.

- the Climate Policy Council submits within three months of the government's submission of its climate policy action plan a report to the government with an assessment of the plan.[66]

The monitoring of the climate emissions is also regulated by international agreements. Therefore, the Swedish EPA each year in March and April reports the official statistics of climate emissions to both the EU and to the UNFCCC Secretariat. There is a two-year delay in these statistics in order to make them robust. Hence, in March 2019, the statistics for the territorial climate emissions of 2017 were released.[67] In April each year, the EPA releases a simplified set of statistics for the previous year.

Put together, this scheme makes it possible to continuously follow the development of both emissions levels and policy actions taken. As all reporting is public, any actor and member of society may be informed. Importantly, facts on the climate issue may more easily inform the political debates. When the government reports something by law to Parliament, the Members of Parliament may act, debate the matter and propose actions in addition to what is planned by the government.

IX. The Climate Act and Environmental Permits for Large Emitters

The Swedish Climate Act's obligations are directed at the government and the Act establishes a structure to be followed by the government to ensure that there is enough progress in reaching the Swedish climate targets. The Act does not include legal limitations on individual actors. However, the Act has been referred to in legal action involving the government and concerning road planning procedures and the licensing of oil refineries and gas pipelines,[68] indicating that the Act might also be used in substantive matters where there is a risk of the emission of substantial amounts of climate gases.

In planning for the Södertörn Crosslink Project, a new motorway in the southern Stockholm region, the Swedish Transport Administration (Swedish: Trafikverket) carried out public consultations and prepared an Environmental Impact Assessment (EIA), as required by environmental legislation. In its consultation opinion, the EPA raised several critical points about the project and referred to the Climate Act and the climate targets.[69] It argued for a more comprehensive EIA,

---

[66] Section 5 of the Ordinance.

[67] The statistics are available on the Swedish EPA website: https://www.naturvardsverket.se/Sa-mar-miljon/Statistik-A-O/Vaxthusgaser-territoriella-utslapp-och-upptag.

[68] See the following paragraphs and references below.

[69] Swedish Environmental Protection Agency, consultation opinion Södertörn Crosslink Project 2019-02-15 no NV-03101-16.

which must include figures on the amount of increased traffic and emissions expected from the project. As 93 per cent of Swedish climate emissions from domestic transport stem from road transport, this is of relevance to the national climate targets. Under the environmental law, the Swedish government can choose to decide on the permissibility of activities that may have a considerable negative effect on the environment.[70] The EPA thus argued for letting the government decide on the permissibility of the project instead of having ordinary decision procedure. The EPA underscored the importance of the environmental standards that apply to the project by referring to the CPF and specifically the target to decrease greenhouse gas emissions from the transport sector – 'a target decided in accordance with the climate law'.[71] The road planning process is ongoing within the Swedish Transport Administration and there has been no action taken so far by the government in response to the EPA opinion.

Another ongoing project that includes a discussion related to the Climate Act is a licensing process for the enlargement of an oil refinery in Lysekil on the Swedish west coast. The petroleum company Preem has applied for an environmental permit to handle 2.5 million tonnes of residual high-sulphur oil products to make diesel and gasoline with a low sulphur content. This would raise climate emissions from the process in the refinery from 1.7 million tonnes to 3.4 million tonnes of CO_2, which would make the refinery the single biggest emitter of climate gases in Sweden. The emissions from the refinery are included in the EU ETS and according to the Swedish Environmental Code, such emissions shall not be limited by conditions in the environmental permit.[72] The Swedish regulation is an implementation of Article 9(1) of the EU Industrial Emission Directive (IED).[73] However, as described above, the Swedish long-term climate goal also covers emissions from Swedish industries within the EU ETS. Therefore, a significant increase in emissions from those industries will affect the possibility of achieving the climate targets set in the CPF and the long-term target referred to in the Climate Act.

In the *Preem* case, the Swedish Association of Nature Conservation (Swedish: Naturskyddsföreningen (NF)), which is the biggest member-based environmental NGO in Sweden, has appealed the decision by the Land and Environment Court in Vänersborg to grant the refinery an environmental permit for increased production.[74] In its appeal, NF has claimed that the permit should be denied because of the potential negative climate effects, arguing that the Climate Act makes it necessary to change the conditions for the climate emitters.[75]In June 2019, the

---

[70] Chapter 17, s 3 of the Environmental Code.

[71] Swedish Environmental Protection Agency, consultation opinion Södertörn Crosslink Project 2019-02-15 no NV-03101-16.

[72] Swedish Environmental Code 16, ch 2 c §.

[73] Directive 2010/75/EU of the European Parliament and of the Council of 24 November 2010 on industrial emissions.

[74] The Land and Environment Court at the District Court in Vänersborg, judgment of 9 November 2018, Case no M 4708-16, permit application for enlarged operation at Preemraff in Lysekil.

[75] Appeal from the Swedish Association of Nature Conservation in Case no M 11730-18, Land and Environment Court of Appeal.

EPA notified the government of the refinery's permit application with reference to Chapter 17, section 3 of the Environmental Code, and argued in an opinion, referring inter alia to the new climate targets decided in accordance with the Climate Act, that the government should use its right to decide on the permissibility of the enlarged activity.[76] In August 2019, the government announced that it would decide on the permissibility after guidance provided by the Land and Environment Court of Appeal's judgment.[77] In June 2020, the Land and Environment Court of Appeal issued its advisory opinion to the government, stating: (i) that a permit for the enlarged refinery can be approved; and (ii) that the Climate Act does not apply on the Preem permit process, as the Act contains guidelines for the government's climate policy work and does not apply to the permit procedure of individual operations. The next step is for the government to decide whether the permit for the enlarged refinery shall be approved or not.[78]

In October 2019, the government decided to reject an application from Swedgas for a 40-year concession for a pipeline of gas from a harbour in Gothenburg that was to be connected to the main gas network.[79] The main argument from the government to deny the pipeline was that such long-lived infrastructure designed for natural gas was not in line with the climate policies to go climate neutral by 2045, and the Minister of Climate said the decision shows that the government 'takes the Climate Act seriously'.[80] The expert agency preparing the matter for the government did not analyse the time aspect or the potential conflict with the Climate Act in its opinion.[81] However, the government has a wide level of discretion when deciding such cases, as the law prescribes that a concession can only be allowed if it is appropriate from a general point of view.[82]

The Södertörn Crosslink Project, Preem Oil Refinery and Swedgas Pipeline cases indicate that although the Climate Act does not include legal limitations on individual actors, it is referred to in some legal actions involving the government. Further, the government seems to be able to take the Act into account when deciding individual cases. Notably, in order for the government to be able to fulfil the ambitious national climate targets and the requirements in the Climate Act, additional tools are required to provide the government as well as the legal system

---

[76] Swedish Environmental Protection Agency, opinion to the Government 2019-06-27 no NV-05187-19.

[77] Governmental decision of 23 August 2019, background from Ministry of Environment no M2019/01299/Me.

[78] Land and Environment Court of Appeal 2020-06-15, Case no M-11730-18 https://www.domstol.se/mark--och-miljooverdomstolen/nyheter/2020/06/domstolen-anser-att-verksamheten-vid-preemraff-i-lysekil-kan-tillatas.

[79] Governmental decision of 10 October 2019, background from Ministry of Environment no I2019/00911/E.

[80] Isabella Lövin, Minister of Climate and the Environment, interview for the magazine *Sveriges Natur*, available at: http://www.sverigesnatur.org/aktuellt/tillstandet-for-gasterminalen-i-goteborg-avslas-av-regeringen.

[81] Swedish Energy Market Inspectorate opinion to the Government, 28 June 2018, no 2016-102263.

[82] Law on Natural Gas (2005:403) ch 2, s 5.

with the power to control emissions. The government has appointed a public investigator to investigate and prepare proposals on how to update the Swedish legislation, especially the Environmental Code, in order to better implement the CPF.[83]

X. Conclusions

To conclude, the Swedish CPF with the Climate Act, indicative and long-term climate targets, and the Climate Policy Council have been in force since 2018. They aim to structure the government's work on Swedish climate policies and requests by law so that the government acts to fulfil national targets on climate mitigation. Sweden has decided to reach net-zero emissions by 2045 at the latest and has also set a series of interim targets. This ambition is well ahead of the present EU climate targets and Sweden has intentions as a country to take a leading role in combating climate change.

The Climate Act is general in nature and only includes five sections, with a focus on the government's planning, monitoring and reporting to Parliament. The specific climate policy measures are regulated separately. The role of the Climate Policy Council, which mainly consists of scientists from a broad range of disciplines, is to evaluate the government's progress towards the climate targets. Regular and transparent reporting on policies and their effects on greenhouse gas emissions is seen to contribute to the clarity, continuity and long-term nature of the climate policy. The Climate Act does not provide for a legal review of the government's actions or inactions. However, there is a constitutional obligation for Parliament to control the work of the government and this obligation was highlighted when preparing the Act.

The CPF is based on a broad political agreement that was negotiated in an All-Party Committee, in which experts from both environmental NGOs and the business sector also participated.[84] The CPF had as its models both the UK Climate Change Act 2008 and a Swedish Fiscal Policy Framework which has been in place since the mid-1990s. Another inspiration was the Paris Agreement, as negotiations on the Swedish framework were held in parallel with the process for the global agreement.

To legislate for climate issues with a Climate Act is a novelty in Sweden. The legal form of the Climate Act, which gives the government a general instruction to ensure that climate action is taken, is a new form of legislation, and thus the implications for climate policies and for climate regulation in the Swedish

---

[83] Instructions no 2019:101, decided by the Government 2019-12-17, https://www.regeringen. se/4afb50/contentassets/244f4e7ae3c64b25b2f167077cedee03/oversyn-av-relevant-lagstiftning-for-att-uppna-sveriges-klimatmal-dir.-2019101.

[84] SOU 2016:21, 'A CPF for Sweden', proposal by the Committee of Environmental Quality Goals, March 2016.

Environmental Code are not yet clear. The Climate Policy Council has already pointed out the need for additional legal climate regulation for the government and the legal system in order to have sufficient tools to ensure that the Swedish climate targets are achieved. Going forward, it is clear that legal researchers have an important role to play in order to deepen the understanding of the legal system in the context of national and global climate governance.

8

The Dutch Response to Climate Change

Evaluating the Netherlands' Climate Act and Associated Issues of Importance

OTTO SPIJKERS AND SOFIE OOSTERHUIS

I. Introduction

This chapter provides an analysis of the substantive and procedural elements of the Netherlands Climate Act ('klimaatwet')[1] and the Netherlands Climate Agreement ('klimaatakkoord').[2] First, the Act itself is introduced and then it is critically assessed on its compatibility with international legal obligations binding on the Netherlands, in particular obligations based on the Paris Agreement.[3] Special attention is paid to the role of public participation in the implementation of the Act.[4] We will then look at the Netherlands Climate Agreement and will again pay special attention to the role of public participation in the drafting and implementation thereof. Through this Climate Agreement, governmental bodies, companies and civil society organisations in the Netherlands commit themselves to take specific measures to combat climate change. A separate section is devoted to the relationship between the Climate Act and Agreement, and the *Urgenda* litigation.

---

[1] Climate Act of 2 July 2019, setting out a framework for developing a policy aimed at the irreversible and step-by-step reduction of Dutch greenhouse gas emissions in order to limit global warming and climate change (Climate Act or Act), published in the Official Gazette of the Kingdom of the Netherlands (Staatsblad van het Koninkrijk der Nederlanden), 2019, no 253 (Climate Act of 2 July 2019).

[2] Climate Agreement (Klimaatakkoord) of 28 June 2019 (Climate Agreement or Agreement), https://www.klimaatakkoord.nl/binaries/klimaatakkoord/documenten/publicaties/2019/06/28/klimaatakkoord/klimaatakkoord.pdf (in Dutch).

[3] Paris Agreement, concluded 12 December 2015, entered into force 4 November 2016.

[4] For a more theoretical discussion on (global) public participation, see Otto Spijkers, 'The World's Citizens Get Involved in Global Policymaking: Global Resistance, Global Public Participation, and Global Democracy' (2016) 1(1) *Inter Gentes: McGill Journal of International Law & Legal Pluralism* 18; and Otto Spijkers and Arron Honniball, 'Developing Global Public Participation' (2015) 17(3) *International Community Law Review* 219.

The three instruments discussed – the Climate Act, the Climate Agreement and the judgments in the *Urgenda* case – are closely related to each other.[5] The Climate Act binds the government in its relationship with Parliament and the Senate. The Climate Agreement consists of a series of non-legally binding commitments made by governmental bodies, companies and civil society organisations in the Netherlands. The Act and the Agreement have the same goal – to reduce greenhouse gas emissions from the Netherlands – but they operate in parallel and have been drafted simultaneously through separate processes. A third development, which again runs in parallel with the other two, is a tort case, initiated against the State of the Netherlands by a foundation called Urgenda.[6] The District Court,[7] the Appeals Court[8] and the Supreme Court all agreed with Urgenda that the State of the Netherlands is legally obliged to do more than it currently does to combat climate change.[9] This tort claim is not based on either the Climate Act or the Climate Agreement, because the initiation of this case, which occurred on 18 December 2013, pre-dates the adoption of both the Act and the Agreement.[10] It also pre-dates the entry into force of the Paris Agreement. Initially, Urgenda could thus not rely on any of those legal instruments; instead, its claim was based on a combination of Dutch domestic civil law – primarily Article 162, Book 6 of the Dutch Civil Code[11] – and European and international (human rights) law – primarily Articles 2 and 8 of the European Convention on Human Rights (ECHR).[12] Even

---

[5] See also Tom Smolders, 'Is de Klimaatwet "Urgenda-proof"?' (2019) 1 *Tijdschrift voor Omgevingsrecht* 1; EC van der Maden and AB Vos, 'Klimaatwet en Klimaatakkoord: Verslag van een VMR Themamiddag op 9 oktober 2018' (2018) 110 *Milieu en Recht,* https://www.navigator.nl/document/id1d830c82a7524f4f832bf0b3ba193829/milieu-recht-klimaatwet-en-klimaatakkoord; and CW Backes, 'De Klimaatwet – de meest ambitieuze of de meest minimalistische ter wereld?' (2018) 150 *Tijdschrift voor Bouwrecht* 989.

[6] See also Otto Spijkers, 'The *Urgenda* Case: A Successful Example of Public Interest Litigation for the Protection of the Environment?' in Christina Voigt and Zen Makuch (eds), *Courts and the Environment* (Cheltenham, Edward Elgar, 2018); and Otto Spijkers, 'Urgenda tegen de Staat der Nederlanden: aan wiens kant staat de Nederlandse burger eigenlijk?' [2019] *Ars aequi* 191.

[7] District Court, The Hague, Judgment of 24 June 2015 in the case between the Urgenda foundation and the State of the Netherlands (Ministry of Infrastructure and the Environment). English translation available at: http://deeplink.rechtspraak.nl/uitspraak?id=ECLI:NL:RBDHA:2015:7196 (hereinafter *Urgenda* District Court Judgment).

[8] Appeals Court, The Hague, Judgment of 9 October 2018 in the case between the State of the Netherlands (Ministry of Infrastructure and the Environment) and the Urgenda foundation. English translation available at: http://deeplink.rechtspraak.nl/uitspraak?id=ECLI:NL:GHDHA:2018:2610 (hereinafter *Urgenda* Appeals Court Judgment).

[9] Netherlands Supreme Court, Judgment of 20 December 2019 in the case between the State of the Netherlands (Ministry of Infrastructure and the Environment) and the Urgenda foundation. Judgment available at: http://deeplink.rechtspraak.nl/uitspraak?id=ECLI:NL:HR:2019:2006 (hereinafter *Urgenda* Supreme Court Judgment).

[10] Urgenda's writ of summons can be found on its website: https://www.urgenda.nl/wp-content/uploads/DagvaardingUrgendaKlimaatzaak19-11-13.pdf (in Dutch).

[11] Article 162, Book 6 of the Dutch Civil Code (Burgerlijk Wetboek), https://wetten.overheid.nl/jci1.3:c:BWBR0005289&boek=6&titeldeel=3&afdeling=1&artikel=162&z=2019-04-01&g=2019-04-01 (in Dutch).

[12] Convention for the Protection of Human Rights and Fundamental Freedoms, concluded in Rome, 4 November 1950, entered into force 1953.

though the Climate Act and Agreement are formally unrelated to the *Urgenda* litigation, all three of these set greenhouse gas emissions reduction targets to be met by the Netherlands before a certain deadline; thus, they are closely linked to each other.

II. The Netherlands Climate Act

A. Introduction

The Climate Act has been approved by both Parliament and the Senate. It was subsequently signed into law by the King, was published[13] and entered into force 1 September 2019.[14] The Act aims to provide a long-term legal framework for policy-making relating to climate change in the decades to come.

Looking at the *travaux préparatoires*[15] of the Act, it is interesting to compare the initial proposal of the Climate Act (First Draft of September 2016)[16] with the revised versions (the Second Draft of January 2017[17] and the Third Draft of December 2018[18]) and see what motivated the changes that were made.[19]

The Act sets three general targets. First, it is stipulated that greenhouse gas emissions from the Netherlands must be reduced by at least 95 per cent in 2050 compared to 1990 levels in order to bring a climate-neutral society within reach. This target was included in the initial draft and has not been changed.[20]

Second, an intermediate goal is set: a significant reduction of greenhouse gas emissions from the Netherlands must already be reached by 2030, again measured

---

[13] Climate Act of 2 July 2019.

[14] Except for art 7, which entered into force on 1 January 2020. See Decree of 2 July 2019, determining the time of entry into force of the Climate Act, published in the Official Gazette of the Kingdom of the Netherlands (Staatsblad van het Koninkrijk der Nederlanden), 2019, no 254.

[15] The term *travaux préparatoires* is used to refer to the collection of documents relating to the negotiation, discussions and drafting of the Act. These documents can also be referred to as the negotiating or drafting history of the Act.

[16] First (Original) Draft Act by members Klaver and Samsom, *Establishing a framework for the development of a policy, aimed at irreversible and step-by-step reduction of Dutch greenhouse gas emissions, in order to limit global warming and climate change (Climate Act)*, 34 534, Nr 2, Parliament (Second Chamber), 2015–2016, submitted 12 September 2016 (hereinafter 'First Draft').

[17] Revised Draft Act by members Klaver, Kuiken, Roemer, van Veldhoven and Dik-Faber, revised pursuant to the Advice of the Council of State, Climate Act, 34 534, Nr 6, Parliament (Second Chamber), 2016–17, submitted 27 January 2017 (hereinafter 'Second Draft').

[18] Revised Draft Act by members Klaver, Asscher, Beckerman, Jetten, Dik-Faber, Yesilgöz-Zegerius, Agnes Mulder and Geleijnse, Climate Act, 34 534, A, Senate (First Chamber), 2018–19, submitted 20 December 2018 (hereinafter 'Third Draft').

[19] Note of Change by members Klaver, Asscher, Beckerman, Jetten, Dik-Faber, Yesilgöz-Zegerius and Agnes Mulder, Climate Act, 34 534, Nr 10, Parliament (Second Chamber), 2017–18, submitted 27 June 2018 (hereinafter 'Note of Change'). A Second Note of Change by members Klaver, Asscher, Beckerman, Jetten, Dik-Faber, Yesilgöz-Zegerius, Agnes Mulder and Geleijnse, Climate Act, 34 534, Nr 37, Parliament (Second Chamber), 2018–19, only contains minor technical changes.

[20] First Draft, art 3(2); Second Draft, art 3(2); and Third Draft, art 2(1).

against 1990 levels. This intermediate goal was first set at 55 per cent[21] and was later changed to 49 per cent.[22] The reason for the change was that the latter target was felt to be more in line with European ambitions. It was thought that if the Netherlands set the target at 55 per cent for 2030, while neighbouring countries were less ambitious, then this would carry too great a risk of economic leakage effects. In this context, the metaphor of the 'waterbed' is often used: if one state is too ambitious and is pressing down too hard, then the 'water' simply leaks to another part of the bed, ie, to the state with less ambitious targets.[23] That is why the target was lowered to 49 per cent. The challenge was thus to find an ambitious reduction target, without placing the Dutch economy at a competitive disadvantage.[24]

And third, it was stipulated, in the initial draft of the Climate Act, that the share of renewable energy must be 100 per cent by 2050.[25] The Act borrowed[26] the definition of 'renewable energy' from the European Union (EU), which defined it as 'energy from renewable non-fossil sources, namely wind, solar, aerothermal, geothermal, hydrothermal and ocean energy, hydropower, biomass, landfill gas, sewage treatment plant gas and biogases'.[27] This target was replaced, in the revised version of the Act, by a new target: to achieve complete CO_2-neutral electricity production by 2050.[28] Renewable energy is defined as 'energy from renewable sources'; CO_2-neutral energy production is defined as 'electricity production in which no greenhouse gases are released into the atmosphere'.[29] The difference between the two is that CO_2-neutral electricity production can be achieved by compensating carbon emissions with carbon removal, whilst a target of 100 per cent renewable energy requires a complete elimination of all non-renewable energy. The motivation behind this change is worth quoting:

> The reason for this change lies in the fact that the term renewable energy has too wide a scope. It involves many different processes, whereby it is conceivable that the use of non-renewable sources remains necessary for certain of these processes. For example, it is not clear whether aircraft can fly entirely without (bio)kerosene by 2050. In view of this uncertainty, a goal for 100% renewable energy in 2050 is currently not realistic.[30]

To achieve these long-term targets, the government committed itself to produce a Climate Plan ('klimaatplan') every five years.[31] In brief, the Climate Plan contains

---

[21] First Draft, art 3(1); and Second Draft, art 3(1).

[22] Third Draft, art 2(2).

[23] See, eg, Explanatory Memorandum as Amended Following the Advice of the Advisory Section of the Council of State, Climate Act, 34 534, no 7, Parliament (Second Chamber), 2016–17 (hereinafter 'Amended Explanatory Memorandum', translation from the Dutch original by the authors), 11.

[24] Note of Change, 8.

[25] First Draft, art 3(3); and Second Draft, art 3(3).

[26] First Draft, art 1; and Second Draft, art 1.

[27] Directive 2009/28/EC of the European Parliament and Council, adopted 23 April 2009.

[28] Third Draft, art 2(2).

[29] ibid art 1.

[30] Note of Change, 9 (translation from the Dutch original by the authors).

[31] First Draft, arts 4–6; Second Draft, arts 4–6; and Third Draft, arts 3–5.

the main points of the climate policy to be pursued, aimed at achieving the objectives referred to above, for the next five years, and it gives overall direction to climate policy for the following 10 years. The five-year cycle is in line with the obligations that the Paris Agreement imposes on the contracting parties. Looking ahead to the next 10 years promotes the consistency and predictability of Dutch climate policy.[32]

The Climate Plan must also contain a list of concrete measures that need to be taken in order to achieve these objectives. It must estimate the expected share of renewable energy and the expected saving on primary energy use. An overview of the most recent scientific insights relating to limiting climate change must also be provided in the Plan. The government must further provide an update on global and European developments in the field of climate change mitigation, and offer an honest assessment of the consequences of the government's climate policy for the financial position of households, businesses and governments.[33] The latter, which was added to the Climate Act in the revised version, is meant to ensure 'draagvlak', a typical Dutch word that can be roughly translated into English as 'public support'.

The Netherlands Environmental Assessment Agency ('Planbureau voor de Leefomgeving') must publish a Climate and Energy Exploration ('klimaat- en energieverkenning') once a year.[34] This is a scientific report on the effects of the implementation of the climate policy in the previous calendar year. At the very least, this report must contain an overview of actual greenhouse gas emissions, and the developments and measures that have had an impact on greenhouse gas emissions.[35] The Netherlands Environmental Assessment Agency (NEAA), which was established in 2008, inter alia conducts independent research on the consequences of the government's environmental policies. It is autonomous, but is formally part of the Netherlands Ministry of Infrastructure and Water Management. Instead of creating a brand-new agency, the NEAA was seen as the obvious institute to carry out this new task under the Climate Act, ie, to annually produce a Climate and Energy Exploration.

According to the earlier drafts, it was envisaged that the government would also draw up an annual Climate Budget ('klimaatbegroting'), indicating which concrete policy measures the government expected to take.[36] The Climate Budget was supposed to provide insight into how much greenhouse gas is emitted that year and how this relates to achieving the targets in the Climate Plan. In the revised version of the Climate Act, the provisions relating to the Climate Budget were replaced with a provision on a so-called Climate Memo ('klimaatnota').[37]

---

[32] Third Draft, art 3(1); and Amended Explanatory Memorandum, 29.
[33] Third Draft, art 3(2).
[34] First Draft, arts 11–12; Second Draft, arts 14–15; and Third Draft, art 6.
[35] Third Draft, art 6. Earlier drafts also required the production of an annual Climate Report ('klimaatjaarverslag'). See First Draft, arts 9–10; and Second Draft, arts 9–10.
[36] First Draft, arts 7–8; and Second Draft, arts 7–8.
[37] Third Draft, art 7.

The minister must send a Climate Memo to both chambers of the States-General (Parliament and the Senate). This Climate Memo must provide the overall picture of the implementation of the climate policy, as described in the Climate Plan; an overview of the consequences of this climate policy for departmental budgets; and an overview of the financial consequences of significant developments in climate policy that deviate from the Climate Plan, for households, companies and governments.

A second draft of the Climate Act provided for the establishment of a Climate Commission ('klimaatcommissie'), modelled after the UK Committee on Climate Change.[38] This Commission was meant to provide authoritative advice, but this was removed from the third draft. Instead, the Commission's tasks were assigned to an already-existing institution: the Council of State. The Advisory Division of the Council of State must be consulted on the Climate Plan and on the Climate Memo.[39]

From the above, it becomes clear that the Climate Act is a framework law ('kaderwet'), which is to a large extent 'empty'. It only sets very generally formulated targets, but it does not say anything about how these targets are to be achieved, what specific measures need to be taken, what the financial and other consequences might be and so on. All this must be provided later by the Climate Agreement (more on this below) and the Climate Plans that are to be adopted every five years.

An often-heard critique is that the Climate Act contains only procedural rules on how to come to an agreement, but does not constitute an agreement itself.[40] This does not accord well with one of the foundational principles of Dutch democracy, namely that substantive rules should, as far as possible, be laid down in formal legislation and should not be left to lower laws and regulations, let alone to policy. Democratic control is then bypassed.

Another often-heard criticism is that adopting a framework law would be a convenient way to avoid having to make difficult decisions. This criticism is reinforced by the fact that the Climate Agreement, which is not a democratically established law, *does* contain the 'hard', substantive, material and concrete agreements and objectives. This Climate Agreement was adopted with little involvement of Parliament (more on this below).[41]

Jesse Klaver, leader of the Green Party (Groenlinks) and one of the initiators of the Climate Act, explained why he chose to give the Climate Act the shape of a framework law:

> [T]ackling climate change will take at least another thirty years. This path that we take is not an easy one. The only thing I know for sure is that we can get there, if we agree with

---

[38] Second Draft, arts 12–13.
[39] See Third Draft, arts 5(3) and 7(4), respectively. See also Note of Change, 14–16.
[40] See, eg, Yvonne Hofs, 'Klimaatwet zeilt moeiteloos door Eerste Kamer' (*Volkskrant*, 29 May 2019).
[41] Discussion of Climate Act in the Senate, 21 May 2019, available at: https://www.eerstekamer.nl/verslag/20190521/verslag (in Dutch).

each other on the rules of the game. That is what this law does … As soon as we start discussing concrete measures, you will immediately see the differences come to the fore. But there too, I have hope that we will find each other. I think this Climate Act helps us achieve such agreement. That is why we chose a framework law.[42]

In other words, the Climate Act is a useful first step that will facilitate future discussions.

B. Public Participation

In the First Draft, the word 'participation' was not mentioned. In the Second Draft, a special provision on participation was added.[43] The addition of this provision on public participation is justified as follows by the drafters of the Act:

> [This article] is an expression of the general principle that the Government must involve society in the preparation and implementation of regulations. By explicitly incorporating this principle into the Act, it is possible to expressly address the Government about this. The basic idea of [this article] is that consultations are to be held with all relevant parties for the implementation of this Act. The consultation therefore not only concerns the drafting of the Climate Plan and the Climate Budget, but also the implementation of the measures included therein.[44]

Article 8 of the Climate Act prescribes that regular consultations are to be held, with 'administrative bodies of provinces, water boards, municipalities and other relevant parties', for the implementation of this Act. Article 5(2) of the Climate Act is also important to mention, which declares section 3.4 of the General Administrative Law Act of the Netherlands ('Algemene wet bestuursrecht') to be applicable to the preparation of the Climate Plan and adds that 'views [on the Climate Plan] can be put forward by everyone'.[45] This section contains rules for a 'uniform public preparation procedure', with a focus on public participation therein.

Rob Jetten of the Liberals (D66), one of the initiators of the Climate Act, said that one of the challenges in relation to public participation was to avoid a scenario where only the 'usual suspects' would participate and exploit the possibilities for citizen participation. To avoid this, he suggested that Parliament could try to involve more people in decision-making by organising hearings and round tables. In his view, the greatest potential for public participation was in regional and provincial decision-making. At this *local* level, energy transition strategies were already being prepared. This was, he explained, an excellent opportunity to involve

---

[42] ibid (translation from the Dutch original by the authors).

[43] Second Draft, art 11.

[44] Amended Explanatory Memorandum, 35–36 (translation from the Dutch original by the authors).

[45] First Draft, art 6(2); Second Draft, art 6(2); and Third Draft, art 5(2). The formulation has not changed.

as many people as possible, at the local and regional levels, in deciding what the region's objectives should be for sustainable energy generation. What means are we prepared to use? Wind? Sun? Are there other options? Where exactly in our region do we want to place the next wind turbine or solar panel? Such questions are best discussed at the regional level.

In Jetten's view, the big test for citizen participation in climate policy will arise in the context of the energy transition in the coming years. 'You can see that by trial and error we are learning how to take our citizens onboard in a good way', he concluded, and one must not forget 'to manage their expectations'.[46] His colleagues in the Green Party had some good advice for him:

> One of the things we learned in our past experience with citizen participation is that people, who initially have opposite views on something, can get much closer to each other if you choose a form of participation that involves deliberation and dialogue instead of a form which encourages disagreements, like a debate.[47]

Article 8 of the Climate Act does not detail the exact method of participation to be used and thus it certainly allows for deliberation and dialogue.

The provision on public participation in the Climate Act constitutes an important bridge between the Act and the Climate Agreement. It provides the Climate Agreement with a legal foundation. In other words, the adoption of the Climate Agreement can be seen as the implementation of Article 8 of the Climate Act.[48]

III. The Climate Act and its Compatibility with International Law

Before we begin our discussion of the Climate Agreement, let us assess whether the Climate Act is good enough to ensure the Netherlands meets its international obligations. In 2015, the Netherlands, both as an EU Member State and in its own capacity, became party to the Paris Agreement. In the Paris Agreement, states committed themselves to limiting the global average temperature rise to well below 2°C compared to pre-industrial levels, in an attempt to mitigate the risks and impact of climate change. The Paris Agreement is a framework agreement and covers issues relating to climate mitigation, climate adaptation, financing and capacity-building. The Climate Act aims to provide a domestic law framework that assists in the implementation of the obligations under the Paris Agreement, at least with regard to the so-called mitigation elements. On 6 March 2015, Latvia and the

---

[46] Discussion of Climate Act in the Senate, 21 May 2019 (translation from the Dutch original by the authors).

[47] ibid.

[48] See also Anne Vos and Valerie van 't Lam, 'Heeft de Klimaatwet toegevoegde waarde naast de al in ontwikkeling zijnde Omgevingswet en het Klimaatakkoord?' (2018) 76 *Bouwrecht* 507.

European Commission submitted the following Intended Nationally Determined Contribution of the EU and its Member States under the Paris Agreement.[49] They did so on behalf of the EU and all its Member States:

> The EU and its Member States are committed to a binding target of an at least 40% domestic reduction in greenhouse gas emissions by 2030 compared to 1990, to be fulfilled jointly.

The international (Paris) and domestic (Climate Act) legal frameworks must operate as one and must not run separately. The procedures and deadlines in the Dutch Climate Act are thus, where possible, aligned with the procedures and deadlines of the Paris Agreement, and the climate policy of the EU. For example, the aim is to coordinate the periods for the five-year Climate Plans with the periods that apply to the Intended Nationally Determined Contributions (INDCs) introduced in the Paris Agreement.

We must also refer to the Sustainable Development Goals (SDGs).[50] In 2015, essentially all states in the world got together, at the United Nations General Assembly in New York, to adopt a set of 17 goals and related targets, which together constituted a global ambition to strive towards more sustainable development. All states committed themselves to use these aspirational and global targets as a basis for the development of national development strategies. It is thus a bit surprising that little reference is made to the SDGs in the *travaux préparatoires* of the Climate Act or in the *Urgenda* litigation (for more on the latter, see below). This could be explained by the fact that the SDGs are only aspirational and not legally binding. But despite their legally non-binding character, they have proved in practice to successfully motivate states to strive towards achieving their ends, and to constantly monitor and report on progress in doing so. This is something many legally binding treaties fail to achieve.[51]

Sustainable Development Goal 13 (SDG13) is of particular note for the present purposes. It calls on all states to take urgent action to combat climate change and its impacts. Target number 2 of SDG13 requires all states to 'integrate climate change measures into national policies, strategies and planning'. It could be argued that the Climate Act provides the framework for the Netherlands to meet this international SDG target. The indicator of progress in realising this target is as follows:

> [It is to measure] the number of countries that have communicated the establishment or operationalization of an integrated policy/strategy/plan which increases their ability

---

[49] Intended Nationally Determined Contribution of the EU and its Member States, Submission by Latvia and the European Commission on Behalf of the European Union and its Member States, Riga, 6 March 2015, LV-03-06-EU INDC.

[50] Transforming Our World: The 2030 Agenda for Sustainable Development, United Nations General Assembly Resolution, adopted 21 October 2015, UN Doc A/RES/70/1.

[51] See, eg, Otto Spijkers, 'The Cross-fertilization between the Sustainable Development Goals and International Water Law' (2016) 25(1) *Review of European, Comparative and International Environmental Law* 39.

to adapt to the adverse impacts of climate change, and foster climate resilience and *low greenhouse gas emissions development* in a manner that does not threaten food production (including a national adaptation plan, nationally determined contribution, national communication, biennial update report or other). (Emphasis added)[52]

Individual countries are urged to report regularly on the progress they make in contributing to the global effort to realize these SDG13 targets. In the latest progress report of the Netherlands, one reads that, in realising the SDGs, the over-all picture is that the Netherlands is doing well compared to many other countries, but that there are some 'points for attention', particularly in the areas of the environment, energy and especially climate.[53] Indeed, 'of all European countries, the Netherlands has the fifth highest greenhouse gas emissions per capita'.[54] How can the Netherlands do better? The progress report does not tell us more than 'climate policy is an important issue for the new government'.[55]

Finally, it is important to mention international human rights law. Increasingly, human rights courts and tribunals refer to a human right to a healthy environment, and see some of the consequences of climate change as a direct threat to the enjoyment of this right. Somewhat surprisingly, perhaps, not much reference is made to human rights in the *travaux préparatoires* leading up to the adoption of the Climate Act. However, human rights law did figure very prominently in the *Urgenda* litigation, especially at the Appeals and Supreme Court stage.

IV. The Climate Agreement

Before we get to our discussion of the *Urgenda* litigation, we shall look at the Climate Agreement. Again, the focus will be on public participation.

A. Introduction

The Netherlands Climate Agreement sets out the Dutch implementation strategy for its obligations under the Paris Agreement. The measures included in the Climate Agreement aim to reduce Dutch CO_2 emissions by at least 49 per cent in 2030 compared to 1990 levels.[56] Unlike the Climate Act, the Climate Agreement was negotiated by private and public parties together, not by the legislator alone. More than 100 parties were involved in the negotiation process.

---

[52] Transforming Our World, SDG13.
[53] Netherlands Central Bureau of Statistics, *Duurzame ontwikkelingsdoelen: de Stand voor Nederland (Sustainable Development Goals: Where Does the Netherlands Stand)* (2018) 11.
[54] ibid 49.
[55] ibid 51.
[56] Proposal Framework Climate Agreement, 10 July 2018, 7; Climate Agreement, 28 June 2019, 4.

These included environmental organisations, academic institutions, companies, representatives of industries, trade unions, governmental organisations and the financial sector. The Ministry of Economic Affairs and Climate Policy and the Social and Economic Council (SEC) supervised these negotiations. The Climate Agreement was announced in October 2017 by the Dutch government in its coalition agreement.[57] The Minister of Economic Affairs and Climate Policy gave the starting shot for the negotiations in his letter to Parliament of 23 February 2018.[58] With this letter, the Minister set out the framework for the Climate Agreement. The first framework of the Agreement was presented to Parliament on 10 July 2018,[59] and a first draft, outlining the specific measures, was presented on 21 December 2018.[60] A final version of the Climate Agreement was presented on 28 June 2019, after which the parties had to confirm their commitment to the Climate Agreement with a signature.[61] The government submitted the Climate Agreement to Parliament for approval. The Senate was not involved in this procedure because it is only involved in legislative procedures, and the Agreement is not a legislative act. The debate in Parliament on the Climate Agreement was held on 3 July 2019.[62] Parliament called for different motions, which were voted for on 4 July 2019. Most of the passed motions stipulated a fast implementation of the Agreement and a further assessment of its financial implications. The Labour Party (Partij van de Arbeid) and the Green Party (GroenLinks) demanded some further changes before supporting the Agreement.

The structure of the negotiation procedure was as follows: the Climate Council ('klimaatberaad') was the coordinating organ of the Climate Agreement negotiations.[63] The Climate Council consisted of the chairmen of each sector platform,[64] civil organisations, local and regional governments, and non-governmental organisations (NGOs).[65] The negotiations about the measures were held within five sector platforms: electricity, the built environment ('gebouwde omgeving'), industry, agriculture and land use, and mobility.[66] These sector platforms included corporations, NGOs and governmental organisations.[67] Each platform had an independent chair and included two secretaries, one from the

---

[57] Coalition Agreement 'Trust in the Future' ('Vertrouwen in de Toekomst'), 10 October 2017, 37.

[58] Parliamentary documents II 2017/18, 32 813, nr 157.

[59] Parliamentary documents II 2017/18, 32 813, nr 193.

[60] Parliamentary documents II 2017/18, 32 813, nr 263.

[61] Letter from Ed Nijpels, chairman of the Climate Council, to the participating parties about presenting the Climate Agreement, 28 June 2019; letter from the Minister of Economic Affairs and Climate Policy to Parliament presenting the draft Climate Agreement, 28 June 2019.

[62] For a transcript of the debate, see: https://www.tweedekamer.nl/kamerstukken/plenaire_verslagen/detail/904f9f02-9893-440b-aa00-f5bdfa8a5986#id67ced40b.

[63] Proposal Framework Climate Agreement, 10 July 2018, 20.

[64] The five industrial sectors included in the Climate Agreement – electricity, the built environment, industry, agriculture and land use, and mobility – had their own sector platform with representatives from NGOs, the industries and governmental organisations.

[65] Proposal Framework Climate Agreement, 10 July 2018, 20.

[66] ibid.

[67] ibid.

SEC and one from the responsible ministry.[68] Besides these sector platforms, three taskforces were set up to negotiate overarching measures on the labour market and education, financing, and innovation.[69]

The goals within the specific sectors are formulated in reductions of Megatons (Mtons), which contribute to the 49 per cent reduction of CO_2 emissions by 2030. In each of the sectors, specific measures were negotiated to reach this reduction. The goal for the electricity sector is a reduction of 20.2 Mtons. To reach this goal, 70 per cent of all electricity will have to be produced by renewable sources by 2030. This includes deploying wind energy on sea and land, and solar panels.[70] The goal for the built environment is a reduction of 3.4 Mtons. Besides using renewable energy sources, the built environment will also have to be natural gas-free.[71] This will be achieved via a community-based approach (which is discussed further below). In addition, a large part of the measures are concerned with making the existing built environment more sustainable, for example, via insulation.[72] The goal for the industry sector is a reduction of 14.3 Mtons. This includes the use of renewable energy sources as well as the obligation to deliver residual industrial heat to the built environment, and storage of CO_2.[73] The goal for the agriculture and land use sector is a reduction of 3.5 Mtons. This includes the reduction of methane gas.[74] The goal for the mobility sector is a reduction of 7.3 Mtons. This reduction is mainly focused on transitioning to electric vehicles.[75]

An important aspect of all of these measures is that the government will have to change several laws to make these transitions possible. An example is changing the Dutch Civil Code to include a provision to make the financing of sustainability measures in the built environment easier.[76] On 17 September 2019, the Minister of Economic Affairs and Climate Policy sent a letter to Parliament with an overview of the proposed legislative changes following the Climate Agreement and their intended dates for discussion in Parliament and intended entry into force.[77]

In a letter answering questions from Parliament, Ed Nijpels, the chairman of the Climate Council, stated that the Agreement will not be legally enforceable.[78] This means that the parties cannot go to court to enforce performance of the measures in the Agreement. According to Nijpels, the strength of the Agreement is the

---

[68] ibid.
[69] ibid.
[70] Climate Agreement, 28 June 2019, 157–58.
[71] ibid 15–16.
[72] ibid 16.
[73] ibid 83–84.
[74] ibid 117–21.
[75] ibid 45–47.
[76] ibid 21.
[77] Letter from the Minister of Economic Affairs and Climate Policy to Parliament on the proposed legislative changes following from the Climate Agreement and their intended entry into force, 17 September 2019.
[78] Annex 2: 'Questions and Answers' belonging to *Parliamentary Documents*, 32 813, nr 190, question 6.

commitment of the parties towards each other.[79] Although the Climate Agreement will not be legally enforceable, it is not without any obligations. One of the underlying principles is that intervention measures will be implemented when one of the parties does not comply with the Agreement.[80] The ministers will organise sectoral implementation consultations to discuss the progress of the execution of the Climate Agreement.[81]

B. Relationship to the Climate Act

As previously stated, the Climate Act stipulates a reduction of Dutch CO_2 emissions of at least 49 per cent by 2030. The Climate Act is legally binding on all future governments, unless the law is changed. However, the Climate Act does not include any concrete measures. To achieve this goal, the government must commit itself to a Climate Plan indicating which concrete policy measures the government expects to take. The Climate Agreement is a social agreement. This means that it is concluded between governmental organisations and societal organisations, where both types of organisations have commitments towards each other. The Climate Agreement sets out the same reduction goal as the Climate Act. The Climate Agreement does include concrete measures on the reduction of CO_2 emissions. On 29 November 2019, the Minister of Economic Affairs and Climate Policy sent a proposal for the Climate Plan to Parliament.[82] Following this proposal, the Climate Plan is largely determined by the Climate Agreement.[83] The Climate Plan will not solely be based on the Agreement because the Agreement is only limited to five specific sectors.[84] In addition to measures coming from the Climate Agreement, the Climate Plan also includes policies arising out of European obligations, current Dutch policies, and other policies announced in the Coalition Agreement that were not part of the Climate Agreement.[85]

C. Public Participation in the Formation of the Climate Agreement

In this section, we will delve into the negotiation process preceding the conclusion of the Climate Agreement. The most important aspect of the Agreement is that all the proposed measures in the five sectors should be feasible and affordable

---

[79] ibid.
[80] ibid.
[81] Central Government, 'The Climate Agreement in (More Than) 70 Questions', 28 June 2019, 2.
[82] *Parliamentary Documents II* 2019–20, 32 813, nr 400 (Annex).
[83] ibid 5; Climate Agreement, 28 June 2019, 9.
[84] Vos and van 't Lam (n 48).
[85] *Parliamentary Documents II* 2019–20, 32 813, nr 400 (Annex), 5.

for everyone, and that there is public support for the measures.[86] Throughout the negotiation process, the parties acknowledged that these measures also affect persons not involved in the drafting of the Climate Agreement. The parties stated that citizens will be particularly affected by these measures, since the measures include a transition in the energy sources used by households.[87]

Public participation in the drafting process happened in two ways. Five regional meetings were organised throughout the Netherlands in which a total of 800 citizens participated. These regional meetings gave citizens the opportunity to submit their ideas.[88] The meetings were organised by the chairman of the Climate Council together with the chairman of the sector platforms and a representative of a local organisation.[89] The main conclusion from these meetings was that most citizens wanted to actively participate in the energy transition measures, but that most did not feel that they were taken seriously.[90] Based on these meetings, three conditions for an active role for citizens were formulated.[91] First, the Climate Agreement must provide a stable policy framework in which the goals and preconditions are set, but must also provide enough flexibility for regional approaches. Second, the local and regional level should be given leading roles in executing these measures. Third, the local approaches in the Climate Agreement should focus on individual citizens and local communities. These measures were included in the initial outline of the Climate Agreement.

Besides these regional meetings, the Ministry of Economic Affairs and Climate Policy and the SEC asked three public participation organisations to research both the critique citizens have of the Climate Agreement and the measures or conditions that should be included according to them. The National Platform for Public Participation in Environmental Policy, in collaboration with Buurkracht and the climate agency HIER,[92] organized several smaller-scale interviews, in which a total of about 200 citizens took part.[93] No explanation was provided on why these three agencies were approached (and not others). We assume it is because these organisations are concerned with the energy transition/climate and public participation in general. The meetings were

---

[86] Draft Climate Agreement, 21 December 2018, 2; Climate Agreement, 28 June 2019, 216.

[87] ibid.

[88] Proposal Framework Climate Agreement, 10 July 2018, 20.

[89] ibid 73.

[90] ibid 73–74.

[91] ibid 73–75.

[92] HIER is not an abbreviation, but the name of the agency.

[93] Proposal Framework Climate Agreement, 73; Nederlands Platform Burgerparticipatie en Overheid (NPBO) and Klimaatavontuur, 'Meedenken om mee te doen: Burgers aan het woord over het klimaatakkoord' ('Thinking Along Participating: Citizens Speaking about the Climate Agreement' 10 July 2018; NPBO, HIER, Buurkracht, ('Klimaatakkoord 2018: Maatschappelijke acceptatie en participatie' ('Climate Agreement 2018: Social Acceptance and Participation'), 4 July 2018. The report also posed the question of whether this is a representative sample; the authors acknowledged that it was not, but that it nevertheless provided important results.

complementary to the regional meetings. The central question brought up in these meetings was which issues should be included in the Climate Agreement to stimulate its acceptance by the citizens.[94] One of the findings was that the citizens had a considerable need for information, but that they did not trust the information provided by the government. This lack of trust in the government was linked to its actions in the procedures for placing wind turbines on land. The citizens did not feel informed about where these wind turbines would be placed or how they could be involved in the decision-making process. This has reinforced the 'not in my backyard' phenomenon among citizens.[95] Another issue is the apparent inconsistency in governmental policies observed by citizens: on the one hand, the government wants to reduce CO_2 emissions, whilst on the other hand, it was presenting plans for an expansion of Lelystad Airport.[96] The majority of the participants also questioned the legitimacy of the Climate Agreement. Because it was predominantly concluded with the corporate sector and activist environmental groups, they felt that it was mostly a compromise of those particular interests instead of representing the public interest.[97] In the recommendations, a distinction was made between acceptance and participation, and citizen participation (joining in on existing projects) and citizens' initiative (taking action themselves).[98] These last two forms in particular, it was argued, should be integrated into the Climate Agreement: citizen participation leads to a citizens' initiative, and citizens' initiative leads to citizen participation.[99] The essence of the recommendations provided by these organisations was that the Climate Agreement should not regulate citizen participation and a citizens' initiative itself, but should point out what is possible in order to have successful citizen participation and citizens' initiative.[100] Akerboom argues that public participation could have been more successful if a draft of the Climate Agreement was presented as a public consultation in order to enable citizens to express their views on the proposed measures.[101]

D. Public Participation in the Governance Mechanisms of the Climate Agreement

Following the public participation meetings, the draft Climate Agreement presented in December 2018 included provisions on public participation in specific sectors.

---

[94] NPBO, HIER, Buurkracht, 'Climate Agreement 2018: Social Acceptance and Participation', 4 July 2018, 3.

[95] ibid 8; Sanne Akerboom, 'Participatie en de energietransitie: juridisch instrumentarium in een veranderende context' (2019) 3 *Tijdschrift voor Omgevingsrecht* 75.

[96] NPBO, HIER, Buurkracht, 'Climate Agreement 2018: Social Acceptance and Participation', 4 July 2018, 8.

[97] ibid 9.

[98] ibid 11.

[99] ibid.

[100] ibid.

[101] Akerboom (n 95) 83.

This was further elaborated upon in the final version of the Climate Agreement, which includes a specific section on public participation. On a more overarching level, the Agreement aims for a citizen dialogue on a continuing basis and a public campaign to stimulate citizens to get involved.[102] One of the measures includes a 'citizens monitor' by the Netherlands Institute for Social Research, which keeps track of the expectations, behaviour, attitudes and motives of the citizens in relation to the transition. Moreover, a public campaign will be held to make the citizens aware of their role in the transition and to stimulate them to change their behaviour.[103] Public participation is also included in the specific sector sections of the Climate Agreement. The electricity section states that participation and public support are necessary for the transition to renewable energy sources.[104] The affected citizens have to be included in the decision-making procedure and have to be offered the opportunity to financially participate in renewable projects. The ambition is that 50 per cent of Dutch renewable energy production will be owned by local communities.[105] Also, the built environment section includes measures for a more regional approach, in which citizens will be more involved.[106] The main aspect is the community-based approach to making houses natural gas-free.[107] Citizens should also be able to participate[108] in the heat plan, which will also be concluded on a more local level by Regional Energy Strategies.[109]

E. Democratic Legitimacy

An important gap in the Climate Agreement is an arguable lack of democratic legitimacy in the drafting process. As previously stated, the Climate Agreement has been negotiated between private and public parties, but it did not directly include debates with the elected representatives on the municipal, provincial and national levels. This was also observed during the public participation meetings. Further, the Dutch Council of State already observed this problem in its annual report of 2013 and elaborated on it again in 2018.[110]

This leads to the following question: are these social agreements democratically legitimised? Social agreements, like the Climate Agreement, can be regarded

---

[102] Draft Climate Agreement, 21 December 2018, 207–11; Climate Agreement, 28 June 2019, 217–18. One of the campaigns has already started on 9 September 2019, 'everybody does something', which aims to help citizens make more sustainable choices in and around their house. See https://www.klimaatakkoord.nl/documenten/videos/2019/09/09/iedereen-doet-wat.

[103] Climate Agreement, 28 June 2019, 216–17.

[104] Draft Climate Agreement, 21 December 2018, 156 ff; Climate Agreement, 28 June 2019, 219.

[105] ibid.

[106] Draft Climate Agreement, 21 December 2018, 31 ff; Climate Agreement, 28 June 2019, 218.

[107] ibid.

[108] Climate Agreement, 28 June 2019, 218.

[109] ibid 26.

[110] Ruud A Koole, 'Is een "akkoorden-democratie" wel een democratie?' (2019) 34 *Regelmaat* 2; Jaarverslag Raad van State 2013, 13.

as network governance. This indicates an involvement of stakeholders, partnerships and 'joint' governance efforts. The emergence of network governance can be particularly observed in sustainability transitions because these often necessitate an actor-network revolution.[111] The Climate Agreement uses such a network governance approach.[112] This is not a new development, but the large extent to which it is currently used is new.[113] The problem with this development is that it runs the risk of weakening the position of Parliament in the legislative process, and thus limiting the democratic legitimacy of social agreements like the Climate Agreement.[114]

The Dutch Council of State observed in its annual report of 2018 that the government brings in other parties, such as NGOs with an interest in the legislation or branches of industries affected by the legislation, in the preparation of legislation. The consequence is that these parties have a greater influence on the legislative process and thus may largely reflect the interests of NGOs or the industrial sector. Although the Climate Agreement is not legislation itself, it does contain measures for the government and thus indirectly leads to the proposal of new legislation or the adaptation of existing legislation. This could lead to the risk that these legislative proposals would only be judged on the merits for those parties and not on their contribution to the Dutch legal framework as such.[115] The Dutch Council of State further observed that the current political landscape is highly fragmented and thus it is difficult to find a political consensus for legislation. This has led to a shift from legislative processes to the formation of social agreements, such as the Climate Agreement and the Energy Agreement.[116] The problem is that parties to these social agreements cannot be expected to properly balance public interests with their own interests. Moreover, these parties do not always have an equal position within these negotiations, which has an unfortunate consequence that some interests weigh heavier than others. Because the use of such social agreements is increasing, the agreement in question gets an independent, public value. According to the Dutch Council of State, because other parties are also increasingly involved in policy-making and the ensuing legislative process, it seems as if the preparation of these documents and the balancing of interests is done by the non-governmental parties, such as industries.[117]

---

[111] Menno Ottens and Jurian Edelenbos, 'Political Leadership as Meta-governance in Sustainability Transitions: A Case Study Analysis of Meta-governance in the Case of the Dutch National Agreement on Climate' (2019) 11 *Sustainability* 3.

[112] ibid.

[113] Koole (n 110).

[114] ibid.

[115] Annual Report Dutch Council of State 2018, 15.

[116] Similar to the Climate Agreement, the Energy Agreement is a social agreement concluded between Dutch (local) governments, employers' associations and unions, environmental organisations, financial institutions, NGOs and other stakeholders in 2013. The Energy Agreement contains a long-term vision and policy on energy, eg, energy efficiency saving and renewable energy. For a broad summary of the Energy Agreement, see: https://www.ser.nl/-/media/ser/downloads/engels/2013/energy-agreement.pdf.

[117] ibid 18.

In its annual report, the Dutch Council of State also paid special attention to the process of the Climate Agreement. It observed that the Climate Agreement has a very peculiar decision-making process because the government is itself a party to the Agreement.[118] As a result, the government was already 'bound' to the Climate Agreement. Parliament only played a small role in commenting on the negotiating position of the government via so-called 'cockpit-consultations'.[119] Another complicating factor concerning the Climate Agreement is that the interpretation of the Climate Act seems to be dependent on the Climate Agreement.[120]

How can one solve this problem? The obvious solution is to provide a significant role for Parliament in the negotiation process, since involving the elected representatives is a central feature of a democracy. It should monitor governmental action.[121] Parliament only had a very limited role in the negotiations preceding the conclusion of the Climate Agreement. Currently, the only role Parliament has is in debating the changes in legislation that are necessary for the execution of the Climate Agreement, such as changing the environmental, gas, heat, electricity and mining acts to enable the community-based approach to making houses natural gas-free.[122] Another solution would be to increase the role of public participation. Although private citizens are not democratically elected representatives, they do represent the public interest and moreover will lead to more public support for plans and policies once adopted.[123]

Although the negotiation process that has led to the Climate Agreement arguably lacked democratic legitimacy, Parliament and the Senate are still involved in the legislative changes that are necessary to enable the measures of the Agreement. This means that the measures to which the government has bound itself in the Agreement are still subject to the consent of the democratically elected representatives and are thus democratically legitimised.

V. The Climate Act and Agreement and the *Urgenda* Litigation

In this section, we will look at the links between the Climate Act, the Climate Agreement and the *Urgenda* litigation.[124] We start by providing a brief description

[118] ibid.
[119] ibid 17.
[120] ibid 19.
[121] Koole (n 110).
[122] Climate Agreement, 28 June 2019, 29.
[123] Spijkers and Honniball (n 4) 222–50.
[124] See also Otto Spijkers, 'The Urgenda Decision of the Dutch District Court: Using Tort Law to Urge the State to Do More in Combating Climate Change' (*Rights! Blog*, 22 May 2017), https://rightsblog.net/2017/05/22/the-urgenda-decision-of-the-dutch-district-court-using-tort-law-to-urge-the-state-to-do-more-in-combating-climate-change; and Otto Spijkers, 'The Urgenda Decision of the Dutch Appeals Court: Using International Human Rights Law to Urge the State to Do More in Combating Climate Change' (*Rights! Blog*, 5 November 2018).

of the *Urgenda* litigation. This case started at the District Court level, then moved up to the Appeals level and ended before the Supreme Court of the Netherlands. These three levels will be discussed in chronological order. Subsequently, the relationship between the *Urgenda* litigation and the Act and the Agreement will be analysed.

A. The District Court

Urgenda, an association established under Dutch law, persuaded the District Court[125] in The Hague to rule on 24 June 2015 that in order not to contribute to dangerous climate change, the Dutch State had to reduce greenhouse gas emissions in and from the Netherlands by at the very least 25 per cent in 2020 when compared with 1990 emissions levels. If the State would not do its utmost to achieve such drastic reduction, it would be in breach of its duty of care towards Urgenda. The duty of care is a legal obligation imposed on the State, requiring it to adhere to a standard of reasonable care in its relationship with those natural and legal persons under its jurisdiction and control.

Urgenda could initially not base its claim on the Paris Agreement, the Climate Act on the Climate Agreement. All three became legally operative *after* Urgenda initiated the legal proceedings against the Netherlands. But this does not mean that the litigants, and the Court, made no reference whatsoever to these instruments. In fact, the Paris Agreement is referred to extensively in the judgment of the Appeals Court and the Supreme Court, but not as a formal basis of its decision.

The provisions of international law that Urgenda did invoke successfully before the District Court included certain articles in the United Nations Framework Convention on Climate Change[126] and the Kyoto Protocol,[127] as well as the no harm principle of customary international environmental law,[128] and Article 191 of the Treaty on the Functioning of the European Union, which states that:

> [European] Union policy on the environment shall contribute to pursuit of [inter alia] promoting measures at international level to deal with regional or worldwide environmental problems, and in particular combating climate change.[129]

---

[125] In the Netherlands, there exist three levels: District Court (court of first instance); Appeals Court; and Supreme Court. The Supreme Court does not reassess the facts, but only checks to make sure that the law is correctly applied to the facts.

[126] United Nations Framework Convention on Climate Change, concluded in New York on 9 May 1992, entered into force 21 March 1994.

[127] Kyoto Protocol to the United Nations Framework Convention on Climate Change, adopted in Kyoto on 11 December 1997, entered into force 16 February 2005.

[128] See the Trail Smelter Case, United States v Canada, Decision of 11 March 1941.

[129] Article 191 of the Treaty on the Functioning of the European Union. The Treaty of Lisbon amending the Treaty on European Union and the Treaty establishing the European Community entered into force on 1 December 2009.

The Dutch District Court held that this provision and the other international provisions referred to above were not suitable to be invoked directly by an association against the State before a Dutch court because they were not sufficiently precise and had no direct effect.[130] However, these norms could be used to give concrete meaning to the duty of care as it exists in Dutch domestic civil law (Article 162 of Book 6 of the Dutch Civil Code to be more precise). Articles 2 and 8 of the ECHR, which the Dutch District Court determined could not be invoked directly because Urgenda was not itself a victim of a breach of these provisions, served a similar function.

Breaching the duty of care is a tort, a wrongful act under Dutch civil law. To assess whether the State had committed a tort by not doing enough to prevent further climate change, the District Court considered, inter alia, the nature and extent of the damage ensuing from climate change, the knowledge and foreseeability of this damage, and the onerousness of taking precautionary measures. Basing itself on the reports of the Intergovernmental Panel on Climate Change, the District Court concluded that the damage was 'catastrophic',[131] that the Netherlands was fully aware of this and that taking measures to combat climate change would be burdensome, but not disproportionally onerous.[132] Finding for Urgenda, the District Court ruled that the Dutch State must reduce greenhouse gas emissions in and from the Netherlands by at the very least 25 per cent in 2020 when compared with 1990 emissions levels, to comply with its duty of care vis-a-vis Urgenda.[133]

B. The Appeals Court

On 9 October 2018, the Appeals Court upheld the ruling of the District Court, finding that the State had acted in breach of its obligations by not taking effective action to protect its population from dangerous climate change. This time, the legal argumentation was based on a direct application of international human rights law. Contrary to the District Court, the Appeals Court *did* allow Urgenda to invoke Articles 2 and 8 ECHR directly.[134]

Articles 2 and 8 ECHR do not *explicitly* protect individuals from the effects of dangerous climate change. Article 2 ECHR says that 'everyone's right to life shall be protected by law' and that 'no one shall be deprived of his life intentionally',

---

[130] For a discussion on the conditions for direct effect of international law in the Dutch domestic legal order, see Willem van Rossem and Otto Spijkers, 'Rechtstreekse werking van internationale verdragen – een Hollands probleem met een Amerikaanse of Franse oplossing?' (2016) 177(3) *Rechtsgeleerd Magazijn Themis* 136.

[131] *Urgenda* District Court Judgment (n 7) para 4.1.1.

[132] ibid paras 4.67–4.73.

[133] ibid para 5.1.

[134] *Urgenda* Appeals Court Judgment (n 8) para 35.

and Article 8 ECHR says that 'everyone has the right to respect for his private and family life, his home and his correspondence'. Using these provisions as a legal basis for the individual's protection from dangerous climate change thus requires some interpretation. The Appeals Court stated in its *Urgenda* ruling that:

> The interest protected by Article 2 ECHR is the right to life, which includes environment-related situations that affect or threaten to affect the right to life. Article 8 ECHR protects the right to private life, family life, home and correspondence. Article 8 ECHR may also apply in environment-related situations. The latter is relevant if (1) an act or omission has an adverse effect on the home and/or private life of a citizen and (2) if that adverse effect has reached a certain minimum level of severity.[135]

With respect to Article 8 ECHR in particular, the Appeals Court asserted that 'if the government knows that there is a real and imminent threat, the State must take precautionary measures to prevent infringement as far as possible'.[136] In other words, there is also an obligation to prevent future infringements of this right. After assessing the relevant facts, the Appeals Court concluded that 'it is appropriate to speak of a real threat of dangerous climate change, resulting in the serious risk that the current generation of citizens will be confronted with loss of life and/or a disruption of family life' and thus 'it follows from Articles 2 and 8 ECHR that the State has a duty to protect [everyone within its jurisdiction] against this real threat'.[137] The Appeals Court thus concluded that 'the State fails to fulfil its duty of care pursuant to Articles 2 and 8 ECHR by not wanting to reduce emissions by at least 25% at the end of 2020'.[138]

The Dutch government made the argument, already referred to above, that it was compliant with the EU's commitment under the Paris Agreement, ie, to reduce emissions by 49 per cent in 2030. This, so it argued, did not require a 25 per cent reduction already by the end of 2020. But the Appeals Court was not persuaded and explained that each Megaton of CO_2 which is emitted into the atmosphere in the short term contributes to global warming, and that the Paris Agreement was never meant to allow business as usual up to 2030.[139]

C. The Supreme Court

The Supreme Court of the Netherlands issued its judgment on 20 December 2019. Article 162(2), Book 6 of the Dutch Civil Code, which was the key provision in the District Court's ruling, did not play any role whatsoever in the Supreme Court's

---

[135] ibid para 40.
[136] ibid para 43.
[137] ibid para 45.
[138] ibid para 73, repeated in para 76.
[139] ibid para 47.

reasoning.[140] Instead, the Supreme Court followed the Appeals Court and relied fully on the ECHR. It allowed Urgenda to directly invoke Articles 2 and 8 ECHR before the Dutch court.[141] Article 2 ECHR obliged the Netherlands to take appropriate measures to safeguard the lives of those residing within the jurisdiction of the Netherlands,[142] while Article 8 ECHR obliged the Netherlands to take reasonable and appropriate measures to protect individuals within its jurisdiction against potentially serious damage to their environment.[143] This obligation to take appropriate measures applied not only with regard to specific, identifiable persons, but also when the risk was due to environmental hazards that threaten large groups of people, or even the entire population of the Netherlands.[144]

D. *Urgenda* and the Climate Act and the Climate Agreement

What is the relationship between *Urgenda* and the Climate Act and Climate Agreement? Most importantly, the reduction target of the *Urgenda* ruling is different from the targets agreed in the Climate Act and the Climate Agreement. The intermediate target in the Act and the Climate Agreement (49 per cent reduction) is to be achieved by 2030, and the target set by the Court in *Urgenda* (25 per cent reduction) must already be achieved by 2020.

The judgment of the Supreme Court referred only once to the Climate Act. In the relevant paragraph, the Court noted that in the Climate Act, the Netherlands had set a reduction target of 49 per cent for 2030 and 95 per cent for 2050. It cleverly noted that the target of 49 per cent for 2030 was linearly derived from the target of 95 per cent for 2050, and if this line would have been extended to the end of 2020, then this would have resulted in a reduction target for that year of 28 per cent. The Supreme Court asked the State why it instead opted for a mere 20 per cent reduction instead of 28 per cent. The State's reply was that a target for 20 per cent could be set for the end of 2020 because afterwards, the reduction would had to be speeded up.[145] The Supreme Court was clearly not persuaded.[146] Thus, it insisted that in order to comply with Articles 2 and 8 ECHR, the State had to reduce emissions by at least 25 per cent in 2020; this was an absolute minimum.

---

[140] Urgenda consistently argued along both lines, ie, it argued that the Netherlands acted both (1) in breach of the duty of care (Article 6:162(2) of the Dutch Civil Code) and (2) in breach of arts 2 and 8 ECHR. See Urgenda Supreme Court, para 2.2.2.
[141] Urgenda Supreme Court Judgment (n 9) para 5.9.3.
[142] ibid, para 5.2.2.
[143] ibid, para 5.2.3.
[144] ibid, para 5.3.1.
[145] ibid para 7.4.5.
[146] ibid para 7.4.6.

The State had not managed to substantiate its claim that it was justified in deviating from that objective.[147]

This created an immediate problem for the government. The Climate Agreement merely provided for a CO_2 reduction of 4 Megatons in 2020, while 9 Megatons is needed to comply with *Urgenda*.[148] The Minister of Economic Affairs and Climate Policy announced that a specific set of measures for the execution of the *Urgenda* ruling will be presented.[149] These specific measures are based on the same principles as the Climate Agreement; the measures have to be cost-efficient and should have broad societal and political support. These measures should strengthen the Climate Agreement.[150] The Minister emphasised in the debate on the Climate Agreement that the government still aims to meet the goal set by *Urgenda*.[151]

VI. Conclusion

What is the relationship between the Climate Act and the Climate Agreement in short? The Climate Act is the legal framework in which the Climate Agreement operates. This has two important consequences. First, the intermediate target for 2030, as set in the Climate Act, determines the aim of the Climate Agreement. Second, the Climate Plan, in which the government outlines its climate policy for the upcoming 10-year period, and the Climate Agreement, in which various partners commit to making their particular contributions, are closely related. There is one important difference between Act and the Agreement, and that is that only the former is, strictly speaking, legally binding. This implies that if the parties to the Climate Agreement cannot come up with supported proposals, the government bears ultimate legal responsibility for making those decisions that ensure the Netherlands reduces its greenhouse gas emissions enough to meet the target. The Climate Act sets the target of a 49 per cent reduction in 2030 and a 95 per cent reduction in 2050 compared to 1990 *by law*. Every newly elected government between today and 2050 is therefore bound by these targets, unless the Act is amended or repealed. Having said that, the Climate Act is not about the substantive measures that must be taken to achieve these targets. In the Climate Agreement, these measures were agreed, together with all social partners.

An important aspect in both the Climate Act and the Climate Agreement is the focus on public participation. Again, the Climate Act provides for the framework for public participation, while the Climate Agreement contains specific measures

---

[147] ibid para 7.5.1.

[148] 'Urgenda: kabinet lapt vonnis van de rechter aan zijn laars' (NOS, 28 June 2019); also discussed by Jesse Klaver, the party chairman of the Green Party (GroenLinks) in the debate on 3 July 2019.

[149] Letter from the Minister of Economic Affairs and Climate Policy to Parliament on the execution of the *Urgenda* ruling, 28 June 2019.

[150] *Parliamentary Documents I*, 32 813, nr H.

[151] Debate held in Parliament on 3 July 2019.

on how citizens can be involved in the transition. However, both documents have attracted criticism.

The Climate Act is often portrayed as being merely symbolic because it does not include specific measures, while the Climate Agreement is seen to be lacking democratic legitimacy. Nevertheless, future governments are still held to the set reduction target, and the execution of the Climate Agreement depends on the willingness of future governments to create new legislation or change existing legislation.

The Christian Democrats (CDA) raised an interesting point when the Climate Act was discussed in the Senate. Why is it, they asked the initiators of the Act, that only a limited number of countries have so far adopted a climate law? The process started in the UK and a few other countries followed suit. At the time, the Netherlands was only the seventh country in the world to prepare a Climate Act. Why is it that only a handful of the nearly 200 states that have ratified the Paris Agreement have followed the UK's example?[152] This is an interesting question, but to provide an answer to this is beyond the scope of this chapter.

---

[152] Discussion of Climate Act in the Senate, 21 May 2019.

9

The New Zealand Legislation

Pursuing the 1.5°C Target Using a Net Zero Approach

PRUE TAYLOR

Author's Editorial Note

On 7 November 2019, 119 of 120 members of the New Zealand Parliament voted to pass the Climate Bill into law (the Climate Change Response (Zero Carbon) Amendment Act 2019 – hereinafter 'the Act'). It received Royal Assent a few days later and has come into force. Politicians made much of their efforts to achieve consensus and spoke of compromises on all sides. However, if political consensus is intended to achieve regulatory certainty, then this has not necessarily been the outcome. The largest opposition party (the New Zealand National Party) clearly stated that they would amend the Act within the first 100 days should they form the next government after the 2020 elections. At least there is some certainty about the reforms they propose: delayed introduction of a biogenic methane target based on advice from the Climate Change Commission; enhanced consideration of economic impacts; and ability to adjust the Act's emissions reduction target downwards based on levels of international action. The government rejected these suggestions, including the last on the basis that New Zealand should not be a 'slow follower'.

Very few substantive changes were made to the Bill that is examined below. Those of particular note are as follows: (1) the Commission must give greater consideration to the Crown–Maori relationship when performing its functions; (2) the use of offshore mitigation is further constrained, enabling its use only in limited circumstances; (3) the treatment of aviation and shipping emissions is to be reviewed in 2024; and (4) consideration of the target and budgets remains a permissive consideration for entities performing a public function, power or duty. However, the clause stating that failure to do so 'does not invalidate anything done' has been removed. The apparent justification was that removal of this clause will enable the common law to develop regarding the status of the budget and targets, and how they should be considered.

I. Background

In May 2019, the New Zealand Minister for Climate Change announced the release of the nation's new legislative response to climate change. Initially intended to be separate or stand-alone legislation, the government introduced it as an amendment to the Climate Change Response Act 2002.[1] As a consequence, the draft legislation is entitled the Climate Change Response (Zero Carbon) Amendment Bill (hereinafter 'Zero Carbon Bill' or 'Bill'). The Bill's stated purpose is to create a 'framework for the development and implementation of clear and stable climate change policies that contribute to the global effort under the Paris Agreement to limit the global average temperature increase to 1.5 [degrees] Celsius above pre-industrial levels'.[2] According to the Minister for Climate Change, it will be the first legislation in the world to create a legally binding commitment to 'living within 1.5 degrees Celsius of global warming'.[3] Some 23 years after the ratification of the 1992 United Nations Framework Convention on Climate Change, it is the first time that a New Zealand government has gone beyond non-binding policies and committed itself and future governments to legally binding reduction targets.[4]

Public reception of the long-awaited Bill was mixed and emotive. Described by the government as a 30-year plan to secure the future of New Zealanders,[5] commentators have called it 'toothless',[6] 'hopeful but troubling'[7] and 'frustratingly cruel'.[8] The Bill's primary political backers, the Green Party of Aotearoa New Zealand, described it as reflecting acceptable costs of achieving the necessary bi-partisanship.[9] This was a reference to the need to include methane emissions from the agricultural sector, but to regulate them in a manner that secures support from farmers.

---

[1] This is the framework legislation for the National Emissions Trading Scheme.

[2] Explanatory Note to the Climate Change Response (Zero Carbon) Amendment Bill 2019, para 1.

[3] Ministry for the Environment, *Climate Change Response (Zero Carbon) Amendment Bill: Summary* (ME 1410, Wellington, Ministry for the Environment, 2018) 4. Other states have committed to net zero targets. For example, Scotland committed to a net zero target (by 2045) in May 2019 and the UK government committed to net zero by 2050 in June 2019; see Roger Harrabin, 'Climate Change: UK Government to Commit to 2050 Target' (*BBC*, 12 June 2019), www.bbc.com/news/science-environment-48596775; UK Climate Change Act 2008 (2050 Target Amendment) Order 2019.

[4] In 2011, the government notified a non-binding target: reduction of greenhouse gases by 50 per cent below 1990 levels by 2050. 'The Climate Change Response (2050 Emissions Target) Notice 2011' (2011) 41 *New Zealand Gazette* 987.

[5] Ministry for the Environment (n 3) 5.

[6] Greenpeace New Zealand, quoted in Thomas Coughlan, 'Zero Carbon Bill Lives or Dies on Politics' (*Newsroom*, 9 May 2019), www.newsroom.co.nz/2019/05/09/575599/zero-carbon-bill-lives-or-dies-on-politics#.

[7] Bronwyn Hayward, 'Government's Climate Change Plan Does Not Go Far Enough' (*Tertiary Education Union*, 27 May 2019), https://teu.ac.nz/news/governments-climate-enough. Hayward is a New Zealand academic and the lead author on the Intergovernmental Panel on Climate Change Report on 1.5°C of global warming (2018).

[8] Federated Farmers, quoted in Coughlan (n 6).

[9] Coughlan (n 6).

Based on the UK's Climate Change Act 2008 (CCA), but with some unique elements, the Bill will do four key things:

(1) Set a long-term greenhouse gas emissions reduction target, to reduce all greenhouse gases (except biogenic methane) to net zero by 2050. Methane is subject to a separate reduction regime employing a 'split gases approach'.

(2) Set a series of emissions budgets to create stepping stones for achieving the long-term target.

(3) Require the government to develop and implement adaptation measures including risk assessments and plans.

(4) Establish an independent Climate Change Commission to provide expert advice and monitoring, and to keep governments on track in order to meet mitigation and adaptation goals.

The legislative process has moved rapidly since the Bill's introduction in May 2019. It received its first reading in the House of Representatives (hereinafter 'the House') on 21 May before being sent to the Environment Select Committee.[10] At the time of writing, the Committee is hearing a large number of public submissions on the Bill (but note also the update provided the in 'Author's Editorial Note' above).[11] The Select Committee process normally takes up to six months, resulting in recommendations to the House. A bill will then receive two further readings before a final vote and, if successful, it is presented to the Governor General for final assent before passing into force. These steps normally take many months. The government has set a very ambitious agenda to see the Bill enter into force by the end of 2019.[12] Given public interest, contention around key elements of the Bill and the government's reliance on coalition parties to achieve a majority vote, this timetable seems optimistic.

As the Bill is still draft legislation, its content will change as it passes through the legislative process. This prevents detailed analysis of its content and implementation. This chapter will begin by discussing the emergence of the Bill. This is of historic interest, but is also critical to understanding key aspects of the Bill and whether current bi-partisan political support will continue. An overview of the basic architecture of the Bill follows, with an emphasis on elements unique to New Zealand. The chapter concludes with a discussion of some emerging issues, based on a sample of public submissions to the Select Committee and the author's own analysis.[13]

---

[10] The Bill received a majority of 119 votes to 1. An overview of New Zealand's legislative process is available at 'Parliament Brief: The Legislative Process' (*New Zealand Parliament*, 21 March 2014), www.parliament.nz/en/visit-and-learn/how-parliament-works/fact-sheets/pbrief6.

[11] Parliament's website lists over 10,000 written submissions. A total of 800 submitters have asked to be heard in person. Ministry for the Environment, 'Climate Change Response (Zero Carbon) Amendment Bill', www.mfe.govt.nz/climate-change/zero-carbon-amendment-bill.

[12] ibid.

[13] Prue Taylor and Kate Scanlen, 'The UK Climate Change Act: An Act to Follow?' (2018) 14(3) *Policy Quarterly* 66; Donald A Brown et al, 'A Four-Step Process for Formulating and Evaluating Legal Commitments under the Paris Agreement' [2018] *Carbon and Climate Law Review* 98. See also Prue

II. Emergence

New Zealand's most recent general election was held in September 2017. The outcome required three political parties (New Zealand Labour, New Zealand First and the Green Party of Aotearoa New Zealand) to form a coalition to secure a majority of 61 seats in the House. The creation of zero carbon legislation was a keystone policy pledge in the agreement between New Zealand Labour and the Green Party Aotearoa New Zealand (hereinafter 'Green Party').[14] Climate change had been a policy concern of the Green Party for many years; however, their minority status, together with the nine-year dominance of a centre-right government (the National Party and supporting political parties), prevented them from acting. The political landscape changed radically when the Labour leader, Jacinda Ardern, announced climate change as her generation's 'nuclear-free' moment. In doing so, she was referring to the powerful 1980s social movement that led to New Zealand becoming a nuclear-free nation.[15] Her statement let the public know that Labour would prioritise climate change if elected.

In making this statement, Ardern would have been well aware of the growing political momentum for climate change legislation. The youth climate organisation Generation Zero worked hard to popularise and advocate for law based on the CCA ahead of the 2017 general election.[16] In early 2017, Lord Deben, Chair of the UK's Climate Change Committee, toured New Zealand raising awareness of the successes of the CCA and highlighting the importance of bi-partisan support. His visit built upon the efforts of some New Zealand politicians to build cross-party consensus and demonstrate how the economy could transition to achieve radical emission reductions. This momentum was supported by successive reports of the Parliamentary Commissioner for the Environment[17] and the New Zealand Productivity Commission,[18] all of which highlighted the urgency of climate change and expressed general favour for legislation similar to the CCA.

Taylor, 'Climate Change and Local Government' in Jean Drage (ed), *Local Government in New Zealand: Challenges & Choices* (Auckland, Dunmore Publishing, 2016).

[14] Cabinet Office Circular, 'Labour-New Zealand First Coalition, with Confidence and Supply from the Green Party: Consultation and Operating Arrangements' (15 December 2017) CO (17) 10.

[15] New Zealand Nuclear Free Zone, Disarmament and Arms Control Act 1987.

[16] The select committee submissions of the Sustainability Council of New Zealand and Generation Zero trace some of this history. See Sustainability Council of New Zealand, 'Submission to the Environment Select Committee on the Climate Change Response (Zero Carbon) Amendment Bill 2019'; Generation Zero, 'Submission to the Environment Select Committee on the Climate Change Response (Zero Carbon) Amendment Bill 2019'.

[17] Parliamentary Commissioner for the Environment, 'Stepping Stones to Paris and Beyond: Climate Change, Progress and Predictability' (2017), www.pce.parliament.nz/media/1724/stepping-stones-web-oct-2017.pdf; Parliamentary Commissioner for the Environment, 'A Zero Carbon Act for New Zealand: Revisiting Stepping Stones to Paris and Beyond' (2018), www.pce.parliament.nz/media/196427/zero-carbon-act-for-nz-web.pdf.

[18] New Zealand Productivity Commission, *Low-Emissions Economy: Final Report* (2018), www.productivity.govt.nz/assets/Documents/lowemissions/4e01d69a83/Productivity-Commission_Low-emissions-economy_Final-Report_FINAL_2.pdf; New Zealand Productivity Commission,

Behind this activity was the ugly spectre of New Zealand's growing greenhouse gas emissions profile. New Zealanders have the fifth highest per capita emissions profile in the Organisation for Economic Co-operation and Development (OECD).[19] New Zealand's latest official Greenhouse Gas Inventory figures show continuing increases in both gross and net emissions.[20] Gross emissions increased by 2.2 per cent between 2016 and 2017, accounting for around 80.9 million tonnes of CO_2 equivalent. This brought the increase in gross emissions from 1990 to 2017 to 23.1 per cent. Net emissions, which take into account CO_2 absorbed by forestry, increased by 65 per cent compared to 1990 levels. The two largest sectors for gross emissions in 2017 were agriculture (48.1 per cent) and energy (40.7 per cent). Emissions from electricity generation and transport continue to grow significantly, as do emissions from agriculture, primarily methane from ruminant livestock and nitrous oxide. A 70 per cent increase in the dairy herd between 1994 and 2017, together with a sixfold increase in the use of nitrogen fertiliser since 1990, are behind the continuing surge in agriculture emissions.[21] With 48.1 per cent of emissions coming from agriculture, of which around 35.2 per cent is methane, New Zealand will not achieve its ambitions unless it takes robust action to reduce methane emissions. The political and economic power of the agricultural sector in New Zealand is a major barrier to addressing methane emissions.

New Zealand's growing emissions profile is the legacy of years of domestic inaction by successive governments. In 2015, the Parliamentary Commissioner for the Environment reported that there was no coherent national plan or process for moving New Zealand towards a low carbon economy.[22] The emissions trading scheme (ETS) was introduced in 2008, but has not performed as expected. It aimed to cap and progressively reduce emissions of all greenhouse gases and create a market for the trade of emission permits. However, problems included the failure to include methane emissions, the absence of a reducing cap and very low market prices for carbon emissions. In addition to problems with the ETS, local government has been prevented from taking emissions into account as part of its regulatory and planning functions.[23]

Low-Emissions Economy: Issues Paper (2017), www.productivity.govt.nz/assets/Documents/50449807ff/ Low-emissions-economy-issues-paper.pdf.

[19] 'Total Greenhouse Gas Emissions per Capita in OECD Countries', https://figure.nz/chart/ jMoS5wjQpAHSYx33.

[20] Ministry for the Environment, *New Zealand's Greenhouse Gas Inventory: 1990–2017* (2019), www. mfe.govt.nz/sites/default/files/media/Climate%20Change/nz-greenhouse-gas-inventory-2019.pdf.

[21] Ministry for the Environment, 'Environment Aotearoa 2019 Summary' (Issue 4, 2019), www.mfe. govt.nz/Environment-Aotearoa-2019-Summary.

[22] Parliamentary Commissioner for the Environment, 'New Zealand's Contribution to the New International Climate Agreement: Submission to the Minister for Climate Change Issues and the Minister for the Environment' (2015), www.pce.parliament.nz/media/1226/climate-change-agreemeent-submission-june-2015.pdf.

[23] New Zealand Productivity Commission, *Low-Emissions Economy: Final Report* (n 18); Julia Harker, Prue Taylor and Stephen Knight-Lenihan, 'Multi-level Governance and Climate Change Mitigation in New Zealand: Lost Opportunities' (2017) 17 *Climate Policy* 485.

Internationally, New Zealand has taken advantage of a uniquely low obligation under the Kyoto Protocol's first commitment period (2008–12). Unlike other developed nations, New Zealand's obligation was limited to reducing emissions to 1990 levels by 2000. New Zealand chose not to make any commitments under the Protocol's second commitment period (2013–20). In 2015, the government announced a modest nationally determined contribution (NDC) of reducing emissions to 30 per cent below 2005 levels by 2030 under the 2015 Paris Agreement.[24] An important official acknowledgement of New Zealand's situation appears in the government's Regulatory Impact Statement for the Bill, which acknowledges the 'substantial increase in greenhouse gas emissions since 1990' and states that '[t]he existing framework has fallen short of providing a stable and credible policy environment to enable necessary long-term planning, decision-making and investment by the private sector and civil society'.[25]

As regards climate change adaptation, evidence and understanding of climate change impacts and risks have grown rapidly in recent years. However, policy and planning responses have been slow and piecemeal. Local government authorities have the primary legal responsibility, but their work has been restricted by the absence of national policy. Successive national governments have provided non-statutory guidance, but none has produced a national adaptation strategy or risk assessment.[26]

Returning to the emergence of the Zero Carbon Bill, a public consultation document was released in mid-2018 asking for comments on key aspects of proposed legislation.[27] A record 15,000 submissions were received.[28] There was widespread public support for zero emission legislation for all gases, together with the establishment of an independent commission to provide expert advice and oversight.[29] Between December 2018 and the Bill's release in May 2019, the government worked with interest groups and the National Party in opposition to develop the draft legislation around a broad consensus across New Zealand society. The Minister acknowledged the National Party (the traditional supporter of the farming sector) for its constructive engagement.[30] In a statement, the National Party stated that they had 'serious reservations about the expected rate of reduction for methane'.[31] 'We are not convinced that the proposed 24–47% reduction for

---

[24] This target is equivalent to 11 per cent below 1990 levels by 2030.

[25] Ministry for the Environment, *Regulatory Impact Statement: Zero Carbon Bill* (January 2019) 1.

[26] Ministry for the Environment, 'Climate Change Adaptation Technical Working Group' (2018), www.mfe.govt.nz/climate-change/climate-change-and-government/adapting-climate-change/climate-change-adaptation.

[27] Ministry for the Environment, *Our Climate Your Say: Consultation on the Zero Carbon Bill* (ME 1371, 2018).

[28] Ministry for the Environment, *Zero Carbon Bill Consultation: Summary of Submissions* (ME 1386, 2018). Consultation occurred between June and July 2018.

[29] ibid.

[30] Toby Manhire, 'Zero Carbon Bill Revealed: Everything You Need to Know' (*The Spinoff*, 8 May 2019), https://thespinoff.co.nz/politics/08-05-2019/zero-carbon-bill-revealed-everything-you-need-to-know.

[31] ibid

methane meets our test in terms of science, economic impact or global response.'[32] Nevertheless, they did support its passage through the House to the select committee phase.

III. The Basic Architecture of the Bill

This section summarises the basic architecture of the Bill. This provides the context for the discussion of selected issues that follows.

A. Long-Term Emissions Reduction Target

The Bill's purpose section states that it provides a 'framework by which New Zealand can develop and implement clear and stable climate change policies that contribute to the global effort under the Paris Agreement to limit the global average temperature increase to 1.5 [degrees] Celsius above pre-industrial levels'.[33] A key mechanism to achieve this is the 2050 emissions reduction target. Following a 'split gases approach', this target has two primary elements:

(1) reducing all greenhouse gases (except biogenic methane) to *net zero* by 2050; and

(2) reducing *gross* emissions of biogenic methane (defined as produced by agricultural and waste sectors) within the range of 24–47 per cent below 2017 levels by 2050, including to 10 per cent below 2017 levels by 2030.[34]

The Bill's explanatory note states that the target was based on the results of public consultation, economic analysis, climate science and New Zealand's greenhouse gas profile.[35] The 2050 target's timeframe and emission levels are reviewable at the Minister's request and subject to the advice of the Climate Change Commission (hereinafter 'the Commission').[36] The Commission can only recommend revision if there has been a significant change in circumstances relevant to climate change. These are stated to include: global action; scientific understanding; New Zealand's obligations under international agreements; fiscal or economic circumstances; technological developments; distributional impacts; and equity implications (including generational equity).[37] The Commission's recommendation (if any) must be made publicly available and presented to Parliament by the Minister.

---

[32] ibid.
[33] Bill, cl 4.
[34] ibid cl 5O.
[35] Explanatory Note to the Climate Change Response (Zero Carbon) Amendment Bill 2019, 4.
[36] Bill, cls 5P–5R. The role and establishment of the Commission are described below.
[37] ibid cl 5Q.

However, the final decision on review remains with the Minister, who has 12 months to provide the Commission (and subsequently Parliament) with a written response. Amending legislation would be required to implement a new target.

The 2050 target, including its distinction between biogenic methane[38] and other greenhouse gases (primarily CO_2 and nitrous oxide), is primarily justified on scientific and policy work supporting the achievement of the Paris Agreement's aim to holding 'the increase in the global average temperature to well below 2°C above pre-industrial levels and pursuing efforts to limit the temperature increase to 1.5°C above pre-industrial levels'.[39] Drawing on the 2018 special report of the Intergovernmental Panel on Climate Change (IPCC), the government stated that it has used the following IPCC scenarios (or emission pathways) for limiting warming to 1.5°C, with limited or no overshoot:[40]

- reduce global emissions of CO_2 to net zero by 2050 and below zero (negative emissions) thereafter;

- reduce global emissions of agricultural methane by 24–47 per cent from 2010 levels by 2050;

- expressed together,[41] reduce global greenhouse gas emissions by 81–93 per cent over 2010 levels by 2050.

Using this work,[42] together with advice from New Zealand experts, the government has explained that biogenic methane can be treated differently because although more potent than other greenhouse gases, it is much shorter lived in the atmosphere – ie, it degrades over decades. This means that: 'Once in equilibrium, it can continue to be emitted at a stable rate without increasing its concentration in the atmosphere.'[43] Other greenhouse gases (notably CO_2) remain in the atmosphere for hundreds of thousands of years, 'meaning further emissions will increase its concentration in the atmosphere.'[44] Accordingly, long-lived gases need to be progressively reduced to net zero.

This approach to formulating the 2050 target gives the government flexibility to continue a *net approach* up until 2050 rather than requiring it to pursue absolute reductions in gross emissions. Tree planting, land use changes and purchase of international carbon credits are all likely to be utilised. The exception is biogenic methane, which is expressed as a gross emissions reduction target. Here the Bill uses the same reduction target (24–47 per cent by 2050), but uses a different baseline year than the IPCC, ie, 2017 as opposed to 2010.

---

[38] Produced from biological (plant and animal) sources; Ministry for the Environment (n 3) 10.

[39] Paris Agreement to the United Nations Framework Convention on Climate Change, 12 December 2015, TIAS No 16-1104, entered into force 4 November 2016, art 2.

[40] Ministry for the Environment, (n 3) 8–9.

[41] Using the GWP 100 equivalence metric; ibid 9.

[42] Explanatory Note to the Climate Change Response (Zero Carbon) Amendment Bill 2019, 4.

[43] Ministry for the Environment, (n 3) 10.

[44] ibid.

B. Emission Budgets and Reduction Plans

The Bill requires the Minister for Climate Change to establish budgets to form step-ping stones to reach the 2050 target.[45] Budgets are intended to provide certainty to the transition, a tool for monitoring progress and creating accountability across successive governments. The Bill explicitly provides that 'emission budgets must be met, as far as possible, through domestic emissions reductions and domestic removals'.[46]

Budgets are set for five-year periods and quantify net emissions permitted for all greenhouse gases as a CO_2 equivalent. The Bill requires three budgets to be in place at any one time, meaning that they will be set 10–15 years in advance from 2022 onwards.[47] The process for setting budgets and reduction plans (the primary tool to achieve them) involves both the Minister and the Commission. The process begins with the Commission recommending a permissible quantity of emissions for a budget period, together with its recommendations on how to achieve it, including pricing mechanisms (eg, the carbon price under the ETS) and regulatory tools.[48] These recommendations must be presented to Parliament by the Minister within a 12-week timeframe.[49] The Minister must provide a written response to the advice of the Commission and present this response to Parliament.[50] Budgets and plans require Cabinet approval and will be gazetted and tabled before Parliament following consultation with the 'appropriate representative of each of the politi-cal parties' in the House.[51] They are not treated as legislative instruments.[52] The Minister may reject the Commission's budget recommendations, but is required to give reasons for rejection and may need to consult with 'persons likely to have an interest in the emissions budget'.[53] In setting budgets, the Commission and the Minister are required to consider an extensive list of factors, including scientific advice, ambition and technical/economic feasibility, public consultation, distribu-tional impacts, technological developments and global responses.[54]

As noted above, reduction plans are the key tool for meeting budgets. The Bill contains little detail on the content of these plans on the basis that while the Commission makes recommendations on 'how the budgets may realistically be met',[55] these are ultimately policy and regulatory decisions that are the prerogative

---

[45] This is very different from the CCA, where the UK Parliament makes the final decision on budgets (s 8). Budgets are expressed as a net quantity of CO_2 equivalent; Bill, cl 5V.

[46] Bill, cl 5W(1).

[47] ibid cl 5U.

[48] ibid cls 5W and 5X.

[49] ibid cl 5X.

[50] ibid cl 5Y.

[51] ibid cl 5ZA.

[52] ibid.

[53] ibid cl 5Y. The Minister is not required to explain the rationale behind the budget chosen and why the Minister is satisfied that it will produce the trajectory needed to achieve the target.

[54] ibid cl 5Z. There is no explicit inclusion of NDCs in this clause, but they may (potentially) be read into the list of matters. Another omission is reference to the national risk assessment.

[55] ibid cl 5X(1)(c) 'including pricing and policy methods'.

of the elected government. The Bill merely provides that plans, outlining policies and strategies for achieving budgets, must be prepared and published informed by advice from the Commission and other agencies. The Bill does not elaborate on the legal effect of plans or their impact on other relevant statutory planning and decision-making processes.[56]

In acknowledgement of 'just transition' concerns, reduction plans must include a strategy to mitigate impacts on 'workers, regions, iwi and Māori, and wider communities',[57] including funding. Both the Minister and the Commission must consult widely on plans. The Minister has additional consultation obligations regarding (but not limited to) iwi and Māori, consistent with Te Tiriti o Waitangi.[58]

As noted above, budgets will 'primarily be met through domestic action – that is, the reduction and removal (eg, through forestry) of domestic greenhouse gas emissions'.[59] On the issue of 'offshore mitigation' (ie, international carbon credits), these can be used in limited circumstances[60] and subject to some oversight by the Commission.[61] New Zealand's ETS will be a key tool for meeting budgets. However, the government acknowledges that significant improvements will need to be made to ensure that the ETS drives reductions 'in line with' budgets.[62] These changes may include a specified reducing emissions cap, together with a more effective carbon price (currently $25 per unit) and (most controversially) bringing agricultural emissions into the scheme.[63] The Commission will also be given a role to advise government on ETS settings as part of the ETS improvements. Interestingly, the government states that changes may also 'enable domestic emitters to buy international units'.[64] Presumably, this would be constrained to 'very limited circumstances' in order to avoid past problems with credibility and to ensure reductions are 'primarily met through domestic action'.

C. Flexibility Mechanisms

As described above, the 2050 target is reviewable in specified circumstances. In order to maintain certainty and integrity, but retain some flexibility, budgets can

---

[56] ibid cl 5ZK – this states that the target and budgets are permissive but not mandatory considerations for government officials.

[57] ibid cl 5ZD. The term 'iwi' is used to refer to tribal groupings.

[58] ibid cl 5ZF. This is discussed in more detail below.

[59] Ministry for the Environment (n 3) 12.

[60] Bill, cl 6.

[61] ibid cl 5X(1). This is discussed in more detail below.

[62] Ministry for the Environment (n 3) 14.

[63] Some of this work is already being conducted by the Interim Climate Change Committee. Legislative changes to the ETS are expected by the end of 2019. Delays in bringing agricultural emissions into the ETS are controversial. The Productivity Commission has done analysis on carbon pricing in New Zealand; see New Zealand Productivity Commission, *Low-Emissions Economy: Final Report* (n 18).

[64] Ministry for the Environment (n 3) 11.

also be amended. However, this can only occur when changes significantly affect the basis on which the budget was established.[65] If the budget period has begun, amendment can only occur in exceptional circumstances and following a process that includes an explanation of reasons for the change. Banking and borrowing between budgets is enabled, with the latter being subject to restrictions to facilitate transitions between budget periods.[66]

D. Monitoring and Enforcement

The Commission plays a role in the setting/amending of budgets and creating reduction plans via its expert recommendatory advice. It also contributes to transparency and accountability. It is tasked with monitoring progress through annual reports and by conducting a full review at the end of each budget period.[67] This monitoring role relates to both progress towards meeting budgets and the 2050 target. Additional provisions enable it to access information that is relevant to this task. The Commission must make review documents available to the Minister and to the public. Annual reports must be presented to the House by the Minister, following which the Minister must write a response to annual reports within two months of receipt. Failure to meet the 2050 target or any budget must be explained by the Minister (in a report presented to Parliament), but this failure is *not* otherwise legally enforceable beyond a declaratory judgment from the courts and an award for costs related to bringing the legal action:

5ZJ Effect of Failure to Meet 2050 Target and Emissions Budgets

(1)   No remedy or relief is available for failure to meet the 2050 target or an emissions budget, and the 2050 target and emissions budgets are not enforceable in a court of law, except as set out in this section.

(2)   If the 2050 target or an emissions budget is not met, a court may make a declaration to that effect, together with an award of costs.

(3)   If a declaration is made and becomes final after all appeals or rights of appeal expire or are disposed of, the Minister must, as soon as practicable, present to the House of Representatives a document that –

(a)   brings the declaration to the attention of the House of Representatives; and

(b)   contains advice on the Government's response to the declaration.

This is followed by a perplexing clause stating that the target and budgets *may* be taken into account, in the exercise or performance of a public function, power or duty. However, a failure to do so (including failure to follow government guidance)

---

[65] Bill, cl 5ZB, as set out in cl 5Z(2).

[66] ibid cl 5ZC. If the total quantity of emissions in a budget period is less than provided for in that budget, the excess may be carried forward to the next budget period (banked). If the total quantity of emissions in a budget period is greater than provided for in that budget, up to 1 per cent may be carried back (borrowed) from the next emissions budget.

[67] ibid cls 5ZG–5ZI.

'does not invalidate anything done by that person or body'.[68] As discussed below, the intention seems to be to restrict the ability of courts to conduct judicial review in respect of budget and target implementation, but the language chosen is ambiguous.

E. Adaptation

Following the approach of the CCA, the Bill makes some provision for improving action on adaptation policy and planning. As previously noted, to date, little action has been taken by central government. The primary legal obligation has fallen upon local government with little guidance from central government. The Bill makes an effort to fill this gap and provide an enhanced legislative framework for climate change adaptation action.

The Bill requires the Commission to carry out national climate change risk assessments at intervals of no more than six years.[69] This involves assessing a range of risks to New Zealand's economy, society, environment and ecology for current and future climate change effects. A broad array of factors are to be considered when evaluating risks. These include: climate trends; international obligations; distribution of effects taking particular account of vulnerable groups or sectors; alignment with other national risk assessments; and scientific/technical advice.[70] Assessments must be made publicly available, following which the Minister will present them to Parliament.[71] The government is responsible to create national adaptation plans within two years of a risk assessment, following public consultation and using factors similar to those used for the risk assessment.[72] The Commission's role is to monitor and report on plan implementation through bi-annual progress reporting, to which the Minister must respond.[73] It may also make recommendations to the government.[74]

F. The Climate Change Commission

The Zero Carbon Bill establishes an independent expert Climate Change Commission which provides advice and performs a monitoring role, similar to that of the UK Climate Change Committee.[75] As outlined above, the Commission's

---

[68] ibid cls 5ZK and 5ZL.

[69] ibid cl 5ZM. The first assessment is to be undertaken by the Minister and thereafter by the Commission to maintain independence.

[70] ibid cl 5ZN.

[71] ibid cl 5ZO.

[72] ibid cl 5ZQ.

[73] ibid cls 5ZS–U.

[74] ibid cl 5ZS.

[75] ibid subparts 1 and 2.

primary role is to give expert advice that is independent of the government and any sector or interest groups.[76] It also plays an important monitoring role. In line with the CCA, it does not have any decision-making or enforcement powers. The justification is to ensure that the elected government determines, and remains responsible and ultimately politically accountable for, policy choices and implementation.

The Commission will be established as an independent Crown entity, the status of which is provided for in separate legislation.[77] However, the government has retained a legislative power to *direct* the Commission to consider government policy in two specific instances; when giving advice on the ETS and *if* asked for advice on an NDC under the Paris Agreement.[78] Appointment and required member expertise is tightly prescribed by the Bill. The Minister will recommend a board of seven commissioners (with five-year terms), but appointments will be made by the Governor-General following consultation with other political parties.[79] The nominations process[80] and expertise provisions attempt to give effect to government obligations under Te Tiriti o Waitangi (the Treaty of Waitangi).[81] Collectively, the Bill requires the Commissioners to have:[82]

- an understanding of climate change mitigation and adaptation (including the effects of responses to climate change);
- experience of working in or with local and central government;
- knowledge of public and regulatory policy processes and implementation;
- technical and professional skills, experience, and expertise in:
  - ○ environmental, ecological, social, economic and distributional effects of climate change and policy interventions; and
  - ○ te Tiriti o Waitangi and te ao Māori (including tikanga Māori, tereo Māori, mātauranga Māori and Māori economic activity);[83] and
- a range of sectors and industries at the regional and local levels.

---

[76] ibid cl 5N.
[77] ibid cl 5C; Crown Entities Act 2004.
[78] Bill, cl 5N(2).
[79] ibid cl 5E.
[80] The Minister is to seek nominations from Māori and Iwi representative organisations: ibid cl 5C(2).
[81] Te Tiriti o Waitangi (the Treaty of Waitangi) is the partnership agreement made between the Crown and Māori in 1840. The Climate Change Response Act 2002 already had a treaty section recognising the Crown's obligation to respect Treaty principles. Treaty obligations are discussed in more detail below.
[82] Bill, cl 5H.
[83] ibid cl 5H(2) provides the following definitions: 'mātauranga Māori means traditional Māori knowledge, te ao Māori means the Māori world, te reo Māori means the Māori language, tikanga Māori means Māori custom and protocol'.

IV. Selected Issues

This section will provide some discussion of issues concerning the Bill, drawing on public submission documents and the author's own analysis. Its primary focus is the mitigation components of the Bill. This does not mean that the national risk assessment and adaptation planning components are of any less significance; indeed, mitigation and adaptation are inextricably linked, and this needs to be clearly provided for in law and policy to ensure good outcomes.[84]

A. The 2050 Target

As discussed above, the Bill sets a target of reducing *net emissions* (excluding biogenic methane) *to zero by 2050*.[85] Net emissions means 'gross emissions combined with emissions and removals from land use, land use change, and the forestry sector'.[86] This is said to be based on scenarios developed by the IPCC's 2018 report, which aimed at limiting global atmospheric warming to 1.5°C. A number of issues have been raised about this target, including the following:

- The target omits any reference to the need to go below zero (ie, achieve negative emissions) after 2050.[87]

- The target's emphasis on *net* emissions to 2050 (and beyond) is not stringent enough. For example, it enables gross emissions to increase, provided they are offset by removals. A net approach provides flexibility, but the target should identify an intention to move away from net emissions to a low or zero-emissions economy.[88] Emphasis on net emissions for another 30 years (and beyond) potentially delays the profound transformations required and is unfair to future generations. There is a significant difference between a low or zero-emissions economy and a *net*-emissions economy.[89] There are also significant

---

[84] Stephen Knight-Lenihan and Kate Scanlen, 'Climate-Compatible Development in New Zealand' (2018) 14(4) *Policy Quarterly* 41. The Bill's Explanatory Note states that: 'Situating adaptation measures in the Bill alongside those for mitigation is designed to address their shared intergenerational implications. It will provide an integrated and holistic approach to the problem and ensure that policies and long-term decision making are appropriately co-ordinated.' Explanatory Note to the Climate Change Response (Zero Carbon) Amendment Bill 2019, 5. A thorough analysis is needed to see if the Bill delivers on this intention.

[85] Bill, cl 5O(1)(a).

[86] ibid cl 6(1).

[87] Environmental Defence Society, 'Submission to the Environment Select Committee on the Climate Change Response (Zero Carbon) Amendment Bill 2019' 3; Parliamentary Commissioner for the Environment, 'Submission to the Environment Select Committee on the Climate Change Response (Zero Carbon) Amendment Bill 2019' 9; Generation Zero (n 16) 12.

[88] Environmental Defence Society (n 87) 3.

[89] ibid. Referring to an earlier report, the Parliamentary Commissioner for the Environment concluded that 'any target for carbon dioxide emissions had to be zero – at some point'. Parliamentary Commissioner for the Environment (n 87) 3. The earlier report referred to is Parliamentary Commissioner

concerns about the use of forestry for offsetting,[90] with submissions suggesting that its use be prohibited or strictly limited.[91]

- The omission of a 2030 target (as suggested by the IPCC) to achieve the Paris Agreement's 1.5°C warming limit and 2050 net zero target. Modelling indicates that global emissions need to decline by about 45 per cent over 2010 levels by 2030 and then begin to drop steeply to net zero by 2050.[92] On the face of it, New Zealand's NDC reflects this, pledging a 30 per cent reduction in greenhouse gases by 2030 (using 2005 as a baseline year), but this interim target is not reflected in the Bill. Only one gas (biogenic methane) has a 2030 reduction target, that of 10 per cent, using a 2017 as the baseline year. If the government is serious about using the Bill's target to meet its NDC, then this approach would place a *much greater burden* on non-agricultural emitters of greenhouse gases (such as transport emitters). This burden has been calculated as a reduction of over 40 per cent below 2005 levels by 2030.[93]

- The target adopts a controversial split gases approach.[94] This is explicitly justified on the grounds that methane is a short-lived gas. The premise is that a stable rate of emissions will not lead to increases in atmospheric concentrations.[95] However, a decision about a fair target for methane is not solely a question of stabilising the temperature impact of a gas by a given year. Given methane's potency and short-lived nature, reducing methane emissions will contribute to rapid atmospheric cooling. As the Parliamentary Commissioner for the Environment notes: 'Given the need to head off peak global temperatures by *whatever means we can, contributions are needed from wherever they can be found*' (emphasis added).[96] The Commissioner suggests a minimum

---

for the Environment, 'Farms, Forests and Fossil Fuels: The Next Great Landscape Transformation?' (2019).

[90] These include the difficulty of maintaining forests given the effects of climate change (eg, water scarcity, fires and disease), the effects on rural communities, the impacts of land-use change and forests being a default solution used at the cost of gross emission reductions. See Parliamentary Commissioner for the Environment (n 87) 6–7.

[91] ibid; Wise Response, 'Submission to the Environment Select Committee on the Climate Change Response (Zero Carbon) Amendment Bill 2019' 15.

[92] Generation Zero (n 16) 9, quoting the 2018 IPCC Special Report on Global Warming: 'In model pathways with no or limited overshoot of 1.5°C, global net anthropogenic CO_2 emissions decline by about 45% from 2010 levels by 2030 (40–60% interquartile range), reaching net zero around 2050 (2045–2055 interquartile range).' IPCC, 2018: Summary for Policymakers in: Valerie Masson-Delmotte, Panmao Zhai, Hans.-O. Pörtner, et al (eds), 'Global Warming of 1.5°C. An IPCC Special Report on the impacts of global warming of 1.5°C above pre-industrial levels and related global greenhouse gas emission pathways, in the context of strengthening the global response to the threat of climate change, sustainable development, and efforts to eradicate poverty,' *World Meteorological Organization, Geneva, Switzerland, at C.2.*

[93] Parliamentary Commissioner for the Environment (n 87) 7–8. The Parliamentary Commissioner for the Environment generously states: if this is not the intention, then the 2030 methane target needs to be reconsidered (ibid 8).

[94] ibid 7.

[95] Explanatory Note to the Climate Change Response (Zero Carbon) Amendment Bill 2019, 4.

[96] Parliamentary Commissioner for the Environment (n 87) 8.

percentage reduction (instead of a range), but notes progression below that minimum becomes a matter of technology, capacity and international credibility: 'Simply attempting to "grandfather" our existing contribution to warming from methane [using a 2017 baseline] could be seen to be self-serving.'[97] A Climate Analytics report notes that stabilisation of methane is not sufficient; a global reduction of 30–50 per cent below 2010 levels by 2030 and around 50 per cent by 2050 is required by science.[98] Accordingly, New Zealand's approach will 'not set the comprehensive policy targets required, and will not be consistent with achieving the Paris Agreement Goals'.[99] These views contrast with those of Federated Farmers, who strongly oppose the Bill's treatment of methane. In their opinion, it imposes a burden which will have a devastating impact on the agricultural sector and provincial economies because it will require (in the short to medium term) significant stock reduction.[100]

• The failure to use a global carbon budgeting approach. This requires: (a) determination of New Zealand's share of the remaining global carbon budget[101] (for keeping within 1.5°C) using both science and equity principles; (b) alignment of New Zealand's target and budgets with both the temperature goal and keeping within New Zealand's share of the remaining global carbon budget; (c) setting a 2030 target for 50 per cent net reductions of non-methane emissions from 2010 levels (consistent with the IPCC's 2030 advice);[102] and (d) setting a specific methane reduction target for 2050 using IPCC science for achievement of the 1.5°C goal.[103]

The above discussion is a simplified analysis of issues and debate concerning the Bill's target. The Parliamentary Commissioner for the Environment notes that while there will always be debate and disagreement, the Bill's target needs to be well understood by the public to ensure longevity and success. Given the

---

[97] ibid. The Wise Response submission is more straightforward: given the considerable scientific uncertainties around global methane emissions, it is essential that New Zealand reduces them immediately. Wise Response (n 91) 14.

[98] Climate Analytics, 'New Zealand's Zero Carbon Bill – Getting the Paris Agreement right' 5. The Generation Zero submission cites a report of the Biological Emissions Reference Group, which found that New Zealand's methane emissions could feasibly be reduced by 22–48 per cent by 2050; Generation Zero (n 16) 11.

[99] Climate Analytics (n 98) 2. This approach places an additional burden on other countries to compensate for the lack of action by New Zealand to reduce its non-CO_2 gases (at 5).

[100] Federated Farmers of New Zealand, 'Submission to the Environment Select Committee on the Climate Change Response (Zero Carbon) Amendment Bill 2019' 4–6.

[101] Calculating this figure is highly complex. For some of the more recent research, see Joeri Rogelj et al, 'Estimating and Tracking the Remaining Carbon Budget for Stringent Climate Targets' (2019) 571 *Nature* 335.

[102] IPCC, 2018: Summary for Policymakers in: Valerie Masson-Delmotte, Panmao Zhai, Hans.-O. Pörtner, et al (eds.) 'Global Warming of 1.5°C. An IPCC Special Report on the impacts of global warming of 1.5°C above pre-industrial levels and related global greenhouse gas emission pathways, in the context of strengthening the global response to the threat of climate change, sustainable development, and efforts to eradicate poverty' *World Meteorological Organization, Geneva, Switzerland, at C.1.*

[103] Generation Zero (n 16) 9–11.

important issues raised by many submitters, it is questionable whether the split target is well understood. The Commissioner recommends that the best way to secure public confidence is for the target to be determined by a robust and transparent process enabling the various trade-offs to be understood. To this end, the Commissioner suggests that the Bill be enacted without a target in place. The Commission should (within 12 months) advise the Minister on the initial 2050 target following a framework based on science *and* a list of specific factors, including equity principles.[104]

B. Integration with Other Legislative Frameworks: A Robust Cross-sectoral Approach

In 2018, the Productivity Commission concluded that New Zealand's current legislative framework:

> [I]s not underpinned by a credible commitment to a domestic low-emissions transition. The current systems architecture lacks long-term stability and predictability about the nature and pace of New Zealand's low-emissions transition, *lacks a clear plan for reducing domestic emissions, and exhibits poor policy coherence.* (Emphasis added)[105]

In its current form, there is concern that the Bill does not provide adequate integration with other legislative frameworks and policy sectors. These frameworks create a wide range of government strategic and regulatory planning and decision-making, which can either significantly contribute to achieving the target and budgets or undermine and frustrate their achievement. Strengthened integration between the Bill and a wide range of relevant policy sectors has been suggested by a number of submitters. For example, one submission recommends that the target and budget (together with ministerial guidance) be changed from permissive to *mandatory considerations* 'in the exercise or performance of' public functions, powers and duties under *specified legislation*.[106] In addition to being mandatory considerations, the Parliamentary Commissioner for the Environment recommends that public authorities be required to demonstrate how the target and budgets have been taken into account.[107] Applying these requirements could greatly strengthen integration between policy and regulatory sectors if scoped to include both national and sub-national levels of governance. The Paris Agreement explicitly recognises the growing role of sub-national actors, but this important governance development is not reflected in the Bill.

---

[104] Parliamentary Commissioner for the Environment (n 87) 3–4, Annex A. See also Brown et al (n 13). This work demonstrates how a national target can be calculated using both science and equity principles.

[105] New Zealand Productivity Commission, *Low-Emissions Economy: Final Report* (n 18).

[106] Lawyers for Climate Action, 'Submission to the Environment Select Committee on the Climate Change Response (Zero Carbon) Amendment Bill 2019' 3.

[107] Parliamentary Commissioner for the Environment (n 87) 15.

Rapid transition to a low emissions economy and society will require radical transformations across virtually all policy sectors. This calls for explicit consideration of climate change in all relevant social, economic and environmental policies and actions. An indicative list of specified legislation for which consideration of the target and budget is a mandatory consideration includes legislation for commerce, electricity, waste management, energy conservation, conservation estate, reserves management, tax, health, labour policy and fiscal management. A list of specified legislation is likely to be extensive and to increase over time.[108] Some key examples in New Zealand include legislation regulating the use of land, air and water, including coastal waters and biodiversity (the Resource Management Act 1991), managing land transport planning and funding (the Land Transport Management Act 2003), regulating onshore and offshore mining (the Crown Minerals Act 1991 and the Exclusive Economic Zone and Continental Shelf (Environmental Effects) Act 2012), regulating the building sector (the Building Act 2004), and defining the role and powers of local government (the Local Government Act 2002). To enhance integration occurring across sectors and legislation, one submission suggests that the Commission and Minister be given enhanced roles. For example, the Minister could be required to issue mandatory guidance to government departments on how to take the target and budgets into account.[109]

In the absence of strong integration across other sectors, the Bill gives the impression that it will be primarily reliant on an enhanced ETS for reductions and forestry for removals. If so, this may only deliver a modest improvement on business as usual, and not all of the economic and societal transformations required. In the Productivity Commission's evaluation, transition to a low-emissions economy must be 'profound and widespread'. This will require 'rapid, far-reaching and unprecedented changes'[110] supported by social transformation.

The Generation Zero submission makes the case that the Bill should be a stand-alone framework (as in the UK) and not part of the ETS legislative framework. They argue that this would provide separate 'systems architecture', which is clear, certain, accessible and not directly entwined with one particular tool (the ETS), which itself is more subject to amendment in line with political agendas.[111]

A related and urgent issue is the Bill's silence on dealing with existing inconsistencies under other primary legislation. A key example is the Resource

---

[108] Lawyers for Climate Action suggest the Commission should scrutinise all existing and new legislation for consistency with the Bill and propose amendments to other legislation, if necessary; Lawyers for Climate Action (n 106) 2–4.

[109] ibid 4–5.

[110] New Zealand Productivity Commission, *Low-Emissions Economy: Final Report* (n 18) 19.

[111] Generation Zero (n 16) 17. The current Fijian Climate Change Bill provides a very interesting example of a comprehensive approach to climate change, including integration with oceans policy, displacement and use of the sustainable development principle; Climate Change Bill 2019 (Fiji), www.economy.gov.fj/images/CCIC/uploads/BILL/Draft-Climate-Change-Bill.pdf?fbclid=IwAR1m7qxAZFuFy0uovYh3AOVEg-l_Utr14EgDKTYPDxoTOquhMqryxRVHhqM.

Management Act 1991. This Act explicitly prevents local government from taking into account greenhouse gas emissions from activities when conducting a wide range of planning and permitting functions. Councils cannot, for example, decline air discharge permits and land use consents when activities (eg, coal-fired power stations, coal mines and urban development) contribute to climate change. Many submissions have suggested that the Resource Management Act 1991 be promptly amended to ensure that local government is no longer obstructed from addressing the climate change effects of permits, land use development plans and a wide range of environmental management plans, including plans for water, biodiversity management and urban development. The government recently announced a major policy and law reform across the resource management sector which will consider interaction between the Bill and the Resource Management Act 1991, the Land Transport Management Act 2003 and the Local Government Act 2002. While this may result in stronger integration (eg, the removal of some barriers), the reform's terms of reference do not include strengthening the Bill's interaction with these other Acts. Given the critical importance of local government in delivering climate change action in both urban and rural communities, this is a significant limitation of the Bill.[112] The submission from local government states that: 'The Government must, in partnership with local government, undertake additional work to identify the policies, tools, incentives and guidance that local government needs in order to be able to meaningfully contribute to emissions reductions.'[113]

Some submissions have focused on the legal effect of emission reduction plans as a means of achieving better integration with other legislation.[114] These plans set out the policies and strategies for meeting a budget. They should include sector-specific and multi-sector policies, and set out *how* the government intends budgets to be met. However, the Bill is silent on the legal effect of these plans and their impact on other statutory processes and agencies.[115] In addition, the government is not required to demonstrate how the policies and strategies identified in reduction plans will actually add up to deliver on either the total budget (expressed as a net quantity of CO_2 equivalent) or portions of the total budget to be achieved through a combination of reductions, removals or offshore mitigation.[116] The combined impact of these aspects gives the impression that reduction plans will be non-binding action plans or strategic policy documents.[117]

---

[112] Taylor (n 13); Harker, Taylor and Knight-Lenihan (n 23). Internationally, the role of local authorities was enhanced through the 'Marrakech Partnership for Global Climate Action' (United Nations Framework Convention on Climate Change, 2016), https://unfccc.int/files/paris_agreement/application/pdf/marrakech_partnership_for_global_climate_action.pdf.

[113] Local Government New Zealand, 'Submission to the Environment Select Committee on the Climate Change Response (Zero Carbon) Amendment Bill 2019' 10. The composition of the Climate Change Commission does include reference to local government expertise; Bill, cl 5H(1)(b).

[114] Environmental Defence Society (n 87) 8–9.

[115] ibid.

[116] Taylor and Scanlen (n 13); Generation Zero (n 16) 18.

[117] Environmental Defence Society (n 87) 9.

C. Offshore Mitigation or International Carbon Credits

The main issues concerning offshore mitigation, defined as 'emission reductions, removals or allowances',[118] are their credibility, potential use as an alternative to achieving domestic reductions, and price variability. The Bill attempts to deal with the credibility issue by defining offshore mitigation as tools that are 'robustly accounted for', ensuring 'double accounting is avoided' and 'represent an actual additional, measurable, and verifiable reduction of an amount of carbon dioxide equivalent'.[119] One submission has suggested that transparency be enhanced by requiring the Commission and the Minister to demonstrate how transparency requirements are met by any offshore mitigation used.[120] On the relationship with domestic action, prior to setting a budget, the Commission must advise on the proportion of a budget to be met by offshore mitigation and the appropriate limit on the amount used. However, the Minister has the final decision. To create greater clarity ahead of a budget period, it has been suggested that the Minister's response to the Commission should include an explicit limit on the amount of offshore mitigation to be used to achieve the budget.[121] Other submissions have gone further, suggesting total prohibition, statutory limits or specification (of offshore mitigation) as a quantity of CO_2 equivalent in budget information.[122]

D. Legal Enforceability

Compared to the CCA, the Bill takes a novel approach to the enforceability of targets and budgets. The CCA is silent on the legal enforceability of targets and budgets and for government fulfilment of related statutory duties; however, there is a strong view that the door is open for judicial review proceedings.[123] Furthermore, the CCA does not preclude the UK Climate Change Committee's involvement in judicial review proceedings. Many submissions have commented that the Bill goes much further than the CCA by explicitly excluding any legal remedy or relief beyond a declaratory judgment and an associated award of costs.[124] As one submission explains, while it is understandable that government departments should not be exposed to damages claims for failing to meet the target or budgets,

---

[118] Bill, cl 6(1).
[119] Bill, cl 6(1).
[120] Lawyers for Climate Action (n 106) 5.
[121] ibid 5–6.
[122] See, eg, Generation Zero (n 16) 15–16.
[123] See generally Thomas L Muinzer, 'Is the Climate Change Act 2008 a Constitutional Statute?' (2018) 24(4) *European Public Law* 733, 747; however, note the potential limitation on available remedies at 749.
[124] Bill, cl 5ZJ. It should be noted that it is not clear whether this privative clause extends beyond substantive obligations (to meet the target and budgets) to include procedural obligations, including those in respect of the reduction plans.

the Bill goes too far 'because it ousts the courts from applying or creating remedies in appropriate cases in a proportionate and reasonable manner'.[125] It notes that courts are capable of developing new remedies appropriate to the failing at issue and that the opportunity for legal development over the next 30 years should not be curtailed.[126] The recommendation is to delete the clause or limit its scope to damages claims.

Another submission makes the point that the adequacy of current aspects of the Bill, including the Commission's recommendatory powers and institutional settings giving the government final decision-making powers on the target, budgets and policies, are dependent upon the ability to enforce legislative targets and budgets once set. The recommendation is for an appeal pathway enabling courts to direct the government to put in place measures to achieve the target or budget. This would not extend to directing the government to act in a specific way. Requiring the government to comply with the law (a numerical target or budget) is not a radical constitutional proposition.[127]

A legal analysis suggests that the Bill's privative clause goes too far, potentially offending against: developing climate justice litigation; international law principles; the right to natural justice in New Zealand's Bill of Rights 1990; and constitutional principles.[128] In general terms, the concern is that, given the urgency and existential risks of climate change, media scrutiny, political accountability and parliamentary oversight are important but not sufficient.[129] In this respect, more consideration should be given to timely scrutiny (including through judicial processes if needed) of reductions plans,[130] including their capability to meet the target and budget, *before* any failure to meet a budget occurs.

The restrictions on legal enforceability have to be viewed alongside the related clause making the target and budgets *non-mandatory* considerations which officials 'may, if they think fit' take into account.[131] A Greenpeace New Zealand press statement calls the Bill 'reasonably ambitious legislation with its teeth ripped out'.[132] They note that a declaratory judgment does not actually require the government to do anything.[133] Such weak provisions seem at odds with the growing understanding of the global climate emergency and the willingness of citizens to take legal and direct action on climate change.[134]

---

[125] Lawyers for Climate Action (n 106) 5.

[126] ibid.

[127] Environmental Defence Society (n 87) 6–7.

[128] Trevor Daya-Winterbottom, 'Zero Carbon, Climate Justice and Privative Clauses' (2019) 12 *Resource Management Bulletin* 173, 173–74. See also Generation Zero (n 16) 18–19.

[129] Daya-Winterbottom (n 87) 173–74.

[130] Generation Zero (n 16) 18.

[131] Bill, cl 5ZK.

[132] Greenpeace, 'Russel Norman: Toothless Zero Carbon Bill Has Bark But No Bite' (press release, 8 May 2019).

[133] ibid.

[134] *Thomson v Minister for Climate Change Issues* [2017] New ZealandHC 733 was an important New Zealand case that considered international obligations in the context of domestic legislation.

E. The Climate Change Commission

The Commission must be granted and retain a high degree of independence in order for its advisory and monitoring role to be credible and trusted. It is established as an independent Crown Entity and 'must act independently in performing its functions and duties'.[135] Most submitters are satisfied with the Commission's status, but some suggest removing the government's explicit policy control for (a) settings under the ETS and (b) NDCs,[136] together with adding safeguards for adequate and independent funding.[137] In terms of monitoring via annual progress reports and end of budget reports, the Commission is less independent than its UK counterpart because it does not report directly to Parliament; it reports to the Minister and the public.[138] If this element is changed, then the Commission would have some powers similar to other parliamentary officers, including the Parliamentary Commissioner for the Environment.

As previously noted, the ETS will be a primary regulatory tool for meeting budgets. The Commission has a role to advise on the necessary ETS settings to meet the target and budgets. If the government refuses to take advice on this matter, it has been suggested that the Commission be given the power to introduce the policy settings into the ETS, including the power to directly set the carbon price in a manner analogous to the Reserve Bank's ability to set interest rates.[139] This suggestion would give the Commission significantly more power than is currently intended by the government.

F. A Broader Mandate

As currently drafted, the Commission has a very specific role regarding the target, budgets and adaption provisions in the Bill. Some submitters have suggested broadening its mandate to include providing information, public education and advocacy.[140] One submission went further, recommending that the Commission provide assistance and advice to groups engaged in mitigation and adaptation, including local government and civil society.[141]

---

[135] Bill, cl 5N(1).

[136] Environmental Defence Society (n 87) 5–6; Lawyers for Climate Action (n 106) 6–7.

[137] Environmental Defence Society (n 87) 5–6; Generation Zero (n 16) 21; Wise Response (n 91) 7. Some submissions also recommend an independent secretariat be established to serve the Commission.

[138] Wise Response (n 91) 10–11. They also suggest the release of reports to all parties at the same time to reduce potential for political intervention. See also Generation Zero (n 16) 20–21.

[139] Greenpeace, 'Greenpeace New Zealand Submission on Zero Carbon Bill' (2018) 19, https://storage.googleapis.com/planet4-new-zealand-stateless/2018/07/c4fbc4ed-substantive-greenpeace-submission-on-zero-carbon-bill-2018.pdf.

[140] Generation Zero (n 16) 22; Environmental Defence Society (n 87) 6.

[141] Environmental Defence Society (n 87) 6.

G. Expertise

There is support for the current identification of expertise, but some submissions identify refinements and gaps – for example, greater scientific expertise (including atmospheric chemistry and climate modelling) to assist with analysis of information and identification of gaps, and specific expertise on public health.[142]

H. Policy Scrutiny and Advice: Decisions on Budgets and Reduction Plans

A very important element of the Bill is the government's full control over the final budget decision. In comparison, the CCA provides for Parliament to make the final decision on emission budgets.[143] The Parliamentary Commissioner for the Environment is highly critical of this element, noting that budget decisions involve significant discretion and have very far-reaching consequences.[144] He notes that important policy should be a matter for Parliament to determine, following an open democratic process. He further argues that full debate and scrutiny (following expert Commission advice) will contribute to transparency and consensus. He recommends that 'Parliament can and should make the final decision on emission budgets'.[145]

As previously discussed, the government has full control over policy and strategies to deliver on the target and budget, but is required to seek and 'consider' the Commission's advice on its reduction plan.[146] The timing will be important, ensuring that the Commission has adequate time to evaluate and advise on the proposed plan. In addition, the scope and direction of the Commission's scrutiny could usefully be strengthened without interfering with the role of government. The Commission currently provides 'advice on the direction of the policy' required in the plan.[147] It could play a much stronger role if it were able to evaluate the ability of the plan to meet the target and budget. Furthermore, the government should be required to respond to the Commission's advice, giving reasons when there is a clear discrepancy between advice on reduction plans and government policy decisions. The Bill provides only that the Minister must 'consider' the Commission's advice.[148] This additional transparency may go some way towards exposing where

---

[142] Wise Response (n 91) 8. Wise Response also suggests the need for greater separation between setting budgets (science role) and reduction mechanisms (policy and economics role). While science may suggest major change, 'there is a history of pushback from those with direct political and/or economic investment in the status quo' (ibid 8–9).

[143] Climate Change Act 2008 (UK), s 8.

[144] Parliamentary Commissioner for the Environment (n 87) 12–13.

[145] ibid.

[146] Bill, cl 5ZF.

[147] ibid cl 5ZE.

[148] ibid cl 5ZF.

and why there have been policy 'trade-offs' between what the science requires (in terms of budgets) and what the government has decided (in terms of policy settings), having regard to matters such as 'economic feasibility' and 'economic circumstances'.[149] It may also require the government to explicitly address conflicting policies on issues such as continued mining and fossil fuel subsidies.

I. Just Transitions

The Bill makes a number of references to the need to consider justice issues, without using the phrase 'just transitions'. Reduction and adaptation plans and risk assessments must, for example, take into account vulnerable groups and sectors. Distributional justice, future generational equity and other equity principles are also relevant considerations to target and budget-setting. However, the treatment of justice issues is generally muddled and superficial, resulting in the omission of significant principles, including the precautionary principle, human rights and interspecies justice. The Bill could be significantly improved by including a comprehensive set of general justice principles.[150]

J. NDCs and the Paris Agreement

The Bill is explicitly linked to the temperature goal of the Paris Agreement. However, it is not intended to be domestic law for the direct and express implementation of NDCs and other Agreement obligations. This clear separation between international commitments and domestic mitigation is intentional.[151] This means that the Bill's target and budgets can be set *below* what is required to deliver on New Zealand's NDC. The current NDC is to reduce all greenhouse gas emissions to 30 per cent below 2005 levels by 2030. This modest pledge may increase in time using Paris Agreement mechanisms for progressive increases in ambition.[152] NDCs are explicitly mentioned only once in the Bill, where the Minister can direct the Commission to have regard to government policy on NDCs for the purpose of reports requested by the Minister.[153] More generally, there are references to the Paris Agreement and international obligations as relevant considerations for target

---

[149] ibid cl 5Z.

[150] Generation Zero (n 16) Appendix E; Parliamentary Commissioner for the Environment (n 87) Appendix A (including equity principles relevant to target setting).

[151] The Explanatory Note to the Climate Change Response (Zero Carbon) Amendment Bill 2019 (at 6) provides that the Bill does not impact commitments to communicate and achieve NDCs. Further, limiting use of offshore mitigation to meet the Bill's 2050 target does not preclude New Zealand's ability to use them to achieve its NDC.

[152] This target is equivalent to 11 per cent below 1990 levels by 2030. New Zealand's current NDC is for the period 2021–30.

[153] Bill, cl 5N.

review, budget-setting and review, national risk assessment and adaptation plans. The intention seems to be that NDCs may be taken into account as part of target and budget-setting/review, but they are not a mandatory requirement. This deliberate separation will make it more difficult for domestic litigants to use the target and budgets as a tool for enforcing achievement of New Zealand's NDC. Equally, it will be more difficult to use any global target revision or progressive increase in New Zealand's NDC[154] as a reason for *requiring* (as opposed to recommending) a review or increase in New Zealand's target and matching budgets.[155]

K. Te Tiriti o Waitangi Obligations

The New Zealand government has obligations under Te Tiriti o Waitangi (hereinafter 'the Treaty') including those of active protection to Māori in the use of their land and resources.[156] A claim has been made to test whether the government is in violation of this and other Treaty obligations and principles.[157] This claim will not be decided before the Bill is enacted. As a result, the government will not benefit from a comprehensive and culturally appropriate evaluation of climate change and its special significance for Māori.

The Bill's approach is to expand on the principal Act's existing Treaty section by listing the clauses that explicitly reference the Treaty or Māori.[158] As described above, the Commission nomination and appointment process is required to ensure Treaty experience and expertise. This will be an important element for integrating an indigenous worldview into the Commission's role, however much more needs to be done. At present, substantive provisions take an ad hoc approach, focusing more on the impacts of policies than on how Māori interests might be relevant to determining the content of budgets and reduction plans. For example, the 'economic, social, health, environmental, ecological, and cultural interests' of Māori are not explicitly relevant to setting budgets.[159] Reduction plans do not have

[154] The current IPCC scenarios (including net zero by 2050) could change radically if rapid action to reduce emissions from all sources is not achieved by 2030. UNEP, *The Emissions Gap Report 2017: A UN Environment Synthesis Report* (United Nations Environment Programme, 2017), https://wedocs.unep.org/bitstream/handle/20.500.11822/22070/EGR_2017.pdf?sequence=1.

[155] In the UK, the Climate Change Committee was able to use a general reference to international obligations as grounds for advising that the UK target should be increased from 80 per cent below 1990 levels by 2050 to net zero by 2050. Committee on Climate Change, 'UK Climate Action Following the Paris Agreement' (Committee on Climate Change, 2016), www.theccc.org.uk/wp-content/uploads/2016/10/UK-climate-action-following-the-Paris-Agreement-Committee-on-Climate-Change-October-2016.pdf.

[156] *New Zealand Maori Council v Attorney General* [1987] 1 New Zealand LR 641. See also Statement of Claim (WAI 2607) to the Waitangi Tribunal; Paul, Potter and Paterson, 'Statement of Claim WAI 2607' (dated 30 May 2016, received 27 September 2016).

[157] Paul, Potter and Paterson (n 157).

[158] Bill, cl 5.

[159] ibid cl 5Z.

to be developed with specific reference to these interests; however, the impacts of emissions reduction policies do.[160] Plans must include a 'strategy to mitigate the impacts that reducing emissions and increasing removals will have on … iwi and Māori'.[161] Most attention is given to Māori interests in the context of national adaptation plans;[162] however, there is an apparent disjunction here because these interests are not explicitly relevant to national risk assessment.[163]

At the time of writing, it appears that much more work needs to be done, including evaluating the Bill from a perspective that actively acknowledges tikanga (Māori custom and practice), mātauranga Māori (traditional knowledge) and kaitiakitanga (guardianship responsibilities of Māori).[164] One commentator opined that she did not see any encouraging signs of this in the Bill. Full recognition of Māori as a Treaty partner (not just a stakeholder) merits, for example, the *co-development* of reduction and adaptation plans to acknowledge Treaty rights, mātauranga Māori and 'the fact that we are the indigenous people here and have a key role to play'.[165]

L. What's Missing?

A number of submissions have highlighted the omission of international aviation and shipping emissions from the regulatory framework, notwithstanding the current lack of international consensus on how to treat these emissions. Suggestions have been made on ways to include these emissions to future-proof the scope of the Bill. For example, the Commission's annual reports could record these emission levels using a range of suggested criteria, including New Zealand aircraft/vessel registration.[166] Given New Zealand's economic reliance on international tourism, this is a significant omission from the Bill's scope.

M. Adaptation

In comparison with the Bill's mitigation elements, submissions gave far less attention to adaptation provisions. One of the more comprehensive was provided by

---

[160] Talisa Kupenga, 'Climate Change Plan "a Start" but "Lacks Detail" – Iwi Chairs Leader' (*Te Ao Māori News*, 8 May 2019), https://teaomaori.news/climate-change-plan--start-lacks-detail--iwi-chairs-leader.
[161] Bill, cl 5ZD(3)(c).
[162] ibid cl 5ZQ.
[163] Compare cl 5ZN(2)(a) with cl 5ZQ(4)(a) of the Bill.
[164] Dale Husband, 'A Tika Māori Approach to Climate Change Action' (*E-Tangata*, 4 August 2019), https://e-tangata.co.nz/comment-and-analysis/a-tika-maori-approach-to-climate-change-action. See also Generation Zero (n 16) 8; Maria Bargh, 'A Tika Transition' in David Hall (ed), *A Careful Revolution: Towards a Low-Emissions Future* (Wellington, Bridget Williams Books, 2019).
[165] Husband (n 164). For further analysis on the strengthening of the Bill, see Bargh (n 164).
[166] Lawyers for Climate Action (n 106) 8; Generation Zero (n 16) 13.

Local Government New Zealand, reflecting the current legal responsibilities of New Zealand local authorities. This submission welcomed central government's engagement in ensuring central framework documents such as the national risk assessment (NRA) and national adaptation plans (NAP). However, Local Government New Zealand argues that these tools will not be sufficient:

> As a matter of urgency, considerable additional work needs to be done to support local governments to … undertake adaptive action at the local level. Local government needs central government to work in partnership with it to allocate roles and responsibilities for climate change adaptation; apportion risk between central government, local government and communities; develop a legal framework that supports councils to take adaptive action, and reduces their liability risks; develop consistent national direction on how to approach adaptation; and to address issues related to funding and financing of the costs of climate change adaptation.[167]

At the very least, it recommends NAPs (including their purpose and outcomes) be developed in 'partnership' with local government to ensure it is workable and reflective of what can be achieved locally.[168]

V. Conclusions: The Bigger Picture

New Zealand's gross emissions increased by 23.1 per cent between 1990 and 2017. Net emissions have also increased by 65 per cent since 1990. The government has acknowledged that significant change is needed. As global emissions climb, the timeframe for reductions shortens and the need for steeper cuts increases. The public mandate to take rapid and strong action is apparent in support for zero carbon legislation, declarations of emergency and in public protests.[169] The government is creating high expectations of the Bill's ability to create policies that contribute to the Paris Agreement 1.5°C goal. On the other hand, there is disagreement about whether the 2050 net zero target and split gases approach will deliver

---

[167] Local Government New Zealand (n 113) 4.

[168] ibid 5–6. Close analysis is also needed to ensure that the Bill's provisions go beyond more planning for adaptation to delivering on-the-ground action. For example, NAPs can be implemented via national policy statements which local government 'must give effect to' at regional and city/district levels, but the government has chosen not to make this explicit in the Bill (Explanatory Note, 5). For additional analysis on appropriate measures beyond NRAs and NAPs, see Judy Lawrence, 'The Adaptation Gap' in Hall (n 164).

[169] Ministry for the Environment (n 28). The media reports a growing list of local governments declaring climate emergencies: Felix Desmarais, 'Councils Declare Climate Emergencies, But Will it Result in Any Real Change?' (*Stuff*, 28 June 2019), www.stuff.co.nz/environment/climate-news/113747732/councils-declare-climate-emergencies-but-will-it-result-in-any-real-change. Recent climate strikes may have been attended by 170,000 people, making it one of the nation's biggest strikes: Brittney Deguara, 'Crunching the Numbers behind the National Climate Change Strike Turnout' (*Stuff*, 28 September 2019), www.stuff.co.nz/environment/climate-news/116172915/crunching-the-numbers-behind-the-national-climate-change-strike-turnout.

on the Bill's purpose. There is also uncertainty as to whether bi-partisan support will continue.[170] Questions remain about ETS reform and its ability to deliver significant emission reductions at source. This is especially contentious given the government's intention to delay bringing agricultural emissions into the ETS until 2025.[171] The effort to gain political consensus recently resulted in a further deal enabling the farming sector and government to co-develop an emissions pricing scheme as an alternative to the ETS. This arrangement will not displace the interim 10 per cent methane reduction target.[172]

Despite these significant difficulties, the Bill is not the government's only climate change initiative.[173] Others include: the one billion trees programme; a Green Investment Finance Fund; $14.5 billion investment in public transport; a phase-out of new offshore oil and gas exploration; and a blue hydrogen initiative.[174] It is considering incentives for electric vehicles and means to increase renewable energy generation (from a current level of 80 per cent) by 2035. The government has also signalled some phase-out of fossil fuel subsidies. It is not clear if some or all of these initiatives will be additional to policies developed to meet the 2050 target.

Given all these complexities and uncertainties, it seems very likely that progress in the short term will be driven by a range of other economic and social factors, including investment decisions, consumer choice and (regarding adaptation) insurance retreat and legal accountability. Nevertheless, the Bill is a starting point and a general framework for addressing climate change. After decades of policy failure, it may provide New Zealanders with new and important legislation that can be used to hold governments politically accountable.

---

[170] In a public address on 8 October 2019 at the University of Auckland, the Prime Minister expressed significant concern about maintaining bipartisan support, but pledged to pass the legislation regardless.

[171] Ministry for the Environment, 'Consensus Reached on Reducing Agricultural Emissions' (16 July 2019), www.mfe.govt.nz/news-events/consensus-reached-reducing-agricultural-emissions; Greenpeace, 'Govt at Risk of Capitulating to Dairy over Climate Pollution' (press release, 16 July 2019), www.greenpeace.org/new-zealand/press-release/govt-at-risk-of-capitulating-to-dairy-over-climate-pollution.

[172] Alex Braae, 'The Bulletin: Shaw, Farmers Now Own Agriculture Emissions Deal' (*The Spinoff*, 25 October 2019), https://thespinoff.co.nz/the-bulletin/25-10-2019/the-bulletin-shaw-farmers-now-own-agriculture-emissions-deal.

[173] For an overview, see Ministry for the Environment, 'Government Response to the New Zealand Productivity Commission Low Emissions Economy Report' (3 August 2019), www.mfe.govt.nz/productivity-commission-report-government-response.

A recent tax review process recommended better use of environmental taxes: Tax Working Group, *Future of Tax: Final Report Volume 1* (Wellington, New Zealand Government, 2019), https://taxworkinggroup.govt.nz/sites/default/files/2019-03/twg-final-report-voli-feb19-v1.pdf. The government has not yet signalled a willingness to follow this recommendation with respect to emissions.

[174] See the government's climate change programme: Ministry for the Environment, 'The Transition to a Low-Emissions and Climate-Resilient Aotearoa New Zealand' (2 August 2019), www.mfe.govt.nz/climate-change/climate-change-and-government/climate-change-programme. Regarding blue hydrogen, see Ministry of Business, Innovation & Employment, *A Vision for Hydrogen in New Zealand* (2019), www.mbie.govt.nz/dmsdocument/6798-a-vision-for-hydrogen-in-new-zealand-green-paper.

10

Conceptualising and Formulating National Climate Change Acts

THOMAS L MUINZER

I. Introduction

This chapter addresses and explores the conceptualisation of Climate Change Acts in generalised, abstracted terms. On one level, it seeks to draw together emergent understandings arising from this book in order to draw conceptual lessons and conclusions. This provides an opportunity for additional, cumulative critical comment to be drawn on major issues arising in the book, while also permitting the commonalities and divergences, as well as the perceived strengths and weaknesses, that underpin national regimes in this complex area of law and governance to be addressed.

In addition, this chapter engages with a generalised consideration of the sorts of features that might usefully underpin a legislative regime when one seeks to formulate optimal national framework climate legislation. Although the evidential basis for this aspect of the chapter is informed by existing commentary, in conjunction with additional doctrinal legal research and associated analysis undertaken for the purposes of this chapter, it is the case that this issue has received little direct treatment in scholarship and research to date. Thus, the discussion relies in particular for evidence on the emergent understandings arising and accumulating across this book's preceding chapters, which were researched and written with these sorts of concerns in mind. To this end, the deep-dive case studies set out over Chapters 3–9 are particularly useful, due to the manner in which they have illuminated a range of major national Climate Change Acts in states that are presently in the vanguard of pioneering the form.

The general insights emerging from this overall consideration of optimally formulated national framework climate legislation are abstract and conceptual in nature, and they have a normative character. However, as has been noted, this generality is also grounded in the experience and understanding of existing national framework climate legislation. In 'The Normative Foundations of Climate Legislation', Green points out that: 'Legislation, including on climate change, is inherently normative. It prescribes, permits and prohibits conduct, and it defines and allocates society's resources. Laws are necessarily both grounded in, and expressive of, values and ideals.'[1] The general impression of optimally formulated regime design that emerges in this chapter strives to highlight and emphasise what appear to be particularly essential elements of this new form of legislative architecture based on the current condition of knowledge and normative experience.

It is hoped that the conceptual model that emerges, which seeks to point to an optimum–form type of national Climate Change Act, might usefully inform development in countries that are seeking to adopt a Climate Change Act for the first time. It could also be of assistance where a country with an existing Climate Change Act is seeking to review its framework with a view to enhancing it. Furthermore, it can also contribute to the discussion where this type of regime, or key aspects of it, might be exported 'upwards' in instances where a framework Climate Change Act-style approach is due to be operationalised or otherwise inform regime design at international or supranational levels of governance.

II. National Climate Change Acts:
Lessons Learned and Emerging Issues

A. The National–International Context

The refrain of 'the personal is political' that emerged out of second-wave feminism is well known.[2] Drawing on that species of phraseology for present purposes, it might be said that 'the national is international', in the sense that a national Climate Change Act has a fundamental *inter*national significance by virtue of its character and intended outcomes. This significance is galvanised to a substantial extent by the nature of anthropogenic climate change itself, where, in this sort of instance, law is operationalised by a national legislature in an attempt to deal within its internal state arena with a fundamentally international issue that impacts humanity across the globe, including future as well as present generations. As Bodansky et al put it, climate change is 'planetary in scope and – due to its long-term and potentially irreversible consequences – intergenerational in its impacts.'[3] It has been evidenced in general terms across this book as a whole that

---

[1] Fergus Green, 'The Normative Foundations of Climate Legislation' in Alina Averchenkova, Sam Fankhauser and Michal Nachmany (eds), *Trends in Climate Change Legislation* (Cheltenham, Edward Elgar, 2017) 85.

[2] Frances Rogan, and Shelley Budgeon, 'The Personal is Political: Assessing Feminist Fundamentals in the Digital Age' (2018) 7(8) *Social Sciences* 132.

[3] Daniel Bodansky, Jutta Brunnée and Lavanya Rajamani, *International Climate Change Law* (Oxford, Oxford University Press 2017) 2.

each of the modest but growing number of countries to have set national frame-work climate legislation in place to date has, in doing so, done something that goes beyond national relevance.

Townshend and Matthews highlight the following generally overlooked point: 'Increasingly it is being realised that advancing domestic climate change legis-lation can help to create the conditions that enable an international deal to be reached.'[4] Yet the international significance of national framework climate legisla-tion ranges significantly beyond even this type of parameter. In this complex and challenging area of law and governance, each existing state framework provides lessons for every other existing state framework, and each of the national regimes in operation now provides lessons for those to come. Due to the gradual passage of time since the implementation of the first Climate Change Act in the UK in 2008,[5] it is increasingly possible for those lessons to range meaningfully beyond foundational matters including regime emergence and substantive design to extend to and encompass key issues such as regime performance in practice (ie, has a particular Climate Change Act actually succeeded over time in reducing greenhouse gas emissions, in remedying or engaging with identifiable adaptation problems etc?). Thus, Nash emphasises with reference to the Danish legislation that 'it will be interesting to observe' whether that legislation might be 'used as a model for other legislation that is developed' and whether it can 'drive higher ambition elsewhere'.[6]

Chapter 1 in this volume engages with the extent to which national frame-work climate legislation can be deemed as significant in the broader context of international climate law.[7] It is concluded that this nationally oriented model does have a substantial global significance in principle. The chief points are drawn out with particular reference to the ICL Regime concept,[8] which embodies an international climate law order predicated in part upon identifiable 'milestone' developments that have lately been subject to an arguably undesirable degree of 'weakening'. The extent of the important cumulative contribution that Climate Change Acts have a capacity to make in the overall setting of global climate governance will depend on the degree to which potential opportunities afforded by this type of model are recognised and embraced by the individual states that could benefit from its application. Moreover, it will also depend on the extent to which international diplomats and legislators recognise and embrace benefits in importing characteristics or lessons derived from those frameworks within nations 'upward' to international/supranational governance levels as a means of informing international climate law. Green has probed the normative theoretical spheres of

---

[4] Terry Townshend and Adam C Matthews, *National Climate Change Legislation: The Key to More Ambitious International Agreements* (London, CDKN/Globe International, 2013) 3.

[5] Climate Change Act 2008 (UK).

[6] Sarah Louise Nash, ch 5 in this volume.

[7] Thomas L Muinzer, ch 1 in this volume.

[8] ibid section IV.

climate justice and economic efficiency, arguing that both spheres have exerted a strong influence on the normative framing underpinning climate legislation.[9] He also isolates and discusses the normative influence of international climate change law, which, he writes, 'constitutes a separate normative foundation. It provides legal reasons for specific courses of climate action, including domestic legislation, by states'.[10] It is also possible that the steering force that national framework climate legislation might conceivably project upward to the international domain as the regime form continues to emerge could have a significant capacity to be estimable in its own right.

In Chapter 2, Duwe and Bodle further elucidate international-national dimensions of Climate Change Acts. The authors situate their exploration of national framework climate legislation in the context of international climate governance and conclude that the Paris Agreement is acting as a significant prompt towards the creation of climate legislation nationally.[11] They also argue that those countries:

> [W]ho take the collective temperature goal of the Paris Agreement seriously will want to direct their national policies towards this goal. This suggests establishing corresponding governance procedures that facilitate goal-directed action – and overarching climate change laws are the most robust way of doing so.[12]

These insights serve to emphasise that the creation of national framework climate legislation within a particular state can be a very useful means for the state in question to ensure that it will contribute to the Paris requirements in a meaningful way over time. Duwe and Bodle also state that:

> The obligation for all ministries involved to deliver policies is included in more than one existing climate framework law (e.g. see the laws in Mexico and Finland). Moreover, the framework climate law in Germany is particularly innovative; it establishes sector specific targets for 2030 and annual allocations for each of the respective ministries in charge of policies for each sector.[13]

Here, the authors catch the spirit of the manner in which the burgeoning Climate Change Act model may differ in certain foundational approaches across states and how, in doing so, these Acts provide opportunities for insights to be drawn through acknowledging, studying and interpreting that diversity.

The notion of the potential usefulness of Climate Change Acts in the challenging national-international setting of global climate governance becomes all the more salient where it is recognised that states' climate goals and aspirations tend to be ensnared in, and impacted by, a complex web of political spin,[14] media

---

[9] Green (n 1).

[10] ibid 93.

[11] Matthias Duwe and Ralph Bodle, ch 2 in this volume.

[12] ibid.

[13] ibid.

[14] Josh Greenberg, Graham Knight and Elizabeth Westersund, 'Spinning Climate Change: Corporate and NGO Public Relations Strategies in Canada and the United States' (2011) 73(1–2) *International*

(mis)representation[15] and so on. Where national framework climate legislation is passed by a national parliament or equivalent national assembly, it serves to introduce a greater degree of clarity and certainty into this contested environment, through the hard edge of binding law. In Chapter 6, for example, Jackson has evoked a snapshot of contrary messaging being projected by influential actors in the period where the Irish Climate Change Act was being passed: to Senator Sean D Barrett, the process constituted 'a very unsatisfactory way in which to make legislation … as there are too many vested interests involved'; to *Friends of the Earth Ireland*, the emergent Irish regime was a 'significant milestone' albeit 'weaker than it should be'; to the Green Party, it was a 'charade'; agricultural and business lobby groups were 'broadly satisfied' etc.[16] The extent to which the completed passage of a Climate Change Act serves to introduce sharpened legal commitments and concrete longer-term certainty into what tends to be a contested and frequently unclear national–international governance arena provides a degree of value in its own right. This position reflects current understandings in the literature, as where Neuweg and Averchenkova consider the US in a comparative international context with particular reference to the EU and China.[17] They find that '[t]he US example shows that the lack of an overarching climate law opens the door for business opposition and court rulings against climate regulation', noting that 'a bottom-up, sub-national approach to climate legislation can drive action despite the lack of a federal law, although it cannot fully compensate for its absence'.[18]

B. The Relationship between Law and Policy

The chapters in this book clarify that the adoption of national framework climate legislation can make a very important contribution to a state's internal efforts to respond to the problem of climate change. Clare et al, drawing on Townshend and others[19] to define framework legislation as 'wide-ranging laws that define a strategic approach to climate policy',[20] have emphasised that framework laws play

---

Communication Gazette 65; Aaron M McCright, Riley E Dunlap and Sandra T Marquart-Pyatt, 'Political Ideology and Views about Climate Change in the European Union' (2016) 25(2) *Environmental Politics* 338.

[15] Elisabeth Eide and Risto Kunelius (eds), *Media Meets Climate: The Global Challenge for Journalism* (Gothenburg, Nordicom, 2012).

[16] Andrew Jackson, ch 6 in this volume.

[17] Isabella Neuweg and Alina Averchenkova, 'Climate Change Legislation and Policy in China, the European Union, and the United States' in Averchenkova, Fankhauser and Nachmany (n 1) 37–58.

[18] ibid 53.

[19] Terry Townshend, Sam Fankhauser, Adam Matthews, Clément Feger, Jin Liu and Thais Narciso, 'Legislating Climate Change on a National Level' (2011) 53(5) *Environment: Science and Policy for Sustainable Development* 5.

[20] Abbie Clare, Sam Fankhauser and Caterina Gennaioli, 'The National and International Drivers of Climate Change Legislation' in Averchenkova, Fankhauser and Nachmany (n 1) 19, 23.

an important role in 'codify[ing] a policy consensus around which political actors can coalesce, creating clarity about the future direction of travel'.[21] However, while the adoption of such legislation is generally to be recommended,[22] this is not to say that it is absolutely necessary where a state intends to take robust legislative action. Thus, for example, a state might endeavour to rely on a cumulative legislative regime predicated on a diverse range of legislation that intersects around the issue of climate change in a common and strategically targeted way rather than endeavouring to establish a centre of legislative gravity in a major framework law. A further alternative, which is commonly employed by most climate-conscious states around the world at present, is to substantially de-emphasise the role of law and drive the national response to climate change primarily through a suite of intermeshed climate-sensitive policies[23] or indeed through an overarching framework policy.[24]

While leading on the climate change issue through policy can permit significant outcomes to be achieved, advantages that tend to arise through employing hard law as a primary regime driver over softer policy approaches have been emphasised at a number of points across this collection, including in Chapter 1:

> [W]here newly emerging targets and decarbonisation trajectories can be locked into national framework climate legislation, this serves to put states' decarbonisation intentions on a more robust, stable and predictable footing appropriate to the challenge by anchoring them in hard law rather than positioning them in, for example, soft policy.[25]

That said, it is also notable that once a substantial Climate Change Act is set in place, its primary substantive design value will tend to some extent to be determined with reference to its relationship to contiguous policy developments. Moreover, and related to this, it is evident that states have a tendency to employ policy sources strategically in order to locate important provisions within policy, which might otherwise have been situated within Climate Change Act legislation.

---

[21] ibid 30.

[22] See Duwe and Bodle, ch 2 in this volume; and Muinzer, ch 1 in this volume.

[23] The UK largely operated in this conventional tradition prior to the passage of the Climate Change Act 2008; the shift that occurred is covered in Thomas L Muinzer, 'Background to the Climate Change Framework' in *Climate and Energy Governance for the UK Low Carbon Transition: The Climate Change Act 2008* (Dordrecht, Springer, 2018).

[24] A policy framework approach rather than a legislative framework approach is employed by China, partly by active choice but also due in part to the country's particular governance setting and the Chinese Communist Party's constitutional tradition of issuing extensive five-year plans. Birney has conceptualised important aspects of the Chinese system as a 'rule of mandates': Mayling Birney, 'Decentralization and Veiled Corruption under China's "Rule of Mandates"' (2014) *World Development* 55. See further, eg, Alun Gu, Fei Teng and Xiangzhao Feng, 'Effects of Pollution Control Measures on Carbon Emission Reduction in China: Evidence from the 11th and 12th Five-Year Plans' (2018) 18(2) *Climate Policy* 198. Neuweg and Averchenkova find that 'a national climate change law would certainly help affirm the political priority placed on climate action' in China: Neuweg and Averchenkova (n 17) 53.

[25] Muinzer, ch 1 in this volume.

As a consequence, such elements are typically established in a softer policy form that is devoid of the sharper edge of 'hard' law. An example is provided in the Irish study in this volume. In the following, Jackson addresses the relationship between the creation of the Irish Climate Change Act (law) and a National Policy Position (policy):

> On 23 April 2014, Minister Hogan published revised (and final) heads of the Climate Bill together with a separate National Policy Position, which he said 'brings clarity and certainty to the national low-carbon transition objective for 2050'. The National Policy Position, *which would sit outside the legislation*, set out a long-term vision based on 'an aggregate reduction in carbon dioxide emissions of at least 80% (compared to 1990 levels) by 2050 across the electricity generation, built environment and transport sectors; and, in parallel, an approach to carbon neutrality in the agriculture and land-use sector, including forestry, which does not compromise capacity for sustainable food production'. (Emphasis added)[26]

Here, one finds elements including a crucial 80 per cent multi-sectoral mitigation target for 2050 framed within soft policy, thus positioned conspicuously beyond the rigours of the legislation. As Spijkers and Oosterhuis emphasise, making reference to the Climate Agreement that operates in the Netherlands in conjunction with the Dutch Climate Change Act: 'There is one important difference between Act and the Agreement, and that is that only the former is, strictly speaking, legally binding.'[27]

In addition to lacking the binding force of legislation in the courts and beyond, policy commitments are typically much more easily subject to change, which undermines the more robust degree of long-term certainty provided by Climate Change Acts. Alteration to primary legislation of this kind typically requires amending or repealing legislation to be passed through a national parliament or equivalent national assembly by a parliamentary or assembly majority, whereas policy changes tend to be implemented much more easily at the behest of governments. Averchenkova has emphasised this aspect in her examination of the creation of the Mexican Climate Change Act: 'one of the main objectives for these efforts was to protect long-term climate policy objectives against future political change, so that they are mandatory for the government regardless of the political orientation of those who are in power in the future'.[28]

That said, it is also notable that the relationship between Climate Change Acts and policy-based documents, schemes and strategies is considerably more complex than a mere headline 'law versus policy' choice where the consideration of optimal flagship governance responses to climate change is at issue. The UK's Climate Change Act is an extensive primary framework that assists in setting a general 'policy' direction for the UK, but that also stands relatively coherently

---

[26] Jackson, ch 6 in this volume.
[27] Otto Spijkers and Sofie Oosterhuis, ch 8 in this volume.
[28] Alina Averchenkova, ch 4 in this volume.

on its own two feet as an independent legislative regime;[29] however, other states might opt to build their Climate Change Act into a broader regime or, indeed, endeavour to establish their framework Act as a subsidiary component of some variety of wider governance architecture. Nash's examination of the Danish experience in this volume is particularly notable in relation to the potentially novel underpinnings of this law–policy relationship in the context of Climate Change Acts. Here, she elaborates upon the role and importance of Denmark's Comments on the Bill agreement. Discussing the Danish Climate Change Act, she outlines that 'additional provisions are added by a subsidiary document, 'Comments on the Bill' ('Bemærkninger til lovforslaget'), which is a non-binding policy decision made between a number of political parties before the act had passed'.[30] She finds that the Comments on the Bill document has an important ongoing policy-oriented bearing and impact on the Danish Act, and notes that 'the comments on the bill is not part of the legislation but rather is an adjacent political agreement'.[31] Given the less entrenched nature of policy, one consequence here is that it 'means that changes can be made to these provisions without having to legislate for it in Parliament'.[32]

This type of quasi-co-dependent stress placed on a purpose-built political or policy agreement on one hand, and a state's Climate Change Act on the other hand, is present in a richly developed form in the case of the Dutch climate regime.[33] Indeed, Spijkers and Oosterhuis not only address law and policy with reference to the issues just raised, but also integrate substantial consideration of litigation into their framing of the Dutch architecture, such that *legislation–policy–litigation* are construed to a significant extent as conjoined elements of their primary regime analysis. Here, the authors provide detailed analysis of the Netherlands Climate Change Act ('klimaatwet') and the similarly important Netherlands Climate Agreement ('klimaatakkoord') that, taken together, embody a cumulative headline Dutch climate regime. They state that: 'The Climate Act sets the target of a 49 per cent reduction in 2030 and a 95 per cent reduction in 2050 compared to 1990, *by law*. Every newly elected government between today and 2050 is therefore bound by these targets, unless the Act is amended or repealed' (emphasis in original).[34] However, they also add that: 'Having said that, the Climate Act is not about the substantive measures that must be taken to achieve these targets. In the Climate Agreement, these measures were agreed, together with all social partners.'[35]

This strategically co-designed and interdependent legal-political architecture extends to become wider still when one factors in important developments in the courts, namely the *Urgenda* litigation, which has resulted in the imposition

---

[29] Richard Macrory and Thomas L Muinzer, ch 3 in this volume.
[30] Nash, ch 5 in this volume.
[31] ibid.
[32] ibid.
[33] Spijkers and Oosterhuis, ch 8 in this volume.
[34] ibid.
[35] ibid.

of distinct emissions reduction obligations on the government in its own right. One result of these circumstances has been the emergence in the Netherlands of a multiplicity of climate change target sources, involving legislation (the Climate Change Act), policy (the Climate Agreement) and litigation (*Urgenda*). Of course, while the Climate Change Act and the Climate Agreement have been strategically and purposefully co-designed, the *Urgenda* outcomes have arisen independently through pressure in the courts, and in this sense *Urgenda* stands apart. However, as the authors also note: 'Even though the Climate Act and Agreement are formally unrelated to the *Urgenda* litigation, all three of these set greenhouse gas emission reduction targets to be met by the Netherlands before a certain deadline.'[36] In this respect, the Dutch Climate Change Act is to be interpreted in concert with the Netherlands Climate Agreement, but it is also to be usefully interpreted with reference to the *Urgenda* outcomes.

Romson and Forsbacka's Swedish analysis provides another salient example of strategically designed pronounced interaction between a Climate Change Act and a partner policy agreement.[37] In this case, the policy dimension is strongly to the fore; Romson and Forsbacka elaborate Sweden's Climate Change Act as being nested within Sweden's Climate Policy Framework. The Swedish Act itself is very short and generalised, consisting 'of only one page with five paragraphs'.[38] It does not embed climate targets within its provisions or articulate specific policy measures, nor is it part of the state's important Environmental Code that consolidates major environmental Acts. As such, where the Swedish Act is juxtaposed in isolation with other examples of national framework climate legislation treated in this volume, it is an extremely weak instrument. However, as Romson and Forsbacka note, it is nested within a three-pronged Climate Policy Framework, comprising the Climate Change Act itself, 'new ambitious interim and long-term climate targets' that sit independently outside of the Act, and a Climate Policy Council;[39] interpreted from this nested position as part of the wider Swedish regime, it can be seen to play a stronger and more important role.

In principle, these sorts of design choices have certain doctrinal and interpretive legal implications. This can be illustrated helpfully with reference to the issue of *adaptation*.[40] In addition to various major features including reduction targets being situated outside of the Swedish Act, Romson and Forsbacka outline that both the Act itself and the Climate Policy Framework more widely avoid the issue of adaptation. This omission is driven by domestic circumstances:

> This reflects the fact that domestic climate adaptation is considered to be part of another area of environmental policy, somewhat connected to water management and overall

---

[36] ibid.
[37] Åsa Romson and Kristina Forsbacka, ch 7 in this volume.
[38] ibid.
[39] 'The [Climate Policy Framework] adopted consists of three parts: (i) a Climate Act; (ii) new ambitious interim and long-term climate targets; and (iii) a Climate Policy Council.' ibid.
[40] ibid.

environmental protection. In this sense, the Swedish national framework stands apart from climate governance in many other countries, where capacity-building for adaptation is inter-related with the development of mitigating actions.[41]

The circumstances elaborated here suggest that where one seeks to interpret Sweden's Climate Policy Framework in order to better understand Sweden's overall approach to key climate issues, in spite of being cast as the *Climate Policy* Framework, the scheme makes it possible to trace and interpret legal-political headline responses to *mitigation*, but not adaptation. In principle, the logical implication in this sort of case is that one must depart from the Climate Policy Framework or equivalent climate regime in question in order to interpret adaptation provisions from other sources. Thus, an assumption also arises that one must both depart fairly substantially from the Climate Change Act itself and introduce additional complex legal-political sources pertinent to adaptation in order to begin to construct an overall picture of the state's headline mitigation–adaptation climate components. While such interpretive consequences may prove appropriate to some important degree due to the particular national legal–political governance circumstances in question, one merit of rolling headline adaptation provisions into a core legislative climate regime is that it makes it possible to avoid going down this type of rabbit hole to such a pronounced extent.

Here, then, one can identify in principle two stand-out advantages of the more expansive and developed national framework climate legislative regimes first pioneered in the developing world and the developed world by the Mexican[42] and UK[43] Climate Change Acts, respectively. First, expanded and consolidated legislative approaches of this kind contribute towards effectively cohering national climate change strategies, drawing them together under the terms of a centred legislative framework. Second, this expanded, consolidated type of regime also extends the force and stability of law across a wider climate governance range than a more diminutive regime can typically achieve, as demonstrated by the Swedish Climate Change Act in the context of the Swedish policy regime. At any rate, Climate Change Acts clearly have a value to offer,[44] whether a Climate Change Act may be relatively free-standing, substantial and robustly internally developed (eg, in the UK), co-partnered with a substantial policy agreement (eg, in the Netherlands) or cast in a subsidiary partnership where it is subordinate to another legal–political source(s)/nested within a broader scheme (eg, in Sweden).

---

[41] ibid.

[42] General Law on Climate Change 2012 (Mexico).

[43] Climate Change Act 2008 (UK).

[44] See further, eg, Averchenkova's summary of the Mexican Act's 'major impact' on Mexican climate change governance in ch 4 in this volume.

C. 'First-Generation' Climate Change Acts and the Future

Going forward, many questions open up in the realm of research and practice. The vast majority of the world's countries do not (yet) have national framework climate legislation in place. However, it is also notable that in spite of the fact that Climate Change Acts are still very much in their infancy relative to more typical forms of legislation, more than a decade has elapsed since the passage of the first regime in the UK. Such circumstances, working in conjunction with the passage of time, will increasingly create opportunities for the enactment of 'second-generation Climate Change Acts'.[45] A second-generation Climate Change Act might take the form of a new Act that repeals and replaces an existing Climate Change Act, such as where one of the Acts covered in this volume could be repealed and replaced by a subsequent Climate Change Act, or it might take the form of an Act that amends an existing Climate Change Act to such an extent that it fundamentally alters the character of the pre-existing Act.

In order to avoid introducing definitional uncertainty here, which has tended to trouble the field of climate law and policy,[46] it is submitted that in order to amount to a second-generation Act where this latter method has been utilised – that is, the 'amending' method rather than the 'repeal and replace' method – the amendments should do one of two things. They should:

(1)   make such an extensive range of alterations to the original Climate Change Act that its overall substance is fundamentally changed in a broad manner; or
(2)   make a narrower range of alterations to the original Climate Change Act that nevertheless serve to fundamentally alter the substance of the pre-existing Act, because they result in ample or otherwise sweeping changes to a range of the framework's major components.

In relation to the 'range of the framework's major components' element raised in point (2) above, based on the components that underpin serious Climate Change Acts at present and as evidenced across this book, the 'major components' requiring substantial changes in order to meet the point (2) test would involve 'ample or otherwise sweeping changes' to a number of the following sorts of features: emissions reduction targets, carbon budget levels or budget design, adaptation/mitigation planning processes, justiciability/enforceability elements, public participation/engagement components, Climate Committee composition and functions etc.[47]

---

[45] In the sphere of policy, see, eg, on so-called 'second generation' climate policies Barry G Rabe, 'Second-Generation Climate Policies in the States: Proliferation, Diffusion, and Regionalization' in Simone Pulver, Barry G Rabe and Peter J Stoett, *Changing Climates in North American Politics: Institutions, Policymaking, and Multilevel governance* (Cambridge, MA, MIT Press, 2009).

[46] See Muinzer, ch 1 in this volume, sections II and III.

[47] See further the discussion of major Climate Change Act components in sections III.B and III.C below.

Discussion of the notion of new legislation arises in a number of chapters in this book, eg, concerning Ireland[48] and Denmark.[49] It will be interesting to see if first-generation regimes evolve into second-generation regimes going forward. To the author's knowledge, this has not yet occurred anywhere in the world based on the criteria just outlined (note that amendment or replacement of the Danish or Irish regimes has not yet occurred at the time of writing). It is notable that the Mexican Parliament did amend its Climate Change Act significantly in 2018 in order to make it responsive to the Paris Agreement 2015.[50] Averchenkova summarises that this 'was motivated by bringing emission targets in consistency with the NDC. It recognised the need to keep global temperature rise to within 2ºC above pre-industrial levels and to undertake efforts to keep this increase below 1.5ºC'.[51] The amendments are significant, but may not have 'fundamentally altered the substance' of the original Act itself to an extent that satisfies the second-generation criteria set out above, due to important amendments targeting the Act's transitory articles. A Spanish-speaking lawyer would be required to analyse the legislation and amendments carefully against the criteria above in order to answer this question definitively.

Against the backdrop of this line of thinking, it is notable that it has been seen in Taylor's treatment of New Zealand's Climate Change Act in this volume that New Zealand's legislation is something of a joker in the pack.[52] The New Zealand Climate Change Act was initially 'intended to be separate or stand-alone legislation', but the government ultimately 'introduced it as an amendment to the Climate Change Response Act 2002'.[53] Thus, in the end, New Zealand's Climate Change Act did not appear as a free-standing Act in its own right, but rather took the form of an amending instrument entitled the Climate Change Response (Zero Carbon) Amendment Act 2019, which made alterations to pre-existing framework legislation that sketched out New Zealand's emissions trading scheme.[54] Taylor outlines that this emissions trading scheme was introduced in 2008, but has 'not performed as expected'.[55] The introduction of the state's flagship national framework climate legislation in the form of a swathe of amendments to pre-existing legislation pertaining to a trading scheme that has been struggling has partially

---

[48] Jackson, ch 6 in this volume.

[49] Nash, ch 5 in this volume.

[50] Carlos Del Razo, 'Amendment to the General Law on Climate Change and its Implications in the Markets' (*Lexology*, 24 July 2018), https://www.lexology.com/library/detail.aspx?g=381e50d1-23bd-4feb-a6a9-c713c6b4215e.

[51] Averchenkova, ch 4 in this volume.

[52] Prue Taylor, ch 9 in this volume.

[53] ibid.

[54] Climate Change Response Act 2002 (New Zealand).

[55] Taylor, ch 9 in this volume.

undermined aspects of the new Climate Change Act's potential to emblematise a free-standing 'fresh start' in New Zealand's efforts to combat climate change.[56]

In this respect, and while the New Zealand framework remains both important and sophisticated, where its emergence and initial application are juxtaposed with other major frameworks covered in this volume, there is some sense that its introduction as an amendment to an existing Act has served to put the cart (the pre-existing emissions trading scheme framework) before the horse (the Climate Change Act proper). Taylor cites Generation Zero, which (at the Bill stage) has emphasised various associated shortcomings arising from this type of approach:

> [T]he Bill should be a standalone framework (as in the UK) and not part of the ETS legislative framework … this would provide separate 'systems architecture', which is clear, certain, accessible and not directly entwined with one particular tool (the ETS), which itself is more subject to amendment in line with political agendas.[57]

In relation to the consideration of first- and second-generation Climate Change Acts outlined above, it appears to be the case that New Zealand is the only country at the time of writing to have constructed a major first-generation Climate Change Act via an amendment to a less extensive pre-existing regime (here, an emissions trading scheme framework).

III. National Climate Change Acts: Foundations, Components and Development

A. Regime Emergence from the UK's Climate Change Act 2008 Onwards

As the founding example of national framework climate legislation, it is little surprise that the UK's Climate Change Act, passed in 2008, has served as something of an inspiration and partial practical guide for the other examples of these regimes emerging to date. Various aspects of the drivers that helped to bring the UK Act into being (discussed by Macrory and Muinzer)[58] have also proven influential. Jackson, for example, notes that 'Friends of the Earth's "The Big Ask" campaign … first called for framework climate legislation in the UK before the campaign rolled out across Europe', and this had an influence in Ireland when 'in 2009, the Labour TD Eamon Gilmore introduced into the Dáil (the lower house) a Climate Change

---

[56] Compare, for example, the significant social engagement and public importance attaching to the creation of the UK's Climate Change Act; see 'Background to the Climate Change Framework' in Muinzer, *Climate and Energy Governance for the UK Low Carbon Transition* (n 23).

[57] Taylor, ch 9 in this volume.

[58] See further Macrory and Muinzer, ch 3 in this volume.

Bill that was clearly modelled on the UK's Climate Change Act 2008'.[59] However, this is not to say that states adopting such regimes have blankly followed the UK template; far from it (including in the case of Ireland).[60] Averchenkova notes in this volume in reference to the Mexican legislation that: 'According to experts who were directly involved in the process, the development of Mexico's climate legislation benefited from close examination of and learning from the UK's Climate Change Act of 2008'.[61] Yet the outcome legislation produced in Mexico is very different from the UK Act in terms of both the way in which the law is constructed doctrinally and much of the content that it lays down.[62] In most if not all cases, the pertinent process to date appears to have been chiefly one where other countries have learned consciously from the UK regime, internalised an understanding of its design and approaches, and proceeded in a largely independent manner to construct an Act in their own spirit and traditions, informed by aspects of this learning process. Thus, Taylor notes in reference to New Zealand's legislation – possibly the closest regime to the UK's to date – that it has been '[b]ased on the UK Climate Change Act 2008, but with some unique elements'.[63]

Furthermore, although the UK framework has had a fairly universal influence to date, multiple major legislative influences will potentially be in operation where a state seeks to construct a Climate Change Act, interacting with the UK example to varying degrees in a manner that helps to influence the form and content of the final outcome Act. This is illustrated in this volume, for example, by Romson and Forsbacka, who note with reference to the Swedish Climate Change Act that: 'The framework had as its models both the UK Climate Change Act 2008 and a Swedish Fiscal Policy Framework which has been in place since the mid-1990s'.[64] In addition to these major external national (UK) and internal national (Swedish) framework schemes, the authors add that: 'Another inspiration was the Paris Agreement as negotiations on the Swedish framework were held in parallel with the process for a global framework'.[65] Here, then, major national–international legal determinants have influenced the form of what will become the Swedish outcome legislation in very substantial direct terms.

Where the acceptance or rejection of *specific* components or elements of the UK framework arises over the course of a subsequent Climate Change Act's

---

[59] Jackson, ch 6 in this volume. See also Neil Carter and Mike Childs, 'Friends of the Earth as a Policy Entrepreneur: "The Big Ask" Campaign for a UK Climate Change Act' (2018) 27(6) *Environmental Politics* 994.

[60] Ultimately, there was significant and successful pressure in Ireland to depart substantially from the UK Act; see further Jackson, ch 6 in this volume.

[61] Averchenkova, ch 4 in this volume.

[62] See further the General Law on Climate Change 2012 (Mexico) and the Climate Change Act 2008 (UK), and the discussion of these frameworks in this volume in Averchenkova, ch 4 in this volume and Macrory and Muinzer, ch 3 in this volume.

[63] Taylor, ch 9 in this volume.

[64] Romson and Forsbacka, ch 7 in this volume.

[65] ibid.

construction, this can involve complicated and contested manoeuvring on the part of legislators and others. Spijkers and Oosterhuis raise the case of the inclusion and then removal of a UK-style free-standing Climate Committee in the proposed Dutch legislation prior to its passage:

> A second draft of the Climate Act provided for the establishment of a Climate Commission ('klimaatcommissie'), modelled after the UK Committee on Climate Change. This Commission was meant to provide authoritative advice, but this was removed from the third draft. Instead, the Commission's tasks were assigned to an already-existing institution: the Council of State.[66]

Similarly, and related to these sorts of matters, it is also notable that it is relatively straightforward to cite an existing regime like the UK Act as inspiration for a forthcoming new Climate Change Act without fleshing out the substance of how that inspiration will manifest itself in terms of specific components. This is emphasised by Nash with reference to the early stages of the Danish regime's development, who has noted that the 'Platform for Government sets up … goals as the foundation for a CCA, specifying that "the goals will be written into a climate law – inspired by the British and Scottish laws"'; however, she adds that it 'does not contain any more details as to the proposed contents of this law or the timeframe in which the legislative process was planned'.[67]

More generally, where one steps back and views the development of national Climate Change Acts from a distance, and with the benefit of well over a decade having passed since the creation of the first framework Climate Change Act in the UK, it is logical that one might anticipate the manifestation of certain challenges. In particular, where the UK's Climate Change Act has served as a direct inspiration to various additional national Acts of a similar character, one might reasonably anticipate a substantial risk of problems or uncertainties underpinning the UK regime being imported into those other regimes as a matter of course.[68] The evidence that has emerged from the deep-dive chapters in this book suggests that this phenomenon is detectible in certain identifiable instances. For example, a particular concern that has arisen in relation to various elements of the UK Act pertains to the issue of *enforceability*.[69] Jackson raises this same issue in his treatment of the Irish legislation in this volume in the following terms:

> A key sticking point was the question of whether the inclusion of targets could result in litigation against the state if the targets were not met. The fudge adopted in the end was that targets would be included in the Bill, but they would be expressly non-justiciable.[70]

---

[66] Spijkers and Oosterhuis, ch 8 in this volume.
[67] Nash, ch 5 in this volume.
[68] See the summative outline of problems raised in the literature on the UK's Climate Change Act in Thomas L Muinzer and Gavin McLeod Little, 'A Stocktake of Legal Research on the United Kingdom's Climate Change Act: Present Understandings, Future Opportunities' (2020) XIII *European Energy Law Report* 421.
[69] As outlined in Macrory and Muinzer, ch 3 in this volume.
[70] Jackson, ch 6 in this volume.

In other words, there was concern in Ireland amongst the government and certain others that if binding greenhouse gas emissions reduction targets were to be included in the Irish legislation, their legally binding nature would render them enforceable against the state. As noted here, a shift occurred that permitted this potential outcome to be avoided, whereby the targets were to be included, but a stipulation would render them non-justiciable (note that such a stipulation has been included in the New Zealand framework). Ultimately, the targets were removed from the Irish legislation altogether.[71] A momentum against the inclusion of targets on enforceability grounds was substantial in Ireland, with Linehan asserting that: 'It is difficult to think of any other prior legislative effort in Ireland – in any sphere – where such a direct ouster of the courts' jurisdiction was attempted.'[72] As a partial consequence of these factors, the final-form Irish legislative regime did not contain targets and was much weaker than the UK framework. Thus, Jackson notes that: 'There is a consensus that Ireland's Climate Act does not measure up well against the UK's Climate Change Act 2008, which is widely regarded as the gold standard.'[73]

Romson and Forsbacka also highlight substantial concern pertaining to enforceability and sanctions-related matters that arose as the Swedish legislation was being crafted, noting that:

> There were opinions disagreeing on the legal character of the Climate Act, especially voiced by the legal community. Most important was the opinion of the Council of Legislation (Swedish: Lagrådet), which suggested that the Climate Act be rejected on the basis that the legal form did not serve the purpose, since there were no legal sanctions.[74]

In some respects, this lack of sanctions arguably renders the Act as 'weak':

> Looking at the Act alone using traditional legal dogmatic methodology, many would say that it is in itself weak, especially so as its provisions are very general and it does not include an enforcement mechanism or any other legal effects in case the government does not fulfil its obligations.[75]

On the other hand, while 'stronger' Climate Change Acts may arguably contain overt sanctions that the courts can apply in the event that a legal duty is breached, the general impact of such sanction omissions, while raising legitimate concerns, ought not to be over-stated due to other factors that serve to assist in driving compliance.[76] Further, in the narrower setting of Sweden itself, Romson

---

[71] Climate Action and Low Carbon Development Act 2015 (Ireland).

[72] Conor Linehan, 'UK and Irish Domestic Greenhouse Gas Reduction Targets: Justiciability, Enforceability and Political Context' (2013) 21(2) *Environmental Liability* 59, quoted in Jackson, ch 6 in this volume.

[73] Jackson, ch 6 in this volume.

[74] Romson and Forsbacka, ch 7 in this volume.

[75] ibid.

[76] Muinzer, *Climate and Energy Governance for the UK Low Carbon Transition* (n 23) 20–21 and 25–26.

and Forsbacka note that the Swedish Act is best studied in the context of the Environmental Code and with reference to other mitigating policies in order to get a fuller view of overall weaknesses and strengths.[77] There may also be different forms of sanction that may operate in relation to particular Climate Change Acts, arising as a consequence of diverse legal-political national settings. Thus, in the case of the UK's Act, the legislation itself does not contain sanctions for a breach of the framework's major duties, but judicial review is available,[78] and this in itself is thought by some to amount to a sanction on governmental non-compliance in its own right.[79] Taylor's chapter indicates that New Zealand's legislators have paid careful attention to these dimensions of the UK regime and, rather than strengthening the presence of sanctions in the event of a breach of major duties, they have strategically weakened their framework's enforceability elements even further.[80]

Problematic features and uncertainties that potentially constrain the success of aspects of the UK regime and that have a potential to be exported into other regimes that the UK Act has helped to inspire are not necessarily limited to narrow specific problems such as enforceability and sanctions. One broad and relatively sweeping concern crystallising across this book, which transcends specific technical or micro-issues arising within the framework regimes, pertains to the wider relationship between *law* and *action*. A capacity for gaps to emerge between the framework laws as set out in Climate Change Acts and the action required to realise the laws' mandatory objectives can amount to a potentially problematic feature of these regimes. In particular, challenges can emerge around institutional and financial capacity, and political will; this is well demonstrated with reference to Averchenkova's chapter in particular.[81]

B. The General Substance of an Optimum Climate Change Act

In continuing to draw on Romson and Forsbacka's use of the word 'weak' raised in the preceding section, it might be observed that the weaknesses and strengths in national framework climate legislation might be conceptualised as existing on a sliding scale. By way of an example, take a hypothetical Climate Change Act that contains no emissions reduction targets, carbon budgets or other (partially)

---

[77] '[M]ore comprehensive scientific questions around the correlation between the new Act and the general environmental legislation, as well as the Act's impact on mitigating policies, need to be investigated.' Romson and Forsbacka, ch 7 in this volume.

[78] See further Michael Fordham, *Judicial Review Handbook* (London, Bloomsbury, 2012).

[79] Colin T Reid, 'A New Sort of Duty? The Significance of "Outcome" Duties in the Climate Change and Child Poverty Acts' (2012) 4 *Public Law* 749, 757.

[80] See the discussion in Taylor, ch 9 in this volume, section VII.

[81] See further Averchenkova, ch 4 in this volume, who devotes considerable attention to Mexico's need 'to close the gap between what is set out in the Law and the actual policy arrangements, processes and practices'.

comparable 'hard' mitigation devices (eg, carbon taxes or emissions trading schemes). Taken in isolation, this Act will be relatively 'weak' on mitigation in comparison to a Climate Change Act that does contain effectively operational versions of these devices, unless the Act incorporates some new device(s) that can be applied as a robust and effective alternative to these hitherto conventional sorts of mechanisms.[82] A Climate Change Act that is 'weak' on mitigation in this type of manner is sub-optimal on logical grounds: anthropogenic greenhouse gas emissions pose a serious problem to humanity and thus there is a need to mitigate them; the absence of robust measures for this purpose in a given Climate Change Act compels the logical conclusion that the Act in question is not suitably developed to a level where it is appropriately fit for purpose.

An answer to this criticism might be that the Act is co-partnered with a substantial policy agreement (or equivalent) or cast in a subsidiary partnership to a substantial policy Agreement. This does not shield the Act itself from the criticism per se, but may dissolve the broader underlying concerns if the partner agreement permits the overall Act-Agreement architecture to engage with mitigation in a more fulsome way. On the same thinking, if national framework climate legislation omits to deal meaningfully with the similarly crucial issue of adaptation, then it is weaker – and by extension less optimal – on that major point in comparison to national framework climate legislation that engages with adaptation meaningfully. Overall, therefore, it follows as a point of general principle that a Climate Change Act is most optimal where it engages both dimensions of the climate mitigation–adaptation binary within its provisions robustly.

It is duly assumed here, then, that the two major thematic elements of *mitigation* and *adaptation* should underlie an optimum Climate Change Act. This conclusion is driven by the nature of the problem – anthropogenic climate change – which requires both elements to be remedied;[83] it follows logically that a framework law that endeavours to respond to climate change in a truly comprehensive 'framework' fashion is subject to an assumed burden to engage meaningfully with both elements. The features of an optimum Climate Change Act may range legitimately and indeed considerably beyond these concerns,[84] but it is submitted that its substantive design may not overlook one (or both) of them and yet be interpreted to embody some form of comprehensive framework response to climate change.

---

[82] That is, some new component that is not yet employed to date typically within this type of legislation.

[83] As Mimura summarises: 'To address global warming there are two basic countermeasures: mitigation and adaptation.' 'Mitigation' pertains to 'measures to reduce the emission and strengthen the absorption of GHGs', and 'adaptation' pertains to 'measures to increase preparedness for the adverse effects of climate change.' Nobuo Mimura, 'Scope and Roles of Adaptation to Climate Change' in Akisama Sumi, Kensuke Fukushi and Ai Hiramatsu (eds), *Adaptation and Mitigation Strategies for Climate Change* (Berlin, Springer Science & Business Media, 2010) 131.

[84] For example, the mobilisation and streaming of (national/international) climate finance might be construed as a major thematic element. See further Alina Averchenkova, Sam Fankhauser and Michal Nachmany, 'Introduction' in Averchenkova, Fankhauser and Nachmany (n 1) 11.

Where one moves beyond the relatively broad-brush consideration of headline strengths and weaknesses embodied by the *mitigation–adaptation* binary here and narrows the focus of investigation to inquire into the sorts of particular features or mechanisms that one might expect to find represented in a roughly optimum Climate Change Act within such headline parameters, one enters a complex area. Part of this complexity is driven by the fact that differing national circumstances will vary, and any particular national Climate Change Act must be grounded in those concrete circumstances. This requirement for a given Climate Change Act to be grounded of necessity in the concrete legal-political circumstances in which it operates in turn drives variation and diversity, and means in essence that there is no such thing as a 'one-size-fits-all' Climate Change Act. Furthermore, specific granular components within such Acts that might be construed as 'strengths' or 'weaknesses' in normative terms are by their nature evaluative and partially contestable.[85] This means, in effect, that there is 'no right answer' in any broad sense to the question of what a most appropriately constructed, optimal Climate Change Act should look like. Nevertheless, based on current approaches to the problem, something resembling an indicative picture of an approximation to an optimum-form Act can be generated from the preceding chapters in this book where they are taken collectively; this can be drawn together usefully for analytical purposes and supplemented by existing commentaries.

Part II of the book *Trends in Climate Change Legislation* is devoted to the subject of 'What Climate Change Legislation Should Contain'.[86] The extensive three-chapter section provides an illuminating series of outlines and analyses engaging important issues pertinent to climate law and governance, and is highly recommended to climate scholars, but it does not really delineate or probe specific features that should be contained in climate legislation directly. The third of the three chapters in particular expressly gives itself over to policy rather than legislation, as its title suggests ('Good Practice in Low-Carbon Policy').[87] The present discussion endeavours to advance the groundwork laid by this work by pointing more narrowly to specific elements and components that might usefully be contained in national Climate Change Acts.

---

[85] An emphasis where Climate Change Act 'flagship' legislation is concerned tends to fall on producing a wide-ranging consensus item of climate legislation that places a primary onus on defining a country's broad approach to climate change. This emphasis on breadth and general direction tends to mitigate the pronounced contestation that might otherwise arise were the primary emphasis to be placed instead on narrow granular regime components. On the notion of wide-ranging flagship legislation that defines a country's approach to climate change, see further Sam Fankhauser, Caterina Gennaioli, and Murray Collins, 'The Political Economy of Passing Climate Change Legislation: Evidence from a Survey' (2015) 35 *Global Environmental Change* 52; Terry Townshend, Sam Fankhauser, Raffael Aybar et al, 'How National Legislation Can Help to Solve Climate Change' (2013) 3(5) *Nature Climate Change* 430.

[86] Averchenkova, Fankhauser and Nachmany (n 1) pt II (covering chs 5–7).

[87] Alex Bowen and Sam Fankhauser, 'Good Practice in Low-Carbon Policy' in Averchenkova, Fankhauser and Nachmany (n 1). The authors summarise that: 'This chapter explores the policies and measures that are needed to make low-carbon (and ultimately zero-carbon) economies a reality. These are the interventions that constitute the core content of climate change legislation and of regulatory efforts to combat climate change more broadly. The focus is on emission reduction policies' (at 123).

Jackson in his chapter in this volume provides a useful opening point, where he summarises what he perceives to be the major design weaknesses that stand out in the Irish Climate Change Act based on the passage and operation of that legislation in Ireland:

> While Ireland's Act is by no means alone in all the following regards, the absence of targets and carbon budgets, the absence of meaningful sanctioning mechanisms, the Act's weak 'have regard to' obligations when it comes to adopting Mitigation and Adaptation Plans … and the composition and functions of the Advisory Council are all evident weaknesses.[88]

Here, then, are a range of features that Jackson identifies would benefit the Irish legislation either through inclusion in the regime or, where a feature is included already, through greater stringency of design. The components Jackson highlights here are unsurprising, given the current condition of knowledge concerning Climate Change Acts.[89]

This is reinforced by the work of Duwe and Bodle in this volume, who identify similar or identical core components based on their interpretation of the current condition of knowledge:

> The existing literature on climate governance frameworks and climate laws has identified a set of core elements, which include, inter alia: short-term and long-term *targets*, long-term *planning*, identification and adoption of specific *measures* (ie, policy instruments), monitoring and reporting procedures to measure *progress*, and independent *institutions* to support transparency and scientific underpinnings, plus opportunities for *public participation*.[90]

Thus, an identifiable range of core components can be detected based on the current condition of knowledge and experience, some or all of which will likely predominate in a sophisticated Climate Change Act.[91] These features echo in part the sorts of building blocks that predominate at the international level. Again, this is captured in the work of Duwe and Bodle, who in the following brief quotation describe the themes underpinning the Paris Agreement, as derived from the

---

[88] Jackson, ch 6 in this volume.

[89] Sarah Louise Nash and Reinhard Steurer, 'Taking Stock of Climate Change Acts in Europe: Living Policy Processes or Symbolic Gestures?' (2019) 19(8) *Climate Policy* 1052.

[90] Duwe and Bodle, ch 2 in this volume.

[91] These components are echoed by Taylor's summary of the 'four key things' that the New Zealand Climate Change Act is designed to do: 'Based on the UK's Climate Change Act 2008 (CCA), but with some unique elements, the Bill will do four key things: (1) Set a long-term greenhouse gas emissions reduction target, to reduce all greenhouse gases (except biogenic methane) to net zero by 2050. Methane is subject to a separate reduction regime employing a 'split gases approach'. (2) Set a series of emissions budgets to create stepping stones for achieving the long-term target. (3) Require the government to develop and implement adaptation measures including risk assessments and plans. (4) Establish an independent Climate Change Commission to provide expert advice and monitoring, and to keep governments on track in order to meet mitigation and adaptation goals.' Taylor, ch 9 in this volume.

UNFCCC tradition, which echo familiar trends in national framework climate legislation: 'Each article of the [Paris] Agreement covers one of the UNFCCC's traditional thematic areas: mitigation, adaptation, support and finance, technology capacity-building, accounting and reporting and also other issues, such as loss and damage. They define thematic objectives and what parties are to do to achieve them.'[92]

Drawing together the predominant useful features that have been mentioned above in relation to the nationally focused indicative lists, these features include the following:

- *Jackson*: targets and carbon budgets; meaningful sanctioning mechanisms; robust obligations where Mitigation and Adaptation Plans are being adopted (ie, obligations that go beyond weak 'have regard to' legislative framing); an adequately composed Advisory Council or equivalent Climate Committee with suitable functional capacities (including capacities that render it immune from substantial government interference).[93]

- *Duwe and Bodle* (additional points): short-term and long-term targets; long-term planning; monitoring and reporting procedures to measure progress; institutional transparency; opportunities for public participation.[94]

It has been emphasised that the particular features one would anticipate as appearing in an optimal Climate Change Act, construed in a general sense, are contestable. Nor are the indicative features pointed to here by the present writer via the work of Jackson, Duwe, Bodle and others, and in the following section, intended to be exhaustive. Based on the current condition of knowledge and experience, they are merely indicative of an optimum Climate Change Act's likely essential characteristics and not a complete statement of them. The intention is to summarise the sorts of emergent expectations arising from our current knowledge, analyses and (thus far limited) experience of these regimes in practice, and relate that thinking to how a Climate Change Act might be helpfully structured in a general sense. With all this in mind, it will be useful to address various key component features in more detail.

---

[92] Duwe and Bodle, ch 2 in this volume.

[93] On matters arising in relation to this point in the UK setting, see Muinzer and McLeod Little (n 68) 429–30. On the general features highlighted by Jackson in the text here, see further Jackson, ch 6 in this volume.

[94] Duwe and Bodle also include identification and adoption of specific 'measures', meaning 'policy instruments'. This is omitted from the list above due both to the broad parameters of this element's meaning and implications, and to the present discussion's concern to focus more sharply on law than on policy issues. Matthias Duwe and Ralph Bodle, ch 2 in this volume. Duwe and Bodle also helpfully emphasise the importance of scientific monitoring and support in the context of national framework climate legislation, which can overlap with the monitoring, advisory and institutional components noted above.

C. Key Components Featuring in Climate Change Acts

Key features to date for either actual inclusion in Climate Change Acts, or at the least for careful consideration of inclusion over the course of a national framework's design, include *targets, carbon budgets* and the *creation of plans*. In addition to being identified in the discussion above, these devices have either featured in all national framework climate legislation to date, or, if not, appeared in partner policy agreements,[95] or at the least featured significantly in formal procedural debates, discussions and consultations leading up to a given framework's creation.[96] The UK framework, which contains each of these three components in a substantial form – *targets, carbon budgets* and the *creation of plans* – has set the tone for these devices,[97] creating an implicit assumption that they should be included in subsequent Climate Change Acts or, if not, at the very least consciously considered for inclusion and rejected. The general position that has emerged is that these key devices may not be ignored or overlooked where a state is seriously considering the creation of credible national framework climate legislation.

To date, *targets* typically pertain to the inclusion in the legislation of greenhouse gas emissions reduction targets. So far, in their most prominent, comprehensive form, they typically apply a specific emissions reduction target to targeted greenhouse gases, measure that reduction against levels in a preceding base year and assert in law that the imposed reduction target is to be achieved by a specific future date.[98] For example, in the case of the UK Climate Change Act, Macrory and Muinzer outline that the Act has imposed a 100 per cent greenhouse gas emissions reduction target on the UK for 2050; a 34 per cent target is also applied for 2020, and both target reductions are measured from 1990 baseline emissions levels.[99] There is scope for development and creative thinking around these novel devices in law, such as by incorporating sector-specific targets,[100] and Taylor's discussion

---

[95] See section II.B above.

[96] As, for example, in the case of Ireland outlined in ch 6 in this volume, where *targets* and *carbon budgets* featured heavily in discussions leading up to the creation of the Irish Climate Change Act, but did not appear in the final Act itself (a *creation of plans* element was incorporated into the final Act).

[97] Macrory and Muinzer, ch 3 in this volume.

[98] A similar but differing method is to endeavour to lower emissions per unit of gross domestic product, but this approach has not been incorporated into national Climate Change Acts to date. The method, which focuses on the emissions 'intensity' of the economy, is discussed in Charles D Kolstad, 'The Simple Analytics of Greenhouse Gas Emission Intensity Reduction Targets' (2005) 33(17) *Energy Policy* 2231. On the general expression of mitigation targets in law and policy, see further Alina Averchenkova and Sini Matikainen, 'Climate Legislation and International Commitments' in Averchenkova, Fankhauser and Nachmany (n 1) 195–97.

[99] The 2020 reduction target initially sat at 26 per cent, but the Secretary of State revised it upwards to 34 per cent after receiving parliamentary approval shortly after the Act's creation, via the Climate Change Act 2008 (2020 Target, Credit Limit and Definitions) Order 2009. The 2050 target initially sat at 80 per cent and was revised upwards to 100 per cent ('Net Zero') via the Climate Change Act 2008 (2050 Target Amendment) Order 2019.

[100] As Averchenkova and Matikainen note, domestic framers of mitigation targets face a choice concerning the 'scope of the target, that is, whether the mitigation actions are undertaken on a sectoral or economy-wide level': Averchenkova and Matikainen (n 99) 196. An economy-wide target is

in this volume outlines New Zealand's decision to legislate for a pioneering 'split gases approach', which separates out a distinct methane-specific target from the overall UK-style headline emissions reduction target for 2050 in the New Zealand Climate Change Act.[101] More broadly, and emphasising the *temperature* dimension that also drives – and indeed can form a basis of – target-setting, the New Zealand legislation has been characterised as 'the first legislation in the world to create a legally binding commitment to "living within 1.5 degrees Celsius of global warming".[102] This 1.5°C target draws inspiration from the Paris Agreement and highlights the facility for temperature goals to be integrated as influential legislative targets in their own right.

In contrast, as outlined by Averchenkova[103] and highlighted in the introduction to this collection,[104] it is notable that the Mexican Climate Change Act includes 'transitory articles' that make reference to specific climate targets. Transitory articles are a nuanced device utilised in Mexican law and take the form of articles that are in effect bolted on to the main body of the Climate Act. Thus, they are not fully part of the binding law. As Averchenkova describes it, they have only 'a temporary validity and are viewed as secondary or auxiliary to the main articles … and they cannot stand on their own'.[105] Here one finds that emissions reduction targets are therefore attached to the Mexican Climate Change Act, but feature in such a way that their legal enforceability, and indeed their general legal weight, is subverted.[106] This suggests that careful interpretation is required by international analysts of Climate Change Acts, given that on initial inspection of an Act of this nature, a non-Mexican specialist might assume that the targets appearing there are embedded in conventional legal terms, when in fact they are not.

Macrory and Muinzer have also outlined that the UK has set in place five-yearly *carbon budgets*. This component, which has been incorporated into New Zealand's legislation as a key feature, limits the amount of greenhouse gas that the UK can emit over each five-year period.[107] Macrory and Muinzer also address the *creation of plans*. These include, for example, the legally required proposals

---

preferable because it spreads a more comprehensive net over the economy as a whole (although sector-specific targets can be very useful within that broader bubble). It also keeps (developed) states in line with the Paris Agreement, which asserts that '[d]eveloped country Parties should continue taking the lead by undertaking economy-wide absolute emissions reduction targets' (Article 4(4)).

[101] Taylor, ch 9 in this volume.

[102] ibid (quoting a government minister).

[103] Averchenkova, ch 4 in this volume.

[104] See further the Introduction in this volume.

[105] Averchenkova, ch 4 in this volume.

[106] On the transitory articles and their evolution during the Mexican Act's 2012 creation and 2018 amendments, see further Alina Averchenkova and Sandra L Guzman Luna, *Mexico's General Law on Climate Change: Key Achievements and Challenges Ahead* (London, Grantham, 2018) 13–14.

[107] The budgeting scheme, including the UK's carbon account and carbon units that underpin it, is outlined in Macrory and Muinzer, ch 3 in this volume. While the New Zealand scheme closely resembles that of the UK, it has attracted criticism for imbuing the government with a concentrated power to set carbon budgets, whereas in the UK, the national Parliament is also accorded a substantial role. See also Taylor, ch 9 in this volume, section XI.

and plans directed towards the issue of meeting the five-yearly carbon budgets. Although the substance of these plans is not fleshed out by the legislation itself, the procedural requirement to produce them is a vital feature of the UK legislation, insofar as significant reliance is placed on this process in order to meet the carbon budgets in practice.[108] While the *creation of plans* component arguably seems more nebulous than harder-edged *target* and *carbon budget* devices when considered in the abstract, one should not underestimate this feature's key role in Climate Change Act framing. This is captured by the work of Nash, who has detected an underdeveloped integration of planning devices into the design of the Danish Climate Change Act and concludes overall in this volume that the Danish Act is at the 'weaker end of the spectrum of CCAs that have entered into force in EU Member States'.[109] Such critiques emphasise the importance of the presence and role of planning devices within these regimes.

Moreover, and returning again to Macrory and Muinzer's examination of the UK in this volume by way of an example, the creation of plans is an especially notable feature of the UK regime's approach to the problem of climate change adaptation.[110] Here, a *Risk Assessment* report is required to be produced, followed by an *Adaptation Programme* that endeavours to respond to the risks set out in that preceding report in practical terms. A refreshed *Risk Assessment* then appears in concert with the ongoing carbon budgets, followed by an *Adaptation Programme*, and so the cycle continues. Further, the *creation of plans* (Adaptation Programmes) plays a key role in tackling the problem of adaptation in conjunction with the sorts of *monitoring and reporting* (Risk Assessment) practices noted as being important within Climate Change Acts by Duwe and Bodle above.[111] *Monitoring and reporting* is also key in the context of a comprehensive *target* and *carbon budget* regime like that of the UK, where overall progress and specific emissions levels need to be carefully monitored and reported on in order to track the state's ongoing performance, and to assess the level of action required in relation to pending reduction goals.

Climate Committees, styled with a range of indicative titles and imbued with varying but relatively common sorts of functions, have also emerged as prominent features of major Climate Change Acts. Again, the UK framework set the tone by establishing the Committee on Climate Change.[112] Macrory and Muinzer have outlined that the Committee does not have powers to set policy, but rather is designed to sit at an independent remove from the UK government and scrutinise national mitigation and adaptation progress under the terms of the Act.[113] It has extensive monitoring, reporting and advisory duties that are

---

[108] Climate Change Act 2008, ss 13–14.
[109] Nash, ch 5 in this volume.
[110] See Macrory and Muinzer, ch 3 in this volume, section VI.
[111] See section III.B above.
[112] Macrory and Muinzer, ch 3 in this volume, section V.
[113] ibid.

undertaken for the UK government, the UK Parliament and the UK's devolved administrations. The other case study chapters in this volume evince how such committees are emerging as a common component of national framework climate legislation.

It is clear that in establishing a committee of this sort one invites questions as to how climate legislation should articulate that institution's powers and functions. For example, one concern relates to whether a committee should be imbued with active policy-setting powers or whether its capacities should be restricted to the sorts of monitoring, reporting and advisory responsibilities embodied by the UK-style approach.[114] Thus, for instance, in this volume Jackson outlines the establishment of Ireland's Climate Change Advisory Council under the terms of the Irish Climate Change Act.[115] The Council is constituted in a UK-style tradition, where it is intended as a reporting and advisory institution rather than one that has powers to actively set policy. While this functional remit is fairly clear from the legislation itself,[116] litigation in the Irish courts has touched on the issue of whether the Council's opinions might somehow amount to binding obligations on the government. Jackson has summarised the High Court's rejection of this position[117] as follows: 'While the Council has repeatedly issued strong critiques of the government's failings on climate change, the High Court held in 2019 that "its conclusions and recommendations cannot be equated with the imposition of a legal obligation under the statutory framework".'[118]

A further prominent concern arising where the creation of these committees is at issue relates to the extent to which such committees should or should not sit at an independent remove from government. Jackson also raises this issue in his Irish analysis and it is further evidenced in this volume, eg, where Romson and Forsbacka elaborate on the role of the Climate Policy Council in Sweden, which evaluates the government's work towards achieving its climate targets.[119] The authors outline that the Swedish Council is an 'independent' body that provides important advice on the government's climate progress; however, it is not regulated by the Climate Act itself, but rather has its rules issued separately by the government.[120] Moreover, Romson and Forsbacka note that the Swedish Climate Policy Council 'operates as an agency under the government, meaning that the independence of the Committee in relation to the government could be

---

[114] See, eg, Matthew Lockwood, 'The Political Sustainability of Climate Policy: The Case of the UK Climate Change Act' (2013) 23(5) *Global Environmental Change* 1339, 1343.

[115] Jackson, ch 6 in this volume.

[116] Climate Action and Low Carbon Development Act 2015, ss 11–13.

[117] *Friends of the Irish Environment v. Government of Ireland and Others* [2019] IEHC 747, judgment of the High Court of Ireland (19 September 2019), para 114.

[118] Jackson, ch 6 in this volume (quoting from ibid).

[119] Romson and Forsbacka, ch 7 in this volume, section III.

[120] ibid.

questioned'.[121] In 'Institutional Aspects of Climate Legislation', Averchenkova and Nachmany note that:

> Empirical studies show that governments delegate powers in order to enhance the credibility of their policies. Hence, the existence of dedicated public bodies focusing on climate change, as well as of independent consultative bodies ... is important for effective implementation of climate policy.[122]

An agency operating under the government in the manner described pertaining to Sweden may not appear to be 'independent' in a broadly meaningful sense of the word. The approach certainly contrasts with a UK-style model, where the UK Committee is structured by the foundational national framework climate legislation in a manner that endeavours to carefully establish its meaningful independence from government.[123]

National framework climate legislation may establish a new committee in the UK fashion just outlined (or indeed more than one such committee); however, alternatively, where it seeks to apply functions associated with this new-form type of committee, it may instead place its emphasis on apportioning pertinent functions to an official department or other body that already exists. There may be no perfect answer as to which course is most appropriate in a general sense, insofar as states must ground their options to some extent in their own concrete circumstances and realise their own most suitable 'fit' in practice. In general, existing research suggests that: 'Ideally, the formulation of a country's climate change strategy involves both a dedicated climate change decision-making organisation, as well as an *independent advisory body* that is tasked with carrying out strategic assessments and advice to the decision makers' (emphasis added).[124] This indicates that on balance, it is to be assumed that the creation of an independent committee is the advisable course where a state seeks to legislate a Climate Change Act.

It is notable that lessons pertaining to certain normative difficulties that states might remain usefully on guard for might be drawn from the Mexican experience outlined in this volume.[125] The Mexican Climate Change Act departs from the emerging tradition of locating Committee-style functions in a relatively clearly defined institution in favour of extending a multitude of overlapping functions and associated responsibilities across a diverse range of committees and

---

[121] ibid.

[122] Alina Averchenkova and Michal Nachmany, 'Institutional Aspects of Climate Legislation' in Averchenkova, Fankhauser and Nachmany (n 1) 111–14.

[123] Macrory and Muinzer, ch 3 in this volume, section V. Note that Muinzer and McLeod Little have highlighted that UK government's control over funding could amount to an indirect means of exerting some control over the institution in principle: Muinzer and McLeod Little (n 68) 429.

[124] Averchenkova and Nachmany (n 123) 114.

[125] Averchenkova, ch 4 in this volume.

institutions. These are conjoined within a complex field of multi-level representation.

> Averchenkova summarises that the Mexican Act establishes the 'National System on Climate Change', which includes the Inter-Ministerial Commission on Climate Change, the Consultative Council on Climate Change, the National Institute of Ecology and Climate Change, and provides for participation of the representatives of the state governments, the associations of municipal governments and the representatives of the Mexican Congress. It also mandates Mexico's 32 states and 2,475 municipalities to develop local mitigation and adaptation programmes.[126]

Averchenkova's work clarifies that the full web of councils, departments and the like that have significant roles under the terms of the Act is broader than the range indicated here;[127] however, this quotation captures the spirit of the manner in which the Mexican Act risks resulting in a convoluted bureaucratic structural design. The extent to which Mexico's national framework climate legislation endeavours to work across the large state's multi-levels of governance from the municipal level upwards arguably constitutes an impressive sensitivity to national multi-level governance challenges;[128] however, the legislation's general tendency towards the convoluted interconnection of committees and departments with partially overlapping functions in this setting creates an impression of partial confusion. It is difficult to interpret clearly how diverse administrators and others can act in an effective joined-up way in the context of this legislative framing.

A further notable element to arise as a significant theme and component in the context of Climate Change Acts pertains to what Duwe and Bodle have summarised above as 'opportunities for public participation'.[129] The deep-dive national exploratory chapters set out in this volume suggest that public participation and engagement tend to play a role of some significance in relation to the crafting of Climate Change Acts, most particularly over the course of pre-legislative consultation processes and the like.[130] However, the issue of whether public participation or engagement is incorporated into final outcome legislation as an actual substantive feature of a particular regime amounts to a related but separate matter. Macrory and Muinzer, for example, note the important role of public pressure and input prior to the passage of the UK Climate Change Act,[131] yet there is little to be said on public participation and engagement within the provisions of the substantive

---

[126] ibid, section IV.

[127] Ibid.

[128] Tim Trench, Anne M Larson et al, 'Analyzing Multilevel Governance in Mexico: Lessons for REDD+ from a Study of Land-Use Change and Benefit Sharing in Chiapas and Yucatán' (2018) 236 *Center for International Forestry Research* 1.

[129] Duwe and Bodle, ch 2 in this volume.

[130] See, eg, Macrory and Muinzer, ch 3 in this volume, section II.

[131] ibid.

outcome Act itself, where the matter does not feature as a significant element in the legislation. In the UK setting, these circumstances can be contrasted with the sub-state Climate Change (Scotland) Act 2009, set in place by Scotland's devolved legislature.[132] This sub-national framework legislation integrates significant 'public engagement' elements into its provisions that include a requirement for the devolved Scottish government to produce a *Public Engagement Strategy* pertinent to Scotland.[133]

Public input can assist in driving the achievement of climate objectives and in creating pressure that contributes to the raising of outcome standards.[134] Conventional democratic norms also indicate that the public should have a robust right of input in the context of a major social concern like climate change.[135] Barnes, Newman and Sullivan summarise that:

> More and better public participation is viewed as capable of improving the quality and legitimacy of decisions in government, health services, local government and other public bodies, as well as having the potential to address the 'democratic deficit' and to build community capacity and social capital.[136]

All this suggests in turn that the inclusion of *public participation and engagement* components should be seriously considered where any Climate Change Act is being crafted. The Dutch setting appears to provide a strong example of how public participation and engagement can be integrated in a serious way at the relatively early pre-bill and consultation stages, and then carried forward as a theme and concern through to the outcome legislation itself.[137] The account provided by Spijkers and Oosterhuis in this volume suggests that the Netherlands has a relatively robust citizens' participation process in place at the consultation stage,[138] and that a sense of this public orientation has been brought forward successfully into the state's national climate framework as an ongoing feature:

> An important aspect in both the Climate Act and the Climate Agreement is the focus on public participation. Again, the Climate Act provides for the framework for public

---

[132] Climate Change (Scotland) Act 2009.

[133] ibid s 91, 'Public engagement'.

[134] Public input includes '[d]ecisions by members of the general public' who make 'informed choices' in the context of their daily lives that are important to climate mitigation and adaptation progress, but also ranges beyond this to incorporate 'the power that the public has to influence decisions that are made by governmental, corporate and non-profit actors': National Research Council, *Informing an Effective Response to Climate Change* (Washington DC, National Academies Press, 2011) 129.

[135] It is notable that Jackson alludes to the Citizens' Assembly in Ireland (Jackson, ch 6 in this volume), that is, an assembly of citizens selected from a cross-section of Irish society and established by the Irish Parliament to consider responses to various major issues, including climate change. This bespoke public participatory channel achieved some positive results. See further Martha Coleman, Laura Devaney, Diarmuid Torney and Pat Brereton, 'Ireland's World-Leading Citizens' Climate Assembly. What Worked? What Didn't?' (*Climate Home News*, 27 June 2019).

[136] Marian Barnes, Janet Newman and Helen C Sullivan, *Power, Participation and Political Renewal: Case Studies in Public Participation* (Bristol, Policy Press 2007), 1.

[137] Spijkers and Oosterhuis, ch 8 in this volume.

[138] See generally ibid and in particular sections V.C and V.D.

participation, while the Climate Agreement contains specific measures on how citizens can be involved in the transition.[139]

Although the authors note that both the Dutch Climate Act and the Climate Agreement have nevertheless 'been criticised',[140] the broad emphasis granted to the role of public participation in the Dutch setting serves to highlight a significant feature of climate regime architecture that might otherwise be unhelpfully neglected (as has arguably occurred in the equivalent UK legislation).

A good deal more could be said about specific components that might be included in an optimum Climate Change Act. This section has engaged in an indicative discussion, highlighting various key features that the current condition of knowledge and experience indicates should be considered for incorporation into any new Act of this kind. Not all of the components that have been identified and discussed will necessarily be required in all circumstances, given that states need to fit their national framework climate legislation to their own concrete legal-political contexts and perceived governance demands. A useful general assumption is that legislators and others seeking to craft (or amend) an optimum Climate Change Act that is to be constructed on the basis of current best-practice knowledge and experience must either:

(a) produce a regime that contains each of the following components listed in the table below; or

(b) omit some of the following components, but in the case of each omission provide a rational account as to why the component has been omitted, including with reference to the particular national circumstances driving the decision.

As noted, the following generalised list is indicative and thus may not be viewed as exhaustive. For example, some may suggest that capacities to apply carbon taxes, trading schemes etc directly under the terms of national framework climate legislation could merit inclusion in a list of this kind. Thus, a main feature of South Korea's climate-oriented Framework Act on Low Carbon Green Growth 2010 is its establishment of a cap and trade system.[141] Here it follows to some extent in the tradition of the UK's Climate Change Act, which also opens up substantial trading scheme capacities.[142] However, such measures do not necessarily need to

---

[139] ibid.

[140] ibid. Although the Netherlands is a best-practice jurisdiction in this area, it should be noted that criticism can also be extended to incorporate the pre-Act consultation phase. The Dutch Climate Bill was issued to the public for pre-legislative consultation, but much important regime substance is located in the Climate Agreement rather than the Act, meaning that it was not incorporated into this type of rigorous, public-oriented pre-legislative consultation process. In other words, in spite of its weighty substance, the Climate Agreement itself is not legislation and thus its substance was not subject to pre-legislative consultation procedures.

[141] Framework Act on Low Carbon Green Growth 2010, art 46.

[142] Climate Change Act 2008, pt 3 and scheds 3 and 4.

be anchored in national framework climate legislation, as Bowen and Fankhauser indicate:

> Not all the interventions that are required have to be anchored in formal climate change legislation. High-profile measures such as carbon taxes or emissions trading schemes will often be at the centre of new climate change laws. However, policy makers can also use existing legislative and regulatory powers to strengthen emission reduction incentives.[143]

Others may adjust or expand certain categories appearing in the indicative list below. For example, 'verification' is often referred to alongside 'monitoring' and 'reporting' – so-called 'MRV' – which may indicate that the 'monitoring and reporting procedures' element could be usefully reframed, depending on one's opinion.[144] Conversely, however, Fiji's Climate Change Bill 2019, for example, does make mention of 'monitoring, reporting and verification',[145] but prefers '*measurement*, reporting and verification' (emphasis added) overall, giving this as a headline title to a full part of the Bill.[146]

Table 10.1 Indicative major best-practice components of an optimum Climate Change Act

MAJOR THEMATIC COMPONENTS	
Substantial focus on mitigation	**Substantial focus on adaptation**

GRANULAR COMPONENTS
Targets
Carbon budgets
Long-term planning procedures
Creation of an independent Climate Committee
Adoption of robust Mitigation and Adaptation Plans
Public participation and engagement
Monitoring and reporting procedures
Sanctioning mechanisms
Institutional transparency

---

[143] Bowen and Fankhauser (n 87) 124.

[144] For a legal example, see the EU's Commission Delegated Regulation (EU) 2019/1603, concerning the 'monitoring, reporting and verification' of aspects of aviation emissions. The Paris Agreement has endeavoured to draw MRV into a coherent concept at the international level; see Neelam Singh, Jared Finnegan and Kelly Levin, 'MRV 101: Understanding Measurement, Reporting, and Verification of Climate Change Mitigation' (2016) World Resources Institute Working Paper, August, www.wri.org/publication/mrv-101-understanding-measurement-reporting-and-verification-climate-change-mitigation.

[145] eg, Climate Change Bill 2019 (Fiji), s 4(h).

[146] ibid pt 7.

IV. Conclusions

This chapter has drawn together emergent understandings arising from this book in order to explore national Climate Change Acts, freeing the form from consideration in the context of a particular state in order to explore national framework climate legislation in a more general, abstracted sense. In addition to both providing critical reflection on major issues arising across this volume and to probing the concept of national framework climate legislation more deeply in light of this and other research in the area, the chapter has explored and outlined the various component features that one might usefully expect to underpin an optimum Climate Change Act.

Thus, an indicative statement of major best-practice components of an optimum Climate Change Act is provided. It is argued that this element of the chapter has normative as well as intellectual value. In particular, it is argued that a useful general assumption is that legislators and others seeking to craft (or amend) an optimum Climate Change Act that is to be constructed on the basis of current best-practice knowledge and experience are well advised to either:

(a)   construct a regime that contains some form of each of the major components highlighted in the study above; or

(b)   omit some of the outlined components, but in the case of each omission provide a rational account as to why the component has been omitted, including with reference to the particular national circumstances driving the decision.

Thus, in cases of best-practice regime design, a burden must be understood to exist: each of the crucial components highlighted above should either be incorporated into the national framework climate legislation in question or, if rejected, that rejection should be explicitly accounted for in a reasoned argument: none of the components can be legitimately ignored.

INDEX

A

adaptation to climate change
  Ireland 142, 143, 144, 149, 246
  Mexican LGCC 99–100, 101, 102, 103
  mitigation compared 82
  national climate change acts 235–236,
      244–245, 250, 256
  Netherlands Climate Law 182–183
  New Zealand 201, 204, 210, 220, 224–225
  Paris Agreement 46, 47, 182–183, 247
  Swedish Climate Change Act 165, 235–236
  UK Climate Change Act 70, 74, 82–83, 250
Akerboom, S 189
anthropogenic climate change 13–16, 17–18,
      20, 22, 24, 26, 28, 75, 228, 244
Ardern, Jacinda 202
Armenia
  Law on Energy Efficiency and Renewable
      Energy 2004 14n
Attenborough, Sir David 20
Australia
  Climate Change Authority Act 2011 14
Austria
  Climate Change Act 2011 111
Averchenkova, A 233, 238, 240, 243,
      249, 253
Averchenkova, A and Guzman, S 104, 108
Averchenkova, A and Nachmany, M 252

B

Bacik, Ivana 133
Barnes, M et al 254
Barrett, Sean D 142, 231
Beltrán, Leonardo 109
biofuels
  Denmark 120
  Sweden 169
biogenic methane
  New Zealand 199, 200, 201, 203,
      205–206, 213
Blair, Tony 72
Bodansky, D et al 31–32, 33, 228
Bowen, A and Fankhauser, S 256
Brandeis J 31

C

Calderón, Felipe 96, 107
Cameron, David 72
Canada
  greenhouse gas emissions 27–28
  Kyoto Protocol 27–28
Cancun Agreements 96–97
cap-and-trade schemes *see* **emissions trading**
      schemes
carbon capture and storage
  Netherlands 178
  New Zealand 208, 213, 216, 217, 218, 226
  Sweden 163
carbon dioxide *see* **greenhouse gas emissions**
Carnwath LJ 85
Carter, N 90
Chile
  Ley Marco de Cambio Climatico 45
China
  climate policy 232n
  greenhouse gas emissions 27, 46, 95
  Kyoto Protocol 27
  Paris Agreement 46
  policy framework approach 232n
chlorofluorocarbons (CFCs)
  see also greenhouse gas emissions
  legislation engaging with 22n
Chubb, B 130
Clare, A et al 13, 231
climate change
  adaptation to *see* adaptation to climate
      change
  anthropogenic 13–16, 17, 18, 22, 24, 26, 28,
      75, 228, 244
  global nature of problem 23
  human rights and 176, 192–197
  international law *see* international climate
      law regime
  national laws *see* national climate legislation
  Paris Agreement *see* Paris Agreement
  risk assessment *see* risk assessment
  technology framework, development 36, 47
  UNFCCC *see* United Nations Framework
      Convention on Climate Change

Climate Change Laws of the World
    database 16n
Climate Focus 37
climate justice
    New Zealand 207, 219, 222
    principle, generally 142, 149, 230
climate law
    see also national climate legislation
    abnormal stakes involved 21
    economy-wide transitions 22
    generally 18
    international *see* international climate law
        regime
    Montreal Protocol 22n
    problems for technical/doctrinal law 22
    use of term 16
climate policy
    China 232n
    Denmark 111, 112, 113–114, 127, 234
    Ireland 129–131, 233
    Mexico 95–96, 99–101, 107, 233
    national legislation and 231–236, 244
    Netherlands 178, 179, 197–198, 233,
        234–235
    supranational obligations 43
    Sweden *see* Sweden: Climate Policy
        Framework
    United Kingdom 71–73, 79, 233–234
Connolly, Tara 138
Copenhagen Conference (COP15) 31n, 39,
        57, 96, 134
    European Union 57
Coveney, Simon 134–135
Curtin, Joe 139

D
Daly Clare 152
Deben, Lord 202
decarbonisation *see* **carbon capture and**
        storage; greenhouse gas emissions
Denmark
    biomass, tax and subsidy system 120
    Citizens' Initiative 111, 121–125, 126
    climate policy 111, 112, 113–114, 127, 234
    Energy Agreement 120
    EU Emissions Trading Scheme 112–113
    EU membership 112
    'green realism' 118
    Lov om klima 2020 *see* Denmark: Lov om
        klima 2020
    Lov om Klimarådet 2014 *see* Denmark: Lov
        om Klimarådet 2014

    net zero emissions target 111, 119, 126–127
    new legislation, possible 238
    Paris Agreement 111, 112, 125, 126,
        127, 128
    political consensus 126, 128
    temperature goal 112, 126, 128
    UNFCCC 112
Denmark: Lov om Klimarådet 2014
    2020 law compared 127, 128
    Climate Council 111, 114, 118–120
    climate policy framework 113–114
    Climate Policy Statements 113, 114
    Comments on the Bill 113, 114–115, 234
    compliance 114
    emissions targets 112–113, 114–115, 118–120
    energy transition 115, 119–120
    form and content 113–115, 241
    generally 44, 111–112
    implementing 117–120
    legally binding provisions 113
    national climate objectives 111, 115
    negotiating 115–117
    Platform for Government 115–117, 118, 120
    renewable energy 113, 119–120
    reporting and advisory duties 118–119, 120
    tax system changes 120
    transparency 114
    transport sector 119
    weakness 114, 250
Denmark: Lov om klima 2020
    2014 law compared 127, 128
    adoption 111, 112, 128
    calculation methods 126, 127
    climate action plans 126–127
    Climate Council 125, 126, 127
    Climate Dialogue Forum 127
    global driving force, Denmark as 124, 127
    greenhouse gas emissions targets 111,
        125–128
    interim targets 111, 125–126, 127
    law – policy relationship 234
    legally binding targets 111, 125
    Platform for Government 125
    reporting and advisory duties 126, 127
    temperature goal 126, 127, 128
developed nations
    Kyoto Protocol 26, 27–28, 31n, 33
    UNFCCC 147–148
developing countries
    Adaptation Fund 165
    Green Climate Fund 97, 165
    Paris Agreement 36

Dillon, Sara 129
Dimitrov, R 38
Doha Amendment 29–32, 33, 34
Duwe, M and Bodle, R 230, 246–247, 250, 253

E
emissions *see* emissions trading schemes;
        greenhouse gas emissions
emissions trading schemes
  cap-and-trade 57, 81, 255
  definition 81
  EU Scheme (ETS) 19, 57, 59, 61, 64, 92,
        112–113, 161, 163, 168, 171
  Mexico 102, 106
  national framework legislation 255
  New Zealand 203, 207, 208, 211, 213, 216,
        217, 218, 220, 226, 238–239
  South Korea 255
  UK legislation 19, 74, 81
energy policy
  see also renewable energy
  Denmark 115, 119–120
  European Union 57, 63–67
  Ireland 141, 143, 144, 149–150
  Mexico 94, 104–107, 109–110
  Netherlands 181–182, 186, 189, 190
  New Zealand 226
  UK Climate Change Act 74–75, 80, 88–89
enforcement
  international climate law regime 28, 31–33
  Ireland 241–242
  Mexican Climate Act 109
  New Zealand Climate Act 209–210,
        218–219, 240
  Paris Agreement 67
  Swedish Climate Act 159, 166, 173,
        242–243
European Convention on Human Rights
        (ECHR)
  Climate Case Ireland 147–150
  Urgenda v The Netherlands 176, 192–197
European Union
  2020 targets 137, 139, 143
  Aarhus Convention 66
  Clean Energy for All Europeans 59
  Clean Planet for All 57
  Climate Action Regulation 59, 63
  Climate Change Programme 57
  Climate and Energy Framework 57–59
  Climate and Energy Package 31n, 57
  Climate Law Proposal 60–63, 64, 66, 68
  climate policy 57, 61, 63–67, 183, 195

Copenhagen Conference (COP15) 57
Denmark 112
Doha Amendment 31n
Effort Sharing Regulation 161, 163
Emissions Trading Scheme (ETS) 19, 57,
        59, 61, 63, 64, 92, 112–113, 161, 163,
        168, 171
energy efficiency targets 57–59, 63–64, 66
energy policy 57, 63–67
energy taxation standards 57
European Climate Change Programme 57
European Environment Agency (EEA) 65
European Green Deal 61
fluorinated gases 57
Governance Regulation 59–60, 61, 64–65, 66
greenhouse gas emissions 31n, 57–59,
        61–64, 66–67, 88–89, 163
Industrial Emission Directive 171
Ireland 131
Kyoto Protocol 26, 26n, 27–28, 31n, 57
landfill rules 57
long-term strategies (LTSs) 60, 61, 62–63,
        64, 66
measures, development 64
monitoring and reporting process 64–65
multilevel stakeholder dialogues 66
national Climate Change Acts 65, 67, 68, 111
national climate policies 43, 66, 67
national energy and climate plans
        (NECPs) 59–60, 61, 62–63,
        64–65, 66
national reports 65
national targets 57–58, 63–64
nationally determined contribution
        (NDC) 58, 59, 61–63, 65, 68, 183
Netherlands 182–183, 187
Paris Agreement 46, 57, 58–67, 142, 195
public participation 66–67
renewable energy 57–58, 63–64, 66, 67, 178
reporting system 65
review process 61–62, 63–64, 68
Treaty on Functioning of (TFEU) 193–194
UN climate treaties 57–58
vehicle energy standards 57
Extinction Rebellion 21

F
Fankhauser, S et al 13, 18
Fiji
  Climate Change Act 45, 256
Finland
  Kansallinen ilmastolaki 2015 44, 67

FitzGerald, John   145
fluorinated gases
   European Union   57
France
   Grenelle laws   18
   Loi de transition énergétique pour la
       croissance verte 2015   44
   Low Carbon Strategy   67
   sector specific targets   67
Friends of the Earth   69, 72, 86
   Ireland   132–133, 231
   'The Big Ask'   131, 132, 133, 239

G
Gallagher, M and Marsh, M   131
Germany
   Bundes Klimaschutzgesetz (KSG) 2019   45, 67
   Marrakesh Accords   26
   Offshore Wind Energy Act 2017   14n
   sector specific targets   67
Gilmore, Eamon   133, 239
global warming
   global average   36
   greenhouse gases *see* greenhouse gas emissions
   Paris Agreement *see* Paris Agreement
Gormley, John   137
Green, F   227–228, 229–230
greenhouse gas emissions
   baseline emissions   76, 78
   Canada   27–28
   cap-and-trade schemes   57, 81, 255
   carbon budgeting   70, 74, 76–79, 88,
       122–123, 127, 199, 201, 207–208,
       210, 220, 247, 248, 249, 250, 256
   carbon dioxide   74–75
   carbon dioxide equivalents   26
   carbon removal   163, 178, 208
   China   27, 95
   chlorofluorocarbons   22n
   cumulative   148
   decarbonisation transition   22, 74–75, 80
   Denmark   111, 112–113, 114–115, 118–120,
       125–128
   developed nations   26
   Doha Amendment   29–32, 33, 34
   European Union   31n, 57–59, 61–64, 66–67,
       88–89, 163
   framework legislation   19–20, 112
   global effect   23
   global stocktakes   36, 38, 46, 47, 51, 53,
       55, 56
   human activity, attributable to   75

hydrofluorocarbons   74–75, 76
India   27
IPCC assessment reports   55, 147–148, 194,
       206, 212–213
Ireland   129–131, 133, 140–141, 147–150
Japan   29–30
Kyoto Protocol *see* Kyoto Protocol
legally binding reduction targets   69, 76–79,
       111
Marrakesh Accords   25–26
methane   74–75, 76
Mexico   93–95, 96–97, 100, 103, 104–108
mitigation *see* mitigation of greenhouse
       gases
monitoring *see* monitoring emissions
nationally determined contributions
       (NDCs)   36–37, 38, 40–42, 47–49,
       50, 51, 52, 53, 58, 61, 67, 112, 183,
       220
negative   162–163, 206, 212
net zero emissions target   76, 77, 86, 111,
       119, 126–127, 153, 162–163, 168,
       173, 177, 178, 199–226, 248
Netherlands   176, 177–179, 180, 184, 186,
       187, 192–198, 234–235
New Zealand   30, 199, 201, 203–210,
       213–215, 225–226, 249
nitrous oxide   74–75, 76
Paris Agreement   47; *see also* Paris
       Agreement
perfluorocarbons   74–75, 76
reduction targets   51–52, 53–54, 61, 70,
       243–244, 246, 248–249
removal from atmosphere   70
Russian Federation   30
split gases approach   201, 205, 213–214,
       225–226, 249
sulphur hexafluoride   74–75, 76
Sweden   153, 154, 157, 158–159, 162–163,
       168–170
trading schemes *see* emissions trading
       schemes
UK Climate Change Act   69, 70,
       71–73, 74–75, 76–79, 80,
       88–89, 248
UK Royal Commission report   71–72
UNFCCC *see* United Nations Framework
       Convention on Climate Change
United States   27, 95
Urgenda v The Netherlands   192–197,
       234–235
Greenpeace   86

H
Haigh, N 92
Hanrahan, Gina 139
Heathrow Airport third runway 85
Hogan, Phil 137–139, 140–141, 233
human rights
  ECHR *see* European Convention on Human
    Rights
  international law 184
hydraulic fracturing
  United Kingdom 84
hydrofluorocarbons
  UK Climate Change Act 74–75, 76

I
India
  greenhouse gas emissions 27, 46
  Kyoto Protocol 27
  Paris Agreement 46
Intergovernmental Panel on Climate Change
    (IPCC)
  assessment reports 55, 147–148, 194, 206,
    212–213
  establishment 23
  generally 21
  Paris Agreement 55, 194
international climate law (ICL) regime
  Doha Amendment 29–32, 33
  emergence 23–28
  enforcement 28, 31–33
  generally 11, 23, 38–39, 210, 228–231
  international monitoring and reporting 24
  Kyoto Protocol *see* Kyoto Protocol
  national climate legislation and 24–25, 32,
    39–42
  Netherlands Climate Law,
    compatibility 182–184
  ozone layer protection 22n, 23
  parallel tracks 33, 34–38
  Paris Agreement *see* Paris Agreement
  strengths 32–33, 39
  terminology 11–18, 19
  UNFCCC *see* United Nations Framework
    Convention on Climate Change
  weakness 28–33, 37, 39–41
international law
  Urgenda v The Netherlands 192–197
Ireland
  2009 Effort Sharing Decision 131
  adaptation measures 142, 143, 144, 149, 246
  agriculture lobby 130–131, 135, 136, 141,
    231

built environment 141, 233
business lobby 136, 138, 231
'The Case for Climate Change Law' 134
Citizens' Assembly report 151–152
Climate Action Act *see* Ireland: Climate
    Action and Low Carbon
    Development Act 2015
Climate Action (Amendment) Bill 151–152
Climate Action Plan 2019 151
Climate Case Ireland 147–150, 152
Climate Change Response Bill 2010
    136–137, 138, 146
Climate Change Targets Bill 2005 132
climate policy 129–131, 233
Climate Protection Bill 2007 133
climate strategy 131, 133
Commission on Climate Change 133
cumulative emissions 148
ECHR Act 2003 147–150
energy policy 141, 143, 144, 149–150
Energy Security and Climate Change Bill
    2012 138
Environmental Pillar 140
EU emissions targets 137, 139, 143,
    148–149
EU membership 131
Friends of the Irish Environment 147
global financial crisis 134, 135–136
greenhouse gas emissions 129–131, 133,
    140–141, 147–150
IIEA report 139–140
JOCCA report 151
Joint Committee 134, 136–137, 138,
    140–141, 145–146, 152
judicial review proceedings 147
Kyoto Protocol 131, 148
Marrakesh Accords 26, 26n
mitigation measures 142, 143, 144,
    147–150, 233, 246
National Economic and Social Council
    (NESC) 138–140
National Policy Position 141, 148, 233
new legislation, possible 238
non-ETS emissions 131
Paris Agreement 148
transport sector 141
Tristor case 149
**Ireland: Climate Action and Low Carbon
    Development Act 2015**
absence of sanctions 144
absence of targets 140–142, 144, 145–147,
    150, 241–242

Advisory Council   140, 141, 142, 143,
    144–146, 246, 251
background to   129, 131–143, 239–240
energy transition   143, 144, 150
National Adaptation Frameworks   142, 143,
    144, 149
National Mitigation Plans   142, 143, 144,
    147–150, 233
powers under   146–150
reporting mechanisms   141, 251
stated objective   144, 149–150
symbolic nature   143–146, 150, 152
vested interests   130–131, 135, 136, 141, 142
weakness   140–141, 143–146, 149, 231,
    233, 246
Ivanova, M   39

J
Jackson, A   231, 233, 239, 241, 242, 246,
    247, 251
Japan
    greenhouse gas emissions   29–30
    Kyoto Protocol   29–30
Jetten, Rob   181–182
judicial review
    Ireland   147
    New Zealand   210, 218–219
    United Kingdom   85, 86, 89, 243

K
Kelly, Alan   141
Kennedy, R   135
Kenny, Enda   143
Kirby, Peadar   140
Klaver, Jesse   180–181
Kyoto Protocol
    adoption   25, 39
    Canada   27–28
    developed nations   26, 27–28, 31n, 33
    diminishing prioritisation   38–39
    Doha Amendment   29–32, 33, 34
    European Union   31n, 57
    greenhouse gas emissions   25–28, 26n,
        29, 148
    Ireland   131, 148
    Japan   29–30
    Kyoto II   28–31, 33, 34–35, 37–39
    Marrakesh Accords   25–26, 26n
    New Zealand   30, 204
    Paris Agreement, relationship with   38–39, 46
    Paris Agreement compared   37–38
    phases   27–29

Russian Federation   30
SBSTA   55
soft law status   26–28, 26n, 31–32
strength   33, 39
United States   27, 95
Urgenda v The Netherlands   193

L
Laes, E et al   87
landfill rules
    European Union   57
Leyen, Ursula von der   60–61
Lilleholt, Lars Christian   118, 123
Linehan, C   147, 242
Lockwood, M   87, 88
López Obrador, Andrés Manuel   109

M
McGregor, P et al   80
McHarg, A   91
McManus, Liz   134, 135, 152
McMaster, P   90
Macrory, R and Muinzer, TL   239, 248,
    249–250, 253
Marrakesh Accords   25–26, 26n
media coverage of climate change   21
methane
    biogenic   199, 200, 201, 203, 205–206,
        213–214
    Mexico LGCC   104
    split gases approach   201, 205, 213–214,
        225–226, 249
    UK Climate Change Act   74–75, 76
Mexico
    black carbon emissions   106
    climate policy   95–96, 99–101,
        107, 233
    Commission on Climate Change
        (CICC)   99, 100
    constitutional energy reform   104
    Consultative Council on Climate
        Change (C3)   99, 100
    emissions trading system   102, 106
    Energy Transition Strategy   105–107,
        109–110
    Excellence in Energy Efficiency   105
    federalism   95, 99–100, 107, 109, 253
    greenhouse gas emissions   93–95, 96–97,
        103, 104–108
    INECC   99, 102
    Ley de Transición Energética 2015
        (LTE)   94, 104–105

Ley General de Cambio Climático (LGCC)
    see Mexico: Ley General de Cambio
    Climático 2012
National Climate Change Programme
    101, 102
National Development Plan   96, 101, 109
National Strategy on Climate Change   96,
    100–101, 102
oil production   93, 94, 97
Paris Agreement NDC   94, 105–106, 107
PRONASE   105
renewable energy   94–95, 104–107, 109–110
SEMARNAT   99, 100–102, 103
vulnerability to climate change   94
Mexico: Ley General de Cambio Climático
    2012 (LGCC)
2018 amendment   102, 105–107, 238
accountability and enforcement   109
adoption   97–98, 107
background to   92–97, 240
Climate Change Fund   101, 107
Coordination for Evaluation   99, 102, 103, 107
economic instruments   102
emission reduction goals   93–94, 100, 103,
    104–108, 249
emissions inventory   102
energy transition   104–107, 109–110
financial incentives   100, 102, 104
form and content   98–104
future political change, protection
    against   96, 233
generally   18, 44, 67, 236
impact   107–110
implementation   107–110
methane emissions   104
mitigation and adaptation policies   99–100,
    101, 102, 103–104
monitoring and evaluation   99, 102, 103,
    107, 109
municipalities   100, 107, 109, 253
National Adaptation Policy   102
National System on Climate Change
    (SINACC)   99, 100, 253
objective   94
official standards   102
opposition to   110
policy costs, imposing   100
private sector   100
progression of ambition over time   102, 103
prosecutions and sanctions   103
public funding   109
public participation   102, 103

registry of emissions   101, 102
risk atlas   102, 103
sector targets   106
Special Programme on Climate Change   96,
    102, 108
state programmes   102
transitory articles   103, 249
transparency and access to
    information   102, 106–107
transport sector   100, 104, 106
voluntary implementation   98, 100, 102, 105
waste reduction   100
weakening of provisions   98, 109
mitigation of greenhouse gases
adaptation compared   82
Ireland   142, 143, 144, 147–150, 233, 246
Mexican LGCC   99–100, 101, 102, 103–104,
    107–108
national Climate Change Acts   112,
    235–236, 244–245, 256
Netherlands Climate Law   182–183
New Zealand Climate Act   201
Paris Agreement   46, 47, 54, 68
reduction of emissions   70
removal of emissions from atmosphere   70
Swedish Climate Change Act   161, 165,
    167, 236
UK Climate Change Act   70, 88
voluntary mitigation contributions   37, 40,
    47, 50, 54, 67, 98, 100, 102, 105
monitoring emissions
European Union   64–65
international   24, 36
monitoring, reporting and verification
    (MRV)   256
national climate legislation   54–56, 246, 247,
    250–251, 256
New Zealand   209–211, 220
Paris Agreement   36, 53, 54–56, 67, 247
Sweden   158, 160–162, 163, 164–165,
    167–170, 173
Montreal Protocol   22n
Muinzer, TL   70, 84, 87–88, 89, 91
Murphy, G   130

N
Nash, SL   229, 234, 241, 250
Nash, SL and Steurer, R   19–20, 143
national climate legislation
adaptation measures *see* adaptation to
    climate change
amendments   237–239

carbon budgets   247, 248, 249, 250, 256
chronological list   44–45
core elements   53–56, 246–247, 248–257
definition of climate change act   18–20,
        111–112
economic factors influencing   88, 178
enforceability   241–243
EU standards   57–67
European Climate Law, proposed   60–61
expanded and consolidated   236
first- and second-generation   237–239
framework legislation   11, 18, 19–20, 22,
        40–42, 67, 68, 111–112, 228–229,
        231–232
future political change, protection
        against   96, 233
generally   19, 227–228, 257
greenhouse gas emissions   53–54, 112
independent institutions, monitoring by   53,
        55–56, 247, 250–253, 256
influence of ICL   24–25, 32
influence of UK Climate Change Act   13,
        69, 87–88, 239–243
international climate law regime   23,
        228–231
long- and short-term targets   51–52, 53–54,
        246, 247, 248–249, 250, 256
long-term planning   48, 51–52, 53, 54, 56,
        154, 155, 158, 160–162, 178–179,
        201, 246, 247, 248, 249–250, 256
mitigation *see* mitigation of greenhouse gases
monitoring and reporting process   54–56,
        246, 247, 250
optimum form   227–228, 243–257
Paris Agreement and   43, 49–68, 230,
        246–247
policy and law, relationship   231–236, 244
political sustainability   88, 110, 117–118
public participation *see* public participation
risk assessments *see* risk assessment
sanctions   247, 256
sector specific targets   67, 71
sub-state   14n, 20, 20n, 254
transparency *see* transparency
use of term   11–20
utility   40–42
vested interests   231
Netherlands
Civil Code   176, 186, 194, 195
Climate Council   185
Climate and Energy Exploration   179
Climate Plan   178–180, 181, 197

climate policy   178, 179, 197–198, 233,
        234–235
ECHR   176, 192–197
economic effects of climate policy   178, 179
Energy Agreement   191, 191n
energy transition   181–182, 186, 189, 190
Environmental Assessment Agency
        (NEAA)   179
EU membership   182–183, 187, 193–194
General Administrative Law Act   181
greenhouse gas emissions   176–179, 180,
        184, 186, 192–198
international human rights law   176, 184,
        192–197
international legal obligations   175
Klimaatakkoord *see* Netherlands:
        Klimaatakkoord 2019
Klimaatwet *see* Netherlands: Klimaatwet
        2019
Lelystad Airport expansion   189
net zero emissions target   177, 178
Paris Agreement   175, 176, 179, 182–183,
        193, 195
Regional Energy Strategies   190
State's duty of care   192–197
UN Sustainable Development
        Goals   183–184
UNFCCC   193
Urgenda v The Netherlands   147, 152,
        175–177, 183, 184, 192–197,
        234–235
Netherlands: Klimaatakkoord 2019
built environment   185, 186, 190
carbon removal   178
criticisms of   180–181, 255
democratic legitimacy   190–192
emissions reduction targets   177–178, 180,
        184, 186, 187, 196–198
framework   185
generally   175, 175n, 184–187, 234–235
governance mechanisms   189–190
Klimaatwet and   175–177, 187, 192,
        197–198, 234, 236
legal status   176, 186–187, 233
negotiation   184–190, 192
objective   176
public participation   175, 181–182,
        187–190, 192, 197–198, 254–255
renewable energy   181–182, 186, 189, 190
social agreement, as   187, 190–192
transport sector   190
Urgenda case and   176–177, 192–197

Netherlands: Klimaatwet 2019
Climate Budget 181
Climate Commission 180, 241
Climate Memo 179–180
Climate Plan 178–180, 181, 187
criticisms of 180–181, 255
economic leakage, risk of 178
emissions reduction targets 177–179,
    196–198, 234
First, Second and Third Drafts 177–178,
    180, 181
framework law, as 180–181
generally 45, 175, 175n, 234–235
interim target 177–178, 180
international law, compatibility with 182–184
interpretation 192
Klimaatakkoord and 175–177, 187, 192,
    197–198, 234, 236
legally-binding status 176, 233, 234
long-term targets 177, 178–179, 180, 234
mitigation and adaptation policies 182–183
objective 176, 177–178
public participation 175, 181–182,
    197–198, 254–255
public support 179
renewable energy 178–179
Urgenda case and 176–177, 192–197
Neuweg, I and Averchenkova, A 231
New Zealand
adaptation measures 204, 220
agricultural sector 200, 203, 204–205, 206,
    208, 213, 214, 226
Bill of Rights 219
Building Act 2004 216
Climate Change Response Act *see*
    New Zealand: Climate Change
    Response (Zero Carbon)
    Amendment Act 2019
continental shelf 216
Crown Minerals Act 1991 216
emission trading scheme 203, 207, 208,
    211, 213, 216, 217, 218, 220, 226,
    238–239
exclusive economic zone 216
fossil fuel subsidies 226
Green Investment Finance Fund 226
greenhouse gas emissions 30, 199, 201,
    203–210, 225–226
international aviation and shipping
    emissions 224
international law obligations 210, 222–223
Kyoto Protocol 30, 204

Land Transport Management Act 2003
    216, 217
Local Government Act 2002 216, 217
Maori 199, 208, 211, 223–224
nationally determined contribution
    (NDC) 204, 220, 222–223
net zero emissions target 199–226
Paris Agreement 200, 204, 205–206, 214,
    215, 222–223
Productivity Commission report 215, 216
public support for legislation 204,
    225–226
renewable energy 226
Resource Management Act 1991 216–217
Te Tiriti o Waitangi 211, 223–224
transparency 218, 221–222
transport sector 203, 213, 226
UNFCCC 200
**New Zealand: Climate Change Response
    (Zero Carbon) Amendment Act 2019**
adaptation measures 201, 210, 220,
    224–225
biogenic methane reduction target 199,
    200, 201, 203, 205–206, 213
carbon capture and storage 208, 213, 216,
    218, 226
Climate Change Commission 199, 201,
    209, 210–211, 220–222, 223
emergence 202–205
emissions reduction 199, 201, 207–209,
    210, 213–215, 216–217, 220,
    221–222, 223, 249
enforcement 209–210, 218–219, 240
flexibility mechanisms 208–209, 212
generally 45, 199, 225–226, 238–239
integration with other legislation
    215–217
judicial review proceedings 210, 218–219
just transition 207, 219, 222
legally binding commitments 200
long-term target 199, 201, 205–206,
    208–209, 212–215
mitigation measures 201
monitoring and reporting process
    209–211, 220
offshore mitigation 208, 217, 218
policy scrutiny and advice 221–222
politically accountability 210, 211
public consultation 207
public reception 200, 225–226
purpose 200
risk assessments 201, 210, 222, 223, 224

split gases approach   201, 205, 213–214, 225–226, 249

temperature dimension   199, 200, 205–206, 212, 214, 225–226, 249

Newig, J   144, 146, 150, 152

Nijpels, Ed   186–187

nitrous oxide

UK Climate Change Act   74–75, 76

Norway

Lov om klimamål 2017   44

O

ozone layer protection

chlorofluorocarbons   22n

international response   22n, 23

Montreal Protocol   22n

P

Paris Agreement

absence of compliance mechanism   36

accounting and reporting   36, 47, 53, 54–56, 67, 247

adaptation as goal   46, 47, 182–183, 247

aims and objective   35–36, 44, 46–47

Biennial Transparency Reports   55

capacity-building   47, 55, 165, 182, 247

China   46

collective long-term goals   44, 46, 48, 50–56, 61–63, 67–68, 182–183

Conference of the Parties (COP)   46, 47

core elements of climate change legislation   53–56, 246–247

Denmark   111, 112, 125, 126, 127, 128

developing countries   36

divisive effect   33, 34–38

Enhanced Transparency Framework   55

establishment and ratification   34–35, 37, 39

European Union   46, 57, 58–67, 142, 195

financial flows, goal as to   46, 47, 55, 182–183

flexibility, goals open to   47

global average temperature rise   36–37, 46–47, 51, 55, 85–86, 106, 112, 126, 128, 195

global stocktakes   36, 38, 46, 47, 51, 53, 55, 56

greenhouse gas emissions   47, 53–54, 85–86

impact   32, 35–38, 230

independent institutions, monitoring by   53, 55–56

India   46

international political commitment   50

IPCC reports   55, 147–148, 194, 206, 212–213

Ireland   148–149

Kyoto Protocol, relationship with   38–39, 46

Kyoto Protocol compared   37–38

long-term planning   48, 53, 54, 56

long-term strategies (LTSs)   48, 51–52, 54, 56, 60

Mexico   94, 105–106, 107, 238

mitigation as goal   46, 47, 54, 68, 182–183

momentum created by   43

national inventory reports   55

national legislation and   43, 49–68

nationally determined contributions (NDCs)   36–37, 38, 40–41, 47–49, 50, 51, 52, 53, 58, 61, 67, 112, 183, 204, 220, 222–223

Netherlands   175, 176, 179, 182–183, 193, 195, 214

New Zealand   200, 204, 205–206, 215, 222–223

non-enforceability   67

obligations under   45–48, 50, 54, 67

pledge and review structure   48–49

potential effectiveness   38–39

progression, principle of   47, 51, 53–54

public participation   53, 56–57

ratification   46, 198

rulebook   49, 50, 55

SBSTA   55

soft framing   37

status   34–35, 46

sub-national actors   215

substance   34, 35–38

Sweden   153, 154, 157, 162–163, 165, 173

targets   46–47, 51–52, 53–54, 61–64, 85–86

technology framework, development   36, 47, 55

transparency   56

UNFCCC, relationship with   46, 47

United Kingdom   85–86, 92

United States   46, 46n

utility   40–41

voluntary mitigation contributions   37, 40, 47, 50, 54, 67

weakness   37–39, 40–41, 50, 67

Peña Nieto, Enrique   107

perfluorocarbons

UK Climate Change Act   74–75, 76

Plan B   85–86

plastic carrier bag charges

UK Climate Change Act   74, 84

pollution

legislation engaging with   22n

UK Royal Commission report   71–72

progression, principle of
  Paris Agreement NDCs   47, 51, 53–54
protests, climate
  emergence   21
public participation
  European Union   66–67
  Mexico   102, 103
  national climate legislation, generally   246,
    247, 253–255, 256
  Netherlands   175, 179, 181–182, 187–190,
    192, 197–198, 254–255
  Paris Agreement   53, 56–57
  United Kingdom   73, 253–254
Pulver, S   95–96

R
Reid, C   88–89
renewable energy
  definition   178
  Denmark   113, 119–120
  energy taxation   57
  European Union   57–59, 63–64, 66, 67
  Mexico   94–95, 104–107, 109–110
  Netherlands   178–179, 186, 189, 190
  New Zealand   226
  Sweden   169
  UK Climate Change Act   74, 84
  UK Royal Commission report   71–72
reporting and advisory duties
  European Union   64–65
  international climate law   24
  Ireland   141, 251
  monitoring, reporting and verification
    (MRV)   256
  national climate legislation   54–56, 246, 247,
    250–251, 256
  New Zealand   209–211
  Paris Agreement   36, 54–56, 67, 247
  Sweden   158–159, 160–162, 163, 164–165,
    167–170, 173
  UK Climate Change Act   70, 78–81, 82,
    83–84, 251
risk assessment
  economic leakage effects   178
  Mexico LGCC risk atlas   102, 103
  national climate legislation, generally
    250
  New Zealand Climate Bill   201, 210, 222,
    223, 224
  UK Climate Change Act   82, 250
Romson, A and Forsbacka, K   235–236, 240,
    242–243, 251

Russian Federation
  Kyoto Protocol   30

S
Scotland
  Climate Change (Scotland) Act 2009   14n,
    20, 20n, 117, 254
South Korea
  Framework Act on Low Carbon Green
    Growth 2010   255
Spain
  Ley de Cambio Climático y Transición
    Energética   45
Spijkers, O and Oosterhuis, S   233, 234, 241,
    254–255
**Subsidiary Body for Scientific and
    Technological Advice (SBSTA)**   55
sulphur hexafluoride
  UK Climate Change Act   74–75, 76
Supperstone J   86
Sweden
  2009 climate policy package   154
  annual climate reports   161, 164–165, 167–170
  Association of Nature Conservation   171
  Budget Act 2011   156
  budget policy targets   159, 168
  carbon capture and storage   163
  Climate Policy Framework *see* Sweden:
    Climate Policy Framework
  climate targets   153, 154, 157, 158–159,
    162–163, 172–173
  Committee on Environmental
    Objectives   153, 156–157
  Constitution   157–158
  Energy Agency   169
  Environmental Code   154, 154n, 171, 172,
    173, 174, 235, 243
  Environmental Impact Assessments
    (EIAs)   170–171
  Environmental Protection Agency   169,
    170, 172
  EU Effort Sharing Regulation   161, 163
  EU Emissions Trading Scheme   161, 163,
    168, 171
  EU membership   170, 171
  Fiscal Policy Council   164
  Fiscal Policy Framework   155–156, 168,
    173, 240
  greenhouse gas emissions   153, 154, 155,
    158–160, 161–162, 168–170
  international engagement and climate
    planning   162

Klimat Lag *see* Sweden: Klimat Lag 2017
net zero emissions target   153, 162–163,
    168, 173
Orientational Bills   154
Paris Agreement   153, 154, 157, 162–163,
    165, 173
policies evaluation reports   167–170
Preem Oil Refinery enlargement   171–172
renewable energy   169
responsibility for securing climate
    objectives   153, 155, 158, 159–160,
    166–167, 170
Södertörn Crosslink Project   170–171, 172
sustainable development   157–158
Swedgas Pipeline   172
Swedish Hagainitiativet   157
transport sector   163, 168, 169, 170–171
UNFCCC   157, 158, 170
Sweden: Climate Policy Framework (CPF)
adoption   154, 156
capacity-building for adaptation   165, 235–236
Climate Policy Council   154, 157, 159,
    164–165, 167–170, 173, 174, 235,
    251–252
establishment   153–154
Government Bill   158, 159, 160–161, 162, 163
interim targets   154, 162–163, 173
Klimat Lag   154, 157, 235; *see also* Sweden:
    Klimat Lag 2017
long-term target   154, 155, 158, 160–163,
    168, 171, 173
national climate targets   153, 157, 158,
    162–163, 168, 172–173
proposal for   155–157
purpose   153–154, 235–236
transparency   154, 155, 173
Sweden: Klimat Lag 2017
adoption   158
background to   154, 157–158, 240
budget policy and   159, 168
business sector and   157, 166
capacity-building for adaptation   165, 235–236
climate targets   154, 158–159, 160–163,
    172–173
compliance, responsibility for   153, 158,
    159–160, 166–167, 170
CPF *see* Sweden: Climate Policy Framework
criticisms of   165–167
enforcement   159, 166, 173, 242–243
form and content   154, 158–160, 173
generally   45, 73, 158–159, 235
legal status   158, 166–167, 170–174

mitigation measures   161, 165, 167, 236
monitoring and reporting process   158–159,
    160–162, 163, 164–165, 167–170, 173
objective   154, 158–160
permits for large emitters   170–173
policy action plans   161–162, 164–165,
    168–170, 173
proposal for   155–157
symbolic legislation
Irish Climate Act 2015   143–146, 150, 152

T
taxation
carbon taxes   255
EU energy taxation standards   57
Taylor, P   238, 239, 240, 248–249
Thunberg, Greta   152
Torney, D   132, 135
Townshend, T et al   13, 17–18, 231
Townshend, T and Matthews, AC   229
trading schemes *see* **emissions trading**
    schemes
transparency
Denmark   114
Mexico LGCC   102, 106–107
national climate legislation   56, 246, 247,
    256
New Zealand   218, 221–222
Paris Agreement   55, 56
Sweden   154, 155, 173
UNFCCC   55

U
United Kingdom
Airports National Policy Statement   86
Brexit   91–92
Climate Change Act *see* United Kingdom:
    Climate Change Act 2008
Climate Change (Scotland) Act 2009   14n,
    20, 20n, 117, 254
climate policy   71–73, 79, 233–234
constitution   90–91
constitutional statutes   91
Environment (Wales) Act 2016   14n
EU Emissions Trading Scheme (ETS)   92
Greenhouse Gas Emissions Trading Scheme
    Regulations 2012   19
Heathrow Airport third runway   85
hydraulic fracturing   84
Infrastructure Act 2015   80
Marrakesh Accords   26
Paris Agreement   85–86, 92

parliamentary sovereignty 87
Preston New Road Action Group v SoS
    for Communities and Local
    Government 84
public consultation 73, 253–254
R (Plan B Earth and others) v SoS for
    Business, Energy and Industrial
    Strategy 85–86
R v SoS for Transport 85
Royal Commission on Environmental
    Pollution 71–72
Stern Report 72, 80
White Papers on climate change 71
United Kingdom: Climate Change Act 2008
    10-year review 69
    accountability 90
    adaptation as goal 70, 74, 82–83
    Adaptation Programme 83, 250
    Adaptation Sub-Committee 82
    austerity measures and 88
    background to 71–73
    baseline emissions 76, 78
    carbon trading and budgeting 19, 70,
        74–75, 76–79, 81, 88, 122, 127, 249,
        250, 255
    Committee on Climate Change 74, 77,
        79–81, 82, 164, 180, 210, 250–251,
        252
    criticisms of 69
    decarbonisation transition 74–75, 80
    devolved powers 80, 81, 83n, 86, 200n, 254
    energy generators, distributors and
        suppliers 84
    flexibility 75
    form and content 73–75
    generally 13, 19, 44, 87–92, 111, 229,
        233–234, 236
    human activity, emissions attributable to 75
    impact of climate change 74
    influence 13, 69, 87–88, 97, 115, 122, 127,
        133–134, 135, 143, 155, 156–157,
        173, 180, 201, 239–243
    judicial review proceedings 85, 86, 89, 243
    jurisdiction 84–86
    law – policy relationship 233–234
    legally binding targets 69, 76–79, 87, 88–90
    locked-in long-term nature 69, 72–73,
        76–79, 87–88, 89
    mitigation as goal 70, 88
    net UK emissions level 77
    net zero emissions target 76, 77, 86,
        89–90, 248

penalty regime 81, 89
plastic carrier bag charges 74, 84
powers and duties under 75, 79, 81, 82–83,
    88–91
procedural duties 70
reduction targets 69, 70, 76–79, 85–86,
    88–90, 248
renewable transport fuel obligations 74, 84
reporting and advisory duties 70, 78–81,
    82, 83–84, 250–251
risk assessment 82, 250
socio-economic reach 70–71
strengthening and deepening 70–71
substantive duties 70, 90
Swedish Climate Change Act compared 73
targeted greenhouse gases 74–75, 76–79
trading schemes 19, 74, 81
waste reduction schemes 74, 84
United Nations
    Sustainable Development Goals
        (SDGs) 183–184
    treaties 43
**United Nations Framework Convention on
    Climate Change (UNFCCC)**
    Adaptation Fund 165
    baseline emissions 76
    Cancun Agreements 96–97
    Conference of the Parties 24, 25, 27, 34, 38
    Copenhagen Conference (COP15) 31n, 39,
        57, 96, 134
    Denmark 112
    developed nations 147–148
    Doha Amendment 29–32, 33
    establishment 23–24, 32–33, 39
    European Climate Change
        Programme 57–67
    Green Climate Fund 97, 165
    human activity, emissions attributable to 75
    Kyoto Protocol *see* Kyoto Protocol
    limited powers 24–25, 25n, 27–28, 31–32
    market mechanisms 26
    Marrakesh Accords 25–26, 26n
    New Zealand 200
    objective 24
    Paris Agreement *see* Paris Agreement
    protocols 25
    Secretariat 24
    State sovereignty and 24–25, 25n
    Sweden 157, 158
    transparency arrangements 55
    Urgenda v The Netherlands 193
    weakness 32–33, 39–41

United States
  greenhouse gas emissions   27, 46, 95
  Kyoto Protocol   27, 95
  lack of overarching climate
       law   231
  Paris Agreement   46, 46n

V
Varadkar, Leo   129
vehicles
  EU energy standards   57
  UK Climate Change Act   74–75, 80

W
Wales
  Environment (Wales) Act 2016   14n
waste management   216
waste reduction schemes
  Mexico LGCC   100
  UK Climate Change Act   74, 84
Wijkman, Anders   156
World Climate Conference 1979   23

Z
Zahar, A   32

Lightning Source UK Ltd.
Milton Keynes UK
UKHW020132140922
408840UK00004B/84